DICTIONARY OF

501 FRENCH VERBS
FULLY CONJUGATED IN ALL THE TENSES

by

Christopher Kendris, PH.D.

Chairman, Foreign Language Department
Schenectady Community College
(Under the Program of State University of
New York and Schenectady County)

BARRON'S EDUCATIONAL SERIES,
Woodbury, N. Y.

All inquiries should be addressed to:

Barron's Educational Series, Inc.
113 Crossways Park Drive
Woodbury, New York 11797

Library of Congress Catalog Card No. 73-90072

PRINTED IN THE UNITED STATES OF AMERICA

6 7 8 9 10 11 M 5 4 3

To my wife *Yolanda*

and my two sons, *Alex* and *Ted*

CONTENTS

FOREWORD

AN EVERYDAY DICTIONARY such as this one for students in colleges and high schools and for travelers should assist the user in learning French verbs.

Verb conjugations are usually found in the back pages of French books and, as you know, French grammar books generally present a limited number of verbs fully conjugated. The verbs which grammar books give are usually the most common regular and irregular ones and only a few of them are conjugated fully. Verbs have always been a major problem for students no matter what system or approach the teacher uses. This everyday dictionary will give you the verb form you need to use. If you study this book, you should master verbs.

There is no doubt that it is frustrating to the student when he does not find in a book the conjugation of a verb he needs to use. It is also somewhat annoying to the average student when he is told in many grammar books that one verb is conjugated the same way as another. This means nothing to some students and very little to others. Although this may seem difficult to believe, it is nevertheless true. Furthermore, verbs conjugated in the same way as other verbs are often difficult to find because they are buried somewhere either in footnotes or in some other obscure place in a grammar book. As a student of French, you undoubtedly have had difficulty in finding the verb form you wish to use. At other times, you probably did not find it at all and tossed the book aside in despair.

For reasons stated above, this everyday dictionary has been compiled in order to help you make your task easier and at the same time to teach you how to learn French verbs systematically. It is a useful dictionary which can always be at your fingertips because it provides a quick and easy way to find the full conjugation of many French verbs. The five hundred and one verbs included in this dictionary are arranged alphabetically. Naturally, this book does not include all the verbs in the French language. It includes an enormous number of common verbs of high frequency, both reflexive and non-reflexive. It also contains a great many others which are irregular in some way and also used frequently.

The student can also use this dictionary as a method of self-instruction. *On one single page you will find the verb forms of all the tenses you need to know.* The subject pronouns have been omitted. The first three verb forms before the semicolon are the first, second and third persons of the singular. The three verb forms after the semicolon are the plural forms of the verbs. After a while, you will gain skill in verb use and you will not have to keep referring to the sample English verb.

At the end of this foreword, you will find a sample English verb conjugated in all the tenses. The purpose of this is to give you an idea of the way the verb is expressed in the same tenses in English. Many people do not know one tense from another because they have never learned the use of verbs in a systematic and organized way. How can you, for instance, know that you need the Future Tense when you want to translate "I shall go" or "I will go" into French? The sample verb in English will help you to distinguish one tense from another so that you will know where to find the desired verb form.

Preceding the sample English verb page, you will find a table showing the formation of regular verbs, both simple and compound, in all the tenses. I have included this for those who wish to observe and memorize the regular endings. Also, at the end of this book, you will find an English-French Verb Index. If you do not know the French equivalent of the English verb you have in mind, look it up in the English-French Verb Index at the end of this dictionary. If it is not listed, remember that this book contains five hundred and one French verbs of high frequency and it does not contain all the verbs in the French language. If it did, the book would be encyclopedic.

As you know, the new way to teach modern languages is with an audio-lingual approach, that is to say, conversational. This means that the language is *used*. In this approach, the student's main difficulty is his search for the form of the verb in a particular tense which he wants to use. He will not stop and read *about* French verbs; rather, he will stop to look up the verb in a dictionary, such as this one, in order to find the form he wants quickly and easily.

At the end of this book there is an index of verb forms identified by infinitive. In your readings, perhaps you have had difficulty in recognizing such verb forms. Some are slightly different from their infinitives, others are very different. The purpose of the index is to help you recall infinitives. Once you have the infinitive, you can look it up in this book, where they are all arranged alphabetically, and identify the verb forms.

In conclusion, this dictionary provides students of French in colleges and high schools, and travelers, with the needed information quickly and easily. It is useful, handy and practical. I sincerely hope that it will be of some help to you in learning and using French verbs.

Christopher Kendris, Ph.D.

Chairman, Foreign Language Department

SCHENECTADY COMMUNITY COLLEGE

SCHENECTADY, NEW YORK 12305

VERBS CONJUGATED WITH AVOIR OR ÊTRE

(1) Generally speaking, the French verb is conjugated with AVOIR to form the compound tenses.
(2) Reflexive verbs, such as *se laver*, are conjugated with ÊTRE.
(3) The following is a list of some common non-reflexive verbs which are conjugated with ÊTRE. Refer to this list from time to time until you know them.

aller	*to go*
arriver	*to arrive*
descendre	*to go down*
devenir	*to become*
entrer	*to enter*
monter	*to go up*
mourir	*to die*
naître	*to be born*
partir	*to leave*
rentrer	*to come (go) back home*
rester	*to remain*
retourner	*to go back, return*
revenir	*to come back*
sortir	*to go out, to leave*
tomber	*to fall*
venir	*to come*

LES TEMPS PRIMITIFS DE QUELQUES VERBES

THE PRINCIPAL PARTS OF SOME VERBS

INFINITIF	PARTICIPE PRÉSENT	PARTICIPE PASSÉ	PRÉSENT DE L'INDICATIF	PASSÉ SIMPLE
aller	allant	allé	je vais	j'allai
avoir	ayant	eu	j'ai	j'eus
battre	battant	battu	je bats	je battis
boire	buvant	bu	je bois	je bus
craindre	craignant	craint	je crains	je craignis
croire	croyant	cru	je crois	je crus
devoir	devant	dû	je dois	je dus
dire	disant	dit	je dis	je dis
écrire	écrivant	écrit	j'écris	j'écrivis
être	étant	été	je suis	je fus
faire	faisant	fait	je fais	je fis
lire	lisant	lu	je lis	je lus
mettre	mettant	mis	je mets	je mis
mourir	mourant	mort	je meurs	je mourus
naître	naissant	né	je nais	je naquis
ouvrir	ouvrant	ouvert	j'ouvre	j'ouvris
porter	portant	porté	je porte	je portai
pouvoir	pouvant	pu	je peux	je pus
prendre	prenant	pris	je prends	je pris
recevoir	recevant	reçu	je reçois	je reçus
savoir	sachant	su	je sais	je sus
venir	venant	venu	je viens	je vins
vivre	vivant	vécu	je vis	je vécus
voir	voyant	vu	je vois	je vis
voler	volant	volé	je vole	je volai

INFINITIF	PARTICIPE PRÉSENT	PARTICIPE PASSÉ	PRÉSENT DE L'INDICATIF	PASSÉ SIMPLE
donner	donnant	donné	je donne	je donnai

FUTUR
donner**ai**
donner**as**
donner**a**

donner**ons**
donner**ez**
donner**ont**

CONDITIONNEL
donner**ais**
donner**ais**
donner**ait**

donner**ions**
donner**iez**
donner**aient**

IMPARFAIT DE L'INDICATIF
donn**ais**
donn**ais**
donn**ait**

donn**ions**
donn**iez**
donn**aient**

PASSÉ COMPOSÉ
ai donné
as donné
a donné

avons donné
avez donné
ont donné

PLUS-QUE-PARFAIT DE L'INDICATIF
avais donné
avais donné
avait donné

avions donné
aviez donné
avaient donné

PASSÉ ANTÉRIEUR
eus donné
eus donné
eut donné

eûmes donné
eûtes donné
eurent donné

PRÉSENT DE L'INDICATIF
donn**e**
donn**es**
donn**e**

donn**ons**
donn**ez**
donn**ent**

IMPÉRATIF
donn**e**
donn**ons**
donn**ez**

PRÉSENT DU SUBJONCTIF
donn**e**
donn**es**
donn**e**

donn**ions**
donn**iez**
donn**ent**

PASSÉ SIMPLE
donn**ai**
donn**as**
donn**a**

donn**âmes**
donn**âtes**
donn**èrent**

IMPARFAIT DU SUBJONCTIF
donna**sse**
donna**sses**
donn**ât**

donna**ssions**
donna**ssiez**
donna**ssent**

FUTUR ANTÉRIEUR
aurai donné
auras donné
aura donné

aurons donné
aurez donné
auront donné

CONDITIONNEL PASSÉ
aurais donné
aurais donné
aurait donné

aurions donné
auriez donné
auraient donné

PASSÉ DU SUBJONCTIF
aie donné
aies donné
ait donné

ayons donné
ayez donné
aient donné

PLUS-QUE-PARFAIT DU SUBJONCTIF
eusse donné
eusses donné
eût donné

eussions donné
eussiez donné
eussent donné

INFINITIF	PARTICIPE PRÉSENT	PARTICIPE PASSÉ	PRÉSENT DE L'INDICATIF	PASSÉ SIMPLE
arriver	arrivant	arrivé	j'arrive	j'arrivai

FUTUR
arriverai
arriveras
arrivera

arriverons
arriverez
arriveront

CONDITIONNEL
arriverais
arriverais
arriverait

arriverions
arriveriez
arriveraient

IMPARFAIT DE L'INDICATIF
arrivais
arrivais
arrivait

arrivions
arriviez
arrivaient

PASSÉ COMPOSÉ
suis arrivé(e)
es arrivé(e)
est arrivé(e)

sommes arrivé(e)s
êtes arrivé(e)(s)
sont arrivé(e)s

PLUS-QUE-PARFAIT DE L'INDICATIF
étais arrivé(e)
étais arrivé(e)
était arrivé(e)

étions arrivé(e)s
étiez arrivé(e)(s)
étaient arrivé(e)s

PASSÉ ANTÉRIEUR
fus arrivé(e)
fus arrivé(e)
fut arrivé(e)

fûmes arrivé(e)s
fûtes arrivé(e)(s)
furent arrivé(e)s

PRÉSENT DE L'INDICATIF
arrive
arrives
arrive

arrivons
arrivez
arrivent

IMPÉRATIF
arrive
arrivons
arrivez

PRÉSENT DU SUBJONCTIF
arrive
arrives
arrive

arrivions
arriviez
arrivent

PASSÉ SIMPLE
arrivai
arrivas
arriva

arrivâmes
arrivâtes
arrivèrent

IMPARFAIT DU SUBJONCTIF
arrivasse
arrivasses
arrivât

arrivassions
arrivassiez
arrivassent

FUTUR ANTÉRIEUR
serai arrivé(e)
seras arrivé(e)
sera arrivé(e)

serons arrivé(e)s
serez arrivé(e)(s)
seront arrivé(e)s

CONDITIONNEL PASSÉ
serais arrivé(e)
serais arrivé(e)
serait arrivé(e)

serions arrivé(e)s
seriez arrivé(e)(s)
seraient arrivé(e)s

PASSÉ DU SUBJONCTIF
sois arrivé(e)
sois arrivé(e)
soit arrivé(e)

soyons arrivé(e)s
soyez arrivé(e)(s)
soient arrivé(e)s

PLUS-QUE-PARFAIT DU SUBJONCTIF
fusse arrivé(e)
fusses arrivé(e)
fût arrivé(e)

fussions arrivé(e)s
fussiez arrivé(e)(s)
fussent arrivé(e)s

SAMPLE ENGLISH VERB CONJUGATION

INFINITIVE	**to go—aller**
PRESENT PARTICIPLE	going PAST PARTICIPLE gone
Present Indicative	I go, you go, he (she, it) goes; we go, you go, they go
or:	I do go, you do go, he (she, it) does go; we do go, you do go, they do go
or:	I am going, you are going, he (she, it) is going; we are going, you are going, they are going
Imperfect Indicative	I was going, you were going, he (she, it) was going; we were going, you were going, they were going
or:	I went, you went, he (she, it) went; we went, you went, they went
or:	I used to go, you used to go, he (she, it) used to go; we used to go, you used to go, he (she, it) used to go
Past Definite or Simple Past	I went, you went, he (she, it) went; we went, you went, they went
or:	I did go, you did go, he (she, it) did go; we did go, you did go, they did go
Future	I shall go, you will go, he (she, it) will go; we shall go, you will go, they will go
Conditional	I should go, you would go, he (she, it) would go; we should go, you would go, they would go
Present Subjunctive	that I may go, that you may go, that he (she, it) may go; that we may go, that you may go, that they may go

Imperfect Subjunctive	that I might go, that you might go, that he (she, it) might go; that we might go, that you might go, that they might go
Past Indefinite	I have gone, you have gone, he (she, it) has gone; we have gone, you have gone, they have gone
or:	I went, you went, he (she, it) went; we went, you went, they went
or:	I did go, you did go, he (she, it) did go; we did go, you did go, they did go
Pluperfect or Past Perfect Indicative	I had gone, you had gone, he (she, it) had gone; we had gone, you had gone, they had gone
Past Anterior	I had gone, you had gone, he (she, it) had gone; we had gone, you had gone, they had gone
Future Perfect or Future Anterior	I shall have gone, you will have gone, he (she, it) will have gone; we shall have gone, you will have gone, they will have gone
Conditional Perfect	I should have gone, you would have gone, he (she, it) would have gone; we should have gone, you would have gone, they would have gone
Past Subjunctive	that I may have gone, that you may have gone, that he (she, it) may have gone; that we may have gone, that you may have gone, that they may have gone
Pluperfect or Past Perfect Subjunctive	that I might have gone, that you might have gone, that he (she, it) might have gone; that we might have gone, that you might have gone, that they might have gone
Imperative or Command	go, let us go, go

A SUMMARY OF MEANINGS AND USES OF FRENCH VERB TENSES AND MOODS AS RELATED TO ENGLISH VERB TENSES AND MOODS

A verb is where the action is! A verb is a word that expresses an action (like *go*, *eat*, *write*) or a state of being (like *think*, *believe*, *be*). Tense means time. French and English verb tenses are divided into three main groups of time: past, present and future. A verb tense shows if an action or state of being took place, is taking place or will take place.

French and English verbs are also used in four moods (or modes). Mood has to do with the *way* a person regards an action or a state that he expresses. For example, a person may merely make a statement or ask a question—this is the Indicative Mood, which we use most of the time in French and English. A person may say that he *would do* something if something else were possible or that he *would have done* something if something else had been possible—this is the Conditional Mood. A person may use a verb *in such a way* that he indicates a wish, a fear, a regret, a supposition, or something of this sort—this is the Subjunctive Mood. The Subjunctive Mood is used in French much more than in English. A person may command someone to do something—this is the Imperative Mood.

There are six tenses in English: Present, Past, Future, Present Perfect, Past Perfect, and Future Perfect. The first three are simple tenses. The other three are compound tenses and are based on the simple tenses. In French, however, there are fourteen tenses, seven of which are simple and seven of which are compound.

In the pages that follow, the tenses and moods are given in French and the equivalent name or names in English are given in parentheses. Although some of the names given in English are not considered to be tenses (for there are only six), they are given for the purpose of identification as they are related to the French names. The comparison includes only the essential points you need to know about the meanings and uses of French verb tenses and moods as related to English usage. We shall use examples to illustrate their meanings and uses.

Le Présent de l'Indicatif

(The Present Indicative)

This tense is used most of the time in French and English. It indicates:

(a) An action or a state of being at the present time.

EXAMPLES:

1. Je **vais** à l'école maintenant. I *am going* to school now.
2. Je **pense**; donc, je **suis**. I *think;* therefore, I *am.*

(b) Habitual action.

EXAMPLE:

1. Je **vais** à la bibliothèque tous les jours.
   I *go* to the library every day.

OR:

I *do go* to the library every day.

(c) A general truth, something which is permanently true.

EXAMPLES:

1. Deux et deux **font** quatre. Two and two *are* four.
2. Voir c'**est** croire. Seeing *is* believing.

(d) Vividness when talking or writing about past events. This is called the *historical present.*

EXAMPLE:

Marie-Antoinette **est** condamnée à mort. Elle **entre** dans la charrette et **est** en route pour la guillotine.

Marie-Antoinette *is* condemned to die. She *goes* into the cart and *is* on her way to the guillotine.

(e) A near future.

EXAMPLE:

Il **arrive** demain. He *arrives* tomorrow.

(f) An action or state of being that occurred in the past and *continues up to the present.* In English, this tense is the *Present Perfect.* It is formed with the Present Tense of *to have* (*have* or *has*) plus the past participle of the verb you are using.

EXAMPLES:

1. Je **suis** ici depuis dix minutes.
   I *have been* here for ten minutes. (I am still here at present)
2. Elle **est** malade depuis trois jours.
   She *has been* sick for three days. (She is still sick at present)
3. **J'attends** l'autobus depuis dix minutes.
   I *have been waiting* for the bus for ten minutes.

NOTE: In this example the formation of the English verb tense is slightly different from the other two examples in English. The present participle (*waiting*) is used instead of the past participle (*waited*).

L'Imparfait de l'Indicatif

(The Imperfect Indicative)

This is a past tense. It is used to indicate:

(a) An action that was going on in the past at the same time as another action.

EXAMPLE:

Il **lisait** pendant que j'**écrivais**. He *was reading* while I *was writing*.

(b) An action that was going on in the past when another action occurred.

EXAMPLE:

Il **lisait** quand je suis entré. He *was reading* when I came in.

(c) An action that a person did habitually in the past.

EXAMPLE:

Nous **allions** à la plage tous les jours.
We *used to go* to the beach every day.

OR:

We *would go* to the beach every day.

(d) A description of a mental or physical condition in the past.

EXAMPLES:

(mental condition)	Il **était** triste quand je l'ai vu. He *was* sad when I saw him.
(physical condition)	Quand ma mère **était** jeune, elle **était** belle. When my mother *was* young, she *was* beautiful.

(e) An action or state of being that occurred in the past and *lasted for a certain length of time* prior to another past action. In English, it is usually translated as a Pluperfect tense and is formed with *had been* plus the present participle of the verb you are using. It is like the special use of the **Présent de l'Indicatif** described in the above section in paragraph (f), except that the action or state of being no longer exists at present.

EXAMPLE:

J'attendais l'autobus depuis dix minutes quand il est arrivé.
I *had been waiting* for the bus for ten minutes when it arrived.

Le Passé Simple

(The Past Definite or Simple Past)

This past tense expresses an action that took place at some definite time. This tense is not ordinarily used in conversational French or in informal writing. It is a literary tense. It is used in formal writing, such as history and literature. You should be able merely to recognize this tense when you see it in your French readings. It should be noted that French writers use the **Passé Simple** less and less these days. The **Passé Composé** is taking its place in literature.

EXAMPLES:

(a) Il **alla** en Afrique. He *went* to Africa.

(b) Il **voyagea** en Amérique. He *traveled* to America.

Le Futur

(The Future)

In French and English this tense is used to express an action or a state of being which will take place at some time in the future.

EXAMPLES:

(a) J'**irai** en France l'été prochain.
I *shall go* to France next summer.

OR:

I *will go* to France next summer.

(b) J'y **penserai**.
I *shall think* about it.

OR:

I *will think* about it.

Le Conditionnel Présent

(The Conditional)

The Conditional is used in French and English to express:

(a) An action that you would do if something else were possible.

EXAMPLE:
Je **ferais** le travail si j'avais le temps.
I *would do* the work if I had the time.

(b) A conditional desire. This is the Conditional of courtesy in French.

EXAMPLES:
J'**aimerais** du thé. I *should like* some tea. OR: I *would like* some tea.
Je **voudrais** du café. I *should like* (or *would like*) some coffee.

(c) An obligation or duty.

EXAMPLE:
Je **devrais** étudier pour l'examen. I *should study* for the examination.

NOTE: When the Conditional of the verb **pouvoir** is used in French, it is translated into English as *could* or *would be able.*

EXAMPLE:
Je **pourrais** venir après le dîner. I *could come* after dinner.

OR:
I *would be able* to come after dinner.

Le Présent du Subjonctif

(The Present Subjunctive)

The Subjunctive is used in French much more than in English. It is disappearing in English, except for the following major uses:

(a) The Subjunctive is used in French and English to express a command.

EXAMPLE:
Soyez à l'heure! *Be* on time!

NOTE: In English, the form in the Subjunctive applies mainly to the verb *to be*. Also, note that all verbs in French are not in the Subjunctive when expressing a command. See **L'Impératif** on p. xxviii.

(b) The Subjunctive is commonly used in English to express a condition contrary to fact.

EXAMPLE:

If I *were* you, I would not do it.

NOTE: In French the Subjunctive is not used in this instance. Instead, the **Imparfait de l'Indicatif** is used if what precedes is *si* (*if*). Same example in French: Si j'**étais** vous, je ne le ferais pas.

(c) The Present Subjunctive is used in French and English after a verb that expresses some kind of insistence, preference, or suggestion.

EXAMPLES:

1. J'insiste que vous **soyez** ici à l'heure.
   I insist that *you be* here on time.
2. Je préfère qu'il **fasse** le travail maintenant.
   I prefer that *he do* the work now.
3. J'exige qu'il **soit** puni.
   I demand that *he be* punished.

(d) The Subjunctive is used in French after a verb that expresses doubt, fear, joy, sorrow, or some other emotion. Notice in the following examples that the Subjunctive is not used in English but it is in French.

EXAMPLES:

1. Je doute qu'il **vienne.**
   I doubt that he *is coming*. OR: I doubt that he *will come*.
2. J'ai peur qu'il ne **soit** malade.
   I'm afraid he *is* sick.
3. Je suis heureux qu'il **vienne.**
   I'm happy that he *is coming*.
4. Je regrette qu'il **soit** malade.
   I'm sorry he *is* sick.

(e) The Present Subjunctive is used in French after certain conjunctions. Notice, however, that the Subjunctive is not always used in English.

EXAMPLES:

1. Je partirai **à moins qu'il ne vienne.**
   I shall leave unless he *comes*.
2. Je resterai **jusqu'à ce qu'il vienne.**
   I shall stay until he *comes*.
3. **Quoiqu'elle soit** belle, il ne l'aime pas.
   Although she *is* beautiful, he does not love her.
4. Je l'explique **pour qu'elle comprenne.**
   I'm explaining it *so that she may understand*.

(f) The Present Subjunctive is used in French after certain impersonal expressions that show a need, a doubt, a possibility or an impossibility. Notice, however, that the Subjunctive is not always used in English in the following examples:

1. Il est urgent qu'il **vienne**.
   It is urgent that he *come*.
2. Il vaut mieux qu'il **vienne**.
   It is better that he *come*.
3. Il est possible qu'il **vienne**.
   It is possible that he *will come*.
4. Il est douteux qu'il **vienne**.
   It is doubtful that he *will come*.
5. Il est nécessaire qu'il **vienne**.
   It is necessary that he *come*. OR: He must come.
6. Il faut qu'il **vienne**.
   It is necessary that he *come*. OR: He must come.
7. Il est important que vous **fassiez** le travail.
   It is important that you *do* the work.
8. Il est indispensable qu'elle **fasse** le travail.
   It is required that she *do* the work.

L'Imparfait du Subjonctif

(The Imperfect Subjunctive)

L'Imparfait du Subjonctif is used for the same reasons as the **Présent du Subjonctif**—that is, after certain verbs, conjunctions, and impersonal expressions which were used in examples above under the section, **le Présent du Subjonctif**. The main difference between these two is the time of the action. If present, use the **Présent du Subjonctif**. If the action is related to the past, the **Imparfait du Subjonctif** is used, provided that the action was *not* completed. If the action was completed, the **Plus-que-parfait du Subjonctif** is used. See below under the section, **Plus-que-parfait du Subjonctif**.

Since the Subjunctive Mood is troublesome in French and English, you may be pleased to know that this tense is rarely used in English. It is used in French, however, but only in formal writing and in literature. For that reason, you should merely be familiar with it so you can recognize it when you see it in your French readings. In conversational French and in informal writing, **l'Imparfait du Subjonctif** is avoided. Use, instead, the **Présent du Subjonctif**.

Notice that the **Imparfait du Subjonctif** is used in French in both of the following examples, but is used in English only in the second example (b):

EXAMPLES:

(a) Je voulais qu'il **vînt**. (action not completed; he did not come while I wanted him to come)
I wanted him to come.

NOTE: The Subjunctive of **venir** is used because the verb that precedes is one that requires the Subjunctive *after* it—in this example it is **vouloir**. In conversational French and informal writing, the **Imparfait du Subjonctif** is avoided. Use, instead, the **Présent du Subjonctif**: Je voulais qu'il **vienne**.

(b) Je le lui expliquais **pour qu'elle le comprît**.
I was explaining it to her *so that she might understand it*.
(action not completed; the understanding was not completed at the time of the explaining)

NOTE: The Subjunctive of **comprendre** is used because the conjunction that precedes is one that requires the Subjunctive *after* it—in this example it is **pour que**. In conversational French and informal writing, the **Imparfait du Subjonctif** is avoided. Use, instead, the **Présent du Subjonctif**: Je le lui expliquais pour qu'elle le **comprenne**.

Le Passé Composé

(The Past Indefinite or Compound Past)

This past tense expresses an action that took place at no definite time. It is used in conversational French, correspondence, and other informal writing. The **Passé Composé** is used more and more in literature these days and is taking the place of the **Passé Simple**. It is a compound tense because it is formed with the **Présent de l'Indicatif** of *avoir* or *être* (depending on which of these two auxiliaries is required to form a compound tense) plus the past participle. See page x for the distinction made between verbs conjugated with *avoir* or *être*.

EXAMPLES:

1. Il **est allé** à l'école. He *went* to school.
2. Il **est allé** à l'école. He *did go* to school.
3. Il **est allé** à l'école. He *has gone* to school.
4. J'**ai mangé** dans ce restaurant beaucoup de fois.
I *have eaten* in this restaurant many times.

NOTE: In examples 3 and 4 in English the verb is formed with the Present Tense of *to have* (*have* or *has*) plus the past participle of the verb you are using. In English, this form is called the *Present Perfect*.

5. J'ai **parlé** au garcon. I *spoke* to the boy. OR: I *have spoken* to the boy.

OR:

I *did speak* to the boy.

Le Plus-que-parfait de l'Indicatif

(The Pluperfect or Past Perfect Indicative)

In French and English this tense is used to express an action which happened in the past *before* another past action. Since it is used in relation to another past action, the other past action is expressed in either the **Passé Composé** or the **Imparfait de l'Indicatif** in French. This tense is used in formal writing and literature as well as in conversational French and informal writing. The correct use of this tense is strictly observed in French. In English, however, too often we neglect to use it correctly. It is a compound tense because it is formed with the **Imparfait de l'Indicatif** of *avoir* or *être* (depending on which of these two auxiliaries is required to form a compound tense) plus the past participle. See page x for the distinction made between verbs conjugated with *avoir* or *être*. In English, this tense is formed with the Past Tense of *to have* (*had*) plus the past participle of the verb you are using.

EXAMPLES:

(a) Je me suis rappelé que j'**avais oublié** de le lui dire.
I remembered that I *had forgotten* to tell him.

NOTE: It would be incorrect in English to say: I remembered that I *forgot* to tell him. The point here is that *first* I forgot; then, I remembered. Both actions are in the past. The action that occurred in the past *before* the other past action is in the Pluperfect. And in this example it is *I had forgotten* (**j'avais oublié**).

(b) J'**avais étudié** la leçon que le professeur a expliquée.
I *had studied* the lesson which the teacher explained.

NOTE: *First* I studied the lesson; then, the teacher explained it. Both actions are in the past. The action that occurred in the past *before* the other past action is in the Pluperfect. And in this example it is *I had studied* (**j'avais étudié**).

(c) J'étais fatigué ce matin parce que je n'**avais** pas **dormi**.
I was tired this morning because I *had* not *slept*.

Le Passé Antérieur

(The Past Anterior)

This tense is similar to the **Plus-que-parfait de l'Indicatif.** The main difference is that in French it is a literary tense; that is, it is used in formal writing, such as history and literature. More and more French writers today use the **Plus-que-parfait de l'Indicatif** instead of this tense. Generally speaking, the **Passé Antérieur** is to the **Plus-que-parfait** what the **Passé Simple** is to the **Passé Composé**. The **Passé Antérieur** is a compound tense. In French, it is formed with the **Passé Simple** of *avoir* or *être* (depending on which of these two auxiliaries is required to form a compound tense) plus the past participle. In English, it is formed in the same way as the *Pluperfect* or *Past Perfect*. This tense is ordinarily introduced by conjunctions of time: **après que, aussitôt que, dès que, lorsque, quand.**

EXAMPLE:
Quand il **eut mangé** tout, il partit.
When he *had eaten* everything, he left.

NOTE: In conversational French and informal writing, the **Plus-que-parfait de l'Indicatif** is used instead: Quand il **avait mangé** tout, il est parti. The translation into English is the same.

Le Futur Antérieur

(The Future Perfect or Future Anterior)

In French and English this tense is used to express an action which will happen in the future *before* another future action. Since it is used in relation to another future action, the other future action is expressed in the simple Future in French, but not always in the simple Future in English. In French, it is used in conversation and informal writing as well as in formal writing and in literature. It is a compound tense because it is formed with the **Futur** of *avoir* or *être* (depending on which of these two auxiliaries is required to form a compound tense) plus the past participle of the verb you are using. In English, it is formed by using *shall have* or *will have* plus the past participle of the verb you are using.

EXAMPLES:

(a) Elle arrivera demain et j'**aurai fini** le travail.
She will arrive tomorrow and I *shall have finished* the work.

NOTE: First, I shall finish the work; then, she will arrive. The action that will occur in the future *before* the other future action is in the **Futur Antérieur.**

(b) Quand elle arrivera demain, j'**aurai fini** le travail.
When she arrives tomorrow, I *shall have finished* the work.

NOTE: The idea of future time here is the same as in example (a) above. In English, the Present Tense is used (*When she arrives...*) to express a near future. In French, the **Futur** is used (**Quand elle arrivera...**) because **quand** precedes and the action will take place in the future.

Le Conditionnel Passé

(The Conditional Perfect)

This is used in French and English to express an action that you *would have done* if something else had been possible; that is, you would have done something *on condition* that something else had been possible. It is a compound tense because it is formed with the **Conditionnel Présent** of *avoir* or *être* plus the past participle of the verb you are using. In English, it is formed by using *would have* plus the past participle. Observe the difference between the following examples and the one given for the use of the **Conditionnel Présent** which was explained and illustrated previously.

EXAMPLES:

(a) J'**aurais fait** le travail si j'avais étudié.
I *would have done* the work if I had studied.

(b) J'**aurais fait** le travail si j'avais eu le temps.
I *would have done* the work if I had had the time.

NOTE: Review the **Plus-que-parfait de l'Indicatif** which was explained and illustrated previously in order to understand the use of *if I had studied* (**si j'avais étudié**) and *if I had had the time* (**si j'avais eu le temps**).

Le Passé du Subjonctif

(The Past or Perfect Subjunctive)

This tense is used to express an action which took place in the past in relation to the present time. It is like the **Passé Composé**, except that the auxiliary verb (*avoir* or *être*) is in the **Présent du Subjonctif.** The Subjunctive is used (as was noted in the previous sections of verb tenses in the Subjunctive) because what precedes is a certain verb, a certain conjunction, or a certain impersonal expression. The **Passé du Subjonctif** is also used in relation to a future time when another action will be completed. This tense is rarely used in English. In French, however, this tense is used in formal writing and in literature as well as in conversational French and informal writing. It is a compound tense because it is formed with the **Présent du Subjonctif** of *avoir* or *être* as the auxiliary plus the past participle of the verb you are using.

EXAMPLES:

(a) A past action in relation to the present
Il est possible qu'elle **soit partie.**
It is possible that she *may have left.* OR: It is possible that she *has left.*
Je doute qu'il **ait fait** cela.
I doubt that he *did* that.

(b) An action that will take place in the future
J'insiste que vous **soyez rentré** avant dix heures.
I insist that you *be back* before ten o'clock.

Le Plus-que-parfait du Subjonctif

(The Pluperfect or Past Perfect Subjunctive)

This tense is used for the same reasons as the **Imparfait du Subjonctif** —that is, after certain verbs, conjunctions and impersonal expressions which were used in examples previously under **le Présent du Subjonctif.** The main difference between the **Imparfait du Subjonctif** and this tense is the time of the action in the past. If the action was *not* completed, the **Imparfait du Subjonctif** is used. If the action was completed, this tense is used. It is rarely used in English. In French, it is used only in formal writing and in literature. For that reason, you should merely be familiar with it so you can recognize it in your readings in French literature. In conversational French and in informal writing, this tense is avoided. Use, instead, the **Passé du Subjonctif**. This is a compound tense. It is formed by using the **Imparfait du Subjonctif** of *avoir* or *être* plus the past participle. This tense is like the **Plus-que-parfait de l'Indicatif,** except that the auxiliary verb (*avoir* or *être*) is in the **Imparfait du Subjonctif**. Review the uses of the Subjunctive mood.

EXAMPLES:

(a) Il était possible qu'elle **fût partie**.
It was possible that she *might have left*.

NOTE: Avoid this tense in French. Use, instead, **le Passé du Subjonctif:**
Il était possible qu'elle *soit partie*.

(b) Je ne croyais pas qu'elle **eût dit** cela.
I did not believe that she *had said* that.

NOTE: Avoid this tense in French. Use, instead, **le Passé du Subjonctif:**
Je ne croyais pas qu'elle **ait dit** cela.

(c) Je n'ai pas cru qu'elle **eût dit** cela.
I did not believe that she *had said* that.

NOTE: Avoid this tense in French. Use, instead, **le Passé du Subjonctif:**
Je n'ai pas cru qu'elle **ait dit** cela.

(d) J'ai craint que vous ne **fussiez tombé**.
I was afraid that you *had fallen*.

NOTE: Avoid this tense in French. Use, instead, **le Passé du Subjonctif:**
J'ai craint que vous ne **soyez tombé**.

L'Impératif

(The Imperative)

The Imperative Mood is used in French and English to express a command or a request. It is also used to express an indirect request made in the third person (see the last two examples below). In both languages it is formed by dropping the subject and using the Present tense. There are a few exceptions in both languages when the **Présent du Subjonctif** is used.

EXAMPLES:

(a) Sortez!
Get out!

(b) Entrez!
Come in!

(c) Buvons!
Let's drink!

(d) **Soyez** à l'heure! (Subjunctive is used)
Be on time! (Subjunctive is used)

(e) Dieu le **veuille!** (Subjunctive is used)
May God *grant* it! (Subjunctive is used)

(f) Qu'ils **mangent du** gâteau! (Subjunctive is used)
Let them eat cake!

VERB TENSES AND MOODS IN FRENCH WITH ENGLISH EQUIVALENTS

French	English
Les Temps Simples	**Simple Tenses**
Présent de l'indicatif	*Present Indicative*
Imparfait de l'indicatif	*Imperfect Indicative*
Passé Simple (passé défini)	*Past Definite (Simple Past)*
Futur	*Future*
Conditionnel présent	*Conditional*
Présent du subjonctif	*Present Subjunctive*
Imparfait du subjonctif	*Imperfect Subjunctive*
Les Temps Composés	**Compound Tenses**
Passé composé (passé indéfini)	*Past Indefinite*
Plus-que-parfait de l'indicatif	*Pluperfect or Past Perfect Indicative*
Passé antérieur	*Past Anterior*
Futur antérieur	*Future Perfect or Future Anterior*
Conditionnel passé	*Conditional Perfect*
Passé du subjonctif	*Past Subjunctive*
Plus-que-parfait du subjonctif	*Pluperfect or Past Perfect Subjunctive*
Impératif	*Imperative or Command*

French Verbs Fully Conjugated

Subject Pronouns

The subject pronouns for all the verbs that follow have been omitted in order to emphasize the verb forms. The subject pronouns are, as you know, as follows:

SINGULAR: je, tu, il (elle, on);
PLURAL: nous, vous, ils (elles)

to lower, reduce, humiliate, humble

Pres. Ind.	abaisse, abaisses, abaisse; abaissons, abaissez, abaissent
Imp. Ind.	abaissais, abaissais, abaissait; abaissions, abaissiez, abaissaient
Past Def.	abaissai, abaissas, abaissa; abaissâmes, abaissâtes, abaissèrent
Future	abaisserai, abaisseras, abaissera; abaisserons, abaisserez, abaisseront
Condit.	abaisserais, abaisserais, abaisserait; abaisserions, abaisseriez, abaisseraient
Pres. Subj.	abaisse, abaisses, abaisse; abaissions, abaissiez, abaissent
Imp. Subj.	abaissasse, abaissasses, abaissât; abaissassions, abaissassiez, abaissassent
Past Indef.	ai abaissé, as abaissé, a abaissé; avons abaissé, avez abaissé, ont abaissé
Pluperf.	avais abaissé, avais abaissé, avait abaissé; avions abaissé, aviez abaissé, avaient abaissé
Past Ant.	eus abaissé, eus abaissé, eut abaissé; eûmes abaissé, eûtes abaissé, eurent abaissé
Fut. Perf.	aurai abaissé, auras abaissé, aura abaissé; aurons abaissé, aurez abaissé, auront abaissé
Cond. Perf.	aurais abaissé, aurais abaissé, aurait abaissé; aurions abaissé, auriez abaissé, auraient abaissé
Past Subj.	aie abaissé, aies abaissé, ait abaissé; ayons abaissé, ayez abaissé, aient abaissé
Plup. Subj.	eusse abaissé, eusses abaissé, eût abaissé; eussions abaissé, eussiez abaissé, eussent abaissé
Imperative	abaisse, abaissons, abaissez

to humble oneself, lower oneself, condescend

Pres. Ind.	m'abaisse, t'abaisses, s'abaisse; nous abaissons, vous abaissez, s'abaissent
Imp. Ind.	m'abaissais, t'abaissais, s'abaissait; nous abaissions, vous abaissiez, s'abaissaient
Past Def.	m'abaissai, t'abaissas, s'abaissa; nous abaissâmes, vous abaissâtes, s'abaissèrent
Future	m'abaisserai, t'abaisseras, s'abaissera; nous abaisserons, vous abaisserez, s'abaisseront
Condit.	m'abaisserais, t'abaisserais, s'abaisserait; nous abaisserions, vous abaisseriez, s'abaisseraient
Pres. Subj.	m'abaisse, t'abaisses, s'abaisse; nous abaissions, vous abaissiez, s'abaissent
Imp. Subj.	m'abaissasse, t'abaissasses, s'abaissât; nous abaissassions, vous abaissassiez, s'abaissassent
Past Indef.	me suis abaissé(e), t'es abaissé(e), s'est abaissé(e); nous sommes abaissé(e)s, vous êtes abaissé(e)(s), se sont abaissé(e)s
Pluperf.	m'étais abaissé(e), t'étais abaissé(e), s'était abaissé(e); nous étions abaissé(e)s, vous étiez abaissé(e)(s), s'étaient abaissé(e)s
Past Ant.	me fus abaissé(e), te fus abaissé(e), se fut abaissé(e); nous fûmes abaissé(e)s, vous fûtes abaissé(e)(s), se furent abaissé(e)s
Fut. Perf.	me serai abaissé(e), te seras abaissé(e), se sera abaissé(e); nous serons abaissé(e)s, vous serez abaissé(e)(s), se seront abaissé(e)s
Cond. Perf.	me serais abaissé(e), te serais abaissé(e), se serait abaissé(e); nous serions abaissé(e)s, vous seriez abaissé(e)(s), se seraient abaissé(e)s
Past Subj.	me sois abaissé(e), te sois abaissé(e), se soit abaissé(e); nous soyons abaissé(e)s, vous soyez abaissé(e)(s), se soient abaissé(e)s
Plup. Subj.	me fusse abaissé(e), te fusses abaissé(e), se fût abaissé(e); nous fussions abaissé(e)s, vous fussiez abaissé(e)(s), se fussent abaissé(e)s
Imperative	abaisse-toi, abaissons-nous, abaissez-vous

Pres. Ind.	abandonne, abandonnes, abandonne; abandonnons, abandonnez, abandonnent	*to abandon,*
Imp. Ind.	abandonnais, abandonnais, abandonnait; abandonnions, abandonniez, abandonnaient	*to desert*
Past Def.	abandonnai, abandonnas, abandonna; abandonnâmes, abandonnâtes, abandonnèrent	
Fut. Ind.	abandonnerai, abandonneras, abandonnera; abandonnerons, abandonnerez, abandonneront	
Condit.	abandonnerais, abandonnerais, abandonnerait; abandonnerions, abandonneriez, abandonneraient	
Pres. Subj.	abandonne, abandonnes, abandonne; abandonnions, abandonniez, abandonnent	
Imp. Subj.	abandonnasse, abandonnasses, abandonnât; abandonnassions, abandonnassiez, abandonnassent	
Past Indef.	ai abandonné, as abandonné, a abandonné; avons abandonné, avez abandonné, ont abandonné	
Pluperf.	avais abandonné, avais abandonné, avait abandonné; avions abandonné, aviez abandonné, avaient abandonné	
Past Ant.	eus abandonné, eus abandonné, eut abandonné; eûmes abandonné, eûtes abandonné, eurent abandonné	
Fut. Perf.	aurai abandonné, auras abandonné, aura abandonné; aurons abandonné, aurez abandonné, auront abandonné	
Cond. Perf.	aurais abandonné, aurais abandonné, aurait abandonné; aurions abandonné, auriez abandonné, auraient abandonné	
Past Subj.	aie abandonné, aies abandonné, ait abandonné; ayons abandonné, ayez abandonné, aient abandonné	
Plup. Subj.	eusse abandonné, eusses abandonné, eût abandonné; eussions abandonné, eussiez abandonné, eussent abandonné	
Imperative	abandonne, abandonnons, abandonnez	

to daze, deafen, stun, bewilder, stupefy

Pres. Ind.	abasourdis, abasourdis, abasourdit; abasourdissons, abasourdissez, abasourdissent
Imp. Ind.	abasourdissais, abasourdissais, abasourdissait; abasourdissions, abasourdissiez, abasourdissaient
Past Def.	abasourdis, abasourdis, abasourdit; abasourdîmes, abasourdîtes, abasourdirent
Future	abasourdirai, abasourdiras, abasourdira; abasourdirons, abasourdirez, abasourdiront
Condit.	abasourdirais, abasourdirais, abasourdirait; abasourdirions, abasourdiriez, abasourdiraient
Pres. Subj.	abasourdisse, abasourdisses, abasourdisse; abasourdissions, abasourdissiez, abasourdissent
Imp. Subj.	abasourdisse, abasourdisses, abasourdît; abasourdissions, abasourdissiez, abasourdissent
Past Indef.	ai abasourdi, as abasourdi, a abasourdi; avons abasourdi, avez abasourdi, ont abasourdi
Pluperf.	avais abasourdi, avais abasourdi, avait abasourdi; avions abasourdi, aviez abasourdi, avaient abasourdi
Past Ant.	eus abasourdi, eus abasourdi, eut abasourdi; eûmes abasourdi, eûtes abasourdi, eurent abasourdi
Fut. Perf.	aurai abasourdi, auras abasourdi, aura abasourdi; aurons abasourdi, aurez abasourdi, auront abasourdi
Cond. Perf.	aurais abasourdi, aurais abasourdi, aurait abasourdi; aurions abasourdi, auriez abasourdi, auraient abasourdi
Past Subj.	aie abasourdi, aies abasourdi, ait abasourdi; ayons abasourdi, ayez abasourdi, aient abasourdi
Plup. Subj.	eusse abasourdi, eusses abasourdi, eût abasourdi; eussions abasourdi, eussiez abasourdi, eussent abasourdi
Imperative	abasourdis, abasourdissons, abasourdissez

to dishearten, strike down, knock down

Pres. Ind.	abats, abats, abat; abattons, abattez, abattent
Imp. Ind.	abattais, abattais, abattait; abattions, abattiez, abattaient
Past Def.	abattis, abattis, abattit; abattîmes, abattîtes, abattirent
Fut. Ind.	abattrai, abattras, abattra; abattrons, abattrez, abattront
Condit.	abattrais, abattrais, abattrait; abattrions, abattriez, abattraient
Pres. Subj.	abatte, abattes, abatte; abattions, abattiez, abattent
Imp. Subj.	abattisse, abattisses, abattît; abattissions, abattissiez, abattissent
Past Indef.	ai abattu, as abattu, a abattu; avons abattu, avez abattu, ont abattu
Pluperf.	avais abattu, avais abattu, avait abattu; avions abattu, aviez abattu, avaient abattu
Past Ant.	eus abattu, eus abattu, eut abattu; eûmes abattu, eûtes abattu, eurent abattu
Fut. Perf.	aurai abattu, auras abattu, aura abattu; aurons abattu, aurez abattu, auront abattu
Cond. Perf.	aurais abattu, aurais abattu, aurait abattu; aurions abattu, auriez abattu, auraient abattu
Past Subj.	aie abattu, aies abattu, ait abattu; ayons abattu, ayez abattu, aient abattu
Plup. Subj.	eusse abattu, eusses abattu, eût abattu; eussions abattu, eussiez abattu, eussent abattu
Imperative	abats, abattons, abattez

to abolish, do away with

Pres. Ind.	abolis, abolis, abolit; abolissons, abolissez, abolissent
Imp. Ind.	abolissais, abolissais, abolissait; abolissions, abolissiez, abolissaient
Past Def.	abolis, abolis, abolit; abolîmes, abolîtes, abolirent
Future	abolirai, aboliras, abolira; abolirons, abolirez, aboliront
Condit.	abolirais, abolirais, abolirait; abolirions, aboliriez, aboliraient
Pres. Subj.	abolisse, abolisses, abolisse; abolissions, abolissiez, abolissent
Imp. Subj.	abolisse, abolisses, abolît; abolissions, abolissiez, abolissent
Past Indef.	ai aboli, as aboli, a aboli; avons aboli, avez aboli, ont aboli
Pluperf.	avais aboli, avais aboli, avait aboli; avions aboli, aviez aboli, avaient aboli
Past Ant.	eus aboli, eus aboli, eut aboli; eûmes aboli, eûtes aboli, eurent aboli
Fut. Perf.	aurai aboli, auras aboli, aura aboli; aurons aboli, aurez aboli, auront aboli
Cond. Perf.	aurais aboli, aurais aboli, aurait aboli; aurions aboli, auriez aboli, auraient aboli
Past Subj.	aie aboli, aies aboli, ait aboli; ayons aboli, ayez aboli, aient aboli
Plup. Subj.	eusse aboli, eusses aboli, eût aboli; eussions aboli, eussiez aboli, eussent aboli
Imperative	abolis, abolissons, abolissez

to absolve

Pres. Ind.	absous, absous, absout; absolvons, absolvez, absolvent
Imp. Ind.	absolvais, absolvais, absolvait; absolvions, absolviez, absolvaient
Past Def.	[inemployé]
Future	absoudrai, absoudras, absoudra; absoudrons, absoudrez, absoudront
Condit.	absoudrais, absoudrais, absoudrait; absoudrions, absoudriez, absoudraient
Pres. Subj.	absolve, absolves, absolve; absolvions, absolviez, absolvent
Imp. Subj.	[inemployé]
Past Indef.	ai absous, as absous, a absous; avons absous, avez absous, ont absous
Pluperf.	avais absous, avais absous, avait absous; avions absous, aviez absous, avaient absous
Past Ant.	eus absous, eus absous, eut absous; eûmes absous, eûtes absous, eurent absous
Fut. Perf.	aurai absous, auras absous, aura absous; aurons absous, aurez absous, auront absous
Cond. Perf.	aurais absous, aurais absous, aurait absous; aurions absous, auriez absous, auraient absous
Past Subj.	aie absous, aies absous, ait absous; ayons absous, ayez absous, aient absous
Plup. Subj.	eusse absous, eusses absous, eût absous; eussions absous, eussiez absous, eussent absous
Imperative	absous, absolvons, absolvez

to abstain

Pres. Ind.	m'abstiens, t'abstiens, s'abstient; nous abstenons, vous abstenez, s'abstiennent
Imp. Ind.	m'abstenais, t'abstenais, s'abstenait; nous abstenions, vous abstenez, s'abstenaient
Past Def.	m'abstins, t'abstins, s'abstint; nous abstînmes, vous abstîntes, s'abstinrent
Fut. Ind.	m'abstiendrai, t'abstiendras, s'abstiendra; nous abstiendrons, vous abstiendrez, s'abstiendront
Condit.	m'abstiendrais, t'abstiendrais, s'abstiendrait; nous abstiendrions, vous abstiendriez, s'abstiendraient
Pres. Subj.	m'abstienne, t'abstiennes, s'abstienne; nous abstenions, vous absteniez, s'abstiennent
Imp. Subj.	m'abstinsse, t'abstinsses, s'abstînt; nous abstinssions, vous abstinssiez, s'abstinssent
Past Indef.	me suis abstenu(e), t'es abstenu(e), s'est abstenu(e); nous sommes abstenu(e)s, vous êtes abstenu(e)(s), se sont abstenu(e)s
Pluperf.	m'étais abstenu(e), t'étais abstenu(e), s'était abstenu(e); nous étions abstenu(e)s, vous étiez abstenu(e)(s), s'étaient abstenu(e)s
Past Ant.	me fus abstenu(e), te fus abstenu(e), se fut abstenu(e); nous fûmes abstenu(e)s, vous fûtes abstenu(e)(s), se furent abstenu(e)s
Fut. Perf.	me serai abstenu(e), te seras abstenu(e), se sera abstenu(e); nous serons abstenu(e)s, vous serez abstenu(e)(s), se seront abstenu(e)s
Cond. Perf.	me serais abstenu(e), te serais abstenu(e), se serait abstenu(e); nous serions abstenu(e)s, vous seriez abstenu(e)(s), se seraient abstenu(e)s
Past Subj.	me sois abstenu(e), te sois abstenu(e), se soit abstenu(e); nous soyons abstenu(e)s, vous soyez abstenu(e)(s), se soient abstenu(e)s
Plup. Subj.	me fusse abstenu(e), te fusses abstenu(e), se fût abstenu(e); nous fussions abstenu(e)s, vous fussiez abstenu(e)(s), se fussent abstenu(e)s
Imperative	abstiens-toi, abstenons-nous, abstenez-vous

to abstract

Pres. Ind.	abstrais, abstrais, abstrait; abstrayons, abstrayez, abstraient
Imp. Ind.	abstrayais, abstrayais, abstrayait; abstrayions, abstrayiez, abstrayaient
Past Def.	[inemployé]
Future	abstrairai, abstrairas, abstraira; abstrairons, abstrairez, abstrairont
Condit.	abstrairais, abstrairais, abstrairait; abstrairions, abstrairiez, abstrairaient
Pres. Subj.	abstraie, abstraies, abstraie; abstrayions, abstrayiez, abstraient
Imp. Subj.	[inemployé]
Past Indef.	ai abstrait, as abstrait, a abstrait; avons abstrait, avez abstrait, ont abstrait
Pluperf.	avais abstrait, avais abstrait, avait abstrait; avions abstrait, aviez abstrait, avaient abstrait
Past Ant.	eus abstrait, eus abstrait, eut abstrait; eûmes abstrait, eûtes abstrait, eurent abstrait
Fut. Perf.	aurai abstrait, auras abstrait, aura abstrait; aurons abstrait, aurez abstrait, auront abstrait
Cond. Perf.	aurais abstrait, aurais abstrait, aurait abstrait; aurions abstrait, auriez abstrait, auraient abstrait
Past Subj.	aie abstrait, aies abstrait, ait abstrait; ayons abstrait, ayez abstrait, aient abstrait
Plup. Subj.	eusse abstrait, eusses abstrait, eût abstrait; eussions abstrait, eussiez abstrait, eussent abstrait
Imperative	abstrais, abstrayons, abstrayez

to accept

Pres. Ind.	accepte, acceptes, accepte; acceptons, acceptez, acceptent
Imp. Ind.	acceptais, acceptais, acceptait; acceptions, acceptiez, acceptaient
Past Def.	acceptai, acceptas, accepta; acceptâmes, acceptâtes, acceptèrent
Fut. Ind.	accepterai, accepteras, acceptera; accepterons, accepterez, accepteront
Condit.	accepterais, accepterais, accepterait; accepterions, accepteriez, accepteraient
Pres. Subj.	accepte, acceptes, accepte; acceptions, acceptiez, acceptent
Imp. Subj.	acceptasse, acceptasses, acceptât; acceptassions, acceptassiez, acceptassent
Past Indef.	ai accepté, as accepté, a accepté; avons accepté, avez accepté, ont accepté
Pluperf.	avais accepté, avais accepté, avait accepté; avions accepté, aviez accepté, avaient accepté
Past Ant.	eus accepté, eus accepté, eut accepté; eûmes accepté, eûtes accepté, eurent accepté
Fut. Perf.	aurai accepté, auras accepté, aura accepté; aurons accepté, aurez accepté, auront accepté
Cond. Perf.	aurais accepté, aurais accepté, aurait accepté; aurions accepté, auriez accepté, auraient accepté
Past Subj.	aie accepté, aies accepté, ait accepté; ayons accepté, ayez accepté, aient accepté
Plup. Subj.	eusse accepté, eusses accepté, eût accepté; eussions accepté, eussiez accepté, eussent accepté
Imperative	accepte, acceptons, acceptez

PRES. PART. *acclamant* PAST PART. *acclamé*

acclamer

to acclaim, applaud, cheer

Pres. Ind.	acclame, acclames, acclame; acclamons, acclamez, acclament
Imp. Ind.	acclamais, acclamais, acclamait; acclamions, acclamiez, acclamaient
Past Def.	acclamai, acclamas, acclama; acclamâmes, acclamâtes, acclamèrent
Future	acclamerai, acclameras, acclamera; acclamerons, acclamerez, acclameront
Condit.	acclamerais, acclamerais, acclamerait; acclamerions, acclameriez, acclameraient
Pres. Subj.	acclame, acclames, acclame; acclamions, acclamiez, acclament
Imp. Subj.	acclamasse, acclamasses, acclamât; acclamassions, acclamassiez, acclamassent
Past Indef.	ai acclamé, as acclamé, a acclamé; avons acclamé, avec acclamé, ont acclamé
Plup. Ind.	avais acclamé, avais acclamé, avait acclamé; avions acclamé, aviez acclamé, avaient acclamé
Past Ant.	eus acclamé, eus acclamé, eut acclamé; eûmes acclamé, eûtes acclamé, eurent acclamé
Fut. Perf.	aurai acclamé, auras acclamé, aura acclamé; aurons acclamé, aurez acclamé, auront acclamé
Cond. Perf.	aurais acclamé, aurais acclamé, aurait acclamé; aurions acclamé, auriez acclamé, auraient acclamé
Past Subj.	aie acclamé, aies acclamé, ait acclamé; ayons acclamé, ayez acclamé, aient acclamé
Plup. Subj.	eusse acclamé, eusses acclamé, eût acclamé; eussions acclamé, eussiez acclamé, eussent acclamé
Imperative	acclame, acclamons, acclamez

to accompany

Pres. Ind.	accompagne, accompagnes, accompagne; accompagnons, accompagnez, accompagnent
Imp. Ind.	accompagnais, accompagnais, accompagnait; accompagnions, accompagniez, accompagnaient
Past Def.	accompagnai, accompagnas, accompagna; accompagnâmes, accompagnâtes, accompagnèrent
Fut. Ind.	accompagnerai, accompagneras, accompagnera; accompagnerons, accompagnerez, accompagneront
Condit.	accompagnerais, accompagnerais, accompagnerait; accompagnerions, accompagneriez, accompagneraient
Pres. Subj.	accompagne, accompagnes, accompagne; accompagnions, accompagniez, accompagnent
Imp. Subj.	accompagnasse, accompagnasses, accompagnât; accompagnassions, accompagnassiez, accompagnassent
Past Indef.	ai accompagné, as accompagné, a accompagné; avons accompagné, avez accompagné, ont accompagné
Pluperf.	avais accompagné, avais accompagné, avait accompagné; avions accompagné, aviez accompagné, avaient accompagné
Past Ant.	eus accompagné, eus accompagné, eut accompagné; eûmes accompagné, eûtes accompagné, eurent accompagné
Fut. Perf.	aurai accompagné, auras accompagné, aura accompagné; aurons accompagné, aurez accompagné, auront accompagné
Cond. Perf.	aurais accompagné, aurais accompagné, aurait accompagné; aurions accompagné, auriez accompagné, auraient accompagné
Past Subj.	aie accompagné, aies accompagné, ait accompagné; ayons accompagné, ayez accompagné, aient accompagné
Plup. Subj.	eusse accompagné, eusses accompagné, eût accompagné; eussions accompagné, eussiez accompagné, eussent accompagné
Imperative	accompagne, accompagnons, accompagnez

to run to, run up to

Pres. Ind.	accours, accours, accourt; accourons, accourez, accourent
Imp. Ind.	accourais, accourais, accourait; accourions, accouriez, accouraient
Past Def.	accourus, accourus, accourut; accourûmes, accourûtes, accoururent
Future	accourrai, accourras, accourra; accourrons, accourrez, accourront
Condit.	accourrais, accourrais, accourrait; accourrions, accourriez, accourraient
Pres. Subj.	accoure, accoures, accoure; accourions, accouriez, accourent
Imp. Subj.	accourusse, accourusses, accourût; accourussions, accourussiez, accourussent
Past Indef.	ai accouru, as accouru, a accouru; avons accouru, avez accouru, ont accouru
Plup. Ind.	avais accouru, avais accouru, avait accouru; avions accouru, aviez accouru, avaient accouru
Past Ant.	eus accouru, eus accouru, eut accouru; eûmes accouru, eûtes accouru, eurent accouru
Fut. Perf.	aurai accouru, auras accouru, aura accouru; aurons accouru, aurez accouru, auront accouru
Cond. Perf.	aurais accouru, aurais accouru, aurait accouru; aurions accouru, auriez accouru, auraient accouru
Past Subj.	aie accouru, aies accouru, ait accouru; ayons accouru, ayez accouru, aient accouru
Plup. Subj.	eusse accouru, eusses accouru, eût accouru; eussions accouru, eussiez accouru, eussent accouru
Imperative	accours, accourons, accourez

to hang (on a hanger, a nail, e.g., a coat)

Pres Ind.	accroche, accroches, accroche; accrochons, accrochez, accrochent
Imp. Ind.	accrochais, accrochais, accrochait; accrochions, accrochiez, accrochaient
Past Def.	accrochai, accrochas, accrocha; accrochâmes, accrochâtes, accrochèrent
Future	accrocherai, accrocheras, accrochera; accrocherons, accrocherez, accrocheront
Condit.	accrocherais, accrocherais, accrocherait; accrocherions, accrocheriez, accrocheraient
Pres. Subj.	accroche, accroches, accroche; accrochions, accrochiez, accrochent
Imp. Subj.	accrochasse, accrochasses, accrochât; accrochassions, accrochassiez, accrochassent
Past Indef.	ai accroché, as accroché, a accroché; avons accroché, avez accroché, ont accroché
Pluperf.	avais accroché, avais accroché, avait accroché; avions accroché, aviez accroché, avaient accroché
Past Ant.	eus accroché, eus accroché, eut accroché; eûmes accroché, eûtes accroché, eurent accroché
Fut. Perf.	aurai accroché, auras accroché, aura accroché; aurons accroché, aurez accroché, auront accroché
Cond.	aurais accroché, aurais accroché, aurait accroché; aurions accroché, auriez accroché, auraient accroché
Past Subj.	aie accroché, aies accroché, ait accroché; ayons accroché, ayez accroché, aient accroché
Plup. Subj.	eusse accroché, eusses accroché, eût accroché; eussions accroché, eussiez accroché, eussent accroché
Imperative	accroche, accrochons, accrochez

to increase, make greater

Pres. Ind.	accrois, accrois, accroît; accroissons, accroissez, accroissent
Imp. Ind.	accroissais, accroissais, accroissait; accroissions, accroissiez, accroissaient
Past Def.	accrus, accrus, accrut; accrûmes, accrûtes, accrurent
Future	accroîtrai, accroîtras, accroîtra; accroîtrons, accroîtrez, accroîtront
Condit.	accroîtrais, accroîtrais, accroîtrait; accroîtrions, accroîtriez, accroîtraient
Pres. Subj.	accroisse, accroisses, accroisse; accroissions, accroissiez, accroissent
Imp. Subj.	accrusse, accrusses, accrût; accrussions, accrussiez, accrussent
Past Indef.	ai accru, as accru, a accru; avons accru, avez accru, ont accru
Plup. Ind.	avais accru, avais accru, avait accru; avions accru, aviez accru, avaient accru
Past Ant.	eus accru, eus accru, eut accru; eûmes accru, eûtes accru, eurent accru
Fut. Perf.	aurai accru, auras accru, aura accru; aurons accru, aurez accru, auront accru
Cond. Perf.	aurais accru, aurais accru, aurait accru; aurions accru, auriez accru, auraient accru
Past Subj.	aie accru, aies accru, ait accru; ayons accru, ayez accru, aient accru
Plup. Subj.	eusse accru, eusses accru, eût accru; eussions accru, eussiez accru, eussent accru
Imperative	accrois, accroissons, accroissez

to greet, welcome

Pres. Ind.	accueille, accueilles, accueille; accueillons, accueillez, accueillent
Imp. Ind.	accueillais, accueillais, accueillait; accueillions, accueilliez, accueillaient
Past Def.	accueillis, accueillis, accueillit; accueillîmes, accueillîtes, accueillirent
Fut. Ind.	accueillerai, accueilleras, accueillera; accueillerons, accueillerez, accueilleront
Condit.	accueillerais, accueillerais, accueillerait; accueillerions, accueilleriez, accueilleraient
Pres. Subj.	accueille, accueilles, accueille; accueillions, accueilliez, accueillent
Imp. Subj.	accueillisse, accueillisses, accueillît; accueillissions, accueillissiez, accueillissent
Past Indef.	ai accueilli, as accueilli, a accueilli; avons accueilli, avez accueilli, ont accueilli
Pluperf.	avais accueilli, avais accueilli, avait accueilli; avions accueilli, aviez accueilli, avaient accueilli
Past Ant.	eus accueilli, eus accueilli, eut accueilli; eûmes accueilli, eûtes accueilli, eurent accueilli
Fut. Perf.	aurai accueilli, auras accueilli, aura accueilli; aurons accueilli, aurez accueilli, auront accueilli
Cond. Perf.	aurais accueilli, aurais accueilli, aurait accueilli; aurions accueilli, auriez accueilli, auraient accueilli
Past Subj.	aie accueilli, aies accueilli, ait accueilli; ayons accueilli, ayez accueilli, aient accueilli
Plup. Subj.	eusse accueilli, eusses accueilli, eût accueilli; eussions accueilli, eussiez accueilli, eussent accueilli
Imperative	accueille, accueillons, accueillez

to accuse

Pres. Ind.	accuse, accuses, accuse; accusons, accusez, accusent
Imp. Ind.	accusais, accusais, accusait; accusions, accusiez, accusaient
Past Def.	accusai, accusas, accusa; accusâmes, accusâtes, accusèrent
Future	accuserai, accuseras, accusera; accuserons, accuserez, accuseront
Condit.	accuserais, accuserais, accuserait; accuserions, accuseriez, accuseraient
Pres. Subj.	accuse, accuses, accuse; accusions, accusiez, accusent
Imp. Subj.	accusasse, accusasses, accusât; accusassions, accusassiez, accusassent
Past Indef.	ai accusé, as accusé, a accusé; avons accusé, avez accusé, ont accusé
Plup. Ind.	avais accusé, avais accusé, avait accusé; avions accusé, aviez accusé, avaient accusé
Past Ant.	eus accusé, eus accusé, eut accusé; eûmes accusé, eûtes accusé, eurent accusé
Fut. Perf.	aurai accusé, auras accusé, aura accusé; aurons accusé, aurez accusé, auront accusé
Cond. Perf.	aurais accusé, aurais accusé, aurait accusé; aurions accusé, auriez accusé, auraient accusé
Past Subj.	aie accusé, aies accusé, ait accusé; ayons accusé, ayez accusé, aient accusé
Plup. Subj.	eusse accusé, eusses accusé, eût accusé; eussions accusé, eussiez accusé, eussent accusé
Imperative	accuse, accusons, accusez

to buy, purchase

Pres. Ind.	achète, achètes, achète; achetons, achetez, achètent
Imp. Ind.	achetais, achetais, achetait; achetions, achetiez, achetaient
Past Def.	achetai, achetas, acheta; achetâmes, achetâtes, achetèrent
Fut. Ind.	achèterai, achèteras, achètera; achèterons, achèterez, achèteront
Condit.	achèterais, achèterais, achèterait; achèterions, achèteriez, achèteraient
Pres. Subj.	achète, achètes, achète; achetions, achetiez, achètent
Imp. Subj.	achetasse, achetasses, achetât; achetassions, achetassiez, achetassent
Past Indef.	ai acheté, as acheté, a acheté; avons acheté, avez acheté, ont acheté
Pluperf.	avais acheté, avais acheté, avait acheté; avions acheté, aviez acheté, avaient acheté
Past Ant.	eus acheté, eus acheté, eut acheté; eûmes acheté, eûtes acheté, eurent acheté
Fut. Perf.	aurai acheté, auras acheté, aura acheté; aurons acheté, aurez acheté, auront acheté
Cond. Perf.	aurais acheté, aurais acheté, aurait acheté; aurions acheté, auriez acheté, auraient acheté
Past Subj.	aie acheté, aies acheté, ait acheté; ayons acheté, ayez acheté, aient acheté
Plup. Subj.	eusse acheté, eusses acheté, eût acheté; eussions acheté, eussiez acheté, eussent acheté
Imperative	achète, achetons, achetez

to achieve, finish

Pres. Ind.	achève, achèves, achève; achevons, achevez, achèvent
Imp. Ind.	achevais, achevais, achevait; achevions, acheviez, achevaient
Past Def.	achevai, achevas, acheva; achevâmes, achevâtes, achevèrent
Future	achèverai, achèveras, achèvera; achèverons, achèverez, achèveront
Condit.	achèverais, achèverais, achèverait; achèverions, achèveriez, achèveraient
Pres. Subj.	achève, achèves, achève; achevions, acheviez, achèvent
Imp. Subj.	achevasse, achevasses, achevât; achevassions, achevassiez, achevassent
Past Indef.	ai achevé, as achevé, a achevé; avons achevé, avez achevé, ont achevé
Plup. Ind.	avais achevé, avais achevé, avait achevé; avions achevé, aviez achevé, avaient achevé
Past Ant.	eus achevé, eus achevé, eut achevé; eûmes achevé, eûtes achevé, eurent achevé
Fut. Perf.	aurai achevé, auras achevé, aura achevé; aurons achevé, aurez achevé, auront achevé
Cond. Perf.	aurais achevé, aurais achevé, aurait achevé; aurions achevé, auriez achevé, auraient achevé
Past Subj.	aie achevé, aies achevé, ait achevé; ayons achevé, ayez achevé, aient achevé
Plup. Subj.	eusse achevé, eusses achevé, eût achevé; eussions achevé, eussiez achevé, eussent achevé
Imperative	achève, achevons, achevez

to acquire

Pres. Ind.	acquiers, acquiers, acquiert; acquérons, acquérez, acquièrent
Imp. Ind.	acquérais, acquérais, acquérait; acquérions, acquériez, acquéraient
Past Def.	acquis, acquis, acquit; acquîmes, acquîtes, acquirent
Fut. Ind.	acquerrai, acquerras, acquerra; acquerrons, acquerrez, acquerront
Condit.	acquerrais, acquerrais, acquerrait; acquerrions, acquerriez, acquerraient
Pres. Subj.	acquière, acquières, acquière; acquérions, acquériez, acquièrent
Imp. Subj.	acquisse, acquisses, acquît; acquissions, acquissiez, acquissent
Past Indef.	ai acquis, as acquis, a acquis; avons acquis, avez acquis, ont acquis
Pluperf.	avais acquis, avais acquis, avait acquis; avions acquis, aviez acquis, avaient acquis
Past Ant.	eus acquis, eus acquis, eut acquis; eûmes acquis, eûtes acquis, eurent acquis
Fut. Perf.	aurai acquis, auras acquis, aura acquis; aurons acquis, aurez acquis, auront acquis
Cond. Perf.	aurais acquis, aurais acquis, aurait acquis; aurions acquis, auriez acquis, auraient acquis
Past Subj.	aie acquis, aies acquis, ait acquis; ayons acquis, ayez acquis, aient acquis
Plup. Subj.	eusse acquis, eusses acquis, eût acquis; eussions acquis, eussiez acquis, eussent acquis
Imperative	acquiers, acquérons, acquérez

to adjoin

Pres. Ind.	adjoins, adjoins, adjoint; adjoignons, adjoignez, adjoignent
Imp. Ind.	adjoignais, adjoignais, adjoignait; adjoignions, adjoigniez, adjoignaient
Past Def.	adjoignis, adjoignis, adjoignit; adjoignîmes, adjoignîtes, adjoignirent
Future	adjoindrai, adjoindras, adjoindra; adjoindrons, adjoindrez, adjoindront
Condit.	adjoindrais, adjoindrais, adjoindrait; adjoindrions, adjoindriez, adjoindraient
Pres. Subj.	adjoigne, adjoignes, adjoigne; adjoignions, adjoigniez, adjoignent
Imp. Subj.	adjoignisse, adjoignisses, adjoignît; adjoignissions, adjoignissiez, adjoignissent
Past Indef.	ai adjoint, as adjoint, a adjoint; avons adjoint, avez adjoint, ont adjoint
Plup. Ind.	avais adjoint, avais adjoint, avait adjoint; avions adjoint, aviez adjoint, avaient adjoint
Past Ant.	eus adjoint, eus adjoint, eut adjoint; eûmes adjoint, eûtes adjoint, eurent adjoint
Fut. Perf.	aurai adjoint, auras adjoint, aura adjoint; aurons adjoint, aurez adjoint, auront adjoint
Cond. Perf.	aurais adjoint, aurais adjoint, aurait adjoint; aurions adjoint, auriez adjoint, auraient adjoint
Past Subj.	aie adjoint, aies adjoint, ait adjoint; ayons adjoint, ayez adjoint, aient adjoint
Plup. Subj.	eusse adjoint, eusses adjoint, eût adjoint; eussions adjoint, eussiez adjoint, eussent adjoint
Imperative	adjoins, adjoignons, adjoignez

to admit

Pres. Ind.	admets, admets, admet; admettons, admettez, admettent
Imp. Ind.	admettais, admettais, admettait; admettions, admettiez, admettaient
Past Def.	admis, admis, admit; admîmes, admîtes, admirent
Fut. Ind.	admettrai, admettras, admettra; admettrons, admettrez, admettront
Condit.	admettrais, admettrais, admettrait; admettrions, admettriez, admettraient
Pres. Subj.	admette, admettes, admette; admettions, admettiez, admettent
Imp. Subj.	admisse, admisses, admît; admissions, admissiez, admissent
Past Indef.	ai admis, as admis, a admis; avons admis, avez admis, ont admis
Pluperf.	avais admis, avais admis, avait admis; avions admis, aviez admis, avaient admis
Past Ant.	eus admis, eus admis, eut admis; eûmes admis, eûtes admis, eurent admis
Fut. Perf.	aurai admis, auras admis, aura admis; aurons admis, aurez admis, auront admis
Cond. Perf.	aurais admis, aurais admis, aurait admis; aurions admis, auriez admis, auraient admis
Past Subj.	aie admis, aies admis, ait admis; ayons admis, ayez admis, aient admis
Plup. Subj.	eusse admis, eusses admis, eût admis; eussions admis, eussiez admis, eussent admis
Imperative	admets, admettons, admettez

to admire

Pres. Ind.	admire, admires, admire; admirons, admirez, admirent
Imp. Ind.	admirais, admirais, admirait; admirions, admiriez, admiraient
Past Def.	admirai, admiras, admira; admirâmes, admirâtes, admirèrent
Future	admirerai, admireras, admirera; admirerons, admirerez, admireront
Condit.	admirerais, admirerais, admirerait; admirerions, admireriez, admireraient
Pres. Subj.	admire, admires, admire; admirions, admiriez, admirent
Imp. Subj.	admirasse, admirasses, admirât; admirassions, admirassiez, admirassent
Past Indef.	ai admiré, as admiré, a admiré; avons admiré, avez admiré, ont admiré
Plup. Ind.	avais admiré, avais admiré, avait admiré; avions admiré, aviez admiré, avaient admiré
Past Ant.	eus admiré, eus admiré, eut admiré; eûmes admiré, eûtes admiré, eurent admiré
Fut. Perf.	aurai admiré, auras admiré, aura admiré; aurons admiré, aurez admiré, auront admiré
Cond. Perf.	aurais admiré, aurais admiré, aurait admiré; aurions admiré, auriez admiré, auraient admiré
Past Subj.	aie admiré, aies admiré, ait admiré; ayons admiré, ayez admiré, aient admiré
Plup. Subj.	eusse admiré, eusses admiré, eût admiré; eussions admiré, eussiez admiré, eussent admiré
Imperative	admire, admirons, admirez

to adore

Pres. Ind.	adore, adores, adore; adorons, adorez, adorent
Imp. Ind.	adorais, adorais, adorait; adorions, adoriez, adoraient
Past Def.	adorai, adoras, adora; adorâmes, adorâtes, adorèrent
Future	adorerai, adoreras, adorera; adorerons, adorerez, adoreront
Condit.	adorerais, adorerais, adorerait; adorerions, adoreriez, adoreraient
Pres. Subj.	adore, adores, adore; adorions, adoriez, adorent
Imp. Subj.	adorasse, adorasses, adorât; adorassions, adorassiez, adorassent
Past Indef.	ai adoré, as adoré, a adoré; avons adoré, avez adoré, ont adoré
Plup. Ind.	avais adoré, avais adoré, avait adoré; avions adoré, aviez adoré, avaient adoré
Past Ant.	eus adoré, eus adoré, eut adoré; eûmes adoré, eûtes adoré, eurent adoré
Fut. Perf.	aurai adoré, auras adoré, aura adoré; aurons adoré, aurez adoré, auront adoré
Cond. Perf.	aurais adoré, aurais adoré, aurait adoré; aurions adoré, auriez adoré, auraient adoré
Past Subj.	aie adoré, aies adoré, ait adoré; ayons adoré, ayez adoré, aient adoré
Plup. Subj.	eusse adoré, eusses adoré, eût adoré; eussions adoré, eussiez adoré, eussent adoré
Imperative	adore, adorons, adorez

to soften, appease, smooth

Pres. Ind.	adoucis, adoucis, adoucit; adoucissons, adoucissez, adoucissent
Imp. Ind.	adoucissais, adoucissais, adoucissait; adoucissions, adoucissiez, adoucissaient
Past Def.	adoucis, adoucis, adoucit; adoucîmes, adoucîtes, adoucirent
Future	adoucirai, adouciras, adoucira; adoucirons, adoucirez, adouciront
Condit.	adoucirais, adoucirais, adoucirait; adoucirions, adouciriez, adouciraient
Pres. Subj.	adoucisse, adoucisses, adoucisse; adoucissions, adoucissiez, adoucissent
Imp. Subj.	adoucisse, adoucisses, adoucît; adoucissions, adoucissiez, adoucissent
Past Indef.	ai adouci, as adouci, a adouci; avons adouci, avez adouci, ont adouci
Pluperf.	avais adouci, avais adouci, avait adouci; avions adouci, aviez adouci, avaient adouci
Past Ant.	eus adouci, eus adouci, eut adouci; eûmes adouci, eûtes adouci, eurent adouci
Fut. Perf.	aurai adouci, auras adouci, aura adouci; aurons adouci, aurez adouci, auront adouci
Cond. Perf.	aurais adouci, aurais adouci, aurait adouci; aurions adouci, auriez adouci, auraient adouci
Past Subj.	aie adouci, aies adouci, ait adouci; ayons adouci, ayez adouci, aient adouci
Plup. Subj.	eusse adouci, eusses adouci, eût adouci; eussions adouci, eussiez adouci, eussent adouci
Imperative	adoucis, adoucissons, adoucissez

to happen, occur, come to pass

Pres. Ind.	il advient
Imp. Ind.	il advenait
Past Def.	il advint
Future	il adviendra
Condit.	il adviendrait
Pres.Subj.	qu'il advienne
Imp. Subj.	qu'il advînt
Past Indef.	il est advenu
Plup. Ind.	il était advenu
Past Ant.	il fut advenu
Fut. Perf.	il sera advenu
Cond. Perf.	il serait advenu
Past. Subj.	qu'il soit advenu
Plup. Subj.	qu'il fût advenu
Imperative	[inemployé]

to annoy, irritate, pester

Pres. Ind.	agace, agaces, agace; agaçons, agacez, agacent
Imp. Ind.	agaçais, agaçais, agaçait; agacions, agaciez, agaçaient
Past Def.	agaçai, agaças, agaça; agaçâmes, agaçâtes, agacèrent
Future	agacerai, agaceras, agacera; agacerons, agacerez, agaceront
Condit.	agacerais, agacerais, agacerait; agacerions, agaceriez, agaceraient
Pres. Subj.	agace, agaces, agace; agacions, agaciez, agacent
Imp. Subj.	agaçasse, agaçasses, agaçât; agaçassions, agaçassiez, agaçassent
Past Indef.	ai agacé, as agacé, a agacé; avons agacé, avez agacé, ont agacé
Pluperf.	avais agacé, avais agacé, avait agacé; avions agacé, aviez agacé, avaient agacé
Past Ant.	eus agacé, eus agacé, eut agacé; eûmes agacé, eûtes agacé, eurent agacé
Fut. Perf.	aurai agacé, auras agacé, aura agacé; aurons agacé, aurez agacé, auront agacé
Cond. Perf.	aurais agacé, aurais agacé, aurait agacé; aurions agacé, auriez agacé, auraient agacé
Past Subj.	aie agacé, aies agacé, ait agacé; ayons agacé, ayez agacé, aient agacé
Plup. Subj.	eusse agacé, eusses agacé, eût agacé; eussions agacé, eussiez agacé, eussent agacé
Imperative	agace, agaçons, agacez

to act, behave

Pres. Ind.	agis, agis, agit; agissons, agissez, agissent
Imp. Ind.	agissais, agissais, agissait; agissions, agissiez, agissaient
Past Def.	agis, agis, agit; agîmes, agîtes, agirent
Future	agirai, agiras, agira; agirons, agirez, agiront
Condit.	agirais, agirais, agirait; agirions, agiriez, agiraient
Pres. Subj.	agisse, agisses, agisse; agissions, agissiez, agissent
Imp. Subj.	agisse, agisses, agît; agissions, agissiez, agissent
Past Indef.	ai agi, as agi, a agi; avons agi, avez agi, ont agi
Pluperf.	avais agi, avais agi, avait agi; avions agi, aviez agi, avaient agi
Past Ant.	eus agi, eus agi, eut agi; eûmes agi, eûtes agi, eurent agi
Fut. Perf.	aurai agi, auras agi, aura agi; aurons agi, aurez agi, auront agi
Cond. Perf.	aurais agi, aurais agi, aurait agi; aurions agi, auriez agi, auraient agi
Past Subj.	aie agi, aies agi, ait agi; ayons agi, ayez agi, aient agi
Plup. Subj.	eusse agi, eusses agi, eût agi; eussions agi, eussiez agi, eussent agi
Imperative	agis, agissons, agissez

Pres. Ind.	il s'agit
Imp. Ind.	il s'agissait
Past Def.	il s'agit
Future	il s'agira
Condit.	il s'agirait
Pres. Subj.	qu'il s'agisse
Imp. Subj.	qu'il s'agît
Past Ind.	il s'est agi
Plup. Ind.	il s'était agi
Past Ant.	il se fut agi
Fut. Perf.	il se sera agi
Cond. Perf.	il se serait agi
Past Subj.	qu'il se soit agi
Plup. Subj.	qu'il se fût agi
Imperative	[inemployé]

to be the matter, be a question of

to aid, help, assist

Pres. Ind.	aide, aides, aide; aidons, aidez, aident
Imp. Ind.	aidais, aidais, aidait; aidions, aidiez, aidaient
Past Def.	aidai, aidas, aida; aidâmes, aidâtes, aidèrent
Fut. Ind.	aiderai, aideras, aidera; aiderons, aiderez, aideront
Condit.	aiderais, aiderais, aiderait; aiderions, aideriez, aideraient
Pres. Subj.	aide, aides, aide; aidions, aidiez, aident
Imp. Subj.	aidasse, aidasses, aidât; aidassions, aidassiez, aidassent
Past Indef.	ai aidé, as aidé, a aidé; avons aidé, avez aidé, ont aidé
Pluperf.	avais aidé, avais aidé, avait aidé; avions aidé, aviez aidé, avaient aidé
Past Ant.	eus aidé, eus aidé, eut aidé; eûmes aidé, eûtes aidé, eurent aidé
Fut. Perf.	aurai aidé, auras aidé, aura aidé; aurons aidé, aurez aidé, auront aidé
Cond. Perf.	aurais aidé, aurais aidé, aurait aidé; aurions aidé, auriez aidé, auraient aidé
Past Subj.	aie aidé, aies aidé, ait aidé; ayons aidé, ayez aidé, aient aidé
Plup. Subj.	eusse aidé, eusses aidé, eût aidé; eussions aidé, eussiez aidé, eussent aidé
Imperative	aide, aidons, aidez

to love, like

Pres. Ind.	aime, aimes, aime; aimons, aimez, aiment
Imp. Ind.	aimais, aimais, aimait; aimions, aimiez, aimaient
Past Def.	aimai, aimas, aima; aimâmes, aimâtes, aimèrent
Fut. Ind.	aimerai, aimeras, aimera; aimerons, aimerez, aimeront
Condit.	aimerais, aimerais, aimerait; aimerions, aimeriez, aimeraient
Pres. Subj.	aime, aimes, aime; aimions, aimiez, aiment
Imp. Subj.	aimasse, aimasses, aimât; aimassions, aimassiez, aimassent
Past Indef.	ai aimé, as aimé, a aimé; avons aimé, avez aimé, ont aimé
Pluperf.	avais aimé, avais aimé, avait aimé; avions aimé, aviez aimé, avaient aimé
Past Ant.	eus aimé, eus aimé, eut aimé; eûmes aimé, eûtes aimé, eurent aimé
Fut. Perf.	aurai aimé, auras aimé, aura aimé; aurons aimé, aurez aimé, auront aimé
Cond. Perf.	aurais aimé, aurais aimé, aurait aimé; aurions aimé, auriez aimé, auraient aimé
Past Subj.	aie aimé, aies aimé, ait aimé; ayons aimé, ayez aimé, aient aimé
Plup. Subj.	eusse aimé, eusses aimé, eût aimé; eussions aimé, eussiez aimé, eussent aimé
Imperative	aime, aimons, aimez

to go

Pres. Ind.	vais, vas, va; allons, allez, vont
Imp. Ind.	allais, allais, allait; allions, alliez, allaient
Past Def.	allai, allas, alla; allâmes, allâtes, allèrent
Fut. Ind.	irai, iras, ira; irons, irez, iront
Condit.	irais, irais, irait; irions, iriez, iraient
Pres. Subj.	aille, ailles, aille; allions, alliez, aillent
Imp. Subj.	allasse, allasses, allât; allassions, allassiez, allassent
Past Indef.	suis allé(e), es allé(e), est allé(e); sommes allé(e)s, êtes allé(e)(s), sont allé(e)s
Pluperf.	étais allé(e), étais allé(e), était allé(e); étions allé(e)s, étiez allé(e)(s), étaient allé(e)s
Past Ant.	fus allé(e), fus allé(e), fut allé(e); fûmes allé(e)s, fûtes allé(e)(s), furent allé(e)s
Fut. Perf.	serai allé(e), seras allé(e), sera allé(e); serons allé(e)s, serez allé(e)(s), seront allé(e)s
Cond. Perf.	serais allé(e), serais allé(e), serait allé(e); serions allé(e)s, seriez allé(e)(s), seraient allé(e)s
Past Subj.	sois allé(e), sois allé(e), soit allé(e); soyons allé(e)s, soyez allé(e)(s), soient allé(e)s
Plup. Subj.	fusse allé(e), fusses allé(e), fût allé(e); fussions allé(e)s, fussiez allé(e)(s), fussent allé(e)s
Imperative	va, allons, allez

to go away

Pres. Ind.	m'en vais, t'en vas, s'en va; nous en allons, vous en allez, s'en vont
Imp. Ind.	m'en allais, t'en allais, s'en allait; nous en allions, vous en alliez, s'en allaient
Past Def.	m'en allai, t'en allas, s'en alla; nous en allâmes, vous en allâtes, s'en allèrent
Fut. Ind.	m'en irai, t'en iras, s'en ira; nous en irons, vous en irez, s'en iront
Condit.	m'en irais, t'en irais, s'en irait; nous en irions, vous en iriez, s'en iraient
Pres. Subj.	m'en aille, t'en ailles, s'en aille; nous en allions, vous en alliez, s'en aillent
Imp. Subj.	m'en allasse, t'en allasses, s'en allât; nous en allassions, vous en allassiez, s'en allassent
Past Indef.	m'en suis allé(e), t'en es allé(e), s'en est allé(e); nous en sommes allé(e)s, vous en êtes allé(e)(s), s'en sont allé(e)s
Pluperf.	m'en étais allé(e), t'en étais allé(e), s'en était allé(e); nous en étions allé(e)s, vous en étiez allé(e)(s), s'en étaient allé(e)s
Past Ant.	m'en fus allé(e), t'en fus allé(e), s'en fut allé(e); nous en fûmes allé(e)s, vous en fûtes allé(e)(s), s'en furent allé(e)s
Fut. Perf.	m'en serai allé(e), t'en seras allé(e), s'en sera allé(e); nous en serons allé(e)s, vous en serez allé(e)(s), s'en seront allé(e)s
Cond. Perf.	m'en serais allé(e), t'en serais allé(e), s'en serait allé(e); nous en serions allé(e)s, vous en seriez allé(e)(s), s'en seraient allé(e)s
Past Subj.	m'en sois allé(e), t'en sois allé(e), s'en soit allé(e); nous en soyons allé(e)s, vous en soyez allé(e)(s), s'en soient allé(e)s
Plup. Subj.	m'en fusse allé(e), t'en fusses allé(e), s'en fût allé(e); nous en fussions allé(e)s, vous en fussiez allé(e)(s), s'en fussent allé(e)s
Imperative	va-t'en, allons-nous-en, allez-vous-en

to bring, lead

Pres. Ind.	amène, amènes, amène; amenons, amenez, amènent
Imp. Ind.	amenais, amenais, amenait; amenions, ameniez, amenaient
Past Def.	amenai, amenas, amena; amenâmes, amenâtes, amenèrent
Future	amènerai, amèneras, amènera; amènerons, amènerez, amèneront
Condit.	amènerais, amènerais, amènerait; amènerions, amèneriez, amèneraient
Pres. Subj.	amène, amènes, amène; amenions, ameniez, amènent
Imp. Subj.	amenasse, amenasses, amenât; amenassions, amenassiez, amenassent
Past Indef.	ai amené, as amené, a amené; avons amené, avez amené, ont amené
Plup. Ind.	avais amené, avais amené, avait amené; avions amené, aviez amené, avaient amené
Past Ant.	eus amené, eus amené, eut amené; eûmes amené, eûtes amené, eurent amené
Fut. Perf.	aurai amené, auras amené, aura amené; aurons amené, aurez amené, auront amené
Cond. Perf.	aurais amené, aurais amené, aurait amené; aurions amené, auriez amené, auraient amené
Past Subj.	aie amené, aies amené, ait amené; ayons amené, ayez amené, aient amené
Plup. Sub.	eusse amené, eusses amené, eût amené; eussions amené, eussiez amené, eussent amené
Imperative	amène, amenons, amenez

to amuse, entertain

Pres. Ind.	amuse, amuses, amuse; amusons, amusez, amusent
Imp. Ind.	amusais, amusais, amusait; amusions, amusiez, amusaient
Past Def.	amusai, amusas, amusa; amusâmes, amusâtes, amusèrent
Future	amuserai, amuseras, amusera; amuserons, amuserez, amuseront
Condit.	amuserais, amuserais, amuserait; amuserions, amuseriez, amuseraient
Pres. Subj.	amuse, amuses, amuse; amusions, amusiez, amusent
Imp. Subj.	amusasse, amusasses, amusât; amusassions, amusassiez, amusassent
Past Indef.	ai amusé, as amusé, a amusé; avons amusé, avez amusé, ont amusé
Plup. Ind.	avais amusé, avais amusé, avait amusé; avions amusé, aviez amusé, avaient amusé
Past Ant.	eus amusé, eus amusé, eut amusé; eûmes amusé, eûtes amusé, eurent amusé
Fut. Perf.	aurai amusé, auras amusé, aura amusé; aurons amusé, aurez amusé, auront amusé
Cond. Perf.	aurais amusé, aurais amusé, aurait amusé; aurions amusé, auriez amusé, auraient amusé
Past Subj.	aie amusé, aies amusé, ait amusé; ayons amusé, ayez amusé, aient amusé
Plup. Subj.	eusse amusé, eusses amusé, eût amusé; eussions amusé, eussiez amusé, eussent amusé
Imperative	amuse, amusons, amusez

to have a good time, amuse oneself, enjoy oneself

Pres. Ind.	m'amuse, t'amuses, s'amuse; nous amusons, vous amusez, s'amusent
Imp. Ind.	m'amusais, t'amusais, s'amusait; nous amusions, vous amusiez, s'amusaient
Past Def.	m'amusai, t'amusas, s'amusa; nous amusâmes, vous amusâtes, s'amusèrent
Fut. Ind.	m'amuserai, t'amuseras, s'amusera; nous amuserons, vous amuserez, s'amuseront
Condit.	m'amuserais, t'amuserais, s'amuserait; nous amuserions, vous amuseriez, s'amuseraient
Pres. Subj.	m'amuse, t'amuses, s'amuse; nous amusions, vous amusiez, s'amusent
Imp. Subj.	m'amusasse, t'amusasses, s'amusât; nous amusassions, vous amusassiez, s'amusassent
Past Indef.	me suis amusé(e), t'es amusé(e), s'est amusé(e); nous sommes amusé(e)s, vous êtes amusé(e)(s), se sont amusé(e)s
Pluperf.	m'étais amusé(e), t'étais amusé(e), s'était amusé(e); nous étions amusé(e)s, vous étiez amusé(e)(s), s'étaient amusé(e)s
Past Ant.	me fus amusé(e), te fus amusé(e), se fut amusé(e); nous fûmes amusé(e)s, vous fûtes amusé(e)(s), se furent amusé(e)s
Fut. Perf.	me serai amusé(e), te seras amusé(e), se sera amusé(e); nous serons amusé(e)s, vous serez amusé(e)(s), se seront amusé(e)s
Cond. Perf.	me serais amusé(e), te serais amusé(e), se serait amusé(e); nous serions amusé(e)s, vous seriez amusé(e)(s), se seraient amusé(e)s
Past Subj.	me sois amusé(e), te sois amusé(e), se soit amusé(e); nous soyons amusé(e)s, vous soyez amusé(e)(s), se soient amusé(e)s
Plup. Subj.	me fusse amusé(e), te fusses amusé(e), se fût amusé(e); nous fussions amusé(e)s, vous fussiez amusé(e)(s), se fussent amusé(e)s
Imperative	amuse-toi, amusons-nous, amusez-vous

Pres. Ind.	aperçois, aperçois, aperçoit; apercevons, apercevez, aperçoivent	*to perceive, see*
Imp. Ind.	apercevais, apercevais, apercevait; apercevions, aperceviez, apercevaient	
Past Def.	aperçus, aperçus, aperçut; aperçûmes, aperçûtes, aperçurent	
Fut. Ind.	apercevrai, apercevras, apercevra; apercevrons, apercevrez, apercevront	
Condit.	apercevrais, apercevrais, apercevrait; apercevrions, apercevriez, apercevraient	
Pres. Subj.	aperçoive, aperçoives, aperçoive; apercevions, aperceviez, aperçoivent	
Imp. Subj.	aperçusse, aperçusses, aperçût; aperçussions, aperçussiez, aperçussent	
Past Indef.	ai aperçu, as aperçu, a aperçu; avons aperçu, avez aperçu, ont aperçu	
Pluperf.	avais aperçu, avais aperçu, avait aperçu; avions aperçu, aviez aperçu, avaient aperçu	
Past Ant.	eus aperçu, eus aperçu, eut aperçu; eûmes aperçu, eûtes aperçu, eurent aperçu	
Fut. Perf.	aurai aperçu, auras aperçu, aura aperçu; aurons aperçu, aurez aperçu, auront aperçu	
Cond. Perf.	aurais aperçu, aurais aperçu, aurait aperçu; aurions aperçu, auriez aperçu, auraient aperçu	
Past Subj.	aie aperçu, aies aperçu, ait aperçu; ayons aperçu, ayez aperçu, aient aperçu	
Plup. Subj.	eusse aperçu, eusses aperçu, eût aperçu; eussions aperçu, eussiez aperçu, eussent aperçu	
Imperative	aperçois, apercevons, apercevez	

to appear

Pres. Ind.	apparais, apparais, apparaît; apparaissons, apparaissez, apparaissent
Imp. Ind.	apparaissais, apparaissais, apparaissait; apparaissions, apparaissiez, apparaissaient
Past Def.	apparus, apparus, apparut; apparûmes, apparûtes, apparurent
Fut. Ind.	apparaîtrai, apparaîtras, apparaîtra; apparaîtrons, apparaîtrez, apparaîtront
Condit.	apparaîtrais, apparaîtrais, apparaîtrait; apparaîtrions, apparaîtriez, apparaîtraient
Pres. Subj.	apparaisse, apparaisses, apparaisse; apparaissions, apparaissiez, apparaissent
Imp. Subj.	apparusse, apparusses, apparût; apparussions, apparussiez, apparussent
Past Indef.	ai apparu, as apparu, a apparu; avons apparu, avez apparu, ont apparu
Pluperf.	avais apparu, avais apparu, avait apparu; avions apparu, aviez apparu, avaient apparu
Past Ant.	eus apparu, eus apparu, eut apparu; eûmes apparu, eûtes apparu, eurent apparu
Fut. Perf.	aurai apparu, auras apparu, aura apparu; aurons apparu, aurez apparu, auront apparu
Cond. Perf.	aurais apparu, aurais apparu, aurait apparu; aurions apparu, auriez apparu, auraient apparu
Past Subj.	aie apparu, aies apparu, ait apparu; ayons apparu, ayez apparu, aient apparu
Plup. Subj.	eusse apparu, eusses apparu, eût apparu; eussions apparu, eussiez apparu, eussent apparu
Imperative	apparais, apparaissons, apparaissez

to belong

Pres. Ind.	appartiens, appartiens, appartient; appartenons, appartenez, appartiennent
Imp. Ind.	appartenais, appartenais, appartenait; appartenions, apparteniez, appartenaient
Past Def.	appartins, appartins, appartint; appartînmes, appartîntes, appartinrent
Fut. Ind.	appartiendrai, appartiendras, appartiendra; appartiendrons, appartiendrez, appartiendront
Condit.	appartiendrais, appartiendrais, appartiendrait; appartiendrions, appartiendriez, appartiendraient
Pres. Subj.	appartienne, appartiennes, appartienne; appartenions, apparteniez, appartiennent
Imp. Subj.	appartinsse, appartinsses, appartînt; appartinssions, appartinssiez, appartinssent
Past Indef.	ai appartenu, as appartenu, a appartenu; avons appartenu, avez appartenu, ont appartenu
Pluperf.	avais appartenu, avais appartenu, avait appartenu; avions appartenu, aviez appartenu, avaient appartenu
Past Ant.	eus appartenu, eus appartenu, eut appartenu; eûmes appartenu, eûtes appartenu, eurent appartenu
Fut. Perf.	aurai appartenu, auras appartenu, aura appartenu; aurons appartenu, aurez appartenu, auront appartenu
Cond. Perf.	aurais appartenu, aurais appartenu, aurait appartenu; aurions appartenu, auriez appartenu, auraient appartenu
Past Subj.	aie appartenu, aies appartenu, ait appartenu; ayons appartenu, ayez appartenu, aient appartenu
Plup. Subj.	eusse appartenu, eusses appartenu, eût appartenu; eussions appartenu, eussiez appartenu, eussent appartenu
Imperative	appartiens, appartenons, appartenez

to call, name

Pres. Ind.	appelle, appelles, appelle; appelons, appelez, appellent
Imp. Ind.	appelais, appelais, appelait; appelions, appeliez, appelaient
Past Def.	appelai, appelas, appela; appelâmes, appelâtes, appelèrent
Fut. Ind.	appellerai, appelleras, appellera; appellerons, appellerez, appelleront
Condit.	appellerais, appellerais, appellerait; appellerions, appelleriez, appelleraient
Pres. Subj.	appelle, appelles, appelle; appelions, appeliez, appellent
Imp. Subj.	appelasse, appelasses, appelât; appelassions, appelassiez, appelassent
Past Indef.	ai appelé, as appelé, a appelé; avons appelé, avez appelé, ont appelé
Pluperf.	avais appelé, avais appelé, avait appelé; avions appelé, aviez appelé, avaient appelé
Past Ant.	eus appelé, eus appelé, eut appelé; eûmes appelé, eûtes appelé, eurent appelé
Fut. Perf.	aurai appelé, auras appelé, aura appelé; aurons appelé, aurez appelé, auront appelé
Cond. Perf.	aurais appelé, aurais appelé, aurait appelé; aurions appelé, auriez appelé, auraient appelé
Past Subj.	aie appelé, aies appelé, ait appelé; ayons appelé, ayez appelé, aient appelé
Plup. Subj.	eusse appelé, eusses appelé, eût appelé; eussions appelé, eussiez appelé, eussent appelé
Imperative	appelle, appelons, appelez

to be named, call oneself

Pres. Ind.	m'appelle, t'appelles, s'appelle; nous appelons, vous appelez, s'appellent
Imp. Ind.	m'appelais, t'appelais, s'appelait; nous appelions, vous appeliez, s'appelaient
Past Def.	m'appelai, t'appelas, s'appela; nous appelâmes, vous appelâtes, s'appelèrent
Fut. Ind.	m'appellerai, t'appelleras, s'appellera; nous appellerons, vous appellerez, s'appelleront
Condit.	m'appellerais, t'appellerais, s'appellerait; nous appellerions, vous appelleriez, s'appelleraient
Pres. Subj.	m'appelle, t'appelles, s'appelle; nous appelions, vous appeliez, s'appellent
Imp. Subj.	m'appelasse, t'appelasses, s'appelât; nous appelassions, vous appelassiez, s'appelassent
Past Indef.	me suis appelé(e), t'es appelé(e), s'est appelé(e); nous sommes appelé(e)s, vous êtes appelé(e)(s), se sont appelé(e)s
Pluperf.	m'étais appelé(e), t'étais appelé(e), s'était appelé(e); nous étions appelé(e)s, vous étiez appelé(e)(s), s'étaient appelé(e)s
Past Ant.	me fus appelé(e), te fus appelé(e), se fut appelé(e); nous fûmes appelé(e)s, vous fûtes appelé(e)(s), se furent appelé(e)s
Fut. Perf.	me serai appelé(e), te seras appelé(e), se sera appelé(e); nous serons appelé(e)s, vous serez appelé(e)(s), se seront appelé(e)s
Cond. Perf.	me serais appelé(e), te serais appelé(e), se serait appelé(e); nous serions appelé(e)s, vous seriez appelé(e)(s), se seraient appelé(e)s
Past Subj.	me sois appelé(e), te sois appelé(e), se soit appelé(e); nous soyons appelé(e)s, vous soyez appelé(e)(s), se soient appelé(e)s
Plup. Subj.	me fusse appelé(e), te fusses appelé(e), se fût appelé(e); nous fussions appelé(e)s, vous fussiez appelé(e)(s), se fussent appelé(e)s
Imperative	appelle-toi, appelons-nous, appelez-vous

to bring

Pres. Ind.	apporte, apportes, apporte; apportons, apportez, apportent
Imp. Ind.	apportais, apportais, apportait; apportions, apportiez, apportaient
Past Def.	apportai, apportas, apporta; apportâmes, apportâtes, apportèrent
Fut. Ind.	apporterai, apporteras, apportera; apporterons, apporterez, apporteront
Condit.	apporterais, apporterais, apporterait; apporterions, apporteriez, apporteraient
Pres. Subj.	apporte, apportes, apporte; apportions, apportiez, apportent
Imp. Subj.	apportasse, apportasses, apportât; apportassions, apportassiez, apportassent
Past Indef.	ai apporté, as apporté, a apporté; avons apporté, avez apporté, ont apporté
Pluperf.	avais apporté, avais apporté, avait apporté; avions apporté, aviez apporté, avaient apporté
Past Ant.	eus apporté, eus apporté, eut apporté; eûmes apporté, eûtes apporté, eurent apporté
Fut. Perf.	aurai apporté, auras apporté, aura apporté; aurons apporté, aurez apporté, auront apporté
Cond. Perf.	aurais apporté, aurais apporté, aurait apporté; aurions apporté, auriez apporté, auraient apporté
Past Subj.	aie apporté, aies apporté, ait apporté; ayons apporté, ayez apporté, aient apporté
Plup. Subj.	eusse apporté, eusses apporté, eût apporté; eussions apporté, eussiez apporté, eussent apporté
Imperative	apporte, apportons, apportez

to learn

Pres. Ind.	apprends, apprends, apprend; apprenons, apprenez, apprennent
Imp. Ind.	apprenais, apprenais, apprenait; apprenions, appreniez, apprenaient
Past Def.	appris, appris, apprit; apprîmes, apprîtes, apprirent
Fut. Ind.	apprendrai, apprendras, apprendra; apprendrons, apprendrez, apprendront
Condit.	apprendrais, apprendrais, apprendrait; apprendrions, apprendriez, apprendraient
Pres. Subj.	apprenne, apprennes, apprenne; apprenions, appreniez, apprennent
Imp. Subj.	apprisse, apprisses, apprît; apprissions, apprissiez, apprissent
Past Indef.	ai appris, as appris, a appris; avons appris, avez appris, ont appris
Pluperf.	avais appris, avais appris, avait appris; avions appris, aviez appris, avaient appris
Past Ant.	eus appris, eus appris, eut appris; eûmes appris, eûtes appris, eurent appris
Fut. Perf.	aurai appris, auras appris, aura appris; aurons appris, aurez appris, auront appris
Cond. Perf.	aurais appris, aurais appris, aurait appris; aurions appris, auriez appris, auraient appris
Past Subj.	aie appris, aies appris, ait appris; ayons appris, ayez appris, aient appris
Plup. Subj.	eusse appris, eusses appris, eût appris; eussions appris, eussiez appris, eussent appris
Imperative	apprends, apprenons, apprenez

to approve (of)

Pres. Ind.	approuve, approuves, approuve; approuvons, approuvez, approuvent
Imp. Ind.	approuvais, approuvais, approuvait; approuvions, approuviez, approuvaient
Past Def.	approuvai, approuvas, approuva; approuvâmes, approuvâtes, approuvèrent
Future	approuverai, approuveras, approuvera; approuverons, approuverez, approuveront
Condit.	approuverais, approuverais, approuverait; approuverions, approuveriez, approuveraient
Pres. Subj.	approuve, approuves, approuve; approuvions, approuviez, approuvent
Imp. Subj.	approuvasse, approuvasses, approuvât; approuvassions, approuvassiez, approuvassent
Past Indef.	ai approuvé, as approuvé, a approuvé; avons approuvé, avez approuvé, ont approuvé
Plup. Ind.	avais approuvé, avais approuvé, avait approuvé; avions approuvé, aviez approuvé, avaient approuvé
Past Ant.	eus approuvé, eus approuvé, eut approuvé; eûmes approuvé, eûtes approuvé, eurent approuvé
Fut. Perf.	aurai approuvé, auras approuvé, aura approuvé; aurons approuvé, aurez approuvé, auront approuvé
Cond. Perf.	aurais approuvé, aurais approuvé, aurait approuvé; aurions approuvé, auriez approuvé, auraient approuvé
Past Subj.	aie approuvé, aies approuvé, ait approuvé; ayons approuvé, ayez approuvé, aient approuvé
Plup. Subj.	eusse approuvé, eusses approuvé, eût approuvé; eussions approuvé, eussiez approuvé, eussent approuvé
Imperative	approuve, approuvons, approuvez

to pull up, uproot

Pres. Ind.	arrache, arraches, arrache; arrachons, arrachez, arrachent
Imp. Ind.	arrachais, arrachais, arrachait; arrachions, arrachiez, arrachaient
Past Def.	arrachai, arrachas, arracha; arrachâmes, arrachâtes, arrachèrent
Future	arracherai, arracheras, arrachera; arracherons, arracherez, arracheront
Condit.	arracherais, arracherais, arracherait; arracherions, arracheriez, arracheraient
Pres. Subj.	arrache, arraches, arrache; arrachions, arrachiez, arrachent
Imp. Subj.	arrachasse, arrachasses, arrachât; arrachassions, arrachassiez, arrachassent
Past Indef.	ai arraché, as arraché, a arraché; avons arraché, avez arraché, ont arraché
Plup. Ind.	avais arraché, avais arraché, avait arraché; avions arraché, aviez arraché, avaient arraché
Past Ant.	eus arraché, eus arraché, eut arraché; eûmes arraché, eûtes arraché, eurent arraché
Fut. Perf.	aurai arraché, auras arraché, aura arraché; aurons arraché, aurez arraché, auront arraché
Cond. Perf.	aurais arraché, aurais arraché, aurait arraché; aurions arraché, auriez arraché, auraient arraché
Past Subj.	aie arraché, aies arraché, ait arraché; ayons arraché, ayez arraché, aient arraché
Plup. Subj.	eusse arraché, eusses arraché, eût arraché; eussions arraché, eussiez arraché, eussent arraché
Imperative	arrache, arrachons, arrachez

Pres. Ind.	arrange, arranges, arrange; arrangeons, arrangez, arrangent	*to arrange*
Imp. Ind.	arrangeais, arrangeais, arrangeait; arrangions, arrangiez, arrangeaient	
Past Def.	arrangeai, arrangeas, arrangea; arrangeâmes, arrangeâtes, arrangèrent	
Future	arrangerai, arrangeras, arrangera; arrangerons, arrangerez, arrangeront	
Condit.	arrangerais, arrangerais, arrangerait; arrangerions, arrangeriez, arrangeraient	
Pres. Subj.	arrange, arranges, arrange; arrangions, arrangiez, arrangent	
Imp. Subj.	arrangeasse, arrangeasses, arrangeât; arrangeassions, arrangeassiez, arrangeassent	
Past Indef.	ai arrangé, as arrangé, a arrangé; avons arrangé, avez arrangé, ont arrangé	
Plup. Ind.	avais arrangé, avais arrangé, avait arrangé; avions arrangé, aviez arrangé, avaient arrangé	
Past Ant.	eus arrangé, eus arrangé, eut arrangé; eûmes arrangé, eûtes arrangé, eurent arrangé	
Fut. Perf.	aurai arrangé, auras arrangé, aura arrangé; aurons arrangé, aurez arrangé, auront arrangé	
Cond. Perf.	aurais arrangé, aurais arrangé, aurait arrangé; aurions arrangé, auriez arrangé, auraient arrangé	
Past Subj.	aie arrangé, aies arrangé, ait arrangé; ayons arrangé, ayez arrangé, aient arrangé	
Plup. Subj.	eusse arrangé, eusses arrangé, eût arrangé; eussions arrangé, eussiez arrangé, eussent arrangé	
Imperative	arrange, arrangeons, arrangez	

to arrest, stop (someone or something)

Pres. Ind.	arrête, arrêtes, arrête; arrêtons, arrêtez, arrêtent
Imp. Ind.	arrêtais, arrêtais, arrêtait; arrêtions, arrêtiez, arrêtaient
Past Def.	arrêtai, arrêtas, arrêta; arrêtâmes, arrêtâtes, arrêtèrent
Future	arrêterai, arrêteras, arrêtera; arrêterons, arrêterez, arrêteront
Condit.	arrêterais, arrêterais, arrêterait; arrêterions, arrêteriez, arrêteraient
Pres. Subj.	arrête, arrêtes, arrête; arrêtions, arrêtiez, arrêtent
Imp. Subj.	arrêtasse, arrêtasses, arrêtât; arrêtassions, arrêtassiez, arrêtassent
Past Indef.	ai arrêté, as arrêté, a arrêté; avons arrêté, avez arrêté, ont arrêté
Plup. Ind.	avais arrêté, avais arrêté, avait arrêté; avions arrêté, aviez arrêté, avaient arrêté
Past Ant.	eus arrêté, eus arrêté, eut arrêté; eûmes arrêté, eûtes arrêté, eurent arrêté
Fut. Perf.	aurai arrêté, auras arrêté, aura arrêté; aurons arrêté, aurez arrêté, auront arrêté
Cond. Perf.	aurais arrêté, aurais arrêté, aurait arrêté; aurions arrêté, auriez arrêté, auraient arrêté
Past Subj.	aie arrêté, aies arrêté, ait arrêté; ayons arrêté, ayez arrêté, aient arrêté
Plup. Subj.	eusse arrêté, eusses arrêté, eût arrêté; eussions arrêté, eussiez arrêté, eussent arrêté
Imperative	arrête, arrêtons, arrêtez

to stop

Pres. Ind.	m'arrête, t'arrêtes, s'arrête; nous arrêtons, vous arrêtez, s'arrêtent
Imp. Ind.	m'arrêtais, t'arrêtais, s'arrêtait; nous arrêtions, vous arrêtiez, s'arrêtaient
Past Def.	m'arrêtai, t'arrêtas, s'arrêta; nous arrêtâmes, vous arrêtâtes, s'arrêtèrent
Fut. Ind.	m'arrêterai, t'arrêteras, s'arrêtera; nous arrêterons, vous arrêterez, s'arrêteront
Condit.	m'arrêterais, t'arrêterais, s'arrêterait; nous arrêterions, vous arrêteriez, s'arrêteraient
Pres. Subj.	m'arrête, t'arrêtes, s'arrête; nous arrêtions, vous arrêtiez, s'arrêtent
Imp. Subj.	m'arrêtasse, t'arrêtasses, s'arrêtât; nous arrêtassions, vous arrêtassiez, s'arrêtassent
Past Indef.	me suis arrêté(e), t'es arrêté(e), s'est arrêté(e); nous sommes arrêté(e)s, vous êtes arrêté(e)(s), se sont arrêté(e)s
Pluperf.	m'étais arrêté(e), t'étais arrêté(e), s'était arrêté(e); nous étions arrêté(e)s, vous étiez arrêté(e)(s), s'étaient arrêté(e)s
Past Ant.	me fus arrêté(e), te fus arrêté(e), se fut arrêté(e); nous fûmes arrêté(e)s, vous fûtes arrêté(e)(s), se furent arrêté(e)s
Fut. Perf.	me serai arrêté(e), te seras arrêté(e), se sera arrêté(e); nous serons arrêté(e)s, vous serez arrêté(e)(s), se seront arrêté(e)s
Cond. Perf.	me serais arrêté(e), te serais arrêté(e), se serait arrêté(e); nous serions arrêté(e)s, vous seriez arrêté(e)(s), se seraient arrêté(e)s
Past Subj.	me sois arrêté(e), te sois arrêté(e), se soit arrêté(e); nous soyons arrêté(e)s, vous soyez arrêté(e)(s), se soient arrêté(e)s
Plup. Subj.	me fusse arrêté(e), te fusses arrêté(e), se fût arrêté(e); nous fussions arrêté(e)s, vous fussiez arrêté(e)(s), se fussent arrêté(e)s
Imperative	arrête-toi, arrêtons-nous, arrêtez-vous

to arrive

Pres. Ind.	arrive, arrives, arrive; arrivons, arrivez, arrivent
Imp. Ind.	arrivais, arrivais, arrivait; arrivions, arriviez, arrivaient
Past Def.	arrivai, arrivas, arriva; arrivâmes, arrivâtes, arrivèrent
Fut. Ind.	arriverai, arriveras, arrivera; arriverons, arriverez, arriveront
Condit.	arriverais, arriverais, arriverait; arriverions, arriveriez, arriveraient
Pres. Subj.	arrive, arrives, arrive; arrivions, arriviez, arrivent
Imp. Subj.	arrivasse, arrivasses, arrivât; arrivassions, arrivassiez, arrivassent
Past Indef.	suis arrivé(e), es arrivé(e), est arrivé(e); sommes arrivé(e)s, êtes arrivé(e)(s), sont arrivé(e)s
Pluperf.	étais arrivé(e), étais arrivé(e), était arrivé(e); étions arrivé(e)s, étiez arrivé(e)(s), étaient arrivé(e)s
Past Ant.	fus arrivé(e), fus arrivé(e), fut arrivé(e); fûmes arrivé(e)s, fûtes arrivé(e)(s), furent arrivé(e)s
Fut. Perf.	serai arrivé(e), seras arrivé(e), sera arrivé(e); serons arrivé(e)s, serez arrivé(e)(s), seront arrivé(e)s
Cond. Perf.	serais arrivé(e), serais arrivé(e), serait arrivé(e); serions arrivé(e)s, seriez arrivé(e)(s), seraient arrivé(e)s
Past Subj.	sois arrivé(e), sois arrivé(e), soit arrivé(e); soyons arrivé(e)s, soyez arrivé(e)(s), soient arrivé(e)s
Plup. Subj.	fusse arrivé(e), fusses arrivé(e), fût arrivé(e); fussions arrivé(e)s, fussiez arrivé(e)(s), fussent arrivé(e)s
Imperative	arrive, arrivons, arrivez

to assail, assault

Pres. Ind.	assaille, assailles, assaille; assaillons, assaillez, assaillent
Imp. Ind.	assaillais, assaillais, assaillait; assaillions, assailliez, assaillaient
Past Def.	assaillis, assaillis, assaillit; assaillîmes, assaillîtes, assaillirent
Fut. Ind.	assaillirai, assailliras, assaillira; assaillirons, assaillirez, assailliront
Condit.	assaillirais, assaillirais, assaillirait; assaillirions, assailliriez, assailliraient
Pres. Subj.	assaille, assailles, assaille; assaillions, assailliez, assaillent
Imp. Subj.	assaillisse, assaillisses, assaillît; assaillissions, assaillissiez, assaillissent
Past Indef.	ai assailli, as assailli, a assailli; avons assailli, avez assailli, ont assailli
Pluperf.	avais assailli, avais assailli, avait assailli; avions assailli, aviez assailli, avaient assailli
Past Ant.	eus assailli, eus assailli, eut assailli; eûmes assailli, eûtes assailli, eurent assailli
Fut. Perf.	aurai assailli, auras assailli, aura assailli; aurons assailli, aurez assailli, auront assailli
Cond. Perf.	aurais assailli, aurais assailli, aurait assailli; aurions assailli, auriez assailli, auraient assailli
Past Subj.	aie assailli, aies assailli, ait assailli; ayons assailli, ayez assailli, aient assailli
Plup. Subj.	eusse assailli, eusses assailli, eût assailli; eussions assailli, eussiez assailli, eussent assailli
Imperative	assaille, assaillons, assaillez

to sit down

Pres. Ind.	m'assieds, t'assieds, s'assied; nous asseyons, vous asseyez, s'asseyent
Imp. Ind.	m'asseyais, t'asseyais, s'asseyait; nous asseyions, vous asseyiez, s'asseyaient
Past Def.	m'assis, t'assis, s'assit; nous assîmes, vous assîtes, s'assirent
Fut. Ind.	m'assiérai, t'assiéras, s'assiéra; nous assiérons, vous assiérez, s'assiéront
Condit.	m'assiérais, t'assiérais, s'assiérait; nous assiérions, vous assiériez, s'assiéraient
Pres. Subj.	m'asseye, t'asseyes, s'asseye; nous asseyions, vous asseyiez, s'asseyent
Imp. Subj.	m'assisse, t'assisses, s'assît; nous assissions, vous assissiez, s'assissent
Past Indef.	me suis assis(e), t'es assis(e), s'est assis(e); nous sommes assis(es), vous êtes assis(e)(es), se sont assis(es)
Pluperf.	m'étais assis(e), t'étais assis(e), s'était assis(e); nous étions assis(es), vous étiez assis(e)(es), s'étaient assis(es)
Past Ant.	me fus assis(e), te fus assis(e), se fut assis(e); nous fûmes assis(es), vous fûtes assis(e)(es), se furent assis(es)
Fut. Perf.	me serai assis(e), te seras assis(e), se sera assis(e); nous serons assis(es), vous serez assis(e)(es), se seront assis(es)
Cond. Perf.	me serais assis(e), te serais assis(e), se serait assis(e); nous serions assis(es), vous seriez assis(e)(es), se seraient assis(es)
Past Subj.	me sois assis(e), te sois assis(e), se soit assis(e); nous soyons assis(es), vous soyez assis(e)(es), se soient assis(es)
Plup. Subj.	me fusse assis(e), te fusses assis(e), se fût assis(e); nous fussions assis(es), vous fussiez assis(e)(es), se fussent assis(es)
Imperative	assieds-toi, asseyons-nous, asseyez-vous

to assist (at), be present (at), attend

Pres. Ind.	assiste, assistes, assiste; assistons, assistez, assistent
Imp. Ind.	assistais, assistais, assistait; assistions, assistiez, assistaient
Past Def.	assistai, assistas, assista; assistâmes, assistâtes, assistèrent
Future	assisterai, assisteras, assistera; assisterons, assisterez, assisteront
Condit.	assisterais, assisterais, assisterait; assisterions, assisteriez, assisteraient
Pres. Subj.	assiste, assistes, assiste; assistions, assistiez, assistent
Imp. Subj.	assistasse, assistasses, assistât; assistassions, assistassiez, assistassent
Past Indef.	ai assisté, as assisté, a assisté; avons assisté, avez assisté, ont assisté
Pluperf.	avais assisté, avais assisté, avait assisté; avions assisté, aviez assisté, avaient assisté
Past Ant.	eus assisté, eus assisté, eut assisté; eûmes assisté, eûtes assisté, eurent assisté
Fut. Perf.	aurai assisté, auras assisté, aura assisté; aurons assisté, aurez assisté, auront assisté
Cond. Perf.	aurais assisté, aurais assisté, aurait assisté; aurions assisté, auriez assisté, auraient assisté
Past Subj.	aie assisté, aies assisté, ait assisté; ayons assisté, ayez assisté, aient assisté
Plup. Subj.	eusse assisté, eusses assisté, eût assisté; eussions assisté, eussiez assisté, eussent assisté
Imperative	assiste, assistons, assistez

to assure, ensure, insure, guarantee

Pres. Ind.	assure, assures, assure; assurons, assurez, assurent
Imp. Ind.	assurais, assurais, assurait; assurions, assuriez, assuraient
Past Def.	assurai, assuras, assura; assurâmes, assurâtes, assurèrent
Future	assurerai, assureras, assurera; assurerons, assurerez, assureront
Condit.	assurerais, assurerais, assurerait; assurerions, assureriez, assureraient
Pres. Subj.	assure, assures, assure; assurions, assuriez, assurent
Imp. Subj.	assurasse, assurasses, assurât; assurassions, assurassiez, assurassent
Past Indef.	ai assuré, as assuré, a assuré; avons assuré, avez assuré, ont assuré
Plup. Ind.	avais assuré, avais assuré, avait assuré; avions assuré, aviez assuré, avaient assuré
Past Ant.	eus assuré, eus assuré, eut assuré; eûmes assuré, eûtes assuré, eurent assuré
Fut. Perf.	aurai assuré, auras assuré, aura assuré; aurons assuré, aurez assuré, auront assuré
Cond. Perf.	aurais assuré, aurais assuré, aurait assuré; aurions assuré, auriez assuré, auraient assuré
Past Subj.	aie assuré, aies assuré, ait assuré; ayons assuré, ayez assuré, aient assuré
Plup. Subj.	eusse assuré, eusses assuré, eût assuré; eussions assuré, eussiez assuré, eussent assuré
Imperative	assure, assurons, assurez

to make sure, assure oneself, insure oneself

Pres. Ind.	m'assure, t'assures, s'assure; nous assurons, vous assurez, s'assurent
Imp. Ind.	m'assurais, t'assurais, s'assurait; nous assurions, vous assuriez, s'assuraient
Past Def.	m'assurai, t'assuras, s'assura; nous assurâmes, vous assurâtes, s'assurèrent
Future	m'assurerai, t'assureras, s'assurera; nous assurerons, vous assurerez, s'assureront
Condit.	m'assurerais, t'assurerais, s'assurerait; nous assurerions, vous assureriez, s'assureraient
Pres. Subj.	m'assure, t'assures, s'assure; nous assurions, vous assuriez, s'assurent
Imp. Subj.	m'assurasse, t'assurasses, s'assurât; nous assurassions, vous assurassiez, s'assurassent
Past Indef.	me suis assuré(e), t'es assuré(e), s'est assuré(e); nous sommes assuré(e)s, vous êtes assuré(e)(s), se sont assuré(e)s
Plup. Ind.	m'étais assuré(e), t'étais assuré(e), s'était assuré(e); nous étions assuré(e)s, vous étiez assuré(e)(s), s'étaient assuré(e)s
Past Ant.	me fus assuré(e), te fus assuré(e), se fut assuré(e); nous fûmes assuré(e)s, vous fûtes assuré(e)(s), se furent assuré(e)s
Fut. Perf.	me serai assuré(e), te seras assuré(e), se sera assuré(e); nous serons assuré(e)s, vous serez assuré(e)(s), se seront assuré(e)s
Cond. Perf.	me serais assuré(e), te serais assuré(e), se serait assuré(e); nous serions assuré(e)s, vous seriez assuré(e)(s), se seraient assuré(e)s
Past Subj.	me sois assuré(e), te sois assuré(e), se soit assuré(e); nous soyons assuré(e)s, vous soyez assuré(e)(s), se soient assuré(e)s
Plup. Subj.	me fusse assuré(e), te fusses assuré(e), se fût assuré(e); nous fussions assuré(e)s, vous fussiez assuré(e)(s), se fussent assuré(e)s
Imperative	assure-toi, assurons-nous, assurez-vous

to attain

Pres. Ind.	atteins, atteins, atteint; atteignons, atteignez, atteignent
Imp. Ind.	atteignais, atteignais, atteignait; atteignions, atteigniez, atteignaient
Past Def.	atteignis, atteignis, atteignit; atteignîmes, atteignîtes, atteignirent
Fut. Ind.	atteindrai, atteindras, atteindra; atteindrons, atteindrez, atteindront
Condit.	atteindrais, atteindrais, atteindrait; atteindrions, atteindriez, atteindraient
Pres. Subj.	atteigne, atteignes, atteigne; atteignions, atteigniez, atteignent
Imp. Subj.	atteignisse, atteignisses, atteignît; atteignissions, atteignissiez, atteignissent
Past Indef.	ai atteint, as atteint, a atteint; avons atteint, avez atteint, ont atteint
Pluperf.	avais atteint, avais atteint, avait atteint; avions atteint, aviez atteint, avaient atteint
Past Ant.	eus atteint, eus atteint, eut atteint; eûmes atteint, eûtes atteint, eurent atteint
Fut. Perf.	aurai atteint, auras atteint, aura atteint; aurons atteint, aurez atteint, auront atteint
Cond. Perf.	aurais atteint, aurais atteint, aurait atteint; aurions atteint, auriez atteint, auraient atteint
Past Subj.	aie atteint, aies atteint, ait atteint; ayons atteint, ayez atteint, aient atteint
Plup. Subj.	eusse atteint, eusses atteint, eût atteint; eussions atteint, eussiez atteint, eussent atteint
Imperative	atteins, atteignons, atteignez

to wait, wait for

Pres. Ind.	attends, attends, attend; attendons, attendez, attendent
Imp. Ind.	attendais, attendais, attendait; attendions, attendiez, attendaient
Past Def.	attendis, attendis, attendit; attendîmes, attendîtes, attendirent
Fut. Ind.	attendrai, attendras, attendra; attendrons, attendrez, attendront
Condit.	attendrais, attendrais, attendrait; attendrions, attendriez, attendraient
Pres. Subj.	attende, attendes, attende; attendions, attendiez, attendent
Imp. Subj.	attendisse, attendisses, attendît; attendissions, attendissiez, attendissent
Past Indef.	ai attendu, as attendu, a attendu; avons attendu, avez attendu, ont attendu
Pluperf.	avais attendu, avais attendu, avait attendu; avions attendu, aviez attendu, avaient attendu
Past Ant.	eus attendu, eus attendu, eut attendu; eûmes attendu, eûtes attendu, eurent attendu
Fut. Perf.	aurai attendu, auras attendu, aura attendu; aurons attendu, aurez attendu, auront attendu
Cond. Perf.	aurais attendu, aurais attendu, aurait attendu; aurions attendu, auriez attendu, auraient attendu
Past Subj.	aie attendu, aies attendu, ait attendu; ayons attendu, ayez attendu, aient attendu
Plup. Subj.	eusse attendu, eusses attendu, eût attendu; eussions attendu, eussiez attendu, eussent attendu
Imperative	attends, attendons, attendez

to attract, allure

Pres. Ind.	attire, attires, attire; attirons, attirez, attirent
Imp. Ind.	attirais, attirais, attirait; attirions, attiriez, attiraient
Past Def.	attirai, attiras, attira; attirâmes, attirâtes, attirèrent
Future	attirerai, attireras, attirera; attirerons, attirerez, attireront
Condit.	attirerais, attirerais, attirerait; attirerions, attireriez, attireraient
Pres. Subj.	attire, attires, attire; attirions, attiriez, attirent
Imp. Subj.	attirasse, attirasses, attirât; attirassions, attirassiez, attirassent
Past Indef.	ai attiré, as attiré, a attiré; avons attiré, avez attiré, ont attiré
Plup. Ind.	avais attiré, avais attiré, avait attiré; avions attiré, aviez attiré, avaient attiré
Past Ant.	eus attiré, eus attiré, eut attiré; eûmes attiré, eûtes attiré, eurent attiré
Fut. Perf.	aurai attiré, auras attiré, aura attiré; aurons attiré, aurez attiré, auront attiré
Cond. Perf.	aurais attiré, aurais attiré, aurait attiré; aurions attiré, auriez attiré, auraient attiré
Past Subj.	aie attiré, aies attiré, ait attiré; ayons attiré, ayez attiré, aient attiré
Plup. Subj.	eusse attiré, eusses attiré, eût attiré; eussions attiré, eussiez attiré, eussent attiré
Imperative	attire, attirons, attirez

to attract, allure, entice

Pres. Ind.	attrais, attrais, attrait; attrayons, attrayez, attraient
Imp. Ind.	attrayais, attrayais, attrayait; attrayions, attrayiez, attrayaient
Past Def.	[inemployé]
Future	attrairai, attrairas, attraira; attrairons, attrairez, attrairont
Condit.	attrairais, attrairais, attrairait; attrairions, attrairiez, attrairaient
Pres. Subj.	attraie, attraies, attraie; attrayions, attrayiez, attraient
Imp. Subj.	[inemployé]
Past Indef.	ai attrait, as attrait, a attrait; avons attrait, avez attrait, ont attrait
Plup. Ind.	avais attrait, avais attrait, avait attrait; avions attrait, aviez attrait, avaient attrait
Past Ant.	eus attrait, eus attrait, eut attrait; eûmes attrait, eûtes attrait, eurent attrait
Fut. Perf.	aurai attrait, auras attrait, aura attrait; aurons attrait, aurez attrait, auront attrait
Cond. Perf.	aurais attrait, aurais attrait, aurait attrait; aurions attrait, auriez attrait, auraient attrait
Past Subj.	aie attrait, aies attrait, ait attrait; ayons attrait, ayez attrait, aient attrait
Plup. Subj.	eusse attrait, eusses attrait, eût attrait; eussions attrait, eussiez attrait, eussent attrait
Imperative	attrais, attrayons, attrayez

to catch

Pres. Ind.	attrape, attrapes, attrape; attrapons, attrapez, attrapent
Imp. Ind.	attrapais, attrapais, attrapait; attrapions, attrapiez, attrapaient
Past Def.	attrapai, attrapas, attrapa; attrapâmes, attrapâtes, attrapèrent
Future	attraperai, attraperas, attrapera; attraperons, attraperez, attraperont
Condit.	attraperais, attraperais, attraperait; attraperions, attraperiez, attraperaient
Pres. Subj.	attrape, attrapes, attrape; attrapions, attrapiez, attrapent
Imp. Subj.	attrapasse, attrapasses, attrapât; attrapassions, attrapassiez, attrapassent
Past Indef.	ai attrapé, as attrapé, a attrapé; avons attrapé, avez attrapé, ont attrapé
Plup. Ind.	avais attrapé, avais attrapé, avait attrapé; avions attrapé, aviez attrapé, avaient attrapé
Past Ant.	eus attrapé, eus attrapé, eut attrapé; eûmes attrapé, eûtes attrapé, eurent attrapé
Fut. Perf.	aurai attrapé, auras attrapé, aura attrapé; aurons attrapé, aurez attrapé, auront attrapé
Cond. Perf.	aurais attrapé, aurais attrapé, aurait attrapé; aurions attrapé, auriez attrapé, auraient attrapé
Past Subj.	aie attrapé, aies attrapé, ait attrapé; ayons attrapé, ayez attrapé, aient attrapé
Plup. Subj.	eusse attrapé, eusses attrapé, eût attrapé; eussions attrapé, eussiez attrapé, eussent attrapé
Imperative	attrape, attrapons, attrapez

to augment, increase

Pres. Ind.	augmente, augmentes, augmente; augmentons, augmentez, augmentent
Imp. Ind.	augmentais, augmentais, augmentait; augmentions, augmentiez, augmentaient
Past Def.	augmentai, augmentas, augmenta; augmentâmes, augmentâtes, augmentèrent
Future	augmenterai, augmenteras, augmentera; augmenterons, augmenterez, augmenteront
Condit.	augmenterais, augmenterais, augmenterait; augmenterions, augmenteriez, augmenteraient
Pres. Subj.	augmente, augmentes, augmente; augmentions, augmentiez, augmentent
Imp. Subj.	augmentasse, augmentasses, augmentât; augmentassions, augmentassiez, augmentassent
Past Indef.	ai augmenté, as augmenté, a augmenté; avons augmenté, avez augmenté, ont augmenté
Plup. Ind.	avais augmenté, avais augmenté, avait augmenté; avions augmenté, aviez augmenté, avaient augmenté
Past Ant.	eus augmenté, eus augmenté, eut augmenté; eûmes augmenté, eûtes augmenté, eurent augmenté
Fut. Perf.	aurai augmenté, auras augmenté, aura augmenté; aurons augmenté, aurez augmenté, auront augmenté
Cond. Perf.	aurais augmenté, aurais augmenté, aurait augmenté; aurions augmenté, auriez augmenté, auraient augmenté
Past Subj.	aie augmenté, aies augmenté, ait augmenté; ayons augmenté, ayez augmenté, aient augmenté
Plup. Subj.	eusse augmenté, eusses augmenté, eût augmenté; eussions augmenté, eussiez augmenté, eussent augmenté
Imperative	augmente, augmentons, augmentez

to swallow

Pres. Ind.	avale, avales, avale; avalons, avalez, avalent
Imp. Ind.	avalais, avalais, avalait; avalions, avaliez, avalaient
Past Def.	avalai, avalas, avala; avalâmes, avalâtes, avalèrent
Future	avalerai, avaleras, avalera; avalerons, avalerez, avaleront
Condit.	avalerais, avalerais, avalerait; avalerions, avaleriez, avaleraient
Pres. Subj.	avale, avales, avale; avalions, avaliez, avalent
Imp. Subj.	avalasse, avalasses, avalât; avalassions, avalassiez, avalassent
Past Indef.	ai avalé, as avalé, a avalé; avons avalé, avez avalé, ont avalé
Plup. Ind.	avais avalé, avais avalé, avait avalé; avions avalé, aviez avalé, avaient avalé
Past Ant.	eus avalé, eus avalé, eut avalé; eûmes avalé, eûtes avalé, eurent avalé
Fut. Perf.	aurai avalé, auras avalé, aura avalé; aurons avalé, aurez avalé, auront avalé
Cond. Perf.	aurais avalé, aurais avalé, aurait avalé; aurions avalé, auriez avalé, auraient avalé
Past Subj.	aie avalé, aies avalé, ait avalé; ayons avalé, ayez avalé, aient avalé
Plup. Subj.	eusse avalé, eusses avalé, eût avalé; eussions avalé, eussiez avalé, eussent avalé
Imperative	avale, avalons, avalez

to advance, go forward

Pres. Ind.	avance, avances, avance; avançons, avancez, avancent
Imp. Ind.	avançais, avançais, avançait; avancions, avanciez, avançaient
Past Def.	avançai, avanças, avança; avançâmes, avançâtes, avancèrent
Future	avancerai, avanceras, avancera; avancerons, avancerez, avanceront
Condit.	avancerais, avancerais, avancerait; avancerions, avanceriez, avanceraient
Pres. Subj.	avance, avances, avance; avancions, avanciez, avancent
Imp. Subj.	avançasse, avançasses, avançât; avançassions, avançassiez, avançassent
Past Indef.	ai avancé, as avancé, a avancé; avons avancé, avez avancé, ont avancé
Pluperf.	avais avancé, avais avancé, avait avancé; avions avancé, aviez avancé, avaient avancé
Past Ant.	eus avancé, eus avancé, eut avancé; eûmes avancé, eûtes avancé, eurent avancé
Fut. Perf.	aurai avancé, auras avancé, aura avancé; aurons avancé, aurez avancé, auront avancé
Cond. Perf.	aurais avancé, aurais avancé, aurait avancé; aurions avancé, auriez avancé, auraient avancé
Past Subj.	aie avancé, aies avancé, ait avancé; ayons avancé, ayez avancé, aient avancé
Plup. Subj.	eusse avancé, eusses avancé, eût avancé; eussions avancé, eussiez avancé, eussent avancé
Imperative	avance, avançons, avancez

to have

Pres. Ind.	ai, as, a; avons, avez, ont
Imp. Ind.	avais, avais, avait; avions, aviez, avaient
Past Def.	eus, eus, eut; eûmes, eûtes, eurent
Fut. Ind.	aurai, auras, aura; aurons, aurez, auront
Condit.	aurais, aurais, aurait; aurions, auriez, auraient
Pres. Subj.	aie, aies, ait; ayons, ayez, aient
Imp. Subj.	eusse, eusses, eût; eussions, eussiez, eussent
Past Indef.	ai eu, as eu, a eu; avons eu, avez eu, ont eu
Pluperf.	avais eu, avais eu, avait eu; avions eu, aviez eu, avaient eu
Past Ant.	eus eu, eus eu, eut eu; eûmes eu, eûtes eu, eurent eu
Fut. Perf.	aurai eu, auras eu, aura eu; aurons eu, aurez eu, auront eu
Cond. Perf.	aurais eu, aurais eu, aurait eu; aurions eu, auriez eu, auraient eu
Past Subj.	aie eu, aies eu, ait eu; ayons eu, ayez eu, aient eu
Plup. Subj.	eusse eu, eusses eu, eût eu; eussions eu, eussiez eu, eussent eu
Imperative	aie, ayons, ayez

to balance, sway, swing, weigh

Pres. Ind.	balance, balances, balance; balançons, balancez, balancent
Imp. Ind.	balançais, balançais, balançait; balancions, balanciez, balançaient
Past Def.	balançai, balanças, balança; balançâmes, balançâtes, balancèrent
Future	balancerai, balanceras, balancera; balancerons, balancerez, balanceront
Condit.	balancerais, balancerais, balancerait; balancerions, balanceriez, balanceraient
Pres. Subj.	balance, balances, balance; balancions, balanciez, balancent
Imp. Subj.	balançasse, balançasses, balançât; balançassions, balançassiez, balançassent
Past Indef.	ai balancé, as balancé, a balancé; avons balancé, avez balancé, ont balancé
Plup. Ind.	avais balancé, avais balancé, avait balancé; avions balancé, aviez balancé, avaient balancé
Past Ant.	eus balancé, eus balancé, eut balancé; eûmes balancé, eûtes balancé, eurent balancé
Fut. Perf.	aurai balancé, auras balancé, aura balancé; aurons balancé, aurez balancé, auront balancé
Cond. Perf.	aurais balancé, aurais balancé, aurait balancé; aurions balancé, auriez balancé, auraient balancé
Past Subj.	aie balancé, aies balancé, ait balancé; ayons balancé, ayez balancé, aient balancé
Plup. Subj.	eusse balancé, eusses balancé, eût balancé; eussions balancé, eussiez balancé, eussent balancé
Imperative	balance, balançons, balancez

to sweep

Pres. Ind.	balaye, balayes, balaye; balayons, balayez, balayent
Imp. Ind.	balayais, balayais, balayait; balayions, balayiez, balayaient
Past Def.	balayai, balayas, balaya; ballayâmes, balayâtes, balayèrent
Future	balayerai, balayeras, balayera; balayerons, balayerez, balayeront
Condit.	balayerais, balayerais, balayerait; balayerions, balayeriez, balayeraient
Pres. Subj.	balaye, balayes, balaye; balayions, balayiez, balayent
Imp. Subj.	balayasse, balayasses, balayât; balayassions, balayassiez, balayassent
Past Indef.	ai balayé, as balayé, a balayé; avons balayé, avez balayé, ont balayé
Plup. Ind.	avais balayé, avais balayé, avait balayé; avions balayé, aviez balayé, avaient balayé
Past Ant.	eus balayé, eus balayé, eut balayé; eûmes balayé, eûtes balayé, eurent balayé
Fut. Perf.	aurai balayé, auras balayé, aura balayé; aurons balayé, aurez balayé, auront balayé
Cond. Perf.	aurais balayé, aurais balayé, aurait balayé; aurions balayé, auriez balayé, auraient balayé
Past Subj.	aie balayé, aies balayé, ait balayé; ayons balayé, ayez balayé, aient balayé
Plup. Subj.	eusse balayé, eusses balayé, eût balayé; eussions balayé, eussiez balayé, eussent balayé
Imperative	balaye, balayons, balayez

to build, construct

Pres. Ind.	bâtis, bâtis, bâtit; bâtissons, bâtissez, bâtissent
Imp. Ind.	bâtissais, bâtissais, bâtissait; bâtissions, bâtissiez, bâtissaient
Past Def.	bâtis, bâtis, bâtit; bâtîmes, bâtîtes, bâtirent
Fut. Ind.	bâtirai, bâtiras, bâtira; bâtirons, bâtirez, bâtiront
Condit.	bâtirais, bâtirais, bâtirait; bâtirions, bâtiriez, bâtiraient
Pres. Subj.	bâtisse, bâtisses, bâtisse; bâtissions, bâtissiez, bâtissent
Imp. Subj.	bâtisse, bâtisse, bâtît; bâtissions, bâtissiez, bâtissent
Past Indef.	ai bâti, as bâti, a bâti; avons bâti, avez bâti, ont bâti
Pluperf.	avais bâti, avais bâti, avait bâti; avions bâti, aviez bâti, avaient bâti
Past Ant.	eus bâti, eus bâti, eut bâti; eûmes bâti, eûtes bâti, eurent bâti
Fut. Perf.	aurai bâti, auras bâti, aura bâti; aurons bâti, aurez bâti, auront bâti
Cond. Perf.	aurais bâti, aurais bâti, aurait bâti; aurions bâti, auriez bâti, auraient bâti
Past Subj.	aie bâti, aies bâti, ait bâti; ayons bâti, ayez bâti, aient bâti
Plup. Subj.	eusse bâti, eusses bâti, eût bâti; eussions bâti, eussiez bâti, eussent bâti
Imperative	bâtis, bâtissons, bâtissez

to beat, hit, strike

Pres. Ind.	bats, bats, bat; battons, battez, battent
Imp. Ind.	battais, battais, battait; battions, battiez, battaient
Past Def.	battis, battis, battit; battîmes, battîtes, battirent
Fut. Ind.	battrai, battras, battra; battrons, battrez, battront
Condit.	battrais, battrais, battrait; battrions, battriez, battraient
Pres. Subj.	batte, battes, batte; battions, battiez, battent
Imp. Subj.	battisse, battisses, battît; battissions, battissiez, battissent
Past Indef.	ai battu, as battu, a battu; avons battu, avez battu, ont battu
Pluperf.	avais battu, avais battu, avait battu; avions battu, aviez battu, avaient battu
Past Ant.	eus battu, eus battu, eut battu; eûmes battu, eûtes battu, eurent battu
Fut. Perf.	aurai battu, auras battu, aura battu; aurons battu, aurez battu, auront battu
Cond. Perf.	aurais battu, aurais battu, aurait battu; aurions battu, auriez battu, auraient battu
Past Subj.	aie battu, aies battu, ait battu; ayons battu, ayez battu, aient battu
Plup. Subj.	eusse battu, eusses battu, eût battu; eussions battu, eussiez battu, eussent battu
Imperative	bats, battons, battez

to fight

Pres. Ind.	me bats, te bats, se bat; nous battons, vous battez, se battent
Imp. Ind.	me battais, te battais, se battait; nous battions, vous battiez, se battaient
Past Def.	me battis, te battis, se battit; nous battîmes, vous battîtes, se battirent
Fut. Ind.	me battrai, te battras, se battra; nous battrons, vous battrez, se battront
Condit.	me battrais, te battrais, se battrait; nous battrions, vous battriez, se battraient
Pres. Subj.	me batte, te battes, se batte; nous battions, vous battiez, se battent
Imp. Subj.	me battisse, te battisses, se battît; nous battissions, vous battissiez, se battissent
Past Indef.	me suis battu(e), t'es battu(e), s'est battu(e); nous sommes battu(e)s, vous êtes battu(e)(s), se sont battu(e)s
Pluperf.	m'étais battu(e), t'étais battu(e), s'était battu(e); nous étions battu(e)s, vous étiez battu(e)(s), s'étaient battu(e)s
Past Ant.	me fus battu(e), te fus battu(e), se fut battu(e); nous fûmes battu(e)s, vous fûtes battu(e)(s), se furent battu(e)s
Fut. Perf.	me serai battu(e), te seras battu(e), se sera battu(e); nous serons battu(e)s, vous serez battu(e)(s), se seront battu(e)s
Cond. Perf.	me serais battu(e), te serais battu(e), se serait battu(e); nous serions battu(e)s, vous seriez battu(e)(s), se seraient battu(e)s
Past Subj.	me sois battu(e), te sois battu(e), se soit battu(e); nous soyons battu(e)s, vous soyez battu(e)(s), se soient battu(e)s
Plup. Subj.	me fusse battu(e), te fusses battu(e), se fût battu(e); nous fussions battu(e)s, vous fussiez battu(e)(s), se fussent battu(e)s
Imperative	bats-toi, battons-nous, battez-vous

to chat, chatter, babble, gossip

Pres. Ind.	bavarde, bavardes, bavarde; bavardons, bavardez, bavardent
Imp. Ind.	bavardais, bavardais, bavardait; bavardions, bavardiez, bavardaient
Past Def.	bavardai, bavardas, bavarda; bavardâmes, bavardâtes, bavardèrent
Future	bavarderai, bavarderas, bavardera; bavarderons, bavarderez, bavarderont
Condit.	bavarderais, bavarderais, bavarderait; bavarderions, bavarderiez, bavarderaient
Pres. Subj.	bavarde, bavardes, bavarde; bavardions, bavardiez, bavardent
Imp. Subj.	bavardasse, bavardasses, bavardât; bavardassions, bavardassiez, bavardassent
Past Indef.	ai bavardé, as bavardé, a bavardé; avons bavardé, avez bavardé, ont bavardé
Plup. Ind.	avais bavardé, avais bavardé, avait bavardé; avions bavardé, aviez bavardé, avaient bavardé
Past Ant.	eus bavardé, eus bavardé, eut bavardé; eûmes bavardé, eûtes bavardé, eurent bavardé
Fut. Perf.	aurai bavardé, auras bavardé, aura bavardé; aurons bavardé, aurez bavardé, auront bavardé
Cond. Perf.	aurais bavardé, aurais bavardé, aurait bavardé; aurions bavardé, auriez bavardé, auraient bavardé
Past Subj.	aie bavardé, aies bavardé, ait bavardé; ayons bavardé, ayez bavardé, aient bavardé
Plup. Subj.	eusse bavardé, eusses bavardé, eût bavardé; eussions bavardé, eussiez bavardé, eussent bavardé
Imperative	bavarde, bavardons, bavardez

to bless, consecrate

Pres. Ind.	bénis, bénis, bénit; bénissons, bénissez, bénissent
Imp. Ind.	bénissais, bénissais, bénissait; bénissions, bénissiez, bénissaient
Past Def.	bénis, bénis, bénit; bénîmes, bénîtes, bénirent
Future	bénirai, béniras, bénira; bénirons, bénirez, béniront
Condit.	bénirais, bénirais, bénirait; bénirions, béniriez, béniraient
Pres. Subj.	bénisse, bénisses, bénisse; bénissions, bénissiez, bénissent
Imp. Subj.	bénisse, bénisses, bénît; bénissions, bénissiez, bénissent
Past Indef.	ai béni, as béni, a béni; avons béni, avez béni, ont béni
Pluperf.	avais béni, avais béni, avait béni; avions béni, aviez béni, avaient béni
Past Ant.	eus béni, eus béni, eut béni; eûmes béni, eûtes béni, eurent béni
Fut. Perf.	aurai béni, auras béni, aura béni; aurons béni, aurez béni, auront béni
Cond. Perf.	aurais béni, aurais béni, aurait béni; aurions béni, auriez béni, auraient béni
Past Subj.	aie béni, aies béni, ait béni; ayons béni, ayez béni, aient béni
Plup. Subj.	eusse béni, eusses béni, eût béni; eussions béni, eussiez béni, eussent béni
Imperative	bénis, bénissons, bénissez

to blame

Pres. Ind.	blâme, blâmes, blâme; blâmons, blâmez, blâment
Imp. Ind.	blâmais, blâmais, blâmait; blâmions, blâmiez, blâmaient
Past Def.	blâmai, blâmas, blâma; blâmâmes, blâmâtes, blâmèrent
Future	blâmerai, blâmeras, blâmera; blâmerons, blâmerez, blâmeront
Condit.	blâmerais, blâmerais, blâmerait; blâmerions, blâmeriez, blâmeraient
Pres. Subj.	blâme, blâmes, blâme; blâmions, blâmiez, blâment
Imp. Subj.	blâmasse, blâmasses, blâmât; blâmassions, blâmassiez, blâmassent
Past Indef.	ai blâmé, as blâmé, a blâmé; avons blâmé, avez blâmé, ont blâmé
Plup. Ind.	avais blâmé, avais blâmé, avait blâmé; avions blâmé, aviez blâmé, avaient blâmé
Past Ant.	eus blâmé, eus blâmé, eut blâmé; eûmes blâmé, eûtes blâmé, eurent blâmé
Fut. Perf.	aurai blâmé, auras blâmé. aura blâmé; aurons blâmé, aurez blâmé, auront blâmé
Cond. Perf.	aurais blâmé, aurais blâmé, aurait blâmé; aurions blâmé, auriez blâmé, auraient blâmé
Past Subj.	aie blâmé, aies blâmé, ait blâmé; ayons blâmé, ayez blâmé, aient blâmé
Plup. Subj.	eusse blâmé, eusses blâmé, eût blâmé; eussions blâmé, eussiez blâmé, eussent blâmé
Imperative	blâme, blâmons, blâmez

to whiten

Pres. Ind.	blanchis, blanchis, blanchit; blanchissons, blanchissez, blanchissent
Imp. Ind.	blanchissais, blanchissais, blanchissait; blanchissions, blanchissiez, blanchissaient
Past Def.	blanchis, blanchis, blanchit; blanchîmes, blanchîtes, blanchirent
Future	blanchirai, blanchiras, blanchira; blanchirons, blanchirez, blanchiront
Condit.	blanchirais, blanchirais, blanchirait; blanchirions, blanchiriez, blanchiraient
Pres. Subj.	blanchisse, blanchisses, blanchisse; blanchissions, blanchissiez, blanchissent
Imp. Subj.	blanchisse, blanchisses, blanchît; blanchissions, blanchissiez, blanchissent
Past Indef.	ai blanchi, as blanchi, a blanchi; avons blanchi, avez blanchi, ont blanchi
Plup. Ind.	avais blanchi, avais blanchi, avait blanchi; avions blanchi, aviez blanchi, avaient blanchi
Past Ant.	eus blanchi, eus blanchi, eut blanchi; eûmes blanchi, eûtes blanchi, eurent blanchi
Fut. Perf.	aurai blanchi, auras blanchi, aura blanchi; aurons blanchi, aurez blanchi, auront blanchi
Cond. Perf.	aurais blanchi, aurais blanchi, aurait blanchi; aurions blanchi, auriez blanchi, auraient blanchi
Past Subj.	aie blanchi, aies blanchi, ait blanchi; ayons blanchi, ayez blanchi, aient blanchi
Plup. Subj.	eusse blanchi, eusses blanchi, eût blanchi; eussions blanchi, eussiez blanchi, eussent blanchi
Imperative	blanchis, blanchissons, blanchissez

to harm, hurt, injure, wound

Pres. Ind.	blesse, blesses, blesse; blessons, blessez, blessent
Imp. Ind.	blessais, blessais, blessait; blessions, blessiez, blessaient
Past Def.	blessai, blessas, blessa; blessâmes, blessâtes, blessèrent
Future	blesserai, blesseras, blessera; blesserons, blesserez, blesseront
Condit.	blesserais, blesserais, blesserait; blesserions, blesseriez, blesseraient
Pres. Subj.	blesse, blesses, blesse; blessions, blessiez, blessent
Imp. Subj.	blessasse, blessasses, blessât; blessassions, blessassiez, blessassent
Past Indef.	ai blessé, as blessé, a blessé; avons blessé, avez blessé, ont blessé
Plup. Ind.	avais blessé, avais blessé, avait blessé; avions blessé, aviez blessé, avaient blessé
Past Ant.	eus blessé, eus blessé, eut blessé; eûmes blessé, eûtes blessé, eurent blessé
Fut. Perf.	aurai blessé, auras blessé, aura blessé; aurons blessé, aurez blessé, auront blessé
Cond. Perf.	aurais blessé, aurais blessé, aurait blessé; aurions blessé, auriez blessé, auraient blessé
Past Subj.	aie blessé, aies blessé, ait blessé; ayons blessé, ayez blessé, aient blessé
Plup. Subj.	eusse blessé, eusses blessé, eût blessé; eussions blessé, eussiez blessé, eussent blessé
Imperative	blesse, blessons, blessez [ordinairement inemployé]

to hurt oneself, injure oneself, wound oneself

Pres. Ind.	me blesse, te blesses, se blesse; nous blessons, vous blessez, se blessent
Imp. Ind.	me blessais, te blessais, se blessait; nous blessions, vous blessiez, se blessaient
Past Def.	me blessai, te blessas, se blessa; nous blessâmes, vous blessâtes, se blessèrent
Fut. Ind.	me blesserai, te blesseras, se blessera; nous blesserons, vous blesserez, se blesseront
Condit.	me blesserais, te blesserais, se blesserait; nous blesserions, vous blesseriez, se blesseraient
Pres. Subj.	me blesse, te blesses, se blesse; nous blessions, vous blessiez, se blessent
Imp. Subj.	me blessasse, te blessasses, se blessât; nous blessassions, vous blessassiez, se blessassent
Past Indef.	me suis blessé(e), t'es blessé(e), s'est blessé(e); nous sommes blessé(e)s, vous êtes blessé(e)(s), se sont blessé(e)s
Pluperf.	m'étais blessé(e), t'étais blessé(e), s'était blessé(e); nous étions blessé(e)s, vous étiez blessé(e)(s), s'étaient blessé(e)s
Past Ant.	me fus blessé(e), te fus blessé(e), se fut blessé(e); nous fûmes blessé(e)s, vous fûtes blessé(e)(s), se furent blessé(e)s
Fut. Perf.	me serai blessé(e), te seras blessé(e), se sera blessé(e); nous serons blessé(e)s, vous serez blessé(e)(s), se seront blessé(e)s
Cond. Perf.	me serais blessé(e), te serais blessé(e), se serait blessé(e); nous serions blessé(e)s, vous seriez blessé(e)(s), se seraient blessé(e)s
Past Subj.	me sois blessé(e), te sois blessé(e), se soit blessé(e); nous soyons blessé(e)s, vous soyez blessé(e)(s), se soient blessé(e)s
Plup. Subj.	me fusse blessé(e), te fusses blessé(e), se fût blessé(e); nous fussions blessé(e)s, vous fussiez blessé(e)(s), se fussent blessé(e)s
Imperative	[inemployé]

to drink

Pres. Ind.	bois, bois, boit; buvons, buvez, boivent
Imp. Ind.	buvais, buvais, buvait; buvions, buviez, buvaient
Past Def.	bus, bus, but; bûmes, bûtes, burent
Fut. Ind.	boirai, boiras, boira; boirons, boirez, boiront
Condit.	boirais, boirais, boirait; boirions, boiriez, boiraient
Pres. Subj.	boive, boives, boive; buvions, buviez, boivent
Imp. Subj.	busse, busses, bût; bussions, bussiez, bussent
Past Indef.	ai bu, as bu, a bu; avons bu, avez bu, ont bu
Pluperf.	avais bu, avais bu, avait bu; avions bu, aviez bu, avaient bu
Past Ant.	eus bu, eus bu, eut bu; eûmes bu, eûtes bu, eurent bu
Fut. Perf.	aurai bu, auras bu, aura bu; aurons bu, aurez bu, auront bu
Cond. Perf.	aurais bu, aurais bu, aurait bu; aurions bu, auriez bu, auraient bu
Past Subj.	aie bu, aies bu, ait bu; ayons bu, ayez bu, aient bu
Plup. Subj.	eusse bu, eusses bu, eût bu; eussions bu, eussiez bu, eussent bu
Imperative	bois, buvons, buvez

to budge, move

Pres. Ind.	bouge, bouges, bouge; bougeons, bougez, bougent
Imp. Ind.	bougeais, bougeais, bougeait; bougions, bougiez, bougeaient
Past Def.	bougeai, bougeas, bougea; bougeâmes, bougeâtes, bougèrent
Fut. Ind.	bougerai, bougeras, bougera; bougerons, bougerez, bougeront
Condit.	bougerais, bougerais, bougerait; bougerions, bougeriez, bougeraient
Pres. Subj.	bouge, bouges, bouge; bougions, bougiez, bougent
Imp. Subj.	bougeasse, bougeasses, bougeât; bougeassions, bougeassiez, bougeassent
Past Indef.	ai bougé, as bougé, a bougé; avons bougé, avez bougé, ont bougé
Pluperf.	avais bougé, avais bougé, avait bougé; avions bougé, aviez bougé, avaient bougé
Past Ant.	eus bougé, eus bougé, eut bougé; eûmes bougé, eûtes bougé, eurent bougé
Fut. Perf.	aurai bougé, auras bougé, aura bougé; aurons bougé, aurez bougé, auront bougé
Cond. Perf.	aurais bougé, aurais bougé, aurait bougé; aurions bougé, auriez bougé, auraient bougé
Past Subj.	aie bougé, aies bougé, ait bougé; ayons bougé, ayez bougé, aient bougé
Plup. Subj.	eusse bougé, eusses bougé, eût bougé; eussions bougé, eussiez bougé, eussent bougé
Imperative	bouge, bougeons, bougez

to boil

Pres. Ind.	bous, bous, bout; bouillons, bouillez, bouillent
Imp. Ind.	bouillais, bouillais, bouillait; bouillions, bouilliez, bouillaient
Past Def.	bouillis, bouillis, bouillit; bouillîmes, bouillîtes, bouillirent
Fut. Ind.	bouillirai, bouilliras, bouillira; bouillirons, bouillirez, bouilliront
Condit.	bouillirais, bouillirais, bouillirait; bouillirions, bouilliriez, bouilliraient
Pres. Subj.	bouille, bouilles, bouille; bouillions, bouilliez, bouillent
Imp. Subj.	bouillisse, bouillisses, bouillît; bouillissions, bouillissiez, bouillissent
Past Indef.	ai bouilli, as bouilli, a bouilli; avons bouilli, avez bouilli, ont bouilli
Pluperf.	avais bouilli, avais bouilli, avait bouilli; avions bouilli, aviez bouilli, avaient bouilli
Past Ant.	eus bouilli, eus bouilli, eut bouilli; eûmes bouilli, eûtes bouilli, eurent bouilli
Fut. Perf.	aurai bouilli, auras bouilli, aura bouilli; aurons bouilli, aurez bouilli, auront bouilli
Cond. Perf.	aurais bouilli, aurais bouilli, aurait bouilli; aurions bouilli, auriez bouilli, auraient bouilli
Past Subj.	aie bouilli, aies bouilli, ait bouilli; ayons bouilli, ayez bouilli, aient bouilli
Plup. Subj.	eusse bouilli, eusses bouilli, eût bouilli; eussions bouilli, eussiez bouilli, eussent bouilli
Imperative	[inemployé]

to brush

Pres. Ind.	brosse, brosses, brosse; brossons, brossez, brossent
Imp. Ind.	brossais, brossais, brossait; brossions, brossiez, brossaient
Past Def.	brossai, brossas, brossa; brossâmes, brossâtes, brossèrent
Future	brosserai, brosseras, brossera; brosserons, brosserez, brosseront
Condit.	brosserais, brosserais, brosserait; brosserions, brosseriez, brosseraient
Pres. Subj.	brosse, brosses, brosse; brossions, brossiez, brossent
Imp. Subj.	brossasse, brossasses, brossât; brossassions, brossassiez, brossassent
Past Indef.	ai brossé, as brossé, a brossé; avons brossé, avez brossé, ont brossé
Plup. Ind.	avais brossé, avais brossé, avait brossé; avions brossé, aviez brossé, avaient brossé
Past Ant.	eus brossé, eus brossé, eut brossé; eûmes brossé, eûtes brossé, eurent brossé
Fut. Perf.	aurai brossé, auras brossé, aura brossé; aurons brossé, aurez brossé, auront brossé
Cond. Perf.	aurais brossé, aurais brossé, aurait brossé; aurions brossé, auriez brossé, auraient brossé
Past Subj.	aie brossé, aies brossé, ait brossé; ayons brossé, ayez brossé, aient brossé
Plup. Subj.	eusse brossé, eusses brossé, eût brossé; eussions brossé, eussiez brossé, eussent brossé
Imperative	brosse, brossons, brossez

to brush oneself

Pres. Ind.	me brosse, te brosses, se brosse; nous brossons, vous brossez, se brossent
Imp. Ind.	me brossais, te brossais, se brossait; nous brossions, vous brossiez, se brossaient
Past Def.	me brossai, te brossas, se brossa; nous brossâmes, vous brossâtes, se brossèrent
Fut. Ind.	me brosserai, te brosseras, se brossera; nous brosserons, vous brosserez, se brosseront
Condit.	me brosserais, te brosserais, se brosserait; nous brosserions, vous brosseriez, se brosseraient
Pres. Subj.	me brosse, te brosses, se brosse; nous brossions, vous brossiez, se brossent
Imp. Subj.	me brossasse, te brossasses, se brossât; nous brossassions, vous brossassiez, se brossassent
Past Indef.	me suis brossé(e), t'es brossé(e), s'est brossé(e); nous sommes brossé(e)s, vous êtes brossé(e)(s), se sont brossé(e)s
Pluperf.	m'étais brossé(e), t'étais brossé(e), s'était brossé(e); nous étions brossé(e)s, vous étiez brossé(e)(s), s'étaient brossé(e)s
Past Ant.	me fus brossé(e), te fus brossé(e), se fut brossé(e); nous fûmes brossé(e)s, vous fûtes brossé(e)(s), se furent brossé(e)s
Fut. Perf.	me serai brossé(e), te seras brossé(e), se sera brossé(e); nous serons brossé(e)s, vous serez brossé(e)(s), se seront brossé(e)s
Cond. Perf.	me serais brossé(e), te serais brossé(e), se serait brossé(e); nous serions brossé(e)s, vous seriez brossé(e)(s), se seraient brossé(e)s
Past Subj.	me sois brossé(e), te sois brossé(e), se soit brossé(e); nous soyons brossé(e)s, vous soyez brossé(e)(s), se soient brossé(e)s
Plup. Subj.	me fusse brossé(e), te fusses brossé(e), se fût brossé(e); nous fussions brossé(e)s, vous fussiez brossé(e)(s), se fussent brossé(e)s
Imperative	brosse-toi, brossons-nous, brossez-vous

to drizzle

Pres. Ind.	il bruine
Imp. Ind.	il bruinait
Past Def.	il bruina
Future	il bruinera
Condit.	il bruinerait
Pres. Subj.	qu'il bruine
Imp. Subj.	qu'il bruinât
Past Indef.	il a bruiné
Plup. Ind.	il avait bruiné
Past Ant.	il eut bruiné
Fut. Perf.	il aura bruiné
Cond. Perf.	il aurait bruiné
Past Subj.	qu'il ait bruiné
Plup. Subj.	qu'il eût bruiné
Imperative	[inemployé]

to burn

Pres. Ind.	brûle, brûles, brûle; brûlons, brûlez, brûlent
Imp. Ind.	brûlais, brûlais, brûlait; brûlions, brûliez, brûlaient
Past Def.	brûlai, brûlas, brûla; brûlâmes, brûlâtes, brûlèrent
Fut. Ind.	brûlerai, brûleras, brûlera; brûlerons, brûlerez, brûleront
Condit.	brûlerais, brûlerais, brûlerait; brûlerions, brûleriez, brûleraient
Pres. Subj.	brûle, brûles, brûle; brûlions, brûliez, brûlent
Imp. Subj.	brûlasse, brûlasses, brûlât; brûlassions, brûlassiez, brûlassent
Past Indef.	ai brûlé, as brûlé, a brûlé; avons brûlé, avez brûlé, ont brûlé
Pluperf.	avais brûlé, avais brûlé, avait brûlé; avions brûlé, aviez brûlé, avaient brûlé
Past Ant.	eus brûlé, eus brûlé, eut brûlé; eûmes brûlé, eûtes brûlé, eurent brûlé
Fut. Perf.	aurai brûlé, auras brûlé, aura brûlé; aurons brûlé, aurez brûlé, auront brûlé
Cond. Perf.	aurais brûlé, aurais brûlé, aurait brûlé; aurions brûlé, auriez brûlé, auraient brûlé
Past Subj.	aie brûlé, aies brûlé, ait brûlé; ayons brûlé, ayez brûlé, aient brûlé
Plup. Subj.	eusse brûlé, eusses brûlé, eût brûlé; eussions brûlé, eussiez brûlé, eussent brûlé
Imperative	brûle, brûlons, brûlez

to hide

Pres. Ind.	cache, caches, cache; cachons, cachez, cachent
Imp. Ind.	cachais, cachais, cachait; cachions, cachiez, cachaient
Past Def.	cachai, cachas, cacha; cachâmes, cachâtes, cachèrent
Fut. Ind.	cacherai, cacheras, cachera; cacherons, cacherez, cacheront
Condit.	cacherais, cacherais, cacherait; cacherions, cacheriez, cacheraient
Pres. Subj.	cache, caches, cache; cachions, cachiez, cachent
Imp. Subj.	cachasse, cachasses, cachât; cachassions, cachassiez, cachassent
Past Indef.	ai caché, as caché, a caché; avons caché, avez caché, ont caché
Pluperf.	avais caché, avais caché, avait caché; avions caché, aviez caché, avaient caché
Past Ant.	eus caché, eus caché, eut caché; eûmes caché, eûtes caché, eurent caché
Fut. Perf.	aurai caché, auras caché, aura caché; aurons caché, aurez caché, auront caché
Cond. Perf.	aurais caché, aurais caché, aurait caché; aurions caché, auriez caché, auraient caché
Past Subj.	aie caché, aies caché, ait caché; ayons caché, ayez caché, aient caché
Plup. Subj.	eusse caché, eusses caché, eût caché; eussions caché, eussiez caché, eussent caché
Imperative	cache, cachons, cachez

to hide oneself

Pres. Ind.	me cache, te caches, se cache; nous cachons, vous cachez, se cachent
Imp. Ind.	me cachais, te cachais, se cachait; nous cachions, vous cachiez, se cachaient
Past Def.	me cachai, te cachas, se cacha; nous cachâmes, vous cachâtes, se cachèrent
Future	me cacherai, te cacheras, se cachera; nous cacherons, vous cacherez, se cacheront
Condit.	me cacherais, te cacherais, se cacherait; nous cacherions, vous cacheriez, se cacheraient
Pres. Subj.	me cache, te caches, se cache; nous cachions, vous cachiez, se cachent
Imp. Subj.	me cachasse, te cachasses, se cachât; nous cachassions, vous cachassiez, se cachassent
Past Indef.	me suis caché(e), t'es caché(e), s'est caché(e); nous sommes caché(e)s, vous êtes caché(e)(s), se sont caché(e)s
Plup. Ind.	m'étais caché(e), t'étais caché(e), s'était caché(e); nous étions caché(e)s, vous étiez caché(e)(s), s'étaient caché(e)s
Past Ant.	me fus caché(e), te fus caché(e), se fut caché(e); nous fûmes caché(e)s, vous fûtes caché(e)(s), se furent caché(e)s
Fut. Perf.	me serai caché(e), te seras caché(e), se sera caché(e); nous serons caché(e)s, vous serez caché(e)(s), se seront caché(e)s
Cond. Perf.	me serais caché(e), te serais caché(e), se serait caché(e); nous serions caché(e)s, vous seriez caché(e)(s), se seraient caché(e)s
Past Subj.	me sois caché(e), te sois caché(e), se soit caché(e); nous soyons caché(e)s, vous soyez caché(e)(s), se soient caché(e)s
Plup. Subj.	me fusse caché(e), te fusses caché(e), se fût caché(e); nous fussions caché(e)s, vous fussiez caché(e)(s), se fussent caché(e)s
Imperative	cache-toi, cachons-nous, cachez-vous

to break

Pres. Ind.	casse, casses, casse; cassons, cassez, cassent
Imp. Ind.	cassais, cassais, cassait; cassions, cassiez, cassaient
Past Def.	cassai, cassas, cassa; cassâmes, cassâtes, cassèrent
Fut. Ind.	casserai, casseras, cassera; casserons, casserez, casseront
Condit.	casserais, casserais, casserait; casserions, casseriez, casseraient
Pres. Subj.	casse, casses, casse; cassions, cassiez, cassent
Imp. Subj.	cassasse, cassasses, cassât; cassassions, cassassiez, cassassent
Past Indef.	ai cassé, as cassé, a cassé; avons cassé, avez cassé, ont cassé
Pluperf.	avais cassé, avais cassé, avait cassé; avions cassé, aviez cassé, avaient cassé
Past Ant.	eus cassé, eus cassé, eut cassé; eûmes cassé, eûtes cassé, eurent cassé
Fut. Perf.	aurai cassé, auras cassé, aura cassé; aurons cassé, aurez cassé, auront cassé
Cond. Perf.	aurais cassé, aurais cassé, aurait cassé; aurions cassé, auriez cassé, auraient cassé
Past Subj.	aie cassé, aies cassé, ait cassé; ayons cassé, ayez cassé, aient cassé
Plup. Subj.	eusse cassé, eusses cassé, eût cassé; eussions cassé, eussiez cassé, eussent cassé
Imperative	casse, cassons, cassez

to cause, chat

Pres. Ind.	cause, causes, cause; causons, causez, causent
Imp. Ind.	causais, causais, causait; causions, causiez, causaient
Past Def.	causai, causas, causa; causâmes, causâtes, causèrent
Fut. Ind.	causerai, causeras, causera; causerons, causerez, causeront
Condit.	causerais, causerais, causerait; causerions, causeriez, causeraient
Pres. Subj.	cause, causes, cause; causions, causiez, causent
Imp. Subj.	causasse, causasses, causât; causassions, causassiez, causassent
Past Indef.	ai causé, as causé, a causé; avons causé, avez causé, ont causé
Pluperf.	avais causé, avais causé, avait causé; avions causé, aviez causé, avaient causé
Past Ant.	eus causé, eus causé, eut causé; eûmes causé, eûtes causé, eurent causé
Fut. Perf.	aurai causé, auras causé, aura causé; aurons causé, aurez causé, auront causé
Cond. Perf.	aurais causé, aurais causé, aurait causé; aurions causé, auriez causé, auraient causé
Past Subj.	aie causé, aies causé, ait causé; ayons causé, ayez causé, aient causé
Plup. Subj.	eusse causé, eusses causé, eût causé; eussions causé, eussiez causé, eussent causé
Imperative	cause, causons, causez

to yield

Pres. Ind.	cède, cèdes, cède; cédons, cédez, cèdent
Imp. Ind.	cédais, cédais, cédait; cédions, cédiez, cédaient
Past Def.	cédai, cédas, céda; cédâmes, cédâtes, cédèrent
Fut. Ind.	céderai, céderas, cédera; céderons, céderez, céderont
Condit.	céderais, céderais, céderait; céderions, céderiez, céderaient
Pres. Subj.	cède, cèdes, cède; cédions, cédiez, cèdent
Imp. Subj.	cédasse, cédasses, cédât; cédassions, cédassiez, cédassent
Past Indef.	ai cédé, as cédé, a cédé; avons cédé, avez cédé, ont cédé
Pluperf.	avais cédé, avais cédé, avait cédé; avions cédé, aviez cédé, avaient cédé
Past Ant.	eus cédé, eus cédé, eut cédé; eûmes cédé, eûtes cédé, eurent cédé
Fut. Perf.	aurai cédé, auras cédé, aura cédé; aurons çédé, aurez cédé, auront cédé
Cond. Perf.	aurais cédé, aurais cédé, aurait cédé; aurions cédé, auriez cédé, auraient cédé
Past Subj.	aie cédé, aies cédé, ait cédé; ayons cédé, ayez cédé, aient cédé
Plup. Subj.	eusse cédé, eusses cédé, eût cédé; eussions cédé, eussiez cédé, eussent cédé
Imperative	cède, cédons, cédez

to attest, certify, guarantee

Pres. Ind.	certifie, certifies, certifie; certifions, certifiez, certifient
Imp. Ind.	certifiais, certifiais, certifiait; certifiions, certifiiez, certifiaient
Past Def.	certifiai, certifias, certifia; certifiâmes, certifiâtes, certifièrent
Future	certifierai, certifieras, certifiera; certifierons, certifierez, certifieront
Condit.	certifierais, certifierais, certifierait; certifierions, certifieriez, certifieraient
Pres. Subj.	certifie, certifies, certifie; certifiions, certifiiez, certifient
Imp. Subj.	certifiasse, certifiasses, certifiât; certifiassions, certifiassiez, certifiassent
Past Indef.	ai certifié, as certifié, a certifié; avons certifié, avez certifié, ont certifié
Plup. Ind.	avais certifié, avais certifié, avait certifié; avions certifié, aviez certifié, avaient certifié
Past Ant.	eus certifié, eus certifié, eut certifié; eûmes certifié, eûtes certifié, eurent certifié
Fut. Perf.	aurai certifié, auras certifié, aura certifié; aurons certifié, aurez certifié, auront certifié
Cond. Perf.	aurais certifié, aurais certifié, aurait certifié; aurions certifié, auriez certifié, auraient certifié
Past Subj.	aie certifié, aies certifié, ait certifié; ayons certifié, ayez certifié, aient certifié
Plup. Subj.	eusse certifié, eusses certifié, eût certifié; eussions certifié, eussiez certifié, eussent certifié
Imperative	certifie, certifions, certifiez

to cease

Pres. Ind.	cesse, cesses, cesse; cessons, cessez, cessent
Imp. Ind.	cessais, cessais, cessait; cessions, cessiez, cessaient
Past Def.	cessai, cessas, cessa; cessâmes, cessâtes, cessèrent
Future	cesserai, cesseras, cessera; cesserons, cesserez, cesseront
Condit.	cesserais, cesserais, cesserait; cesserions, cesseriez, cesseraient
Pres. Subj.	cesse, cesse, cesse; cessions, cessiez, cessent
Imp. Subj.	cessasse, cessasses, cessât; cessassions, cessassiez, cessassent
Past Indef.	ai cessé, as cessé, a cessé; avons cessé, avez cessé, ont cessé
Plup. Ind.	avais cessé, avais cessé, avait cessé; avions cessé, aviez cessé, avaient cessé
Past Ant.	eus cessé, eus cessé, eut cessé; eûmes cessé, eûtes cessé, eurent cessé
Fut. Perf.	aurai cessé, auras cessé, aura cessé; aurons cessé, aurez cessé, auront cessé
Cond. Perf.	aurais cessé, aurais cessé, aurait cessé; aurions cessé, auriez cessé, auraient cessé
Past Subj.	aie cessé, aies cessé, ait cessé; ayons cessé, ayez cessé, aient cessé
Plup. Subj.	eusse cessé, eusses cessé, eût cessé; eussions cessé, eussiez cessé, eussent cessé
Imperative	cesse, cessons, cessez

to change

Pres. Ind.	change, changes, change; changeons, changez, changent
Imp. Ind.	changeais, changeais, changeait; changions, changiez, changeaient
Past Def.	changeai, changeas, changea; changeâmes, changeâtes, changèrent
Fut. Ind.	changerai, changeras, changera; changerons, changerez, changeront
Condit.	changerais, changerais, changerait; changerions, changeriez, changeraient
Pres. Subj.	change, changes, change; changions, changiez, changent
Imp. Subj.	changeasse, changeasses, changeât; changeassions, changeassiez, changeassent
Past Indef.	ai changé, as changé, a changé; avons changé, avez changé, ont changé
Pluperf.	avais changé, avais changé, avait changé; avions changé, aviez changé, avaient changé
Past Ant.	eus changé, eus changé, eut changé; eûmes changé, eûtes changé, eurent changé
Fut. Perf.	aurai changé, auras changé, aura changé; aurons changé, aurez changé, auront changé
Cond. Perf.	aurais changé, aurais changé, aurait changé; aurions changé, auriez changé, auraient changé
Past Subj.	aie changé, aies changé, ait changé; ayons changé, ayez changé, aient changé
Plup. Subj.	eusse changé, eusses changé, eût changé; eussions changé, eussiez changé, eussent changé
Imperative	change, changeons, changez

to sing

Pres. Ind.	chante, chantes, chante; chantons, chantez, chantent
Imp. Ind.	chantais, chantais, chantait; chantions, chantiez, chantaient
Past Def.	chantai, chantas, chanta; chantâmes, chantâtes, chantèrent
Fut. Ind.	chanterai, chanteras, chantera; chanterons, chanterez, chanteront
Condit.	chanterais, chanterais, chanterait; chanterions, chanteriez, chanteraient
Pres. Subj.	chante, chantes, chante; chantions, chantiez, chantent
Imp. Subj.	chantasse, chantasses, chantât; chantassions, chantassiez, chantassent
Past Indef.	ai chanté, as chanté, a chanté; avons chanté, avez chanté, ont chanté
Pluperf.	avais chanté, avais chanté, avait chanté; avions chanté, aviez chanté, avaient chanté
Past Ant.	eus chanté, eus chanté, eut chanté; eûmes chanté, eûtes chanté, eurent chanté
Fut. Perf.	aurai chanté, auras chanté, aura chanté; aurons chanté, aurez chanté, auront chanté
Cond. Perf.	aurais chanté, aurais chanté, aurait chanté; aurions chanté, auriez chanté, auraient chanté
Past Subj.	aie chanté, aies chanté, ait chanté; ayons chanté, ayez chanté, aient chanté
Plup. Subj.	eusse chanté, eusses chanté, eût chanté; eussions chanté, eussiez chanté, eussent chanté
Imperative	chante, chantons, chantez

to burden, charge, load

Pres. Ind.	charge, charges, charge; chargeons, chargez, chargent
Imp. Ind.	chargeais, chargeais, chargeait; chargions, chargiez, chargeaient
Past Def.	chargeai, chargeas, chargea; chargeâmes, chargeâtes, chargèrent
Future	chargerai, chargeras, chargera; chargerons, chargerez, chargeront
Condit.	chargerais, chargerais, chargerait; chargerions, chargeriez, chargeraient
Pres. Subj.	charge, charges, charge; chargions, chargiez, chargent
Imp. Subj.	chargeasse, chargeasses, chargeât; chargeassions, chargeassiez, chargeassent
Past Indef.	ai chargé, as chargé, a chargé; avons chargé, avez chargé, ont chargé
Plup. Ind.	avais chargé, avais chargé, avait chargé; avions chargé, aviez chargé, avaient chargé
Past Ant.	eus chargé, eus chargé, eut chargé; eûmes chargé, eûtes chargé, eurent chargé
Fut. Perf.	aurai chargé, auras chargé, aura chargé; aurons chargé, aurez chargé, auront chargé
Cond. Perf.	aurais chargé, aurais chargé, aurait chargé; aurions chargé, auriez chargé, auraient chargé
Past Subj.	aie chargé, aies chargé, ait chargé; ayons chargé, ayez chargé, aient chargé
Plup. Subj.	eusse chargé, eusses chargé, eût chargé; eussions chargé, eussiez chargé, eussent chargé
Imperative	charge, chargeons, chargez

to hunt, pursue, chase, drive out

Pres. Ind.	chasse, chasses, chasse; chassons, chassez, chassent
Imp. Ind.	chassais, chassais, chassait; chassions, chassiez, chassaient
Past Def.	chassai, chassas, chassa; chassâmes, chassâtes, chassèrent
Future	chasserai, chasseras, chassera; chasserons, chasserez, chasseront
Condit.	chasserais, chasserais, chasserait; chasserions, chasseriez, chasseraient
Pres. Subj.	chasse, chasses, chasse; chassions, chassiez, chassent
Imp. Subj.	chassasse, chassasses, chassât; chassassions, chassassiez, chassassent
Past Indef.	ai chassé, as chassé, a chassé; avons chassé, avez chassé, ont chassé
Pluperf.	avais chassé, avais chassé, avait chassé; avions chassé, aviez chassé, avaient chassé
Past Ant.	eus chassé, eus chassé, eut chassé; eûmes chassé, eûtes chassé, eurent chassé
Fut. Perf.	aurai chassé, auras chassé, aura chassé; aurons chassé, aurez chassé, auront chassé
Cond. Perf.	aurais chassé, aurais chassé, aurait chassé; aurions chassé, auriez chassé, auraient chassé
Past Subj.	aie chassé, aies chassé, ait chassé; ayons chassé, ayez chassé, aient chassé
Plup. Subj.	eusse chassé, eusses chassé, eût chassé; eussions chassé, eussiez chassé, eussent chassé
Imperative	chasse, chassons, chassez

to look for, search

Pres. Ind.	cherche, cherches, cherche; cherchons, cherchez, cherchent
Imp. Ind.	cherchais, cherchais, cherchait; cherchions, cherchiez, cherchaient
Past Def.	cherchai, cherchas, chercha; cherchâmes, cherchâtes, cherchèrent
Fut. Ind.	chercherai, chercheras, cherchera; chercherons, chercherez, chercheront
Condit.	chercherais, chercherais, chercherait; chercherions, chercheriez, chercheraient
Pres. Subj.	cherche, cherches, cherche; cherchions, cherchiez, cherchent
Imp. Subj.	cherchasse, cherchasses, cherchât; cherchassions, cherchassiez, cherchassent
Past Indef.	ai cherché, as cherché, a cherché; avons cherché, avez cherché, ont cherché
Pluperf.	avais cherché, avais cherché, avait cherché; avions cherché, aviez cherché, avaient cherché
Past Ant.	eus cherché, eus cherché, eut cherché; eûmes cherché, eûtes cherché, eurent cherché
Fut. Perf.	aurai cherché, auras cherché, aura cherché; aurons cherché, aurez cherché, auront cherché
Cond. Perf.	aurais cherché, aurais cherché, aurait cherché; aurions cherché, auriez cherché, auraient cherché
Past Subj.	aie cherché, aies cherché, ait cherché; ayons cherché, ayez cherché, aient cherché
Plup. Subj.	eusse cherché, eusses cherché, eût cherché; eussions cherché, eussiez cherché, eussent cherché
Imperative	cherche, cherchons, cherchez

to cherish

Pres. Ind.	chéris, chéris, chérit; chérissons, chérissez, chérissent
Imp. Ind.	chérissais, chérissais, chérissait; chérissions, chérissiez, chérissaient
Past Def.	chéris, chéris, chérit; chérîmes, chérîtes, chérirent
Fut. Ind.	chérirai, chériras, chérira; chérirons, chérirez, chériront
Condit.	chérirais, chérirais, chérirait; chéririons, chéririez, chériraient
Pres. Subj.	chérisse, chérisses, chérisse; chérissions, chérissiez, chérissent
Imp. Subj.	chérisse, chérisses, chérît; chérissions, chérissiez, chérissent
Past Indef.	ai chéri, as chéri, a chéri; avons chéri, avez chéri, ont chéri
Pluperf.	avais chéri, avais chéri, avait chéri; avions chéri, aviez chéri, avaient chéri
Past Ant.	eus chéri, eus chéri, eut chéri; eûmes chéri, eûtes chéri, eurent chéri
Fut. Perf.	aurai chéri, auras chéri, aura chéri; aurons chéri, aurez chéri, auront chéri
Cond. Perf.	aurais chéri, aurais chéri, aurait chéri; aurions chéri, auriez chéri, auraient chéri
Past Subj.	aie chéri, aies chéri, ait chéri; ayons chéri, ayez chéri, aient chéri
Plup. Subj.	eusse chéri, eusses chéri, eût chéri; eussions chéri, eussiez chéri, eussent chéri
Imperative	chéris, chérissons, chérissez

to choose, select, pick

Pres. Ind.	choisis, choisis, choisit; choisissons, choisissez, choisissent
Imp. Ind.	choisissais, choisissais, choisissait; choisissions, choisissiez, choisissaient
Past Def.	choisis, choisis, choisit; choisîmes, choisîtes, choisirent
Fut. Ind.	choisirai, choisiras, choisira; choisirons, choisirez, choisiront
Condit.	choisirais, choisirais, choisirait; choisirions, choisiriez, choisiraient
Pres. Subj.	choisisse, choisisses, choisisse; choisissions, choisissiez, choisissent
Imp. Subj.	choisisse, choisisses, choisît; choisissions, choisissiez, choisissent
Past Indef.	ai choisi, as choisi, a choisi; avons choisi, avez choisi, ont choisi
Pluperf.	avais choisi, avais choisi, avait choisi; avions choisi, aviez choisi, avaient choisi
Past Ant.	eus choisi, eus choisi, eut choisi; eûmes choisi, eûtes choisi, eurent choisi
Fut. Perf.	aurai choisi, auras choisi, aura choisi; aurons choisi, aurez choisi, auront choisi
Cond. Perf.	aurais choisi, aurais choisi, aurait choisi; aurions choisi, auriez choisi, auraient choisi
Past Subj.	aie choisi, aies choisi, ait choisi; ayons choisi, ayez choisi, aient choisi
Plup. Subj.	eusse choisi, eusses choisi, eût choisi; eussions choisi, eussiez choisi, eussent choisi
Imperative	choisis, choisissons, choisissez

to whisper

Pres. Ind.	chuchote, chuchotes, chuchote; chuchotons, chuchotez, chuchotent
Imp. Ind.	chuchotais, chuchotais, chuchotait; chuchotions, chuchotiez, chuchotaient
Past Def.	chuchotai, chuchotas, chuchota; chuchotâmes, chuchotâtes, chuchotèrent
Future	chuchoterai, chuchoteras, chuchotera; chuchoterons, chuchoterez, chuchoteront
Condit.	chuchoterais, chuchoterais, chuchoterait; chuchoterions, chuchoteriez, chuchoteraient
Pres. Subj.	chuchote, chuchotes, chuchote; chuchotions, chuchotiez, chuchotent
Imp. Subj.	chuchotasse, chuchotasses, chuchotât; chuchotassions, chuchotassiez, chuchotassent
Past Indef.	ai chuchoté, as chuchoté, a chuchoté; avons chuchoté, avez chuchoté, ont chuchoté
Plup. Ind.	avais chuchoté, avais chuchoté, avait chuchoté; avions chuchoté, aviez chuchoté, avaient chuchoté
Past Ant.	eus chuchoté, eus chuchoté, eut chuchoté; eûmes chuchoté, eûtes chuchoté, eurent chuchoté
Fut. Perf.	aurai chuchoté, auras chuchoté, aura chuchoté; aurons chuchoté, aurez chuchoté, auront chuchoté
Cond. Perf.	aurais chuchoté, aurais chuchoté, aurait chuchoté; aurions chuchoté, auriez chuchoté, auraient chuchoté
Past Subj.	aie chuchoté, aies chuchoté, ait chuchoté; ayons chuchoté, ayez chuchoté, aient chuchoté
Plup. Subj.	eusse chuchoté, eusses chuchoté, eût chuchoté; eussions chuchoté, eussiez chuchoté, eussent chuchoté
Imperative	chuchote, chuchotons, chuchotez

to class, classify, sort

Pres. Ind.	classe, classes, classe; classons, classez, classent
Imp. Ind.	classais, classais, classait; classions, classiez, classaient
Past Def.	classai, classas, classa; classâmes, classâtes, classèrent
Future	classerai, classeras, classera; classerons, classerez, classeront
Condit.	classerais, classerais, classerait; classerions, classeriez, classeraient
Pres. Subj.	classe, classes, classe; classions, classiez, classent
Imp. Subj.	classasse, classasses, classât; classassions, classassiez, classassent
Past Indef.	ai classé, as classé, a classé; avons classé, avez classé, ont classé
Pluperf.	avais classé, avais classé, avait classé; avions classé, aviez classé, avaient classé
Past Ant.	eus classé, eus classé, eut classé; eûmes classé, eûtes classé, eurent classé
Fut. Perf.	aurai classé, auras classé, aura classé; aurons classé, aurez classé, auront classé
Condit.	aurais classé, aurais classé, aurait classé; aurions classé, auriez classé, auraient classé
Past Subj.	aie classé, aies classé, ait classé; ayons classé, ayez classé, aient classé
Plup. Subj.	eusse classé, eusses classé, eût classé; eussions classé, eussiez classé, eussent classé
Imperative	classe, classons, classez

to combat, fight

Pres. Ind.	combats, combats, combat; combattons, combattez, combattent
Imp. Ind.	combattais, combattais, combattait; combattions, combattiez, combattaient
Past Def.	combattis, combattis, combattit; combattîmes, combattîtes, combattirent
Future	combattrai, combattras, combattra; combattrons, combattrez, combattront
Condit.	combattrais, combattrais, combattrait; combattrions, combattriez, combattraient
Pres. Subj.	combatte, combattes, combatte; combattions, combattiez, combattent
Imp. Subj.	combattisse, combattisses, combattît; combattissions, combattissiez, combattissent
Past Indef.	ai combattu, as combattu, a combattu; avons combattu, avez combattu, ont combattu
Plup. Ind.	avais combattu, avais combattu, avait combattu; avions combattu, aviez combattu, avaient combattu
Past Ant.	eus combattu, eus combattu, eut combattu; eûmes combattu, eûtes combattu, eurent combattu
Fut. Perf.	aurai combattu, auras combattu, aura combattu; aurons combattu, aurez combattu, auront combattu
Cond. Perf.	aurais combattu, aurais combattu, aurait combattu; aurions combattu, auriez combattu, auraient combattu
Past Subj.	aie combattu, aies combattu, ait combattu; ayons combattu, ayez combattu, aient combattu
Plup. Subj.	eusse combattu, eusses combattu, eût combattu; eussions combattu, eussiez combattu, eussent combattu
Imperative	combats, combattons, combattez

to command, order

Pres. Ind.	commande, commandes, commande; commandons, commandez, commandent
Imp. Ind.	commandais, commandais, commandait; commandions, commandiez, commandaient
Past Def.	commandai, commandas, commanda; commandâmes, commandâtes, commandèrent
Fut. Ind.	commanderai, commanderas, commandera; commanderons, commanderez, commanderont
Condit.	commanderais, commanderais, commanderait; commanderions, commanderiez, commanderaient
Pres. Subj.	commande, commandes, commande; commandions, commandiez, commandent
Imp. Subj.	commandasse, commandasses, commandât; commandassions, commandassiez, commandassent
Past Indef	ai commandé, as commandé, a commandé; avons commandé, avez commandé, ont commandé
Pluperf.	avais commandé, avais commandé, avait commandé; avions commandé, aviez commandé, avaient commandé
Past Ant.	eus commandé, eus commandé, eut commandé; eûmes commandé, eûtes commandé, eurent commandé
Fut. Perf.	aurai commandé, auras commandé, aura commandé; aurons commandé, aurez commandé, auront commandé
Cond. Perf.	aurais commandé, aurais commandé, aurait commandé; aurions commandé, auriez commandé, auraient commandé
Past Subj.	aie commandé, aies commandé, ait commandé; ayons commandé, ayez commandé, aient commandé
Plup. Subj.	eusse commandé, eusses commandé, eût commandé; eussions commandé, eussiez commandé, eussent commandé
Imperative	commande, commandons, commandez

Pres. Ind.	commence, commences, commence; commençons, commencez, commencent	*to begin, start, commence*
Imp. Ind.	commençais, commençais, commençait; commencions, commenciez, commençaient	
Past Def.	commençai, commenças, commença; commençâmes, commençâtes, commencèrent	
Fut. Ind.	commencerai, commenceras, commencera; commencerons, commencerez, commenceront	
Condit.	commencerais, commencerais, commencerait; commencerions, commenceriez, commenceraient	
Pres. Subj.	commence, commences, commence; commencions, commenciez, commencent	
Imp. Subj.	commençasse, commençasses, commençât; commençassions, commençassiez, commençassent	
Past Indef.	ai commencé, as commencé, a commencé; avons commencé, avez commencé, ont commencé	
Pluperf.	avais commencé, avais commencé, avait commencé; avions commencé, aviez commencé, avaient commencé	
Past Ant.	eus commencé, eus commencé, eut commencé; eûmes commencé, eûtes commencé, eurent commencé	
Fut. Perf.	aurai commencé, auras commencé, aura commencé; aurons commencé, aurez commencé, auront commencé	
Cond. Perf.	aurais commencé, aurais commencé, aurait commencé; aurions commencé, auriez commencé, auraient commencé	
Past Subj.	aie commencé, aies commencé, ait commencé; ayons commencé, ayez commencé, aient commencé	
Plup. Subj.	eusse commencé, eusses commencé, eût commencé; eussions commencé, eussiez commencé, eussent commencé	
Imperative	commence, commençons, commencez	

to commit

Pres. Ind.	commets, commets, commet; commettons, commettez, commettent
Imp. Ind.	commettais, commettais, commettait; commettions, commettiez, commettaient
Past Def.	commis, commis, commit; commîmes, commîtes, commirent
Future	commettrai, commettras, commettra; commettrons, commettrez, commettront
Condit.	commettrais, commettrais, commettrait; commettrions, commettriez, commettraient
Pres. Subj.	commette, commettes, commette; commettions, commettiez, commettent
Imp. Subj.	commisse, commisses, commît; commissions, commissiez, commissent
Past Indef.	ai commis, as commis, a commis; avons commis, avez commis, ont commis
Plup. Ind.	avais commis, avais commis, avait commis; avions commis, aviez commis, avaient commis
Past Ant.	eus commis, eus commis, eut commis; eûmes commis, eûtes commis, eurent commis
Fut. Perf.	aurai commis, auras commis, aura commis; aurons commis, aurez commis, auront commis
Cond. Perf.	aurais commis, aurais commis, aurait commis; aurions commis, auriez commis, auraient commis
Past Subj.	aie commis, aies commis, ait commis; ayons commis, ayez commis, aient commis
Plup. Subj.	eusse commis, eusses commis, eût commis; eussions commis, eussiez commis, eussent commis
Imperative	commets, commettons, commettez

to compare

Pres. Ind.	compare, compares, compare; comparons, comparez, comparent
Imp. Ind.	comparais, comparais, comparait; comparions, compariez, comparaient
Past Def.	comparai, comparas, compara; comparâmes, comparâtes, comparèrent
Future	comparerai, compareras, comparera; comparerons, comparerez, compareront
Condit.	comparerais, comparerais, comparerait; comparerions, compareriez, compareraient
Pres. Subj.	compare, compares, compare; comparions, compariez, comparent
Imp. Subj.	comparasse, comparasses, comparât; comparassions, comparassiez, comparassent
Past Indef.	ai comparé, as comparé, a comparé; avons comparé, avez comparé, ont comparé
Plup. Ind.	avais comparé, avais comparé, avait comparé; avions comparé, aviez comparé, avaient comparé
Past Ant.	eus comparé, eus comparé, eut comparé; eûmes comparé, eûtes comparé, eurent comparé
Fut. Perf.	aurai comparé, auras comparé, aura comparé; aurons comparé, aurez comparé, auront comparé
Cond. Perf.	aurais comparé, aurais comparé, aurait comparé; aurions comparé, auriez comparé, auraient comparé
Past Subj.	aie comparé, aies comparé, ait comparé; ayons comparé, ayez comparé, aient comparé
Plup. Subj.	eusse comparé, eusses comparé, eût comparé; eussions comparé, eussiez comparé, eussent comparé
Imperative	compare, comparons, comparez

to understand

Pres. Ind.	comprends, comprends, comprend; comprenons, comprenez, comprennent
Imp. Ind.	comprenais, comprenais, comprenait; comprenions, compreniez, comprenaient
Past Def.	compris, compris, comprit; comprîmes, comprîtes, comprirent
Fut. Ind.	comprendrai, comprendras, comprendra; comprendrons, comprendrez, comprendront
Condit.	comprendrais, comprendrais, comprendrait; comprendrions, comprendriez, comprendraient
Pres. Subj.	comprenne, comprennes, comprenne; comprenions, compreniez, comprennent
Imp. Subj.	comprisse, comprisses, comprît; comprissions, comprissiez, comprissent
Past Indef.	ai compris, as compris, a compris; avons compris, avez compris, ont compris
Pluperf.	avais compris, avais compris, avait compris; avions compris, aviez compris, avaient compris
Past Ant.	eus compris, eus compris, eut compris; eûmes compris, eûtes compris, eurent compris
Fut. Perf.	aurai compris, auras compris, aura compris; aurons compris, aurez compris, auront compris
Cond. Perf.	aurais compris, aurais compris, aurait compris; aurions compris, auriez compris, auraient compris
Past Subj.	aie compris, aies compris, ait compris; ayons compris, ayez compris, aient compris
Plup. Subj.	eusse compris, eusses compris, eût compris; eussions compris, eussiez compris, eussent compris
Imperative	comprends, comprenons, comprenez

to compromise

Pres. Ind.	compromets, compromets, compromet; compromettons, compromettez, compromettent
Imp. Ind.	compromettais, compromettais, compromettait; compromettions, compromettiez, compromettaient
Past Def.	compromis, compromis, compromit; compromîmes, compromîtes, compromirent
Future	compromettrai, compromettras, compromettra; compromettrons, compromettrez, compromettront
Condit.	compromettrais, compromettrais, compromettrait; compromettrions, compromettriez, compromettraient
Pres. Subj.	compromette, compromettes, compromette; compromettions, compromettiez, compromettent
Imp. Subj.	compromisse, compromisses, compromît; compromissions, compromissiez, compromissent
Past Indef.	ai compromis, as compromis, a compromis; avons compromis, avez compromis, ont compromis
Plup. Ind.	avais compromis, avais compromis, avait compromis; avions compromis, aviez compromis, avaient compromis
Past Ant.	eus compromis, eus compromis, eut compromis; eûmes compromis, eûtes compromis, eurent compromis
Fut. Perf.	aurai compromis, auras compromis, aura compromis; aurons compromis, aurez compromis, auront compromis
Cond. Perf.	aurais compromis, aurais compromis, aurait compromis; aurions compromis, auriez compromis, auraient compromis
Past Subj.	aie compromis, aies compromis, ait compromis; ayons compromis, ayez compromis, aient compromis
Plup. Subj.	eusse compromis, eusses compromis, eût compromis; eussions compromis, eussiez compromis, eussent compromis
Imperative	compromets, compromettons, compromettez

to intend, count

Pres. Ind.	compte, comptes, compte; comptons, comptez, comptent
Imp. Ind.	comptais, comptais, comptait; comptions, comptiez, comptaient
Past Def.	comptai, comptas, compta; comptâmes, comptâtes, comptèrent
Fut. Ind.	compterai, compteras, comptera; compterons, compterez, compteront
Condit.	compterais, compterais, compterait; compterions, compteriez, compteraient
Pres. Subj.	compte, comptes, compte; comptions, comptiez, comptent
Imp. Subj.	comptasse, comptasses, comptât; comptassions, comptassiez, comptassent
Past Indef.	ai compté, as compté, a compté; avons compté, avez compté, ont compté
Pluperf.	avais compté, avais compté, avait compté; avions compté, aviez compté, avaient compté
Past Ant.	eus compté, eus compté, eut compté; eûmes compté, eûtes compté, eurent compté
Fut. Perf.	aurai compté, auras compté, aura compté; aurons compté, aurez compté, auront compté
Cond. Perf.	aurais compté, aurais compté, aurait compté; aurions compté, auriez compté, auraient compté
Past Subj.	aie compté, aies compté, ait compté; ayons compté, ayez compté, aient compté
Plup. Subj.	eusse compté, eusses compté, eût compté; eussions compté, eussiez compté, eussent compté
Imperative	compte, comptons, comptez

to conceive

Pres. Ind.	conçois, conçois, conçoit; concevons, concevez, conçoivent
Imp. Ind.	concevais, concevais, concevait; concevions, conceviez, concevaient
Past Def.	conçus, conçus, conçut; conçûmes, conçûtes, conçurent
Future	concevrai, concevras, concevra; concevrons, concevrez, concevront
Condit.	concevrais, concevrais, concevrait; concevrions, concevriez, concevraient
Pres. Subj.	conçoive, conçoives, conçoive; concevions, conceviez, conçoivent
Imp. Subj.	conçusse, conçusses, conçût; conçussions, conçussiez, conçussent
Past Indef.	ai conçu, as conçu, a conçu; avons conçu, avez conçu, ont conçu
Plup. Ind.	avais conçu, avais conçu, avait conçu; avions conçu, aviez conçu, avaient conçu
Past Ant.	eus conçu, eus conçu, eut conçu; eûmes conçu, eûtes conçu, eurent conçu
Fut. Perf.	aurai conçu, auras conçu, aura conçu; aurons conçu, aurez conçu, auront conçu
Cond. Perf.	aurais conçu, aurais conçu, aurait conçu; aurions conçu, auriez conçu, auraient conçu
Past Subj.	aie conçu, aies conçu, ait conçu; ayons conçu, ayez conçu, aient conçu
Plup. Subj.	eusse conçu, eusses conçu, eût conçu; eussions conçu, eussiez conçu, eussent conçu
Imperative	conçois, concevons, concevez

to conclude

Pres. Ind.	conclus, conclus, conclut; concluons, concluez, concluent
Imp. Ind.	concluais, concluais, concluait; concluions, concluiez, concluaient
Past Def.	conclus, conclus, conclut; conclûmes, conclûtes, conclurent
Fut. Ind.	conclurai, concluras, conclura; conclurons, conclurez, concluront
Condit.	conclurais, conclurais, conclurait; conclurions, concluriez, concluraient
Pres. Subj.	conclue, conclues, conclue; concluions, concluiez, concluent
Imp. Subj.	conclusse, conclusses, conclût; conclussions, conclussiez, conclussent
Past Indef.	ai conclu, as conclu, a conclu; avons conclu, avez conclu, ont conclu
Pluperf.	avais conclu, avais conclu, avait conclu; avions conclu, aviez conclu, avaient conclu
Past Ant.	eus conclu, eus conclu, eut conclu; eûmes conclu, eûtes conclu, eurent conclu
Fut. Perf.	aurai conclu, auras conclu, aura conclu; aurons conclu, aurez conclu, auront conclu
Cond. Perf.	aurais conclu, aurais conclu, aurait conclu; aurions conclu, auriez conclu, auraient conclu
Past Subj.	aie conclu, aies conclu, ait conclu; ayons conclu, ayez conclu, aient conclu
Plup. Subj.	eusse conclu, eusses conclu, eût conclu; eussions conclu, eussiez conclu, eussent conclu
Imperative	conclus, concluons, concluez

to concur

Pres. Ind.	concours, concours, concourt; concourons, concourez, concourent
Imp. Ind.	concourais, concourais, concourait; concourions, concouriez, concouraient
Past Def.	concourus, concourus, concourut; concourûmes, concourûtes, concoururent
Future	concourrai, concourras, concourra; concourrons, concourrez, concourront
Condit.	concourrais, concourrais, concourrait; concourrions, concourriez, concourraient
Pres. Subj.	concoure, concoures, concoure; concourions, concouriez, concourent
Imp. Subj.	concourusse, concourusses, concourût; concourussions, concourussiez, concourussent
Past Indef.	ai concouru, as concouru, a concouru; avons concouru, avez concouru, ont concouru
Plup. Ind.	avais concouru, avais concouru, avait concouru; avions concouru, aviez concouru, avaient concouru
Past Ant.	eus concouru, eus concouru, eut concouru; eûmes concouru, eûtes concouru, eurent concouru
Fut. Perf.	aurai concouru, auras concouru, aura concouru; aurons concouru, aurez concouru, auront concouru
Cond. Perf.	aurais concouru, aurais concouru, aurait concouru; aurions concouru, auriez concouru, auraient concouru
Past Subj.	aie concouru, aies concouru, ait concouru; ayons concouru, ayez concouru, aient concouru
Plup. Subj.	eusse concouru, eusses concouru, eût concouru; eussions concouru, eussiez concouru, eussent concouru
Imperative	concours, concourons, concourez

to lead, drive, conduct

Pres. Ind.	conduis, conduis, conduit; conduisons, conduisez, conduisent
Imp. Ind.	conduisais, conduisais, conduisait; conduisions, conduisiez, conduisaient
Past Def.	conduisis, conduisis, conduisit; conduisîmes, conduisîtes, conduisirent
Fut. Ind.	conduirai, conduiras, conduira; conduirons, conduirez, conduiront
Condit.	conduirais, conduirais, conduirait; conduirions, conduiriez, conduiraient
Pres. Subj.	conduise, conduises, conduise; conduisions, conduisiez, conduisent
Imp. Subj.	conduisisse, conduisisses, conduisît; conduisissions, conduisissiez, conduisissent
Past Indef.	ai conduit, as conduit, a conduit; avons conduit, avez conduit, ont conduit
Pluperf.	avais conduit, avais conduit, avait conduit; avions conduit, aviez conduit, avaient conduit
Past Ant.	eus conduit, eus conduit, eut conduit; eûmes conduit, eûtes conduit, eurent conduit
Fut. Perf.	aurai conduit, auras conduit, aura conduit; aurons conduit, aurez conduit, auront conduit
Cond. Perf.	aurais conduit, aurais conduit, aurait conduit; aurions conduit, auriez conduit, auraient conduit
Past Subj.	aie conduit, aies conduit, ait conduit; ayons conduit, ayez conduit, aient conduit
Plup. Subj.	eusse conduit, eusses conduit, eût conduit; eussions conduit, eussiez conduit, eussent conduit
Imperative	conduis, conduisons, conduisez

to preserve, pickle

Pres. Ind.	confis, confis, confit; confisons, confisez, confisent
Imp. Ind.	confisais, confisais, confisait; confisions, confisiez, confisaient
Past Def.	confis, confis, confit; confîmes, confîtes, confirent
Future	confirai, confiras, confira; confirons, confirez, confiront
Condit.	confirais, confirais, confirait; confirions, confiriez, confiraient
Pres. Subj.	confise, confises, confise; confisions, confisiez, confisent
Imp. Subj.	confisse, confisses, confît; confissions, confissiez, confissent
Past Indef.	ai confit, as confit, a confit; avons confit, avez confit, ont confit
Plup. Ind.	avais confit, avais confit, avait confit; avions confit, aviez confit, avaient confit
Past Ant.	eus confit, eus confit, eut confit; eûmes confit, eûtes confit, eurent confit
Fut. Perf.	aurai confit, auras confit, aura confit; aurons confit, aurez confit, auront confit
Cond. Perf.	aurais confit, aurais confit, aurait confit; aurions confit, auriez confit, auraient confit
Past Subj.	aie confit, aies confit, ait confit; ayons confit, ayez confit, aient confit
Plup. Subj.	eusse confit, eusses confit, eût confit; eussions confit, eussiez confit, eussent confit
Imperative	confis, confisons, confisez

to know, be acquainted with

Pres. Ind.	connais, connais, connaît; connaissons, connaissez, connaissent
Imp. Ind.	connaissais, connaissais, connaissait; connaissions, connaissiez, connaissaient
Past Def.	connus, connus, connut; connûmes, connûtes, connurent
Fut. Ind.	connaîtrai, connaîtras, connaîtra; connaîtrons, connaîtrez, connaîtront
Condit.	connaîtrais, connaîtrais, connaîtrait; connaîtrions, connaîtriez, connaîtraient
Pres. Subj.	connaisse, connaisses, connaisse; connaissions, connaissiez, connaissent
Imp. Subj.	connusse, connusses, connût; connussions, connussiez, connussent
Past Indef.	ai connu, as connu, a connu; avons connu, avez connu, ont connu
Pluperf.	avais connu, avais connu, avait connu; avions connu, aviez connu, avaient connu
Past Ant.	eus connu, eus connu, eut connu; eûmes connu, eûtes connu, eurent connu
Fut. Perf.	aurai connu, auras connu, aura connu; aurons connu, aurez connu, auront connu
Cond. Perf.	aurais connu, aurais connu, aurait connu; aurions connu, auriez connu, auraient connu
Past Subj.	aie connu, aies connu, ait connu; ayons connu, ayez connu, aient connu
Plup. Subj.	eusse connu, eusses connu, eût connu; eussions connu, eussiez connu, eussent connu
Imperative	connais, connaissons, connaissez

to conquer

Pres. Ind.	conquiers, conquiers, conquiert; conquérons, conquérez, conquièrent
Imp. Ind.	conquérais, conquérais, conquérait; conquérions, conquériez, conquéraient
Past Def.	conquis, conquis, conquit; conquîmes, conquîtes, conquirent
Future	conquerrai, conquerras, conquerra; conquerrons, conquerrez, conquerront
Condit.	conquerrais, conquerrais, conquerrait; conquerrions, conquerriez, conquerraient
Pres. Subj.	conquière, conquières, conquière; conquérions, conquériez, conquièrent
Imp. Subj.	conquisse, conquisses, conquît; conquissions, conquissiez, conquissent
Past Indef.	ai conquis, as conquis, a conquis; avons conquis, avez conquis, ont conquis
Pluperf.	avais conquis, avais conquis, avait conquis; avions conquis, aviez conquis, avaient conquis
Past Ant.	eus conquis, eus conquis, eut conquis; eûmes conquis, eûtes conquis, eurent conquis
Fut. Perf.	aurai conquis, auras conquis, aura conquis; aurons conquis, aurez conquis, auront conquis
Cond. Perf.	aurais conquis, aurais conquis, aurait conquis; aurions conquis, auriez conquis, auraient conquis
Past Subj.	aie conquis, aies conquis, ait conquis; ayons conquis, ayez conquis, aient conquis
Plup. Subj.	eusse conquis, eusses conquis, eût conquis; eussions conquis, eussiez conquis, eussent conquis
Imperative	conquiers, conquérons, conquérez

to consent

Pres. Ind.	consens, consens, consent; consentons, consentez, consentent
Imp. Ind.	consentais, consentais, consentait; consentions, consentiez, consentaient
Past Def.	consentis, consentis, consentit; consentîmes, consentîtes, consentirent
Future	consentirai, consentiras, consentira; consentirons, consentirez, consentiront
Condit.	consentirais, consentirais, consentirait; consentirions, consentiriez, consentiraient
Pres. Subj.	consente, consentes, consente; consentions, consentiez, consentent
Imp. Subj.	consentisse, consentisses, consentît; consentissions, consentissiez, consentissent
Past Indef.	ai consenti, as consenti, a consenti; avons consenti, avez consenti, ont consenti
Pluperf.	avais consenti, avais consenti, avait consenti; avions consenti, aviez consenti, avaient consenti
Past Ant.	eus consenti, eus consenti, eut consenti; eûmes consenti, eûtes consenti, eurent consenti
Fut. Perf.	aurai consenti, auras consenti, aura consenti; aurons consenti, aurez consenti, auront consenti
Cond. Perf.	aurais consenti, aurais consenti, aurait consenti; aurions consenti, auriez consenti, auraient consenti
Past Subj.	aie consenti, aies consenti, ait consenti; ayons consenti, ayez consenti, aient consenti
Plup. Subj.	eusse consenti, eusses consenti, eût consenti; eussions consenti, eussiez consenti, eussent consenti
Imperative	consens, consentons, consentez

to ascertain, certify, observe

Pres. Ind.	constate, constates, constate; constatons, constatez, constatent
Imp. Ind.	constatais, constatais, constatait; constations, constatiez, constataient
Past Def.	constatai, constatas, constata; constatâmes, constatâtes, constatèrent
Future	constaterai, constateras, constatera; constaterons, constaterez, constateront
Condit.	constaterais, constaterais, constaterait; constaterions, constateriez, constateraient
Pres. Subj.	constate, constates, constate; constations, constatiez, constatent
Imp. Subj.	constatasse, constatasses, constatât; constatassions, constatassiez, constatassent
Past Indef.	ai constaté, as constaté, a constaté; avons constaté, avez constaté, ont constaté
Plup. Ind.	avais constaté, avais constaté, avait constaté; avions constaté, aviez constaté, avaient constaté
Past Ant.	eus constaté, eus constaté, eut constaté; eûmes constaté, eûtes constaté, eurent constaté
Fut. Perf.	aurai constaté, auras constaté, aura constaté; aurons constaté, aurez constaté, auront constaté
Cond. Perf.	aurais constaté, aurais constaté, aurait constaté; aurions constaté, auriez constaté, auraient constaté
Past Subj.	aie constaté, aies constaté, ait constaté; ayons constaté, ayez constaté, aient constaté
Plup. Subj.	eusse constaté, eusses constaté, eût constaté; eussions constaté, eussiez constaté, eussent constaté
Imperative	constate, constatons, constatez

to construct, build

Pres. Ind.	construis, construis, construit; construisons, construisez, construisent
Imp. Ind.	construisais, construisais, construisait; construisions, construisiez, construisaient
Past Def.	construisis, construisis, construisit; construisîmes, construisîtes, construisirent
Fut. Ind.	construirai, construiras, construira; construirons, construirez, construiront
Condit.	construirais, construirais, construirait; construirions, construiriez, construiraient
Pres. Subj.	construise, construises, construise; construisions, construisiez, construisent
Imp. Subj.	construisisse, construisisses, construisît; construisissions, construisissiez, construisissent
Past Indef.	ai construit, as construit, a construit; avons construit, avez construit, ont construit
Pluperf.	avais construit, avais construit, avait construit; avions construit, aviez construit, avaient construit
Past Ant.	eus construit, eus construit, eut construit; eûmes construit, eûtes construit, eurent construit
Fut. Perf.	aurai construit, auras construit, aura construit; aurons construit, aurez construit, auront construit
Cond. Perf.	aurais construit, aurais construit, aurait construit; aurions construit, auriez construit, auraient construit
Past Subj.	aie construit, aies construit, ait construit; ayons construit, ayez construit, aient construit
Plup. Subj.	eusse construit, eusses construit, eût construit; eussions construit, eussiez construit, eussent construit
Imperative	construis, construisons, construisez

to contain

Pres. Ind.	contiens, contiens, contient; contenons, contenez, contiennent
Imp. Ind.	contenais, contenais, contenait; contenions, conteniez, contenaient
Past Def.	contins, contins, contint; contînmes, contîntes, continrent
Future	contiendrai, continendras, contiendra; contiendrons, contiendrez, contiendront
Condit.	contiendrais, contiendrais, contiendrait; contiendrions, contiendriez, contiendraient
Pres. Subj.	contienne, contiennes, contienne; contenions, conteniez, contiennent
Imp. Subj.	continsse, continsses, contînt; continssions, continssiez, continssent
Past Indef.	ai contenu, as contenu, a contenu; avons contenu, avez contenu, ont contenu
Pluperf.	avais contenu, avais contenu, avait contenu; avions contenu, aviez contenu, avaient contenu
Past Ant.	eus contenu, eus contenu, eut contenu; eûmes contenu, eûtes contenu, eurent contenu
Fut. Perf.	aurai contenu, auras contenu, aura contenu; aurons contenu, aurez contenu, auront contenu
Cond. Perf.	aurais contenu, aurais contenu, aurait contenu; aurions contenu, auriez contenu, auraient contenu
Past Subj.	aie contenu, aies contenu, ait contenu; ayons contenu, ayez contenu, aient contenu
Plup. Subj.	eusse contenu, eusses contenu, eût contenu; eussions contenu, eussiez contenu, eussent contenu
Imperative	contiens, contenons, contenez

to relate

Pres. Ind.	conte, contes, conte; contons, contez, content
Imp. Ind.	contais, contais, contait; contions, contiez, contaient
Past Def.	contai, contas, conta; contâmes, contâtes, contèrent
Future	conterai, conteras, contera; conterons, conterez, conteront
Condit.	conterais, conterais, conterait; conterions, conteriez, conteraient
Pres. Subj.	conte, contes, conte; contions, contiez, content
Imp. Subj.	contasse, contasses, contât; contassions, contassiez, contassent
Past Indef.	ai conté, as conté, a conté; avons conté, avez conté, ont conté
Plup. Ind.	avais conté, avais conté, avait conté; avions conté, aviez conté, avaient conté
Past Ant.	eus conté, eus conté, eut conté; eûmes conté, eûtes conté, eurent conté
Fut. Perf.	aurai conté, auras conté, aura conté; aurons conté, aurez conté, auront conté
Cond. Perf.	aurais conté, aurais conté, aurait conté; aurions conté, auriez conté, auraient conté
Past Subj.	aie conté, aies conté, ait conté; ayons conté, ayez conté, aient conté
Plup. Subj.	eusse conté, eusses conté, eût conté; eussions conté, eussiez conté, eussent conté
Imperative	conte, contons, contez

to continue

Pres. Ind.	continue, continues, continue; continuons, continuez, continuent
Imp. Ind.	continuais, continuais, continuait; continuions, continuiez, continuaient
Past Def.	continuai, continuas, continua; continuâmes, continuâtes, continuèrent
Future	continuerai, continueras, continuera; continuerons, continuerez, continueront
Condit.	continuerais, continuerais, continuerait; continuerions, continueriez, continueraient
Pres. Subj.	continue, continues, continue; continuions, continuiez, continuent
Imp. Subj.	continuasse, continuasses, continuât; continuassions, continuassiez, continuassent
Past Indef.	ai continué, as continué, a continué; avons continué, avez continué, ont continué
Plup. Ind.	avais continué, avais continué, avait continué; avions continué, aviez continué, avaient continué
Past Ant.	eus continué, eus continué, eut continué; eûmes continué, eûtes continué, eurent continué
Fut. Perf.	aurai continué, auras continué, aura continué; aurons continué, aurez continué, auront continué
Cond. Perf.	aurais continué, aurais continué, aurait continué; aurions continué, auriez continué, auraient continué
Past Subj.	aie continué, aies continué, ait continué; ayons continué, ayez continué, aient continué
Plup. Subj.	eusse continué, eusses continué, eût continué; eussions continué, eussiez continué, eussent continué
Imperative	continue, continuons, continuez

to constrain, compel

Pres. Ind.	contrains, contrains, contraint; contraignons, contraignez, contraignent
Imp. Ind.	contraignais, contraignais, contraignait; contraignions, contraigniez, contraignaient
Past Def.	contraignis, contraignis, contraignit; contraignîmes, contraignîtes, contraignirent
Future	contraindrai, contraindras, contraindra; contraindrons, contraindrez, contraindront
Condit.	contraindrais, contraindrais, contraindrait; contraindrions, contraindriez, contraindraient
Pres. Subj.	contraigne, contraignes, contraigne; contraignions, contraigniez, contraignent
Imp. Subj.	contraignisse, contraignisses, contraignît; contraignissions, contraignissiez, contraignissent
Past Indef.	ai contraint, as contraint, a contraint; avons contraint, avez contraint, ont contraint
Plup. Ind.	avais contraint, avais contraint, avait contraint; avions contraint, aviez contraint, avaient contraint
Past Ant.	eus contraint, eus contraint, eut contraint; eûmes contraint, eûtes contraint, eurent contraint
Fut. Perf.	aurai contraint, auras contraint, aura contraint; aurons contraint, aurez contraint, auront contraint
Cond. Perf.	aurais contraint, aurais contraint, aurait contraint; aurions contraint, auriez contraint, auraient contraint
Past Subj.	aie contraint, aies contraint, ait contraint; ayons contraint, ayez contraint, aient contraint
Plup. Subj.	eusse contraint, eusses contraint, eût contraint; eussions contraint, eussiez contraint, eussent contraint
Imperative	contrains, contraignons, contraignez

to contradict

Pres. Ind.	contredis, contredis, contredit; contredisons, contredisez, contredisent
Imp. Ind.	contredisais, contredisais, contredisait; contredisions, contredisiez, contredisaient
Past Def.	contredis, contredis, contredit; contredîmes, contredîtes, contredirent
Future	contredirai, contrediras, contredira; contredirons, contredirez, contrediront
Condit.	contredirais, contredirais, contredirait; contredirions, contrediriez, contrediraient
Pres. Subj.	contredise, contredises, contredise; contredisions, contredisiez, contredisent
Imp. Subj.	contredisse, contredisses, contredît; contredissions, contredissiez, contredissent
Past Indef.	ai contredit, as contredit, a contredit; avons contredit, avez contredit, ont contredit
Plup. Ind.	avais contredit, avais contredit, avait contredit; avions contredit, aviez contredit, avaient contredit
Past Ant.	eus contredit, eus contredit, eut contredit; eûmes contredit, eûtes contredit, eurent contredit
Fut. Perf.	aurai contredit, auras contredit, aura contredit; aurons contredit, aurez contredit, auront contredit
Cond. Perf.	aurais contredit, aurais contredit, aurait contredit; aurions contredit, auriez contredit, auraient contredit
Past Subj.	aie contredit, aies contredit, ait contredit; ayons contredit, ayez contredit, aient contredit
Plup. Subj.	eusse contredit, eusses contredit, eût contredit; eussions contredit, eussiez contredit, eussent contredit
Imperative	contredis, contredisons, contredisez

to convince

Pres Ind.	convaincs, convaincs, convainc; convainquons, convainquez, convainquent
Imp. Ind.	convainquais, convainquais, convainquait; convainquions, convainquiez, convainquaient
Past Def.	convainquis, convainquis, convainquit; convainquîmes, convainquîtes, convainquirent
Future	convaincrai, convaincras, convaincra; convaincrons, convaincrez, convaincront
Condit.	convaincrais, convaincrais, convaincrait; convaincrions, convaincriez, convaincraient
Pres. Subj.	convainque, convainques, convainque; convainquions, convainquiez, convainquent
Imp. Subj.	convainquisse, convainquisses, convainquît; convainquissions, convainquissiez, convainquissent
Past Indef.	ai convaincu, as convaincu, a convaincu; avons convaincu, avez convaincu, ont convaincu
Plup. Ind.	avais convaincu, avais convaincu, avait convaincu; avions convaincu, aviez convaincu, avaient convaincu
Past Ant.	eus convaincu, eus convaincu, eut convaincu; eûmes convaincu, eûtes convaincu, eurent convaincu
Fut. Perf.	aurai convaincu, auras convaincu, aura convaincu; aurons convaincu, aurez convaincu, auront convaincu
Cond. Perf.	aurais convaincu, aurais convaincu, aurait convaincu; aurions convaincu, auriez convaincu, auraient convaincu
Past Subj.	aie convaincu, aies convaincu, ait convaincu; ayons convaincu, ayez convaincu, aient convaincu
Plup. Subj.	eusse convaincu, eusses convaincu, eût convaincu; eussions convaincu, eussiez convaincu, eussent convaincu
Imperative	convaincs, convainquons, convainquez

to suit, be suitable, be appropriate, agree, acknowledge

Pres. Ind.	conviens, conviens, convient; convenons, convenez, conviennent
Imp. Ind.	convenais, convenais, convenait; convenions, conveniez, convenaient
Past Def.	convins, convins, convint; convînmes, convîntes, convinrent
Future	conviendrai, conviendras, conviendra; conviendrons, conviendrez, conviendront
Condit.	conviendrais, conviendrais, conviendrait; conviendrions, conviendriez, conviendraient
Pres. Subj.	convienne, conviennes, convienne; convenions, conveniez, conviennent
Imp. Subj.	convinsse, convinsses, convînt; convinssions, convinssiez, convinssent
Past Indef.	ai convenu, as convenu, a convenu; avons convenu, avez convenu, ont convenu
Pluperf.	avais convenu, avais convenu, avait convenu; avions convenu, aviez convenu, avaient convenu
Past Ant.	eus convenu, eus convenu, eut convenu; eûmes convenu, eûtes convenu, eurent convenu
Fut. Perf.	aurai convenu, auras convenu, aura convenu; aurons convenu, aurez convenu, auront convenu
Cond. Perf.	aurais convenu, aurais convenu, aurait convenu; aurions convenu, auriez convenu, auraient convenu
Past Subj.	aie convenu, aies convenu, ait convenu; ayons convenu, ayez convenu, aient convenu
Plup. Subj.	eusse convenu, eusses convenu, eût convenu; eussions convenu, eussiez convenu, eussent convenu
Imperative	conviens, convenons, convenez

to correct

Pres. Ind.	corrige, corriges, corrige; corrigeons, corrigez, corrigent
Imp. Ind.	corrigeais, corrigeais, corrigeait; corrigions, corrigiez, corrigeaient
Past Def.	corrigeai, corrigeas, corrigea; corrigeâmes, corrigeâtes, corrigèrent
Fut. Ind.	corrigerai, corrigeras, corrigera; corrigerons, corrigerez, corrigeront
Condit.	corrigerais, corrigerais, corrigerait; corrigerions, corrigeriez, corrigeraient
Pres. Subj.	corrige, corriges, corrige; corrigions, corrigiez, corrigent
Imp. Subj.	corrigeasse, corrigeasses, corrigeât; corrigeassions, corrigeassiez, corrigeassent
Past Indef.	ai corrigé, as corrigé, a corrigé; avons corrigé, avez corrigé, ont corrigé
Pluperf.	avais corrigé, avais corrigé, avait corrigé; avions corrigé, aviez corrigé, avaient corrigé
Past Ant.	eus corrigé, eus corrigé, eut corrigé; eûmes corrigé, eûtes corrigé, eurent corrigé
Fut. Perf.	aurai corrigé, auras corrigé, aura corrigé; aurons corrigé, aurez corrigé, auront corrigé
Cond. Perf.	aurais corrigé, aurais corrigé, aurait corrigé; aurions corrigé, auriez corrigé, auraient corrigé
Past Subj.	aie corrigé, aies corrigé, ait corrigé; ayons corrigé, ayez corrigé, aient corrigé
Plup. Subj.	eusse corrigé, eusses corrigé, eût corrigé; eussions corrigé, eussiez corrigé, eussent corrigé
Imperative	corrige, corrigeons, corrigez

to corrupt

Pres. Ind.	corromps, corromps, corrompt; corrompons, corrompez, corrompent
Imp. Ind.	corrompais, corrompais, corrompait; corrompions, corrompiez, corrompaient
Past Def.	corrompis, corrompis, corrompit; corrompîmes, corrompîtes, corrompirent
Future	corromprai, corrompras, corrompra; corromprons, corromprez, corrompront
Condit.	corromprais, corromprais, corromprait; corromprions, corrompriez, corrompraient
Pres. Subj.	corrompe, corrompes, corrompe; corrompions, corrompiez, corrompent
Imp. Subj.	corrompisse, corrompisses, corrompît; corrompissions, corrompissiez, corrompissent
Past Indef.	ai corrompu, as corrompu, a corrompu; avons corrompu, avez corrompu, ont corrompu
Plup. Ind.	avais corrompu, avais corrompu, avait corrompu; avions corrompu, aviez corrompu, avaient corrompu
Past Ant.	eus corrompu, eus corrompu, eut corrompu; eûmes corrompu, eûtes corrompu, eurent corrompu
Fut. Perf.	aurai corrompu, auras corrompu, aura corrompu; aurons corrompu, aurez corrompu, auront corrompu
Cond. Perf.	aurais corrompu, aurais corrompu, aurait corrompu; aurions corrompu, auriez corrompu, auraient corrompu
Past Subj.	aie corrompu, aies corrompu, ait corrompu; ayons corrompu, ayez corrompu, aient corrompu
Plup. Subj.	eusse corrompu, eusses corrompu, eût corrompu; eussions corrompu, eussiez corrompu, eussent corrompu
Imperative	corromps, corrompons, corrompez

to put to bed, lay

Pres. Ind.	couche, couches, couche; couchons, couchez, couchent
Imp. Ind.	couchais, couchais, couchait; couchions, couchiez, couchaient
Past Def.	couchai, couchas, coucha; couchâmes, couchâtes, couchèrent
Future	coucherai, coucheras, couchera; coucherons, coucherez, coucheront
Condit.	coucherais, coucherais, coucherait; coucherions, coucheriez, coucheraient
Pres. Subj.	couche, couches, couche; couchions, couchiez, couchent
Imp. Subj.	couchasse, couchasses, couchât; couchassions, couchassiez, couchassent
Past Indef.	ai couché, as couché, a couché; avons couché, avez couché, ont couché
Plup. Ind.	avais couché, avais couché, avait couché; avions couché, aviez couché, avaient couché
Past Ant.	eus couché, eus couché, eut couché; eûmes couché, eûtes couché, eurent couché
Fut. Perf.	aurai couché, auras couché, aura couché; aurons couché, aurez couché, auront couché
Cond. Perf.	aurais couché, aurais couché, aurait couché; aurions couché, auriez couché, auraient couché
Past Subj.	aie couché, aies couché, ait couché; ayons couché, ayez couché, aient couché
Plup. Subj.	eusse couché, eusses couché, eût couché; eussions couché, eussiez couché, eussent couché
Imperative	couche, couchons, couchez

to go to bed

Pres. Ind.	me couche, te couches, se couche; nous couchons, vous couchez, se couchent
Imp. Ind.	me couchais, te couchais, se couchait; nous couchions, vous couchiez, se couchaient
Past Def.	me couchai, te couchas, se coucha; nous couchâmes, vous couchâtes, se couchèrent
Fut. Ind.	me coucherai, te coucheras, se couchera; nous coucherons, vous coucherez, se coucheront
Condit.	me coucherais, te coucherais, se coucherait; nous coucherions, vous coucheriez, se coucheraient
Pres. Subj.	me couche, te couches, se couche; nous couchions, vous couchiez, se couchent
Imp. Subj.	me couchasse, te couchasses, se couchât; nous couchassions, vous couchassiez, se couchassent
Past Indef.	me suis couché(e), t'es couché(e), s'est couché(e); nous sommes couché(e)s, vous êtes couché(e)(s), se sont couché(e)s
Pluperf.	m'étais couché(e), t'étais couché(e), s'était couché(e); nous étions couché(e)s, vous étiez couché(e)(s), s'étaient couché(e)s
Past Ant.	me fus couché(e), te fus couché(e), se fut couché(e); nous fûmes couché(e)s, vous fûtes couché(e)(s), se furent couché(e)s
Fut. Perf.	me serai couché(e), te seras couché(e), se sera couché(e); nous serons couché(e)s, vous serez couché(e)(s), se seront couché(e)s
Cond. Perf.	me serais couché(e), te serais couché(e), se serait couché(e); nous serions couché(e)s, vous seriez couché(e)(s), se seraient couché(e)s
Past Subj.	me sois couché(e), te sois couché(e), se soit couché(e); nous soyons couché(e)s, vous soyez couché(e)(s), se soient couché(e)s
Plup. Subj.	me fusse couché(e), te fusses couché(e), se fût couché(e); nous fussions couché(e)s, vous fussiez couché(e)(s), se fussent couché(e)s
Imperative	couche-toi, couchons-nous, couchez-vous

to sew

Pres. Ind.	couds, couds, coud; cousons, cousez, cousent
Imp. Ind.	cousais, cousais, cousait; cousions, cousiez, cousaient
Past Def.	cousis, cousis, cousit; cousîmes, cousîtes, cousirent
Fut. Ind.	coudrai, coudras, coudra; coudrons, coudrez, coudront
Condit.	coudrais, coudrais, coudrait; coudrions, coudriez, coudraient
Pres. Subj.	couse, couses, couse; cousions, cousiez, cousent
Imp. Subj.	cousisse, cousisses, cousît; cousissions, cousissiez, cousissent
Past Indef.	ai cousu, as cousu, a cousu; avons cousu, avez cousu, ont cousu
Pluperf.	avais cousu, avais cousu, avait cousu; avions cousu, aviez cousu, avaient cousu
Past Ant.	eus cousu, eus cousu, eut cousu; eûmes cousu, eûtes cousu, eurent cousu
Fut. Perf.	aurai cousu, auras cousu, aura cousu; aurons cousu, aurez cousu, auront cousu
Cond. Perf.	aurais cousu, aurais cousu, aurait cousu; aurions cousu, auriez cousu, auraient cousu
Past Subj.	aie cousu, aies cousu, ait cousu; ayons cousu, ayez cousu, aient cousu
Plup. Subj.	eusse cousu, eusses cousu, eût cousu; eussions cousu, eussiez cousu, eussent cousu
Imperative	couds, cousons, cousez

to cut

Pres. Ind.	coupe, coupes, coupe; coupons, coupez, coupent
Imp. Ind.	coupais, coupais, coupait; coupions, coupiez, coupaient
Past Def.	coupai, coupas, coupa; coupâmes, coupâtes, coupèrent
Future	couperai, couperas, coupera; couperons, couperez, couperont
Condit.	couperais, couperais, couperait; couperions, couperiez, couperaient
Pres. Subj.	coupe, coupes, coupe; coupions, coupiez, coupent
Imp. Subj.	coupasse, coupasses, coupât; coupassions, coupassiez, coupassent
Past Indef.	ai coupé, as coupé, a coupé; avons coupé, avez coupé, ont coupé
Plup. Ind.	avais coupé, avais coupé, avait coupé; avions coupé, aviez coupé, avaient coupé
Past Ant.	eus coupé, eus coupé, eut coupé; eûmes coupé, eûtes coupé, eurent coupé
Fut. Perf.	aurai coupé, auras coupé, aura coupé; aurons coupé, aurez coupé, auront coupé
Cond. Perf.	aurais coupé, aurais coupé, aurait coupé; aurions coupé, auriez coupé, auraient coupé
Past Subj.	aie coupé, aies coupé, ait coupé; ayons coupé, ayez coupé, aient coupé
Plup. Subj.	eusse coupé, eusses coupé, eût coupé; eussions coupé, eussiez coupé, eussent coupé
Imperative	coupe, coupons, coupez

to run

Pres. Ind.	cours, cours, court; courons, courez, courent
Imp. Ind.	courais, courais, courait; courions, couriez, couraient
Past Def.	courus, courus, courut; courûmes, courûtes, coururent
Fut. Ind.	courrai, courras, courra; courrons, courrez, courront
Condit.	courrais, courrais, courrait; courrions, courriez, courraient
Pres. Subj.	coure, coures, coure; courions, couriez, courent
Imp. Subj.	courusse, courusses, courût; courussions, courussiez, courussent
Past Indef.	ai couru, as couru, a couru; avons couru, avez couru, ont couru
Pluperf.	avais couru, avais couru, avait couru; avions couru, aviez couru, avaient couru
Past Ant.	eus couru, eus couru, eut couru; eûmes couru, eûtes couru, eurent couru
Fut. Perf.	aurai couru, auras couru, aura couru; aurons couru, aurez couru, auront couru
Cond. Perf.	aurais couru, aurais couru, aurait couru; aurions couru, auriez couru, auraient couru
Past Subj.	aie couru, aies couru, ait couru; ayons couru, ayez couru, aient couru
Plup. Subj.	eusse couru, eusses couru, eût couru; eussions couru, eussiez couru, eussent couru
Imperative	cours, courons, courez

to cost

Pres. Ind.	il (elle) coûte ils (elles) coûtent
Imp. Ind.	il (elle) coûtait ils (elles) coûtaient
Past Def.	il (elle) coûta ils (elles) coûtèrent
Fut. Ind.	il (elle) coûtera ils (elles) coûteront
Condit.	il (elle) coûterait ils (elles) coûteraient
Pres. Subj.	qu'il (elle) coûte qu'ils (elles) coûtent
Imp. Subj.	qu'il (elle) coûtât qu'ils (elles) coûtassent
Past Indef.	il (elle) a coûté ils (elles) ont coûté
Pluperf.	il (elle) avait coûté ils (elles) avaient coûté
Past Ant.	il (elle) eut coûté ils (elles) eurent coûté
Fut. Perf.	il (elle) aura coûté ils (elles) auront coûté
Cond. Perf.	il (elle) aurait coûté ils (elles) auraient coûté
Past Subj.	qu'il (elle) ait coûté qu'ils (elles) aient coûté
Plup. Subj.	qu'il (elle) eût coûté qu'ils (elles) eussent coûté
Imperative	[inemployé]

to cover

Pres. Ind.	couvre, couvres, couvre; couvrons, couvrez, couvrent
Imp. Ind.	couvrais, couvrais, couvrait; couvrions, couvriez, couvraient
Past Def.	couvris, couvris, couvrit; couvrîmes, couvrîtes, couvrirent
Fut. Ind.	couvrirai, couvriras, couvrira; couvrirons, couvrirez, couvriront
Condit.	couvrirais, couvrirais, couvrirait; couvririons, couvririez, couvriraient
Pres. Subj.	couvre, couvres, couvre; couvrions, couvriez, couvrent
Imp. Subj.	couvrisse, couvrisses, couvrît; couvrissions, couvrissiez, couvrissent
Past Indef.	ai couvert, as couvert, a couvert; avons couvert, avez couvert, ont couvert
Pluperf.	avais couvert, avais couvert, avait couvert; avions couvert, aviez couvert, avaient couvert
Past Ant.	eus couvert, eus couvert, eut couvert; eûmes couvert, eûtes couvert, eurent couvert
Fut. Perf.	aurai couvert, auras couvert, aura couvert; aurons couvert, aurez couvert, auront couvert
Cond. Perf.	aurais couvert, aurais couvert, aurait couvert; aurions couvert, auriez couvert, auraient couvert
Past Subj.	aie couvert, aies couvert, ait couvert; ayons couvert, ayez couvert, aient couvert
Plup. Subj.	eusse couvert, eusses couvert, eût couvert; eussions couvert, eussiez couvert, eussent couvert
Imperative	couvre, couvrons, couvrez

to fear, be afraid

Pres. Ind.	crains, crains, craint; craignons, craignez, craignent
Imp. Ind.	craignais, craignais, craignait; craignions, craigniez, craignaient
Past Def.	craignis, craignis, craignit; craignîmes, craignîtes, craignirent
Fut. Ind.	craindrai, craindras, craindra; craindrons, craindrez, craindront
Condit.	craindrais, craindrais, craindrait; craindrions, craindriez, craindraient
Pres. Subj.	craigne, craignes, craigne; craignions, craigniez, craignent
Imp. Subj.	craignisse, craignisses, craignît; craignissions, craignissiez, craignissent
Past Indef.	ai craint, as craint, a craint; avons craint, avez craint, ont craint
Pluperf.	avais craint, avais craint, avait craint; avions craint, aviez craint, avaient craint
Past Ant.	eus craint, eus craint, eut craint; eûmes craint, eûtes craint, eurent craint
Fut. Perf.	aurai craint, auras craint, aura craint; aurons craint, aurez craint, auront craint
Cond. Perf.	aurais craint, aurais craint, aurait craint; aurions craint, auriez craint, auraient craint
Past Subj.	aie craint, aies craint, ait craint; ayons craint, ayez craint, aient craint
Plup. Subj.	eusse craint, eusses craint, eût craint; eussions craint, eussiez craint, eussent craint
Imperative	crains, craignons, craignez

to create

Pres. Ind.	crée, crées, crée; créons, créez, créent
Imp. Ind.	créais, créais, créait; créions, créiez, créaient
Past Def.	créai, créas, créa; créâmes, créâtes, créèrent
Future	créerai, créeras, créera; créerons, créerez, créeront
Condit.	créerais, créerais, créerait; créerions, créeriez, créeraient
Pres. Subj.	crée, crées, crée; créions, créiez, créent
Imp. Subj.	créasses, créasses, créât; créassions, créassiez, créassent
Past Indef.	ai créé, as créé, a créé; avons créé, avez créé, ont créé
Pluperf.	avais créé, avais créé, avait créé; avions créé, aviez créé, avaient créé
Past Ant.	eus créé, eus créé, eut créé; eûmes créé, eûtes créé, eurent créé
Fut. Perf.	aurai créé, auras créé, aura créé; aurons créé, aurez créé, auront créé
Cond. Perf.	aurais créé, aurais créé, aurait créé; aurions créé, auriez créé, auraient créé
Past Subj.	aie créé, aies créé, ait créé; ayons créé, ayez créé, aient créé
Plup. Subj.	eusse créé, eusses créé, eût créé; eussions créé, eussiez créé, eussent créé
Imperative	crée, créons, créez

to believe

Pres. Ind.	crois, crois, croit; croyons, croyez, croient
Imp. Ind.	croyais, croyais, croyait; croyions, croyiez, croyaient
Past Def.	crus, crus, crut; crûmes, crûtes, crurent
Fut. Ind.	croirai, croiras, croira; croirons, croirez, croiront
Condit.	croirais, croirais, croirait; croirions, croiriez, croiraient
Pres. Subj.	croie, croies, croie; croyions, croyiez, croient
Imp. Subj.	crusse, crusses, crût; crussions, crussiez, crussent
Past Indef.	ai cru, as cru, a cru; avons cru, avez cru, ont cru
Pluperf.	avais cru, avais cru, avait cru; avions cru, aviez cru, avaient cru
Past Ant.	eus cru, eus cru, eut cru; eûmes cru, eûtes cru, eurent cru
Fut. Perf.	aurai cru, auras cru, aura cru; aurons cru, aurez cru, auront cru
Cond. Perf.	aurais cru, aurais cru, aurait cru; aurions cru, auriez cru, auraient cru
Past Subj.	aie cru, aies cru, ait cru; ayons cru, ayez cru, aient cru
Plup. Subj.	eusse cru, eusses cru, eût cru; eussions cru, eussiez cru, eussent cru
Imperative	crois, croyons, croyez

to grow

Pres. Ind.	croîs, croîs, croît; croissons, croissez, croissent
Imp. Ind.	croissais, croissais, croissait; croissions, croissiez, croissaient
Past Def.	crûs, crûs, crût; crûmes, crûtes, crûrent
Fut. Ind.	croîtrai, croîtras, croîtra; croîtrons, croîtrez, croîtront
Condit.	croîtrais, croîtrais, croîtrait; croîtrions, croîtriez, croîtraient
Pres. Subj.	croisse, croisses, croisse; croissions, croissiez, croissent
Imp. Subj.	crûsse, crûsses, crût; crûssions, crûssiez, crûssent
Past Indef.	ai crû, as crû, a crû; avons crû, avez crû, ont crû
Pluperf.	avais crû, avais crû, avait crû; avions crû, aviez crû, avaient crû
Past Ant.	eus crû, eus crû, eut crû; eûmes crû, eûtes crû, eurent crû
Fut. Perf.	aurai crû, auras crû, aura crû; aurons crû, aurez crû, auront crû
Cond. Perf.	aurais crû, aurais crû, aurait crû; aurions crû, auriez crû, auraient crû
Past Subj.	aie crû, aies crû, ait crû; ayons crû, ayez crû, aient crû
Plup. Subj.	eusse crû, eusses crû, eût crû; eussions crû, eussiez crû, eussent crû
Imperative	croîs, croissons, croissez

to gather, pick

Pres. Ind.	cueille, cueilles, cueille; cueillons, cueillez, cueillent
Imp. Ind.	cueillais, cueillais, cueillait; cueillions, cueilliez, cueillaient
Past Def.	cueillis, cueillis, cueillit; cueillîmes, cueillîtes, cueillirent
Fut. Ind.	cueillerai, cueilleras, cueillera; cueillerons, cueillerez, cueilleront
Condit.	cueillerais, cueillerais, cueillerait; cueillerions, cueilleriez, cueilleraient
Pres. Subj.	cueille, cueilles, cueille; cueillions, cueilliez, cueillent
Imp. Subj.	cueillisse, cueillisses, cueillît; cueillissions, cueillissiez, cueillissent
Past Indef.	ai cueilli, as cueilli, a cueilli; avons cueilli, avez cueilli, ont cueilli
Pluperf.	avais cueilli, avais cueilli, avait cueilli; avions cueilli, aviez cueilli, avaient cueilli
Past Ant.	eus cueilli, eus cueilli, eut cueilli; eûmes cueilli, eûtes cueilli, eurent cueilli
Fut. Perf.	aurai cueilli, auras cueilli, aura cueilli; aurons cueilli, aurez cueilli, auront cueilli
Cond. Perf.	aurais cueilli, aurais cueilli, aurait cueilli; aurions cueilli, auriez cueilli, auraient cueilli
Past Subj.	aie cueilli, aies cueilli, ait cueilli; ayons cueilli, ayez cueilli, aient cueilli
Plup. Subj.	eusse cueilli, eusses cueilli, eût cueilli; eussions cueilli, eussiez cueilli, eussent cueilli
Imperative	cueille, cueillons, cueillez

to cook

Pres. Ind.	cuis, cuis, cuit; cuisons, cuisez, cuisent
Imp. Ind.	cuisais, cuisais, cuisait; cuisions, cuisiez, cuisaient
Past Def.	cuisis, cuisis, cuisit; cuisîmes, cuisîtes, cuisirent
Fut. Ind.	cuirai, cuiras, cuira; cuirons, cuirez, cuiront
Condit.	cuirais, cuirais, cuirait; cuirions, cuiriez, cuiraient
Pres. Subj.	cuise, cuises, cuise; cuisions, cuisiez, cuisent
Imp. Subj.	cuisisse, cuisisses, cuisît; cuisissions, cuisissiez, cuisissent
Past Indef.	ai cuit, as cuit, a cuit; avons cuit, avez cuit, ont cuit
Pluperf.	avais cuit, avais cuit, avait cuit; avions cuit, aviez cuit, avaient cuit
Past Ant.	eus cuit, eus cuit, eut cuit; eûmes cuit, eûtes cuit, eurent cuit
Fut. Perf.	aurai cuit, auras cuit, aura cuit; aurons cuit, aurez cuit, auront cuit
Cond. Perf.	aurais cuit, aurais cuit, aurait cuit; aurions cuit, auriez cuit, auraient cuit
Past Subj.	aie cuit, aies cuit, ait cuit; ayons cuit, ayez cuit, aient cuit
Plup. Subj.	eusse cuit, eusses cuit, eût cuit; eussions cuit, eussiez cuit, eussent cuit
Imperative	cuis, cuisons, cuisez

to dance

Pres. Ind.	danse, danses, danse; dansons, dansez, dansent
Imp. Ind.	dansais, dansais, dansait; dansions, dansiez, dansaient
Past Def.	dansai, dansas, dansa; dansâmes, dansâtes, dansèrent
Fut. Ind.	danserai, danseras, dansera; danserons, danserez, danseront
Condit.	danserais, danserais, danserait; danserions, danseriez, danseraient
Pres. Subj.	danse, danses, danse; dansions, dansiez, dansent
Imp. Subj.	dansasse, dansasses, dansât; dansassions, dansassiez, dansassent
Past Indef.	ai dansé, as dansé, a dansé; avons dansé, avez dansé, ont dansé
Pluperf.	avais dansé, avais dansé, avait dansé; avions dansé, aviez dansé, avaient dansé
Past Ant.	eus dansé, eus dansé, eut dansé; eûmes dansé, eûtes dansé, eurent dansé
Fut. Perf.	aurai dansé, auras dansé, aura dansé; aurons dansé, aurez dansé, auront dansé
Cond. Perf.	aurais dansé, aurais dansé, aurait dansé; aurions dansé, auriez dansé, auraient dansé
Past Subj.	aie dansé, aies dansé, ait dansé; ayons dansé, ayez dansé, aient dansé
Plup. Subj.	eusse dansé, eusses dansé, eût dansé; eussions dansé, eussiez dansé, eussent dansé
Imperative	danse, dansons, dansez

to deceive

Pres. Ind.	déçois, déçois, déçoit; décevons, décevez, déçoivent
Imp. Ind.	décevais, décevais, décevait; décevions, déceviez, décevaient
Past Def.	déçus, déçus, déçut; déçûmes, déçûtes, déçurent
Future	décevrai, décevras, décevra; décevrons, décevrez, décevront
Condit.	décevrais, décevrais, décevrait; décevrions, décevriez, décevraient
Pres. Subj.	déçoive, déçoives, déçoive; décevions, déceviez, déçoivent
Imp. Subj.	déçusse, déçusses, déçût; déçussions, déçussiez, déçussent
Past Indef.	ai déçu, as déçu, a déçu; avons déçu, avez déçu, ont déçu
Pluperf.	avais déçu, avais déçu, avait déçu; avions déçu, aviez déçu, avaient déçu
Past Ant.	eus déçu, eus déçu, eut déçu; eûmes déçu, eûtes déçu, eurent déçu
Fut. Perf.	aurai déçu, auras déçu, aura déçu; aurons déçu, aurez déçu, auront déçu
Cond. Perf.	aurais déçu, aurais déçu, aurait déçu; aurions déçu, auriez déçu, auraient déçu
Past Subj.	aie déçu, aies déçu, ait déçu; ayons déçu, ayez déçu, aient déçu
Plup. Subj.	eusse déçu, eusses déçu, eût déçu; eussions déçu, eussiez déçu, eussent déçu
Imperative	déçois, décevons, décevez

to rend, rip, tear

Pres. Ind.	déchire, déchires, déchire; déchirons, déchirez, déchirent
Imp. Ind.	déchirais, déchirais, déchirait; déchirions, déchiriez, déchiraient
Past Def.	déchirai, déchiras, déchira; déchirâmes, déchirâtes, déchirèrent
Future	déchirerai, déchireras, déchirera; déchirerons, déchirerez, déchireront
Condit.	déchirerais, déchirerais, déchirerait; déchirerions, déchireriez, déchireraient
Pres. Subj.	déchire, déchires, déchire; déchirions, déchiriez, déchirent
Imp. Subj.	déchirasse, déchirasses, déchirât; déchirassions, déchirassiez, déchirassent
Past Indef.	ai déchiré, as déchiré, a déchiré; avons déchiré, avez déchiré, ont déchiré
Plup. Ind.	avais déchiré, avais déchiré, avait déchiré; avions déchiré, aviez déchiré, avaient déchiré
Past Ant.	eus déchiré, eus déchiré, eut déchiré; eûmes déchiré, eûtes déchiré, eurent déchiré
Fut. Perf.	aurai déchiré, auras déchiré, aura déchiré; aurons déchiré, aurez déchiré, auront déchiré
Cond. Perf.	aurais déchiré, aurais déchiré, aurait déchiré; aurions déchiré, auriez déchiré, auraient déchiré
Past Subj.	aie déchiré, aies déchiré, ait déchiré; ayons déchiré, ayez déchiré, aient déchiré
Plup. Subj.	eusse déchiré, eusses déchiré, eût déchiré; eussions déchiré, eussiez déchiré, eussent déchiré
Imperative	déchire, déchirons, déchirez

to decay, decline, fall off

Pres. Ind.	déchois, déchois, déchoit; déchoyons, déchoyez, déchoient
Imp. Ind.	[inemployé]
Past Def.	déchus, déchus, déchut; déchûmes, déchûtes, déchurent
Future	déchoirai, déchoiras, déchoira; déchoirons, déchoirez, déchoiront
Condit.	déchoirais, déchoirais, déchoirait; déchoirions, déchoiriez, déchoiraient
Pres. Subj.	déchoie, déchoies, déchoie; déchoyions, déchoyiez, déchoient
Imp. Subj.	déchusse, déchusses, déchût; déchussions, déchussiez, déchussent
Past Indef.	ai déchu, as déchu, a déchu; avons déchu, avez déchu, ont déchu
Plup. Ind.	avais déchu, avais déchu, avait déchu; avions déchu, aviez déchu, avaient déchu
Past Ant.	eus déchu, eus déchu, eut déchu; eûmes déchu, eûtes déchu, eurent déchu
Fut. Perf.	aurai déchu, auras déchu, aura déchu; aurons déchu, aurez déchu, auront déchu
Cond. Perf.	aurais déchu, aurais déchu, aurait déchu; aurions déchu, auriez déchu, auraient déchu
Past Subj.	aie déchu, aies déchu, ait déchu; ayons déchu, ayez déchu, aient déchu
Plup. Subj.	eusse déchu, eusses déchu, eût déchu; eussions déchu, eussiez déchu, eussent déchu
Imperative	[inemployé]

to unsew, unstitch

Pres. Ind.	découds, découds, découd; décousons, décousez, décousent
Imp. Ind.	décousais, décousais, décousait; décousions, décousiez, décousaient
Past Def.	décousis, décousis, décousit; décousîmes, décousîtes, décousirent
Future	découdrai, découdras, découdra; découdrons, découdrez, découdront
Condit.	découdrais, découdrais, découdrait; découdrions, découdriez, découdraient
Pres. Subj.	découse, découses, découse; décousions, décousiez, décousent
Imp. Subj.	décousisse, décousisses, décousît; décousissions, décousissiez, décousissent
Past Indef.	ai décousu, as décousu, a décousu; avons décousu, avez décousu, ont décousu
Plup. Ind.	avais décousu, avais décousu, avait décousu; avions décousu, aviez décousu, avaient décousu
Past Ant.	eus décousu, eus décousu, eut décousu; eûmes décousu, eûtes décousu, eurent décousu
Fut. Perf.	aurai décousu, auras décousu, aura décousu; aurons décousu, aurez décousu, auront décousu
Cond. Perf.	aurais décousu, aurais décousu, aurait décousu; aurions décousu, auriez décousu, auraient décousu
Past Subj.	aie décousu, aies décousu, ait décousu; ayons décousu, ayez décousu, aient décousu
Plup. Subj.	eusse décousu, eusses décousu, eût décousu; eussions décousu, eussiez décousu, eussent décousu
Imperative	découds, décousons, décousez

to discover, uncover

Pres. Ind.	découvre, découvres, découvre; découvrons, découvrez, découvrent
Imp. Ind.	découvrais, découvrais, découvrait; découvrions, découvriez, découvraient
Past Def.	découvris, découvris, découvrit; découvrîmes, découvrîtes, découvrirent
Future	découvrirai, découvriras, découvrira; découvrirons, découvrirez, découvriront
Condit.	découvrirais, découvrirais, découvrirait; découvririons, découvririez, découvriraient
Pres. Subj.	découvre, découvres, découvre; découvrions, découvriez, découvrent
Imp. Subj.	découvrisse, découvrisses, découvrît; découvrissions, découvrissiez, découvrissent
Past Indef.	ai découvert, as découvert, a découvert; avons découvert, avez découvert, ont découvert
Pluperf.	avais découvert, avais découvert, avait découvert; avions découvert, aviez découvert, avaient découvert
Past Ant.	eus découvert, eus découvert, eut découvert; eûmes découvert, eûtes découvert, eurent découvert
Fut. Perf.	aurai découvert, auras découvert, aura découvert; aurons découvert, aurez découvert, auront découvert
Cond. Perf.	aurais découvert, aurais découvert, aurait découvert; aurions découvert, auriez découvert, auraient découvert
Past Subj.	aie découvert, aies découvert, ait découvert; ayons découvert, ayez découvert, aient découvert
Plup. Subj.	eusse découvert, eusses découvert, eût découvert; eussions découvert, eussiez découvert, eussent découvert
Imperative	découvre, découvrons, découvrez

to describe

Pres. Ind.	décris, décris, décrit; décrivons, décrivez, décrivent
Imp. Ind.	décrivais, décrivais, décrivait; décrivions, décriviez, décrivaient
Past Def.	décrivis, décrivis, décrivit; décrivîmes, décrivîtes, décrivirent
Future	décrirai, décriras, décrira; décrirons, décrirez, décriront
Condit.	décrirais, décrirais, décrirait; décririons, décririez, décriraient
Pres. Subj.	décrive, décrives, décrive; décrivions, décriviez, décrivent
Imp. Subj.	décrivisse, décrivisses, décrivît; décrivissions, décrivissiez, décrivissent
Past Indef.	ai décrit, as décrit, a décrit; avons décrit, avez décrit, ont décrit
Pluperf.	avais décrit, avais décrit, avait décrit; avions décrit, aviez décrit, avaient décrit
Past Ant.	eus décrit, eus décrit, eut décrit; eûmes décrit, eûtes décrit, eurent décrit
Fut. Perf.	aurai décrit, auras décrit, aura décrit; aurons décrit, aurez décrit, auront décrit
Cond. Perf.	aurais décrit, aurais décrit, aurait décrit; aurions décrit, auriez décrit, auraient décrit
Past Subj.	aie décrit, aies décrit, ait décrit; ayons décrit, ayez décrit, aient décrit
Plup. Subj.	eusse décrit, eusses décrit, eût décrit; eussions décrit, eussiez décrit, eussent décrit
Imperative	décris, décrivons, décrivez

to decrease, diminish

Pres. Ind.	décrois, décrois, décroît; décroissons, décroissez, décroissent
Imp. Ind.	décroissais, décroissais, décroissait; décroissions, décroissiez, décroissaient
Past Def.	décrus, décrus, décrut; décrûmes, décrûtes, décrurent
Future	décroîtrai, décroîtras, décroîtra; décroîtrons, décroîtrez, décroîtront
Condit.	décroîtrais, décroîtrais, décroîtrait; décroîtrions, décroîtriez, décroîtraient
Pres. Subj.	décroisse, décroisses, décroisse; décroissions, décroissiez, décroissent
Imp. Subj.	décrusse, décrusses, décrût; décrussions, décrussiez, décrussent
Past Indef.	ai décru, as décru, a décru; avons décru, avez décru, ont décru
Plup. Ind.	avais décru, avais décru, avait décru; avions décru, aviez décru, avaient décru
Past Ant.	eus décru, eus décru, eut décru; eûmes décru, eûtes décru, eurent décru
Fut. Perf.	aurai décru, auras décru, aura décru; aurons décru, aurez décru, auront décru
Cond. Perf.	aurais décru, aurais décru, aurait décru; aurions décru, auriez décru, auraient décru
Past Subj.	aie décru, aies décru, ait décru; ayons décru, ayez décru, aient décru
Plup. Subj.	eusse décru, eusses décru, eût décru; eussions décru, eussiez décru, eussent décru
Imperative	décrois, décroissons, décroissez

to deduce, infer, deduct

Pres. Ind.	déduis, déduis, déduit; déduisons, déduisez, déduisent
Imp. Ind.	déduisais, déduisais, déduisait; déduisions, déduisiez, déduisaient
Past Def.	déduisis, déduisis, déduisit; déduisîmes, déduisîtes, déduisirent
Future	déduirai, déduiras, déduira; déduirons, déduirez, déduiront
Condit.	déduirais, déduirais, déduirait; déduirions, déduiriez, déduiraient
Pres. Subj.	déduise, déduises, déduise; déduisions, déduisiez, déduisent
Imp. Subj.	déduisisse, déduisisses, déduisît; déduisissions, déduisissiez, déduisissent
Past Indef.	ai déduit, as déduit, a déduit; avons déduit, avez déduit, ont déduit
Plup. Ind.	avais déduit, avais déduit, avait déduit; avions déduit, aviez déduit, avaient déduit
Past Ant.	eus déduit, eus déduit, eut déduit; eûmes déduit, eûtes déduit, eurent déduit
Fut. Perf.	aurai déduit, auras déduit, aura déduit; aurons déduit, aurez déduit, auront déduit
Cond. Perf.	aurais déduit, aurais déduit, aurait déduit; aurions déduit, auriez déduit, auraient déduit
Past Subj.	aie déduit, aies déduit, ait déduit; ayons déduit, ayez déduit, aient déduit
Plup. Subj.	eusse déduit, eusses déduit, eût déduit; eussions déduit, eussiez déduit, eussent déduit
Imperative	déduis, déduisons, déduisiez

to undo, untie

Pres. Ind.	défais, défais, défait; défaisons, défaites, défont
Imp. Ind.	défaisais, défaisais, défaisait; défaisions, défaisiez, défaisaient
Past Def.	défis, défis, défit; défîmes, défîtes, défirent
Future	déferai, déferas, défera; déferons, déferez, déferont
Condit.	déferais, déferais, déferait; déferions, déferiez, déferaient
Pres. Subj.	défasse, défasses, défasse; défassions, défassiez, défassent
Imp. Subj.	défisse, défisses, défît; défissions, défissiez, défissent
Past Indef.	ai défait, as défait, a défait; avons défait, avez défait, ont défait
Plup. Ind.	avais défait, avais défait, avait défait; avions défait, aviez défait, avaient défait
Past Ant.	eus défait, eus défait, eut défait; eûmes défait, eûtes défait, eurent défait
Fut. Perf.	aurai défait, auras défait, aura défait; aurons défait, aurez défait, auront défait
Cond. Perf.	aurais défait, aurais défait, aurait défait; aurions défait, auriez défait, auraient défait
Past Subj.	aie défait, aies défait, ait défait; ayons défait, ayez défait, aient défait
Plup. Subj.	eusse défait, eusses défait, eût défait; eussions défait, eussiez défait, eussent défait
Imperative	défais, défaisons, défaites

to defend, forbid, prohibit

Pres. Ind.	défends, défends, défend; défendons, défendez, défendent
Imp. Ind.	défendais, défendais, défendait; défendions, défendiez, défendaient
Past Def.	défendis, défendis, défendit; défendîmes, défendîtes, défendirent
Future	défendrai, défendras, défendra; défendrons, défendrez, défendront
Condit.	défendrais, défendrais, défendrait; défendrions, défendriez, défendraient
Pres. Subj.	défende, défendes, défende; défendions, défendiez, défendent
Imp. Subj.	défendisse, défendisses, défendît; défendissions, défendissiez, défendissent
Past Indef.	ai défendu, as défendu, a défendu; avons défendu, avez défendu, ont défendu
Pluperf.	avais défendu, avais défendu, avait défendu; avions défendu, aviez défendu, avaient défendu
Past Ant.	eus défendu, eus défendu, eut défendu; eûmes défendu, eûtes défendu, eurent défendu
Fut. Perf.	aurai défendu, auras défendu, aura défendu; aurons défendu, aurez défendu, auront défendu
Cond. Perf.	aurais défendu, aurais défendu, aurait défendu; aurions défendu, auriez défendu, auraient défendu
Past Subj.	aie défendu, aies défendu, ait défendu; ayons défendu, ayez défendu, aient défendu
Plup. Subj.	eusse défendu, eusses défendu, eût défendu; eussions défendu, eussiez défendu, eussent défendu
Imperative	défends, défendons, défendez

to thaw

Pres. Ind.	il dégèle
Imp. Ind.	il dégelait
Past Def.	il dégela
Future	il dégèlera
Condit.	il dégèlerait
Pres. Subj.	qu'il dégèle
Imp. Subj.	qu'il dégelât
Past Indef.	il a dégelé
Plup. Ind.	il avait dégelé
Past Ant.	il eut dégelé
Fut. Perf.	il aura dégelé
Cond. Perf.	il aurait dégelé
Past Subj.	qu'il ait dégelé
Plup. Subj.	qu'il eût dégelé
Imperative	[inemployé]

to lunch, have lunch

Pres. Ind.	déjeune, déjeunes, déjeune; déjeunons, déjeunez, déjeunent
Imp. Ind.	déjeunais, déjeunais, déjeunait; déjeunions, déjeuniez, déjeunaient
Past Def.	déjeunai, déjeunas, déjeuna; déjeunâmes, déjeunâtes, déjeunèrent
Fut. Ind.	déjeunerai, déjeuneras, déjeunera; déjeunerons, déjeunerez, déjeuneront
Condit.	déjeunerais, déjeunerais, déjeunerait; déjeunerions, déjeuneriez, déjeuneraient
Pres. Subj.	déjeune, déjeunes, déjeune; déjeunions, déjeuniez, déjeunent
Imp. Subj.	déjeunasse, déjeunasses, déjeunât; déjeunassions, déjeunassiez, déjeunassent
Past Indef.	ai déjeuné, as déjeuné, a déjeuné; avons déjeuné, avez déjeuné, ont déjeuné
Pluperf.	avais déjeuné, avais déjeuné, avait déjeuné; avions déjeuné, aviez déjeuné, avaient déjeuné
Past Ant.	eus déjeuné, eus déjeuné, eut déjeuné; eûmes déjeuné, eûtes déjeuné, eurent déjeuné
Fut. Perf.	aurai déjeuné, auras déjeuné, aura déjeuné; aurons déjeuné, aurez déjeuné, auront déjeuné
Cond. Perf.	aurais déjeuné, aurais déjeuné, aurait déjeuné; aurions déjeuné, auriez déjeuné, auraient déjeuné
Past Subj.	aie déjeuné, aies déjeuné, ait déjeuné; ayons déjeuné, ayez déjeuné, aient déjeuné
Plup. Subj.	eusse déjeuné, eusses déjeuné, eût déjeuné; eussions déjeuné, eussiez déjeuné, eussent déjeuné
Imperative	déjeune, déjeunons, déjeunez

to unlace

Pres. Ind.	délace, délaces, délace; délaçons, délacez, délacent
Imp. Ind.	délaçais, délaçais, délaçait; délacions, délaciez, délaçaient
Past Def.	délaçai, délaças, délaça; délaçâmes, délaçâtes, délacèrent
Future	délacerai, délaceras, délacera; délacerons, délacerez, délaceront
Condit.	délacerais, délacerais, délacerait; délacerions, délaceriez, délaceraient
Pres. Subj.	délace, délaces, délace; délacions, délaciez, délacent
Imp. Subj.	délaçasse, délaçasses, délaçât; délaçassions, délaçassiez, délaçassent
Past Indef.	ai délacé, as délacé, a délacé; avons délacé, avez délacé, ont délacé
Plup. Ind.	avais délacé, avais délacé, avait délacé; avions délacé, aviez délacé, avaient délacé
Past Ant.	eus délacé, eus délacé, eut délacé; eûmes délacé, eûtes délacé, eurent délacé
Fut. Perf.	aurai délacé, auras délacé, aura délacé; aurons délacé, aurez délacé, auront délacé
Cond. Perf.	aurais délacé, aurais délacé, aurait délacé; aurions délacé, auriez délacé, auraient délacé
Past Subj.	aie délacé, aies délacé, ait délacé; ayons délacé, ayez délacé, aient délacé
Plup. Subj.	eusse délacé, eusses délacé, eût délacé; eussions délacé, eussiez délacé, eussent délacé
Imperative	délace, délaçons, délacez

to ask (for), request

Pres. Ind.	demande, demandes, demande; demandons, demandez, demandent
Imp. Ind.	demandais, demandais, demandait; demandions, demandiez, demandaient
Past Def.	demandai, demandas, demanda; demandâmes, demandâtes, demandèrent
Fut. Ind.	demanderai, demanderas, demandera; demanderons, demanderez, demanderont
Condit.	demanderais, demanderais, demanderait; demanderions, demanderiez, demanderaient
Pres. Subj.	demande, demandes, demande; demandions, demandiez, demandent
Imp. Subj.	demandasse, demandasses, demandât; demandassions, demandassiez, demandassent
Past Indef.	ai demandé, as demandé, a demandé; avons demandé, avez demandé, ont demandé
Pluperf.	avais demandé, avais demandé, avait demandé; avions demandé, aviez demandé, avaient demandé
Past Ant.	eus demandé, eus demandé, eut demandé; eûmes demandé, eûtes demandé, eurent demandé
Fut. Perf.	aurai demandé, auras demandé, aura demandé; aurons demandé, aurez demandé, auront demandé
Cond. Perf.	aurais demandé, aurais demandé, aurait demandé; aurions demandé, auriez demandé, auraient demandé
Past Subj.	aie demandé, aies demandé, ait demandé; ayons demandé, ayez demandé, aient demandé
Plup. Subj.	eusse demandé, eusses demandé, eût demandé; eussions demandé, eussiez demandé, eussent demandé
Imperative	demande, demandons, demandez

to move, move out, (change residence)

Pres. Ind.	déménage, déménages, déménage; déménageons, déménagez, déménagent
Imp. Ind.	déménageais, déménageais, déménageait; déménagions, déménagiez, déménageaient
Past Def.	déménageai, déménageas, déménagea; déménageâmes, déménageâtes, déménagèrent
Future	déménagerai, déménageras, déménagera; déménagerons, déménagerez, déménageront
Condit.	déménagerais, déménagerais, déménagerait; déménagerions, déménageriez, déménageraient
Pres. Subj.	déménage, déménages, déménage; déménagions, déménagiez, déménagent
Imp. Subj.	déménageasse, déménageasses, déménageât; déménageassions, déménageassiez, déménageassent
Past Indef.	ai déménagé, as déménagé, a déménagé; avons déménagé, avez déménagé, ont déménagé
Pluperf.	avais déménagé, avais déménagé, avait déménagé; avions déménagé, aviez déménagé, avaient déménagé
Past Ant.	eus déménagé, eus déménagé, eut déménagé; eûmes déménagé, eûtes déménagé, eurent déménagé
Fut. Perf.	aurai déménagé, auras déménagé, aura déménagé; aurons déménagé, aurez déménagé, auront déménagé
Cond. Perf.	aurais déménagé, aurais déménagé, aurait déménagé; aurions déménagé, auriez déménagé, auraient déménagé
Past Subj.	aie déménagé, aies déménagé, ait déménagé; ayons déménagé, ayez déménagé, aient déménagé
Plup. Subj.	eusse déménagé, eusses déménagé, eût déménagé; eussions déménagé, eussiez déménagé, eussent déménagé
Imperative	déménage, déménageons, déménagez

to reside, live

Pres. Ind.	demeure, demeures, demeure; demeurons, demeurez, demeurent
Imp. Ind.	demeurais, demeurais, demeurait; demeurions, demeuriez, demeuraient
Past Def.	demeurai, demeuras, demeura; demeurâmes, demeurâtes, demeurèrent
Fut. Ind.	demeurerai, demeureras, demeurera; demeurerons, demeurerez, demeureront
Condit.	demeurerais, demeurerais, demeurerait; demeurerions, demeureriez, demeureraient
Pres. Subj.	demeure, demeures, demeure; demeurions, demeuriez, demeurent
Imp. Subj.	demeurasse, demeurasses, demeurât; demeurassions, demeurassiez, demeurassent
Past Indef.	ai demeuré, as demeuré, a demeuré; avons demeuré, avez demeuré, ont demeuré
Pluperf.	avais demeuré, avais demeuré, avait demeuré; avions demeuré, aviez demeuré, avaient demeuré
Past Ant.	eus demeuré, eus demeuré, eut demeuré; eûmes demeuré, eûtes demeuré, eurent demeuré
Fut. Perf.	aurai demeuré, auras demeuré, aura demeuré; aurons demeuré, aurez demeuré, auront demeuré
Cond. Perf.	aurais demeuré, aurais demeuré, aurait demeuré; aurions demeuré, auriez demeuré, auraient demeuré
Past Subj.	aie demeuré, aies demeuré, ait demeuré; ayons demeuré, ayez demeuré, aient demeuré
Plup. Subj.	eusse demeuré, eusses demeuré, eût demeuré; eussions demeuré, eussiez demeuré, eussent demeuré
Imperative	demeure, demeurons, demeurez

to demolish

Pres. Ind.	démolis, démolis, démolit; démolissons, démolissez, démolissent
Imp. Ind.	démolissais, démolissais, démolissait; démolissions, démolissiez, démolissaient
Past Def.	démolis, démolis, démolit; démolîmes, démolîtes, démolirent
Future	démolirai, démoliras, démolira; démolirons, démolirez, démoliront
Condit.	démolirais, démolirais, démolirait; démolirions, démoliriez, démoliraient
Pres. Subj.	démolisse, démolisses, démolisse; démolissions, démolissiez, démolissent
Imp. Subj.	démolisse, démolisses, démolît; démolissions, démolissiez, démolissent
Past Indef.	ai démoli, as démoli, a démoli; avons démoli, avez démoli, ont démoli
Plup. Ind.	avais démoli, avais démoli, avait démoli; avions démoli, aviez démoli, avaient démoli
Past Ant.	eus démoli, eus démoli, eut démoli; eûmes démoli, eûtes démoli, eurent démoli
Fut. Perf.	aurai démoli, auras démoli. aura démoli; aurons démoli, aurez démoli, auront démoli
Cond. Perf.	aurais démoli, aurais démoli, aurait démoli; aurions démoli, auriez démoli, auraient démoli
Past Subj.	aie démoli, aies démoli, ait démoli; ayons démoli, ayez démoli, aient démoli
Plup. Subj.	eusse démoli, eusses démoli, eût démoli; eussions démoli, eussiez démoli, eussent démoli
Imperative	démolis, démolissons, démolissez

to hurry, hasten

Pres. Ind.	me dépêche, te dépêches, se dépêche; nous dépêchons, vous dépêchez, se dépêchent
Imp. Ind.	me dépêchais, te dépêchais, se dépêchait; nous dépêchions, vous dépêchiez, se dépêchaient
Past Def.	me dépêchai, te dépêchas, se dépêcha; nous dépêchâmes, vous dépêchâtes, se dépêchèrent
Fut. Ind.	me dépêcherai, te dépêcheras, se dépêchera; nous dépêcherons, vous dépêcherez, se dépêcheront
Condit.	me dépêcherais, te dépêcherais, se dépêcherait; nous dépêcherions, vous dépêcheriez, se dépêcheraient
Pres. Subj.	me dépêche, te dépêches, se dépêche; nous dépêchions, vous dépêchiez, se dépêchent
Imp. Subj.	me dépêchasse, te dépêchasses, se dépêchât; nous dépêchassions, vous dépêchassiez, se dépêchassent
Past Indef.	me suis dépêché(e), t'es dépêché(e), s'est dépêché(e); nous sommes dépêché(e)s, vous êtes dépêché(e)(s), se sont dépêché(e)s
Pluperf.	m'étais dépêché(e), t'étais dépêché(e), s'était dépêché(e); nous étions dépêché(e)s, vous étiez dépêché(e)(s), s'étaient dépêché(e)s
Past Ant.	me fus dépêché(e), te fus dépêché(e), se fut dépêché(e); nous fûmes dépêché(e)s, vous fûtes dépêché(e)(s), se furent dépêché(e)s
Fut. Perf.	me serai dépêché(e), te seras dépêché(e), se sera dépêché(e); nous serons dépêché(e)s, vous serez dépêché(e)(s), se seront dépêché(e)s
Cond. Perf.	me serais dépêché(e), te serais dépêché(e), se serait dépêché(e); nous serions dépêché(e)s, vous seriez dépêché(e)(s), se seraient dépêché(e)s
Past Subj.	me sois dépêché(e), te sois dépêché(e), se soit dépêché(e); nous soyons dépêché(e)s, vous soyez dépêché(e)(s), se soient dépêché(e)s
Plup. Subj.	me fusse dépêché(e), te fusses dépêché(e), se fût dépêché(e); nous fussions dépêché(e)s, vous fussiez dépêché(e)(s), se fussent dépêché(e)s
Imperative	dépêche-toi, dépêchons-nous, dépêchez-vous

to depict, describe

Pres. Ind. dépeins, dépeins, dépeint;
dépeignons, dépeignez, dépeignent

Imp. Ind. dépeignais, dépeignais, dépeignait;
dépeignions, dépeigniez, dépeignaient

Past Def. dépeignis, dépeignis, dépeignit;
dépeignîmes, dépeignîtes, dépeignirent

Future dépeindrai, dépeindras, dépeindra;
dépeindrons, dépeindrez, dépeindront

Condit. dépeindrais, dépeindrais, dépeindrait;
dépeindrions, dépeindriez, dépeindraient

Pres. Subj. dépeigne, dépeignes, dépeigne;
dépeignions, dépeigniez, dépeignent

Imp. Subj. dépeignisse, dépeignisses, dépeignît;
dépeignissions, dépeignissiez, dépeignissent

Past Indef. ai dépeint, as dépeint, a dépeint;
avons dépeint, avez dépeint, ont dépeint

Plup. Ind. avais dépeint, avais dépeint, avait dépeint;
avions dépeint, aviez dépeint, avaient dépeint

Past Ant. eus dépeint, eus dépeint, eut dépeint;
eûmes dépeint, eûtes dépeint, eurent dépeint

Fut. Perf. aurai dépeint, auras dépeint, aura dépeint;
aurons dépeint, aurez dépeint, auront dépeint

Cond. Perf. aurais dépeint, aurais dépeint, aurait dépeint;
aurions dépeint, auriez dépeint, auraient dépeint

Past Subj. aie dépeint, aies dépeint, ait dépeint;
ayons déleint, ayez dépeint, aient dépeint

Plup. Subj. eusse dépeint, eusses dépeint, eût dépeint;
eussions dépeint, eussiez dépeint, eussent dépeint

Imperative dépeins, dépeignons, dépeignez

to depend (on), be dependent (on)

Pres. Ind.	dépends, dépends, dépend; dépendons, dépendez, dépendent
Imp. Ind.	dépendais, dépendais, dépendait; dépendions, dépendiez, dépendaient
Past Def.	dépendis, dépendis, dépendit; dépendîmes, dépendîtes, dépendirent
Future	dépendrai, dépendras, dépendra; dépendrons, dépendrez, dépendront
Condit.	dépendrais, dépendrais, dépendrait; dépendrions, dépendriez, dépendraient
Pres. Subj.	dépende, dépendes, dépende; dépendions, dépendiez, dépendent
Imp. Subj.	dépendisse, dépendisses, dépendît; dépendissions, dépendissiez, dépendissent
Past Indef.	ai dépendu, as dépendu, a dépendu; avons dépendu, avez dépendu, ont dépendu
Plup. Ind.	avais dépendu, avais dépendu, avait dépendu; avions dépendu, aviez dépendu, avaient dépendu
Past Ant.	eus dépendu, eus dépendu, eut dépendu; eûmes dépendu, eûtes dépendu, eurent dépendu
Fut. Perf.	aurai dépendu, auras dépendu, aura dépendu; aurons dépendu, aurez dépendu, auront dépendu
Cond. Perf.	aurais dépendu, aurais dépendu, aurait dépendu; aurions dépendu, auriez dépendu, auraient dépendu
Past Subj.	aie dépendu, aies dépendu, ait dépendu; ayons dépendu, ayez dépendu, aient dépendu
Plup. Subj.	eusse dépendu, eusses dépendu, eût dépendu; eussions dépendu, eussiez dépendu, eussent dépendu
Imperative	dépends, dépendons, dépendez

to spend (money)

Pres. Ind.	dépense, dépenses, dépense; dépensons, dépensez, dépensent
Imp. Ind.	dépensais, dépensais, dépensait; dépensions, dépensiez, dépensaient
Past Def.	dépensai, dépensas, dépensa; dépensâmes, dépensâtes, dépensèrent
Future	dépenserai, dépenseras, dépensera; dépenserons, dépenserez, dépenseront
Condit.	dépenserais, dépenserais, dépenserait; dépenserions, dépenseriez, dépenseraient
Pres. Subj.	dépense, dépenses, dépense; dépensions, dépensiez, dépensent
Imp. Subj.	dépensasse, dépensasses, dépensât; dépensassions, dépensassiez, dépensassent
Past Indef.	ai dépensé, as dépensé, a dépensé; avons dépensé, avez dépensé, ont dépensé
Plup. Ind.	avais dépensé, avais dépensé, avait dépensé; avions dépensé, aviez dépensé, avaient dépensé
Past Ant.	eus dépensé, eus dépensé, eut dépensé; eûmes dépensé, eûtes dépensé, eurent dépensé
Fut. Perf.	aurai dépensé, auras dépensé. aura dépensé; aurons dépensé, aurez dépensé, auront dépensé
Cond. Perf.	aurais dépensé, aurais dépensé, aurait dépensé; aurions dépensé, auriez dépensé, auraient dépensé
Past Subj.	aie dépensé, aies dépensé, ait dépensé; ayons dépensé, ayez dépensé, aient dépensé
Plup. Subj.	eusse dépensé, eusses dépensé, eût dépensé; eussions dépensé, eussiez dépensé, eussent dépensé
Imperative	dépense, dépensons, dépensez

to displease

Pres. Ind.	déplais, déplais, déplaît; déplaisons, déplaisez, déplaisent
Imp. Ind.	déplaisais, déplaisais, déplaisait; déplaisions, déplaisiez, déplaisaient
Past Def.	déplus, déplus, déplut; déplûmes, déplûtes, déplurent
Future	déplairai, déplairas, déplaira; déplairons, déplairez, déplairont
Condit.	déplairais, déplairais, déplairait; déplairions, déplairiez, déplairaient
Pres. Subj.	déplaise, déplaises, déplaise; déplaisions, déplaisiez, déplaisent
Imp. Subj.	déplusse, déplusses, déplût; déplussions, déplussiez, déplussent
Past Indef.	ai déplu, as déplu, a déplu; avons déplu, avez déplu, ont déplu
Plup. Ind.	avais déplu, avais déplu, avait déplu; avions déplu, aviez déplu, avaient déplu
Past Ant.	eus déplu, eus déplu, eut déplu; eûmes déplu, eûtes déplu, eurent déplu
Fut. Perf.	aurai déplu, auras déplu, aura déplu; aurons déplu, aurez déplu, auront déplu
Cond. Perf.	aurais déplu, aurais déplu, aurait déplu; aurions déplu, auriez déplu, auraient déplu
Past Subj.	aie déplu, aies déplu, ait déplu; ayons déplu, ayez déplu, aient déplu
Plup. Subj.	eusse déplu, eusses déplu, eût déplu; eussions déplu, eussiez déplu, eussent déplu
Imperative	déplais, déplaisons, déplaisez

to go down, descend, take down, bring down

Pres. Ind.	descends, descends, descend; descendons, descendez, descendent
Imp. Ind.	descendais, descendais, descendait; descendions, descendiez, descendaient
Past Def.	descendis, descendis, descendit; descendîmes, descendîtes, descendirent
Fut. Ind.	descendrai, descendras, descendra; descendrons, descendrez, descendront
Condit.	descendrais, descendrais, descendrait; descendrions, descendriez, descendraient
Pres. Subj.	descende, descendes, descende; descendions, descendiez, descendent
Imp. Subj.	descendisse, descendisses, descendît; descendissions, descendissiez, descendissent
Past Indef.	suis descendu(e), es descendu(e), est descendu(e); sommes descendu(e)s, êtes descendu(e)(s), sont descendu(e)s
Pluperf.	étais descendu(e), étais descendu(e), était descendu(e); étions descendu(e)s, étiez descendu(e)(s), étaient descendu(e)s
Past Ant.	fus descendu(e), fus descendu(e), fut descendu(e); fûmes descendu(e)s, fûtes descendu(e)(s), furent descendu(e)s
Fut. Perf.	serai descendu(e), seras descendu(e), sera descendu(e); serons descendu(e)s, serez descendu(e)(s), seront descendu(e)s
Cond. Perf.	serais descendu(e), serais descendu(e), serait descendu(e); serions descendu(e)s, seriez descendu(e)(s), seraient descendu(e)s
Past Subj.	sois descendu(e), sois descendu(e), soit descendu(e); soyons descendu(e)s, soyez descendu(e)(s), soient descendu(e)s
Plup. Subj.	fusse descendu(e), fusses descendu(e), fût descendu(e); fussions descendu(e)s, fussiez descendu(e)(s), fussent descendu(e)s
Imperative	descends, descendons, descendez

* This verb is conjugated with *avoir* when it has a direct object.
Example: J'ai descendu l'escalier.
J'ai descendu les valises.

to desire

Pres. Ind.	désire, désires, désire; désirons, désirez, désirent
Imp. Ind.	désirais, désirais, désirait; désirions, désiriez, désiraient
Past Def.	désirai, désiras, désira; désirâmes, désirâtes, désirèrent
Fut. Ind.	désirerai, désireras, désirera; désirerons, désirerez, désireront
Condit.	désirerais, désirerais, désirerait; désirerions, désireriez, désireraient
Pres. Subj.	désire, désires, désire; désirions, désiriez, désirent
Imp. Subj.	désirasse, désirasses, désirât; désirassions, désirassiez, désirassent
Past Indef.	ai désiré, as désiré, a désiré; avons désiré, avez désiré, ont désiré
Pluperf.	avais désiré, avais désiré, avait désiré; avions désiré, aviez désiré, avaient désiré
Past Ant.	eus désiré, eus désiré, eut désiré; eûmes désiré, eûtes désiré, eurent désiré
Fut. Perf.	aurai désiré, auras désiré, aura désiré; aurons désiré, aurez désiré, auront désiré
Cond. Perf.	aurais désiré, aurais désiré, aurait désiré; aurions désiré, auriez désiré, auraient désiré
Past Subj.	aie désiré, aies désiré, ait désiré; ayons désiré, ayez désiré, aient désiré
Plup. Subj.	eusse désiré, eusses désiré, eût désiré; eussions désiré, eussiez désiré, eussent désiré
Imperative	[Ordinarily not used]

to draw, sketch

Pres. Ind.	dessine, dessines, dessine; dessinons, dessinez, dessinent
Imp. Ind.	dessinais, dessinais, dessinait; dessinions, dessiniez, dessinaient
Past Def.	dessinai, dessinas, dessina; dessinâmes, dessinâtes, dessinèrent
Future	dessinerai, dessineras, dessinera; dessinerons, dessinerez, dessineront
Condit.	dessinerais, dessinerais, dessinerait; dessinerions, dessineriez, dessineraient
Pres. Subj.	dessine, dessines, dessine; dessinions, dessiniez, dessinent
Imp. Subj.	dessinasse, dessinasses, dessinât; dessinassions, dessinassiez, dessinassent
Past Indef.	ai dessiné, as dessiné, a dessiné; avons dessiné, avez dessiné, ont dessiné
Plup. Ind.	avais dessiné, avais dessiné, avait dessiné; avions dessiné, aviez dessiné, avaient dessiné
Past Ant.	eus dessiné, eus dessiné, eut dessiné; eûmes dessiné, eûtes dessiné, eurent dessiné
Fut. Perf.	aurai dessiné, auras dessiné, aura dessiné; aurons dessiné, aurez dessiné, auront dessiné
Cond. Perf.	aurais dessiné, aurais dessiné, aurait dessiné; aurions dessiné, auriez dessiné, auraient dessiné
Past Subj.	aie dessiné, aies dessiné, ait dessiné; ayons dessiné, ayez dessiné, aient dessiné
Plup. Subj.	eusse dessiné, eusses dessiné, eût dessiné; eussions dessiné, eussiez dessiné, eussent dessiné
Imperative	dessine, dessinons, dessinez

to detest, dislike

Pres. Ind.	déteste, détestes, déteste; détestons, détestez, détestent
Imp. Ind.	détestais, détestais, détestait; détestions, détestiez, détestaient
Past Def.	détestai, détestas, détesta; détestâmes, détestâtes, détestèrent
Future	détesterai, détesteras, détestera; détesterons, détesterez, détesteront
Condit.	détesterais, détesterais, détesterait; détesterions, détesteriez, détesteraient
Pres. Subj.	déteste, détestes, déteste; détestions, détestiez, détestent
Imp. Subj.	détestasse, détestasses, détestât; détestassions, détestassiez, détestassent
Past Indef.	ai détesté, as détesté, a détesté; avons détesté, avez détesté, ont détesté
Plup. Ind.	avais détesté, avais détesté, avait détesté; avions détesté, aviez détesté, avaient détesté
Past Ant.	eus détesté, eus détesté, eut détesté; eûmes détesté, eûtes détesté, eurent détesté
Fut. Perf.	aurai détesté, auras détesté, aura détesté; aurons détesté, aurez détesté, auront détesté
Cond. Perf.	aurais détesté, aurais détesté, aurait détesté; aurions détesté, auriez détesté, auraient détesté
Past Subj.	aie détesté, aies détesté, ait détesté; ayons détesté, ayez détesté, aient détesté
Plup. Subj.	eusse détesté, eusses détesté, eût détesté; eussions détesté, eussiez détesté, eussent détesté
Imperative	déteste, détestons, détestez

to turn aside, turn away

Pres. Ind.	détourne, détournes, détourne; détournons, détournez, détournent
Imp. Ind.	détournais, détournais, détournait; détournions, détourniez, détournaient
Past Def.	détournai, détournas, détourna; détournâmes, détournâtes, détournèrent
Future	détournerai, détourneras, détournera; détournerons, détournerez, détourneront
Condit.	détournerais, détournerais, détournerait; détournerions, détourneriez, détourneraient
Pres. Subj.	détourne, détournes, détourne; détournions, détourniez, détournent
Imp. Subj.	détournasse, détournasses, détournât; détournassions, détournassiez, détournassent
Past Indef.	ai détourné, as détourné, a détourné; avons détourné, avez détourné, ont détourné
Plup. Ind.	avais détourné, avais détourné, avait détourné; avions détourné, aviez détourné, avaient détourné
Past Ant.	eus détourné, eus détourné, eut détourné; eûmes détourné, eûtes détourné, eurent détourné
Fut. Perf.	aurai détourné, auras détourné, aura détourné; aurons détourné, aurez détourné, auront détourné
Cond. Perf.	aurais détourné, aurais détourné, aurait détourné; aurions détourné, auriez détourné, auraient détourné
Past Subj.	aie détourné, aies détourné, ait détourné; ayons détourné, ayez détourné, aient détourné
Plup. Subj.	eusse détourné, eusses détourné, eût détourné; eussions détourné, eussiez détourné, eussent détourné
Imperative	détourne, détournons, détournez

to turn (oneself) aside, away

Pres. Ind.	me détourne, te détourne, se détourne; nous détournons, vous détournez, se détournent
Imp. Ind.	me détournais, te détournais, se détournait; nous détournions, vous détourniez, se détournaient
Past Def.	me détournai, te détournas, se détourna; nous détournâmes, vous détournâtes, se détournèrent
Future	me détournerai, te détourneras, se détournera; nous détournerons, vous détournerez, se détourneront
Condit.	me détournerais, te détournerais, se détournerait; nous détournerions, vous détourneriez, se détourneraient
Pres. Subj.	me détourne, te détournes, se détourne; nous détournions, vous détourniez, se détournent
Imp. Subj.	me détournasse, te détournasses, se détournât; nous détournassions, vous détournassiez, se détournassent
Past Indef.	me suis détourné(e), t'es détourné(e), s'est détourné(e); nous sommes détourné(e)s, vous êtes détourné(e)(s), se sont détourné(e)s
Plup. Ind.	m'étais détourné(e), t'étais détourné(e), s'était détourné(e); nous étions détourné(e)s, vous étiez détourné(e)(s), s'étaient détourné(e)s
Past Ant.	me fus détourné(e), te fus détourné(e), se fut détourné(e); nous fûmes détourné(e)s, vous fûtes détourné(e)(s), se furent détourné(e)s
Fut. Perf.	me serai détourné(e), te seras détourné(e), se sera détourné(e); nous serons détourné(e)s, vous serez détourné(e)(s), se seront détourné(e)s
Cond. Perf.	me serais détourné(e), te serais détourné(e), se serait détourné(e); nous serions détourné(e)s, vous seriez détourné(e)(s), se seraient détourné(e)s
Past Subj.	me sois détourné(e), te sois détourné(e), se soit détourné(e); nous soyons détourné(e)s, vous soyez détourné(e)(s), se soient détourné(e)s
Plup. Subj.	me fusse détourné(e), te fusses détourné(e), se fût détourné(e); nous fussions détourné(e)s, vous fussiez détourné(e)(s), se fussent détourné(e)s
Imperative	détourne-toi, détournons-nous, détournez-vous

to destroy

Pres. Ind.	détruis, détruis, détruit; détruisons, détruisez, détruisent
Imp. Ind.	détruisais, détruisais, détruisait; détruisions, détruisiez, détruisaient
Past Def.	détruisis, détruisis, détruisit; détruisîmes, détruisîtes, détruisirent
Future	détruirai, détruiras, détruira; détruirons, détruirez, détruiront
Condit.	détruirais, détruirais, détruirait; détruirions, détruiriez, détruiraient
Pres. Subj.	détruise, détruises, détruise; détruisions, détruisiez, détruisent
Imp. Subj.	détruisisse, détruisisses, détruisît; détruisissions, détruisissiez, détruisissent
Past Indef.	ai détruit, as détruit, a détruit; avons détruit, avez détruit, ont détruit
Pluperf.	avais détruit, avais détruit, avait détruit; avions détruit, aviez détruit, avaient détruit
Past Ant.	eus détruit, eus détruit, eut détruit; eûmes détruit, eûtes détruit, eurent détruit
Fut. Perf.	aurai détruit, auras détruit, aura détruit; aurons détruit, aurez détruit, auront détruit
Cond. Perf.	aurais détruit, aurais détruit, aurait détruit; aurions détruit, auriez détruit, auraient détruit
Past Subj.	aie détruit, aies détruit, ait détruit; ayons détruit, ayez détruit, aient détruit
Plup. Subj.	eusse détruit, eusses détruit, eût détruit; eussions détruit, eussiez détruit, eussent détruit
Imperative	détruis, détruisons, détruisez

to develop

Pres. Ind.	développe, développes, développe; développons, développez, développent
Imp. Ind.	développais, développais, développait; développions, développiez, développaient
Past Def.	développai, développas, développa; développâmes, développâtes, développèrent
Future	développerai, développeras, développera; développerons, développerez, développeront
Condit.	développerais, développerais, développerait; développerions, développeriez, développeraient
Pres. Subj.	développe, développes, développe; développions, développiez, développent
Imp. Subj.	développasse, développasses, développât; développassions, développassiez, développassent
Past Indef.	ai développé, as développé, a développé; avons développé, avez développé, ont développé
Plup. Ind.	avais développé, avais développé, avait développé; avions développé, aviez développé, avaient développé
Past Ant.	eus développé, eus développé, eut développé; eûmes développé, eûtes développé, eurent développé
Fut. Perf.	aurai développé, auras développé, aura développé; aurons développé, aurez développé, auront développé
Cond. Perf.	aurais développé, aurais développé, aurait développé; aurions développé, auriez développé, auraient développé
Past Subj.	aie développé, aies développé, ait développé; ayons développé, ayez développé, aient développé
Plup. Subj.	eusse développé, eusses développé, eût développé; eussions développé, eussiez développé, eussent développé
Imperative	développe, développons, développez

to become

Pres. Ind.	deviens, deviens, devient; devenons, devenez, deviennent
Imp. Ind.	devenais, devenais, devenait; devenions, deveniez, devenaient
Past Def.	devins, devins, devint; devînmes, devîntes, devinrent
Fut. Ind.	deviendrai, deviendras, deviendra; deviendrons, deviendrez, deviendront
Condit.	deviendrais, deviendrais, deviendrait; deviendrions, deviendriez, deviendraient
Pres. Subj.	devienne, deviennes, devienne; devenions, deveniez, deviennent
Imp. Subj.	devinsse, devinsses, devînt; devinssions, devinssiez, devinssent
Past Indef.	suis devenu(e), es devenu(e), est devenu(e); sommes devenu(e)s, êtes devenu(e)(s), sont devenu(e)s
Pluperf.	étais devenu(e), étais devenu(e), était devenu(e); étions devenu(e)s, étiez devenu(e)(s), étaient devenu(e)s
Past Ant.	fus devenu(e), fus devenu(e), fut devenu(e); fûmes devenu(e)s, fûtes devenu(e)(s), furent devenu(e)s
Fut. Perf.	serai devenu(e), seras devenu(e), sera devenu(e); serons devenu(e)s, serez devenu(e)(s), seront devenu(e)s
Cond. Perf.	serais devenu(e), serais devenu(e), serait devenu(e); serions devenu(e)s, seriez devenu(e)(s), seraient devenu(e)s
Past Subj.	sois devenu(e), sois devenu(e), soit devenu(e); soyons devenu(e)s, soyez devenu(e)(s), soient devenu(e)s
Plup. Subj.	fusse devenu(e), fusses devenu(e), fût devenu(e); fussions devenu(e)s, fussiez devenu(e)(s), fussent devenu(e)s
Imperative	deviens, devenons, devenez

to strip, divest

Pres. Ind.	dévêts, dévêts, dévêt; dévêtons, dévêtez, dévêtent
Imp. Ind.	dévêtais, dévêtais, dévêtait; dévêtions, dévêtiez, dévêtaient
Past Def.	dévêtis, dévêtis, dévêtit; dévêtîmes, dévêtîtes, dévêtirent
Future	dévêtirai, dévêtiras, dévêtira; dévêtirons, dévêtirez, dévêtiront
Condit.	dévêtirais, dévêtirais, dévêtirait; dévêtirions, dévêtiriez, dévêtiraient
Pres. Subj.	dévête, dévêtes, dévête; dévêtions, dévêtiez, dévêtent
Imp. Subj.	dévêtisse, dévêtisses, dévêtît; dévêtissions, dévêtissiez, dévêtissent
Past Indef.	ai dévêtu, as dévêtu, a dévêtu; avons dévêtu, avez dévêtu, ont dévêtu
Pluperf.	avais dévêtu, avais dévêtu, avait dévêtu; avions dévêtu, aviez dévêtu, avaient dévêtu
Past Ant.	eus dévêtu, eus dévêtu, eut dévêtu; eûmes dévêtu, eûtes dévêtu, eurent dévêtu
Fut. Perf.	aurai dévêtu, auras dévêtu, aura dévêtu; aurons dévêtu, aurez dévêtu, auront dévêtu
Cond. Perf.	aurais dévêtu, aurais dévêtu, aurait dévêtu; aurions dévêtu, auriez dévêtu, auraient dévêtu
Past Subj.	aie dévêtu, aies dévêtu, ait dévêtu; ayons dévêtu, ayez dévêtu, aient dévêtu
Plup. Subj.	eusse dévêtu, eusses dévêtu, eût dévêtu; eussions dévêtu, eussiez dévêtu, eussent dévêtu
Imperative	dévêts, dévêtons, dévêtez

Pres. Ind.	dois, dois, doit; devons, devez, doivent	*have to, must, ought, owe, should*
Imp. Ind.	devais, devais, devait; devions, deviez, devaient	
Past Def.	dus, dus, dut; dûmes, dûtes, durent	
Fut. Ind.	devrai, devras, devra; devrons, devrez, devront	
Condit.	devrais, devrais, devrait; devrions, devriez, devraient	
Pres. Subj.	doive, doives, doive; devions, deviez, doivent	
Imp. Subj.	dusse, dusses, dût; dussions, dussiez, dussent	
Past Indef.	ai dû, as dû, a dû; avons dû, avez dû, ont dû	
Pluperf.	avais dû, avais dû, avait dû; avions dû, aviez dû, avaient dû	
Past Ant.	eus dû, eus dû, eut dû; eûmes dû, eûtes dû, eurent dû	
Fut. Perf.	aurai dû, auras dû, aura dû; aurons dû, aurez dû, auront dû	
Cond. Perf.	aurais dû, aurais dû, aurait dû; aurions dû, auriez dû, auraient dû	
Past Subj.	aie dû, aies dû, ait dû; ayons dû, ayez dû, aient dû	
Plup. Subj.	eusse dû, eusses dû, eût dû; eussions dû, eussiez dû, eussent dû	
Imperative	dois, devons, devez	

to diminish, decrease

Pres. Ind.	diminue, diminues, diminue; diminuons, diminuez, diminuent
Imp. Ind.	diminuais, diminuais, diminuait; diminuions, diminuiez, diminuaient
Past Def.	diminuai, diminuas, diminua; diminuâmes, diminuâtes, diminuèrent
Future	diminuerai, diminueras, diminuera; diminuerons, diminuerez, diminueront
Condit.	diminuerais, diminuerais, diminuerait; diminuerions, diminueriez, diminueraient
Pres. Subj.	diminue, diminues, diminue; diminuions, diminuiez, diminuent
Imp. Subj.	diminuasse, diminuasses, diminuât; diminuassions, diminuassiez, diminuassent
Past Indef.	ai diminué, as diminué, a diminué; avons diminué, avez diminué, ont diminué
Plup. Ind.	avais diminué, avais diminué, avait diminué; avions diminué, aviez diminué, avaient diminué
Past Ant.	eus diminué, eus diminué, eut diminué; eûmes diminué, eûtes diminué, eurent diminué
Fut. Perf.	aurai diminué, auras diminué, aura diminué; aurons diminué, aurez diminué, auront diminué
Cond. Perf.	aurais diminué, aurais diminué, aurait diminué; aurions diminué, auriez diminué, auraient diminué
Past Subj.	aie diminué, aies diminué, ait diminué; ayons diminué, ayez diminué, aient diminué
Plup. Subj.	eusse diminué, eusses diminué, eût diminué; eussions diminué, eussiez diminué, eussent diminué
Imperative	diminue, diminuons, diminuez

to dine, have dinner

Pres. Ind.	dîne, dînes, dîne; dînons, dînez, dînent
Imp. Ind.	dînais, dînais, dînait; dînions, dîniez, dînaient
Past Def.	dînai, dînas, dîna; dînâmes, dînâtes, dînèrent
Fut. Ind.	dînerai, dîneras, dînera; dînerons, dînerez, dîneront
Condit.	dînerais, dînerais, dînerait; dînerions, dîneriez, dîneraient
Pres. Subj.	dîne, dînes, dîne; dînions, dîniez, dînent
Imp. Subj.	dînasse, dînasses, dînât; dînassions, dînassiez, dînassent
Past Indef.	ai dîné, as dîné, a dîné; avons dîné, avez dîné, ont dîné
Pluperf.	avais dîné, avais dîné, avait dîné; avions dîné, aviez dîné, avaient dîné
Past Ant.	eus dîné, eus dîné, eut dîné; eûmes dîné, eûtes dîné, eurent dîné
Fut. Perf.	aurai dîné, auras dîné, aura dîné; aurons dîné, aurez dîné, auront dîné
Cond. Perf.	aurais dîné, aurais dîné, aurait dîné; aurions dîné, auriez dîné, auraient dîné
Past Subj.	aie dîné, aies dîné, ait dîné; ayons dîné, ayez dîné, aient dîné
Plup. Subj.	eusse dîné, eusses dîné, eût dîné; eussions dîné, eussiez dîné, eussent dîné
Imperative	dîne, dînons, dînez

to say, tell

Pres. Ind.	dis, dis, dit; disons, dites, disent
Imp. Ind.	disais, disais, disait; disions, disiez, disaient
Past Def.	dis, dis, dit; dîmes, dîtes, dirent
Fut. Ind.	dirai, diras, dira; dirons, direz, diront
Condit.	dirais, dirais, dirait; dirions, diriez, diraient
Pres. Subj.	dise, dises, dise; disions, disiez, disent
Imp. Subj.	disse, disses, dît; dissions, dissiez, dissent
Past Indef.	ai dit, as dit, a dit; avons dit, avez dit, ont dit
Pluperf.	avais dit, avais dit, avait dit; avions dit, aviez dit, avaient dit
Past Ant.	eus dit, eus dit, eut dit; eûmes dit, eûtes dit, eurent dit
Fut. Perf.	aurai dit, auras dit, aura dit; aurons dit, aurez dit, auront dit
Cond. Perf.	aurais dit, aurais dit, aurait dit; aurions dit, auriez dit, auraient dit
Past Subj.	aie dit, aies dit, ait dit; ayons dit, ayez dit, aient dit
Plup. Subj.	eusse dit, eusses dit, eût dit; eussions dit, eussiez dit, eussent dit
Imperative	dis, disons, dites

to discourse

Pres. Ind.	discours, discours, discourt; discourons, discourez, discourent
Imp. Ind.	discourais, discourais, discourait; discourions, discouriez, discouraient
Past Def.	discourus, discourus, discourut; discourûmes, discourûtes, discoururent
Future	discourrai, discourras, discourra; discourrons, discourrez, discourront
Condit.	discourrais, discourrais, discourrait; discourrions, discourriez, discourraient
Pres. Subj.	discoure, discoures, discoure; discourions, discouriez, discourent
Imp. Subj.	discourusse, discourusses, discourût; discourussions, discourussiez, discourussent
Past Indef.	ai discouru, as discouru, a discouru; avons discouru, avez discouru, ont discouru
Plup. Ind.	avais discouru, avais discouru, avait discouru; avions discouru, aviez discouru, avaient discouru
Past Ant.	eus discouru, eus discouru, eut discouru; eûmes discouru, eûtes discouru, eurent discouru;
Future	aurai discouru, auras discouru, aura discouru; aurons discouru, aurez discouru, auront discouru
Cond. Perf.	aurais discouru, aurais discouru, aurait discouru; aurions discouru, auriez discouru, auraient discouru
Past Subj.	aie discouru, aies discouru, ait discouru; ayons discouru, ayez discouru, aient discouru
Plup. Subj.	eusse discouru, eusses discouru, eût discouru; eussions discouru, eussiez discouru, eussent discouru
Imperative	discours, discourons, discourez

to disappear

Pres. Ind.	disparais, disparais, disparaît; disparaissons, disparaissez, disparaissent
Imp. Ind.	disparaissais, disparaissais, disparaissait; disparaissions, disparaissiez, disparaissaient
Past Def.	disparus, disparus, disparut; disparûmes, disparûtes, disparurent
Future	disparaîtrai, disparaîtras, disparaîtra; disparaîtrons, disparaîtrez, disparaîtront
Condit.	disparaîtrais, disparaîtrais, disparaîtrait; disparaîtrions, disparaîtriez, disparaîtraient
Pres. Subj.	disparaisse, disparaisses, disparaisse; disparaissions, disparaissiez, disparaissent
Imp. Subj.	disparusse, disparusses, disparût; disparussions, disparussiez, disparussent
Past Indef.	ai disparu, as disparu, a disparu; avons disparu, avez disparu, ont disparu
Pluperf.	avais disparu, avais disparu, avait disparu; avions disparu, aviez disparu, avaient disparu
Past Ant.	eus disparu, eus disparu, eut disparu; eûmes disparu, eûtes disparu, eurent disparu
Fut. Perf.	aurai disparu, auras disparu, aura disparu; aurons disparu, aurez disparu, auront disparu
Cond. Perf.	aurais disparu, aurais disparu, aurait disparu; aurions disparu, auriez disparu, auraient disparu
Past Subj.	aie disparu, aies disparu, ait disparu; ayons disparu, ayez disparu, aient disparu
Plup. Subj.	eusse disparu, eusses disparu, eût disparu; eussions disparu, eussiez disparu, eussent disparu
Imperative	disparais, disparaissons, disparaissez

to dissuade

Pres. Ind.	dissuade, dissuades, dissuade; dissuadons, dissuadez, dissuadent
Imp. Ind.	dissuadais, dissuadais, dissuadait; dissuadions, dissuadiez, dissuadaient
Past Def.	dissuadai, dissuadas, dissuada; dissuadâmes, dissuadâtes, dissuadèrent
Future	dissuaderai, dissuaderas, dissuadera; dissuaderons, dissuaderez, dissuaderont
Condit.	dissuaderais, dissuaderais, dissuaderait; dissuaderions, dissuaderiez, dissuaderaient
Pres. Subj.	dissuade, dissuades, dissuade; dissuadions, dissuadiez, dissuadent
Imp. Subj.	dissuadasse, dissuadasses, dissuadât; dissuadassions, dissuadassiez, dissuadassent
Past Indef.	ai dissuadé, as dissuadé, a dissuadé; avons dissuadé, avez dissuadé, ont dissuadé
Plup. Ind.	avais dissuadé, avais dissuadé, avait dissuadé; avions dissuadé, aviez dissuadé, avaient dissuadé
Past Ant.	eus dissuadé, eus dissuadé, eut dissuadé; eûmes dissuadé, eûtes dissuadé, eurent dissuadé
Fut. Perf.	aurai dissuadé, auras dissuadé, aura dissuadé; aurons dissuadé, aurez dissuadé, auront dissuadé
Cond. Perf.	aurais dissuadé, aurais dissuadé, aurait dissuadé; aurions dissuadé, auriez dissuadé, auraient dissuadé
Past Subj.	aie dissuadé, aies dissuadé, ait dissuadé; ayons dissuadé, ayez dissuadé, aient dissuadé
Plup. Subj.	eusse dissuadé, eusses dissuadé, eût dissuadé; eussions dissuadé, eussiez dissuadé, eussent dissuadé
Imperative	dissuade, dissuadons, dissuadez

to distract

Pres. Ind.	distrais, distrais, distrait; distrayons, distrayez, distraient
Imp. Ind.	distrayais, distrayais, distrayait; distrayions, distrayiez, distrayaient
Past Def.	[inemployé]
Future	distrairai, distrairas, distraira; distrairons, distrairez, distrairont
Condit.	distrairais, distrairais, distrairait; distrairions, distrairiez, distrairaient
Pres. Subj.	distraie, distraies, distraie; distrayions, distrayiez, distraient
Imp. Subj.	[inemployé]
Past Indef.	ai distrait, as distrait, a distrait; avons distrait, avez distrait, ont distrait
Plup. Ind.	avais distrait, avais distrait, avait distrait; avions distrait, aviez distrait, avaient distrait
Past Ant.	eus distrait, eus distrait, eut distrait; eûmes distrait, eûtes distrait, eurent distrait
Fut. Perf.	aurai distrait, auras distrait, aura distrait; aurons distrait, aurez distrait, auront distrait
Cond. Perf.	aurais distrait, aurais distrait, aurait distrait; aurions distrait, auriez distrait, auraient distrait
Past Subj.	aie distrait, aies distrait, ait distrait; ayons distrait, ayez distrait, aient distrait
Plup. Subj.	eusse distrait, eusses distrait, eût distrait; eussions distrait, eussiez distrait, eussent distrait
Imperative	distrais, distrayons, distrayez

to give

Pres. Ind.	donne, donnes, donne; donnons, donnez, donnent
Imp. Ind.	donnais, donnais, donnait; donnions, donniez, donnaient
Past Def.	donnai, donnas, donna; donnâmes, donnâtes, donnèrent
Fut. Ind.	donnerai, donneras, donnera; donnerons, donnerez, donneront
Condit.	donnerais, donnerais, donnerait; donnerions, donneriez, donneraient
Pres. Subj.	donne, donnes, donne; donnions, donniez, donnent
Imp. Subj.	donnasse, donnasses, donnât; donnassions, donnassiez, donnassent
Past Indef.	ai donné, as donné, a donné; avons donné, avez donné, ont donné
Pluperf.	avais donné, avais donné, avait donné; avions donné, aviez donné, avaient donné
Past Ant.	eus donné, eus donné, eut donné; eûmes donné, eûtes donné, eurent donné
Fut. Perf.	aurai donné, auras donné, aura donné; aurons donné, aurez donné, auront donné
Cond. Perf.	aurais donné, aurais donné, aurait donné; aurions donné, auriez donné, auraient donné
Past Subj.	aie donné, aies donné, ait donné; ayons donné, ayez donné, aient donné
Plup. Subj.	eusse donné, eusses donné, eût donné; eussions donné, eussiez donné, eussent donné
Imperative	donne, donnons, donnez

to sleep

Pres. Ind.	dors, dors, dort; dormons, dormez, dorment
Imp. Ind.	dormais, dormais, dormait; dormions, dormiez, dormaient
Past Def.	dormis, dormis, dormit; dormîmes, dormîtes, dormirent
Fut. Ind.	dormirai, dormiras, dormira; dormirons, dormirez, dormiront
Condit.	dormirais, dormirais, dormirait; dormirions, dormiriez, dormiraient
Pres. Subj.	dorme, dormes, dorme; dormions, dormiez, dorment
Imp. Subj.	dormisse, dormisses, dormît; dormissions, dormissiez, dormissent
Past Indef.	ai dormi, as dormi, a dormi; avons dormi, avez dormi, ont dormi
Pluperf.	avais dormi, avais dormi, avait dormi; avions dormi, aviez dormi, avaient dormi
Past Ant.	eus dormi, eus dormi, eut dormi; eûmes dormi, eûtes dormi, eurent dormi
Fut. Perf.	aurai dormi, auras dormi, aura dormi; aurons dormi, aurez dormi, auront dormi
Cond. Perf.	aurais dormi, aurais dormi, aurait dormi; aurions dormi, auriez dormi, auraient dormi
Past Subj.	aie dormi, aies dormi, ait dormi; ayons dormi, ayez dormi, aient dormi
Plup. Subj.	eusse dormi, eusses dormi, eût dormi; eussions dormi, eussiez dormi, eussent dormi
Imperative	dors, dormons, dormez

to doubt

Pres. Ind.	doute, doutes, doute; doutons, doutez, doutent
Imp. Ind.	doutais, doutais, doutait; doutions, doutiez, doutaient
Past Def.	doutai, doutas, douta; doutâmes, doutâtes, doutèrent
Future	douterai, douteras, doutera; douterons, douterez, douteront
Condit.	douterais, douterais, douterait; douterions, douteriez, douteraient
Pres. Subj.	doute, doutes, doute; doutions, doutiez, doutent
Imp. Subj.	doutasse, doutasses, doutât; doutassions, doutassiez, doutassent
Past Indef.	ai douté, as douté, a douté; avons douté, avez douté, ont douté
Plup. Ind.	avais douté, avais douté, avait douté; avions douté, aviez douté, avaient douté
Past Ant.	eus douté, eus douté, eut douté; eûmes douté, eûtes douté, eurent douté
Fut. Perf.	aurai douté, auras douté, aura douté; aurons douté, aurez douté, auront douté
Cond. Perf.	aurais douté, aurais douté, aurait douté; aurions douté, auriez douté, auraient douté
Past Subj.	aie douté, aies douté, ait douté; ayons douté, ayez douté, aient douté
Plup. Subj.	eusse douté, eusses douté, eût douté; eussions douté, eussiez douté, eussent douté
Imperative	doute, doutons, doutez

to fail

Pres. Ind.	échoue, échoues, échoue; échouons, échouez, échouent
Imp. Ind.	échouais, échouais, échouait; échouions, échouiez, échouaient
Past Def.	échouai, échouas, échoua; échouâmes, échouâtes, échouèrent
Future	échouerai, échoueras, échouera; échouerons, échouerez, échoueront
Condit.	échouerais, échouerais, échouerait; échouerions, échoueriez, échoueraient
Pres. Subj.	échoue, échoues, échoue; échouions, échouiez, échouent
Imp. Subj.	échouasse, échouasses, échouât; échouassions, échouassiez, échouassent
Past Indef.	ai échoué, as échoué, a échoué; avons échoué, avez échoué, ont échoué
Pluperf.	avais échoué, avais échoué, avait échoué; avions échoué, aviez échoué, avaient échoué
Past Ant.	eus échoué, eus échoué, eut échoué; eûmes échoué, eûtes échoué, eurent échoué
Fut. Perf.	aurai échoué, auras échoué, aura échoué; aurons échoué, aurez échoué, auront échoué
Cond. Perf.	aurais échoué, aurais échoué, aurait échoué; aurions échoué, auriez échoué, auraient échoué
Past Subj.	aie échoué, aies échoué, ait échoué; ayons échoué, ayez échoué, aient échoué
Plup. Subj.	eusse échoué, eusses échoué, eût échoué; eussions échoué, eussiez échoué, eussent échoué
Imperative	échoue, échouons, échouez

to listen (to)

Pres. Ind.	écoute, écoutes, écoute; écoutons, écoutez, écoutent
Imp. Ind.	écoutais, écoutais, écoutait; écoutions, écoutiez, écoutaient
Past Def.	écoutai, écoutas, écouta; écoutâmes, écoutâtes, écoutèrent
Fut. Ind.	écouterai, écouteras, écoutera; écouterons, écouterez, écouteront
Condit.	écouterais, écouterais, écouterait; écouterions, écouteriez, écouteraient
Pres. Subj.	écoute, écoutes, écoute; écoutions, écoutiez, écoutent
Imp. Subj.	écoutasse, écoutasses, écoutât; écoutassions, écoutassiez, écoutassent
Past Indef.	ai écouté, as écouté, a écouté; avons écouté, avez écouté, ont écouté
Pluperf.	avais écouté, avais écouté, avait écouté; avions écouté, aviez écouté, avaient écouté
Past Ant.	eus écouté, eus écouté, eut écouté; eûmes écouté, eûtes écouté, eurent écouté
Fut. Perf.	aurai écouté, auras écouté, aura écouté; aurons écouté, aurez écouté, auront écouté
Cond. Perf.	aurais écouté, aurais écouté, aurait écouté; aurions écouté, auriez écouté, auraient écouté
Past Subj.	aie écouté, aies écouté, ait écouté; ayons écouté, ayez écouté, aient écouté
Plup. Subj.	eusse écouté, eusses écouté, eût écouté; eussions écouté, eussiez écouté, eussent écouté
Imperative	écoute, écoutons, écoutez

to write

Pres. Ind.	écris, écris, écrit; écrivons, écrivez, écrivent
Imp. Ind.	écrivais, écrivais, écrivait; écrivions, écriviez, écrivaient
Past Def.	écrivis, écrivis, écrivit; écrivîmes, écrivîtes, écrivirent
Fut. Ind.	écrirai, écriras, écrira; écrirons, écrirez, écriront
Condit.	écrirais, écrirais, écrirait; écririons, écririez, écriraient
Pres. Subj.	écrive, écrives, écrive; écrivions, écriviez, écrivent
Imp. Subj.	écrivisse, écrivisses, écrivît; écrivissions, écrivissiez, écrivissent
Past Indef.	ai écrit, as écrit, a écrit; avons écrit, avez écrit, ont écrit
Pluperf.	avais écrit, avais écrit, avait écrit; avions écrit, aviez écrit, avaient écrit
Past Ant.	eus écrit, eus écrit, eut écrit; eûmes écrit, eûtes écrit, eurent écrit
Fut. Perf.	aurai écrit, auras écrit, aura écrit; aurons écrit, aurez écrit, auront écrit
Cond. Perf.	aurais écrit, aurais écrit, aurait écrit; aurions écrit, auriez écrit, auraient écrit
Past Subj.	aie écrit, aies écrit, ait écrit; ayons écrit, ayez écrit, aient écrit
Plup. Subj.	eusse écrit, eusses écrit, eût écrit; eussions écrit, eussiez écrit, eussent écrit
Imperative	écris, écrivons, écrivez

to frighten

Pres. Ind.	effraye, effrayes, effraye; effrayons, effrayez, effrayent
Imp. Ind.	effrayais, effrayais, effrayait; effrayions, effrayiez, effrayaient
Past Def.	effrayai, effrayas, effraya; effrayâmes, effrayâtes, effrayèrent
Future	effrayerai, effrayeras, effrayera; effrayerons, effrayerez, effrayeront
Condit.	effrayerais, effrayerais, effrayerait; effrayerions, effrayeriez, effrayeraient
Pres. Subj.	effraye, effrayes, effraye; effrayions, effrayiez, effrayent
Imp. Subj.	effrayasse, effrayasses, effrayât; effrayassions, effrayassiez, effrayassent
Past Indef.	ai effrayé, as effrayé, a effrayé; avons effrayé, avez effrayé, ont effrayé
Plup. Ind.	avais effrayé, avais effrayé, avait effrayé; avions effrayé, aviez effrayé, avaient effrayé
Past Ant.	eus effrayé, eus effrayé, eut effrayé; eûmes effrayé, eûtes effrayé, eurent effrayé
Fut. Perf.	aurai effrayé, auras effrayé, aura effrayé; aurons effrayé, aurez effrayé, auront effrayé
Cond. Perf.	aurais effrayé, aurais effrayé, aurait effrayé; aurions effrayé, auriez effrayé, auraient effrayé
Past Subj.	aie effrayé, aies effrayé, ait effrayé; ayons effrayé, ayez effrayé, aient effrayé
Plup. Subj.	eusse effrayé, eusses effrayé, eût effrayé; eussions effrayé, eussiez effrayé, eussent effrayé
Imperative	effraye, effrayons, effrayez

to amuse, cheer up, enliven, entertain

Pres. Ind.	égaye, égayes, égaye; égayons, égayez, égayent
Imp. Ind.	égayais, égayais, égayait; égayions, égayiez, égayaient
Past Def.	égayai, égayas, égaya; égayâmes, égayâtes, égayèrent
Future	égayerai, égayeras, égayera; égayerons, égayerez, égayeront
Condit.	égayerais, égayerais, égayerait; égayerions, égayeriez, égayeraient
Pres. Subj.	égaye, égayes, égaye; égayions, égayiez, égayent
Imp. Subj.	égayasse, égayasses, égayât; égayassions, égayassiez, égayassent
Past Indef.	ai égayé, as égayé, a égayé; avons égayé, avez égayé, ont égayé
Plup. Ind.	avais égayé, avais égayé, avait égayé; avions égayé, aviez égayé, avaient égayé
Past Ant.	eus égayé, eus égayé, eut égayé; eûmes égayé, eûtes égayé, eurent égayé
Fut. Perf.	aurai égayé, auras égayé, aura égayé; aurons égayé, aurez égayé, auront égayé
Cond. Perf.	aurais égayé, aurais égayé, aurait égayé; aurions égayé, auriez égayé, auraient égayé
Past Subj.	aie égayé, aies égayé, ait égayé; ayons égayé, ayez égayé, aient égayé
Plup. Subj.	eusse égayé, eusses égayé, eût égayé; eussions égayé, eussiez égayé, eussent égayé
Imperative	égaye, égayons, égayez

to raise, bring up, rear

Pres. Ind.	élève, élèves, élève; élevons, élevez, élèvent
Imp. Ind.	élevais, élevais, élevait; élevions, éleviez, élevaient
Past Def.	élevai, élevas, éleva; élevâmes, élevâtes, élevèrent
Future	élèverai, élèveras, élèvera; élèverons, élèverez, élèveront
Condit.	élèverais, élèverais, élèverait; élèverions, élèveriez, élèveraient
Pres. Subj.	élève, élèves, élève; élevions, éleviez, élèvent
Imp. Subj.	élevasse, élevasses, élevât; élevassions, élevasssiez, élevassent
Past Indef.	ai élevé, as élevé, a élevé; avons élevé, avez élevé, ont élevé
Plup. Ind.	avais élevé, avais élevé, avait élevé; avions élevé, aviez élevé, avaient élevé
Past Ant.	eus élevé, eus élevé, eut élevé; eûmes élevé, eûtes élevé, eurent élevé
Fut. Perf.	aurai élevé, auras élevé, aura élevé; aurons élevé, aurez élevé, auront élevé
Cond. Perf.	aurais élevé, aurais élevé, aurait élevé; aurions élevé, auriez élevé, auraient élevé
Past Subj.	aie élevé, aies élevé, ait élevé; ayons élevé, ayez élevé, aient élevé
Plup. Subj.	eusse élevé, eusses élevé, eût élevé; eussions élevé, eussiez élevé, eussent élevé
Imperative	élève, élevons, élevez

to elect

Pres. Ind.	élis, élis, élit; élisons, élisez, élisent
Imp. Ind.	élisais, élisais, élisait; élisions, élisiez, élisaient
Past Def.	élus, élus, élut; élûmes, élûtes, élurent
Future	élirai, éliras, élira; élirons, élirez, éliront
Condit.	élirais, élirais, élirait; élirions, éliriez, éliraient
Pres. Subj.	élise, élises, élise; élisions, élisiez, élisent
Imp. Subj.	élusse, élusses, élût; élussions, élussiez, élussent
Past Indef.	ai élu, as élu, a élu; avons élu, avez élu, ont élu
Plup. Ind.	avais élu, avais élu, avait élu; avions élu, aviez élu, avaient élu
Past Ant.	eus élu, eus élu, eut élu; eûmes élu, eûtes élu, eurent élu
Fut. Perf.	aurai élu, auras élu, aura élu; aurons élu, aurez élu, auront élu
Cond. Perf.	aurais élu, aurais élu, aurait élu; aurions élu, auriez élu, auraient élu
Past Subj.	aie élu, aies élu, ait élu; ayons élu, ayez élu, aient élu
Plup. Subj.	eusse élu, eusses élu, eût élu; eussions élu, eussiez élu, eussent élu
Imperative	élis, élisons, élisez

to excite, rouse, stir

Pres. Ind.	émeus, émeus, émeut; émouvons, émouvez, émeuvent
Imp. Ind.	émouvais, émouvais, émouvait; émouvions, émouviez, émouvaient
Past Def.	émus, émus, émut; émûtes, émûtes, émurent
Future	émouvrai, émouvras, émouvra; émouvrons, émouvrez, émouvront
Condit.	émouvrais, émouvrais, émouvrait; émouvrions, émouvriez, émouvraient
Pres. Subj.	émeuve, émeuves, émeuve; émouvions, émouviez, émeuvent
Imp. Subj.	émusse, émusses, émût; émussions, émussiez, émussent
Past Indef.	ai ému, as ému, a ému; avons ému, avez ému, ont ému
Pluperf.	avais ému, avais ému, avait ému; avions ému, aviez ému, avaient ému
Past Ant.	eus ému, eus ému, eut ému; eûmes ému, eûtes ému, eurent ému
Fut. Perf.	aurai ému, auras ému, aura ému; aurons ému, aurez ému, auront ému
Cond. Perf.	aurais ému, aurais ému, aurait ému; aurions ému, auriez ému, auraient ému
Past Subj.	aie ému, aies ému, ait ému; ayons ému, ayez ému, aient ému
Plup. Subj.	eusse ému, eusses ému, eût ému; eussions ému, eussiez ému, eussent ému
Imperative	émeus, émouvons, émouvez

to hinder, prevent

Pres. Ind.	empêche, empêches, empêche; empêchons, empêchez, empêchent
Imp. Ind.	empêchais, empêchais, empêchait; empêchions, empêchiez, empêchaient
Past Def.	empêchai, empêchas, empêcha; empêchâmes, empêchâtes, empêchèrent
Future	empêcherai, empêcheras, empêchera; empêcherons, empêcherez, empêcheront
Condit.	empêcherais, empêcherais, empêcherait; empêcherions, empêcheriez, empêcheraient
Pres. Subj.	empêche, empêches, empêche; empêchions, empêchiez, empêchent
Imp. Subj.	empêchasse, empêchasses, empêchât; empêchassions, empêchassiez, empêchassent
Past Indef.	ai empêché, as empêché, a empêché; avons empêché, avez empêché, ont empêché
Plup. Ind.	avais empêché, avais empêché, avait empêché; avions empêché, aviez empêché, avaient empêché
Past Ant.	eus empêché, eus empêché, eut empêché; eûmes empêché, eûtes empêché, eurent empêché
Fut. Perf.	aurai empêché, auras empêché, aura empêché; aurons empêché, aurez empêché, auront empêché
Cond. Perf.	aurais empêché, aurais empêché, aurait empêché; aurions empêché, auriez empêché, auraient empêché
Past Subj.	aie empêché, aies empêché, ait empêché; ayons empêché, ayez empêché, aient empêché
Plup. Subj.	eusse empêché, eusses empêché, eût empêché; eussions empêché, eussiez empêché, eussent empêché
Imperative	empêche, empêchons, empêchez

to use, employ

Pres. Ind.	emploie, emploies, emploie; employons, employez, emploient
Imp. Ind.	employais, employais, employait; employions, employiez, employaient
Past Def.	employai, employas, employa; employâmes, employâtes, employèrent
Fut. Ind.	emploierai, emploieras, emploiera; emploierons, emploierez, emploieront
Condit.	emploierais, emploierais, emploierait; emploierions, emploieriez, emploieraient
Pres. Subj.	emploie, emploies, emploie; employions, employiez, emploient
Imp. Subj.	employasse, employasses, employât; employassions, employassiez, employassent
Past Indef.	ai employé, as employé, a employé; avons employé, avez employé, ont employé
Pluperf.	avais employé, avais employé, avait employé; avions employé, aviez employé, avaient employé
Past Ant.	eus employé, eus employé, eut employé; eûmes employé, eûtes employé, eurent employé
Fut. Perf.	aurai employé, auras employé, aura employé; aurons employé, aurez employé, auront employé
Cond. Perf.	aurais employé, aurais employé, aurait employé; aurions employé, auriez employé, auraient employé
Past Subj.	aie employé, aies employé, ait employé; ayons employé, ayez employé, aient employé
Plup. Subj.	eusse employé, eusses employé, eût employé; eussions employé, eussiez employé, eussent employé
Imperative	emploie, employons, employez

to borrow

Pres. Ind.	emprunte, empruntes, emprunte; empruntons, empruntez, empruntent
Imp. Ind.	empruntais, empruntais, empruntait; empruntions, empruntiez, empruntaient
Past Def.	empruntai, empruntas, emprunta; empruntâmes, empruntâtes, empruntèrent
Fut. Ind.	emprunterai, emprunteras, empruntera; emprunterons, emprunterez, emprunteront
Condit.	emprunterais, emprunterais, emprunterait; emprunterions, emprunteriez, emprunteraient
Pres. Subj.	emprunte, empruntes, emprunte; empruntions, empruntiez, empruntent
Imp. Subj.	empruntasse, empruntasses, empruntât; empruntassions, empruntassiez, empruntassent
Past Indef.	ai emprunté, as emprunté, a emprunté; avons emprunté, avez emprunté, ont emprunté
Pluperf.	avais emprunté, avais emprunté, avait emprunté; avions emprunté, aviez emprunté, avaient emprunté
Past Ant.	eus emprunté, eus emprunté, eut emprunté; eûmes emprunté, eûtes emprunté, eurent emprunté
Fut. Perf.	aurai emprunté, auras emprunté, aura emprunté; aurons emprunté, aurez emprunté, auront emprunté
Cond. Perf.	aurais emprunté, aurais emprunté, aurait emprunté; aurions emprunté, auriez emprunté, auraient emprunté
Past Subj.	aie emprunté, aies emprunté, ait emprunté; ayons emprunté, ayez emprunté, aient emprunté
Plup. Subj.	eusse emprunté, eusses emprunté, eût emprunté; eussions emprunté, eussiez emprunté, eussent emprunté
Imperative	emprunte, empruntons, empruntez

to encourage

Pres. Ind.	encourage, encourages, encourage; encourageons, encouragez, encouragent
Imp. Ind.	encourageais, encourageais, encourageait; encouragions, encouragiez, encourageaient
Past Def.	encourageai, encourageas, encouragea; encourageâmes, encourageâtes, encouragèrent
Future	encouragerai, encourageras, encouragera; encouragerons, encouragerez, encourageront
Condit.	encouragerais, encouragerais, encouragerait; encouragerions, encourageriez, encourageraient
Pres. Subj.	encourage, encourages, encourage; encouragions, encouragiez, encouragent
Imp. Subj.	encourageasse, encourageasses, encourageât; encourageassions, encourageassiez, encourageassent
Past Indef.	ai encouragé, as encouragé, a encouragé; avons encouragé, avez encouragé, ont encouragé
Plup. Ind.	avais encouragé, avais encouragé, avait encouragé; avions encouragé, aviez encouragé, avaient encouragé
Past Ant.	eus encouragé, eus encouragé, eut encouragé; eûmes encouragé, eûtes encouragé, eurent encouragé
Fut. Perf.	aurai encouragé, auras encouragé, aura encouragé; aurons encouragé, aurez encouragé, auront encouragé
Cond. Perf.	aurais encouragé, aurais encouragé, aurait encouragé; aurions encouragé, auriez encouragé, auraient encouragé
Past Subj.	aie encouragé, aies encouragé, ait encouragé; ayons encouragé, ayez encouragé, aient encouragé
Plup. Subj.	eusse encouragé, eusses encouragé, eût encouragé; eussions encouragé, eussiez encouragé, eussent encouragé
Imperative	encourage, encourageons, encouragez

to run away, slip away, escape, flee, fly

Pres. Ind.	m'enfuis, t'enfuis, s'enfuis; nous enfuyons, vous enfuyez, s'enfuient
Imp. Ind.	m'enfuyais, t'enfuyais, s'enfuyait; nous enfuyions, vous enfuyiez, s'enfuyaient
Past Def.	m'enfuis, t'enfuis, s'enfuit; nous enfuîmes, vous enfuîtes, s'enfuirent
Future	m'enfuirai, t'enfuiras, s'enfuira; nous enfuirons, vous enfuirez, s'enfuiront
Condit.	m'enfuirais, t'enfuirais, s'enfuirait; nous enfuirions, vous enfuiriez, s'enfuiraient
Pres. Subj.	m'enfuie, t'enfuies, s'enfuie; nous enfuyions, vous enfuyiez, s'enfuient
Imp. Subj.	m'enfuisse, t'enfuisses, s'enfuît; nous enfuissions, vous enfuissiez, s'enfuissent
Past Indef.	me suis enfui(e), t'es enfuie(e), s'est enfui(e); nous sommes enfui(e)s, vous êtes enfui(e)(s), se sont enfui(e)s
Plup. Ind.	m'étais enfui(e), t'étais enfui(e), s'était enfui(e); nous étions enfui(e)s, vous étiez enfui(e)(s), s'étaient enfui(e)s
Past Ant.	me fus enfui(e), te fus enfui(e), se fut enfui(e); nous fûmes enfui(e)s, vous fûtes enfui(e)(s), se furent enfui(e)s
Fut. Perf.	me serai enfui(e), te seras enfui(e), se sera enfui(e); nous serons enfui(e)s, vous serez enfui(e)(s), se seront enfui(e)s
Cond. Perf.	me serais enfui(e), te serais enfui(e), se serait enfui(e); nous serions enfui(e)s, vous seriez enfui(e)(s), se seraient enfui(e)s
Past Subj.	me sois enfui(e), te sois enfui(e), se soit enfui(e); nous soyons enfui(e)s, vous soyez enfui(e)(s), se soient enfui(e)s
Plup. Subj.	me fusse enfui(e), te fusses enfui(e), se fût enfui(e); nous fussions enfui(e)s, vous fussiez enfui(e)(s), se fussent enfui(e)s
Imperative	enfuis-toi, enfuyons-nous, enfuyez-vous

to carry away, take away

Pres. Ind.	enlève, enlèves, enlève; enlevons, enlevez, enlèvent
Imp. Ind.	enlevais, enlevais, enlevait; enlevions, enleviez, enlevaient
Past Def.	enlevai, enlevas, enleva; enlevâmes, enlevâtes, enlevèrent
Future	enlèverai, enlèveras, enlèvera; enlèverons, enlèverez, enlèveront
Condit.	enlèverais, enlèverais, enlèverait; enlèverions, enlèveriez, enlèveraient
Pres. Subj.	enlève, enlèves, enlève; enlevions, enleviez, enlèvent
Imp. Subj.	enlevasse, enlevasses, enlevât; enlevassions, enlevassiez, enlevassent
Past Indef.	ai enlevé, as enlevé, a enlevé; avons enlevé, avez enlevé, ont enlevé
Plup. Ind.	avais enlevé, avais enlevé, avait enlevé; avions enlevé, aviez enlevé, avaient enlevé
Past Ant.	eus enlevé, eus enlevé, eut enlevé; eûmes enlevé, eûtes enlevé, eurent enlevé
Fut. Perf.	aurai enlevé, auras enlevé, aura enlevé; aurons enlevé, aurez enlevé, auront enlevé
Cond. Perf.	aurais enlevé, aurais enlevé, aurait enlevé; aurions enlevé, auriez enlevé, auraient enlevé
Past Subj.	aie enlevé, aies enlevé, ait enlevé; ayons enlevé, ayez enlevé, aient enlevé
Plup. Subj.	eusse enlevé, eusses enlevé, eût enlevé; eussions enlevé, eussiez enlevé, eussent enlevé
Imperative	enlève, enlevons, enlevez

to bore, annoy, weary

Pres. Ind.	ennuie, ennuies, ennuie; ennuyons, ennuyez, ennuient
Imp. Ind.	ennuyais, ennuyais, ennuyait; ennuyions, ennuyiez, ennuyaient
Past Def.	ennuyai, ennuyas, ennuya; ennuyâmes, ennuyâtes, ennuyèrent
Fut. Ind.	ennuierai, ennuieras, ennuiera; ennuierons, ennuierez, ennuieront
Condit.	ennuierais, ennuierais, ennuierait; ennuierions, ennuieriez, ennuieraient
Pres. Subj.	ennuie, ennuies, ennuie; ennuyions, ennuyiez, ennuient
Imp. Subj.	ennuyasse, ennuyasses, ennuyât; ennuyassions, ennuyassiez, ennuyassent
Past Indef.	ai ennuyé, as ennuyé, a ennuyé; avons ennuyé, avez ennuyé, ont ennuyé
Pluperf.	avais ennuyé, avais ennuyé, avait ennuyé; avions ennuyé, aviez ennuyé, avaient ennuyé
Past Ant.	eus ennuyé, eus ennuyé, eut ennuyé; eûmes ennuyé, eûtes ennuyé, eurent ennuyé
Fut. Perf.	aurai ennuyé, auras ennuyé, aura ennuyé; aurons ennuyé, aurez ennuyé, auront ennuyé
Cond. Perf.	aurais ennuyé, aurais ennuyé, aurait ennuyé; aurions ennuyé, auriez ennuyé, auraient ennuyé
Past Subj.	aie ennuyé, aies ennuyé, ait ennuyé; ayons ennuyé, ayez ennuyé, aient ennuyé
Plup. Subj.	eusse ennuyé, eusses ennuyé, eût ennuyé; eussions ennuyé, eussiez ennuyé, eussent ennuyé
Imperative	ennuie, ennuyons, ennuyez

to teach

Pres. Ind.	enseigne, enseignes, enseigne; enseignons, enseignez, enseignent
Imp. Ind.	enseignais, enseignais, enseignait; enseignions, enseigniez, enseignaient
Past Def.	enseignai, enseignas, enseigna; enseignâmes, enseignâtes, enseignèrent
Fut. Ind.	enseignerai, enseigneras, enseignera; enseignerons, enseignerez, enseigneront
Condit.	enseignerais, enseignerais, enseignerait; enseignerions, enseigneriez, enseigneraient
Pres. Subj.	enseigne, enseignes, enseigne; enseignions, enseigniez, enseignent
Imp. Subj.	enseignasse, enseignasses, enseignât; enseignassions, enseignassiez, enseignassent
Past Indef.	ai enseigné, as enseigné, a enseigné; avons enseigné, avez enseigné, ont enseigné
Pluperf.	avais enseigné, avais enseigné, avait enseigné; avions enseigné, aviez enseigné, avaient enseigné
Past Ant.	eus enseigné, eus enseigné, eut enseigné; eûmes enseigné, eûtes enseigné, eurent enseigné
Fut. Perf.	aurai enseigné, auras enseigné, aura enseigné; aurons enseigné, aurez enseigné, auront enseigné
Cond. Perf.	aurais enseigné, aurais enseigné, aurait enseigné; aurions enseigné, auriez enseigné, auraient enseigné
Past Subj.	aie enseigné, aies enseigné, ait enseigné; ayons enseigné, ayez enseigné, aient enseigné
Plup. Subj.	eusse enseigné, eusses enseigné, eût enseigné; eussions enseigné, eussiez enseigné, eussent enseigné
Imperative	enseigne, enseignons, enseignez

to hear, understand

Pres. Ind.	entends, entends, entend; entendons, entendez, entendent
Imp. Ind.	entendais, entendais, entendait; entendions, entendiez, entendaient
Past Def.	entendis, entendis, entendit; entendîmes, entendîtes, entendirent
Fut. Ind.	entendrai, entendras, entendra; entendrons, entendrez, entendront
Condit.	entendrais, entendrais, entendrait; entendrions, entendriez, entendraient
Pres. Subj.	entende, entendes, entende; entendions, entendiez, entendent
Imp. Subj.	entendisse, entendisses, entendît; entendissions, entendissiez, entendissent
Past Indef.	ai entendu, as entendu, a entendu; avons entendu, avez entendu, ont entendu
Pluperf.	avais entendu, avais entendu, avait entendu; avions entendu, aviez entendu, avaient entendu
Past Ant.	eus entendu, eus entendu, eut entendu; eûmes entendu, eûtes entendu, eurent entendu
Fut. Perf.	aurai entendu, auras entendu, aura entendu; aurons entendu, aurez entendu, auront entendu
Cond. Perf.	aurais entendu, aurais entendu, aurait entendu; aurions entendu, auriez entendu, auraient entendu
Past Subj.	aie entendu, aies entendu, ait entendu; ayons entendu, ayez entendu, aient entendu
Plup. Subj.	eusse entendu, eusses entendu, eût entendu; eussions entendu, eussiez entendu, eussent entendu
Imperative	entends, entendons, entendez

to bury

Pres. Ind.	enterre, enterres, enterre; enterrons, enterrez, enterrent
Imp. Ind.	enterrais, enterrais, enterrait; enterrions, enterriez, enterraient
Past Def.	enterrai, enterras, enterra; enterrâmes, enterrâtes, enterrèrent
Future	enterrerai, enterreras, enterrera; enterrerons, enterrerez, enterreront
Condit.	enterrerais, enterrerais, enterrerait; enterrerions, enterreriez, enterreraient
Pres. Subj.	enterre, enterres, enterre; enterrions, enterriez, enterrent
Imp. Subj.	enterrasse, enterrasses, enterrât; enterrassions, enterrassiez, enterrassent
Past Indef.	ai enterré, as enterré, a enterré; avons enterré, avez enterré, ont enterré
Plup. Ind.	avais enterré, avais enterré, avait enterré; avions enterré, aviez enterré, avaient enterré
Past Ant.	eus enterré, eus enterré, eut enterré; eûmes enterré, eûtes enterré, eurent enterré
Fut. Perf.	aurai enterré, auras enterré, aura enterré; aurons enterré, aurez enterré, auront enterré
Cond. Perf.	aurais enterré, aurais enterré, aurait enterré; aurions enterré, auriez enterré, auraient enterré
Past Subj.	aie enterré, aies enterré, ait enterré; ayons enterré, ayez enterré, aient enterré
Plup. Subj.	eusse enterré, eusses enterré, eût enterré; eussions enterré, eussiez enterré, eussent enterré
Imperative	enterre, enterrons, enterrez

to undertake, engage upon

Pres. Ind.	entreprends, entreprends, entreprend; entreprenons, entreprenez, entreprennent
Imp. Ind.	entreprenais, entreprenais, entreprenait; entreprenions, entrepreniez, entreprenaient
Past Def.	entrepris, entrepris, entreprit; entreprîmes, entreprîtes, entreprirent
Future	entreprendrai, entreprendras, entreprendra; entreprendrons, entreprendrez, entreprendront
Condit.	entreprendrais, entreprendrais, entreprendrait; entreprendrions, entreprendriez, entreprendraient
Pres. Subj.	entreprenne, entreprennes, entreprenne; entreprenions, entrepreniez, entreprennent
Imp. Subj.	entreprisse, entreprisses, entreprît; entreprissions, entreprissiez, entreprissent
Past Indef.	ai entrepris, as entrepris, a entrepris; avons entrepris, avez entrepris, ont entrepris
Plup. Ind.	avais entrepris, avais entrepris, avait entrepris; avions entrepris, aviez entrepris, avaient entrepris
Past Ant.	eus entrepris, eus entrepris, eut entrepris; eûmes entrepris, eûtes entrepris, eurent entrepris
Fut. Perf.	aurai entrepris, auras entrepris, aura entrepris; aurons entrepris, aurez entrepris, auront entrepris
Cond. Perf.	aurais entrepris, aurais entrepris, aurait entrepris; aurions entrepris, auriez entrepris, auraient entrepris
Past Subj.	aie entrepris, aies entrepris, ait entrepris; ayons entrepris, ayez entrepris, aient entrepris
Plup. Subj.	eusse entrepris, eusses entrepris, eût entrepris; eussions entrepris, eussiez entrepris, eussent entrepris
Imperative	entreprends, entreprenons, entreprenez

to enter, come in, go in

Pres. Ind.	entre, entres, entre; entrons, entrez, entrent
Imp. Ind.	entrais, entrais, entrait; entrions, entriez, entraient
Past Def.	entrai, entras, entra; entrâmes, entrâtes, entrèrent
Fut. Ind.	entrerai, entreras, entrera; entrerons, entrerez, entreront
Condit.	entrerais, entrerais, entrerait; entrerions, entreriez, entreraient
Pres. Subj.	entre, entres, entre; entrions, entriez, entrent
Imp. Subj.	entrasse, entrasses, entrât; entrassions, entrassiez, entrassent
Past Indef.	suis entré(e), es entré(e), est entré(e); sommes entré(e)s, êtes entré(e)(s), sont entré(e)s
Pluperf.	étais entré(e), étais entré(e), était entré(e); étions entré(e)s, étiez entré(e)(s), étaient entré(e)s
Past Ant.	fus entré(e), fus entré(e), fut entré(e); fûmes entré(e)s, fûtes entré(e)(s), furent entré(e)s
Fut. Perf.	serai entré(e), seras entré(e), sera entré(e); serons entré(e)s, serez entré(e)(s), seront entré(e)s
Cond. Perf.	serais entré(e), serais entré(e), serait entré(e); serions entré(e)s, seriez entré(e)(s), seraient entré(e)s
Past Subj.	sois entré(e), sois entré(e), soit entré(e); soyons entré(e)s, soyez entré(e)(s), soient entré(e)s
Plup. Subj.	fusse entré(e), fusses entré(e), fût entré(e); fussions entré(e)s, fussiez entré(e)(s), fussent entré(e)s
Imperative	entre, entrons, entrez

to fly off, take flight, take wing, take off (airplane)

Pres. Ind.	m'envole, t'envoles, s'envole; nous envolons, vous envolez, s'envolent
Imp. Ind.	m'envolais, t'envolais, s'envolait; nous envolions, vous envoliez, s'envolaient
Past Def.	m'envolai, t'envolas, s'envola; nous envolâmes, vous envolâtes, s'envolèrent
Future	m'envolerai, t'envoleras, s'envolera; nous envolerons, vous envolerez, s'envoleront
Condit.	m'envolerais, t'envolerais, s'envolerait; nous envolerions, vous envoleriez, s'envoleraient
Pres. Subj.	m'envole, t'envoles, s'envole; nous envolions, vous envoliez, s'envolent
Imp. Subj.	m'envolasse, t'envolasses, s'envolât; nous envolassions, vous envolassiez, s'envolassent
Past Indef.	me suis envolé(e), t'es envolé(e), s'est envolé(e); nous sommes envolé(e)s, vous êtes envolé(e)(s), se sont envolé(e)s
Plup. Ind.	m'étais envolé(e), t'étais envolé(e), s'était envolé(e); nous étions envolé(e)s, vous étiez envolé(e)(s), s'étaient envolé(e)s
Past Ant.	me fus envolé(e), te fus envolé(e), se fut envolé(e); nous fûmes envolé(e)s, vous fûtes envolé(e)(s), se furent envolé(e)s
Fut. Perf.	me serai envolé(e), te seras envolé(e), se sera envolé(e); nous serons envolé(e)s, vous serez envolé(e)(s), se seront envolé(e)s
Cond. Perf.	me serais envolé(e), te serais envolé(e), se serait envolé(e); nous serions envolé(e)s, vous seriez envolé(e)(s), se seraient envolé(e)s
Past Subj.	me sois envolé(e), te sois envolé(e), se soit envolé(e); nous soyons envolé(e)s, vous soyez envolé(e)(s), se soient envolé(e)s
Plup. Subj.	me fusse envolé(e), te fusses envolé(e), se fût envolé(e); nous fussions envolé(e)s, vous fussiez envolé(e)(s), se fussent envolé(e)s
Imperative	envole-toi, envolons-nous, envolez-vous

to send

Pres. Ind.	envoie, envoies, envoie; envoyons, envoyez, envoient
Imp. Ind.	envoyais, envoyais, envoyait; envoyions, envoyiez, envoyaient
Past Def.	envoyai, envoyas, envoya; envoyâmes, envoyâtes, envoyèrent
Fut. Ind.	enverrai, enverras, enverra; enverrons, enverrez, enverront
Condit.	enverrais, enverrais, enverrait; enverrions, enverriez, enverraient
Pres. Subj.	envoie, envoies, envoie; envoyions, envoyiez, envoient
Imp. Subj.	envoyasse, envoyasses, envoyât; envoyassions, envoyassiez, envoyassent
Past Indef.	ai envoyé, as envoyé, a envoyé; avons envoyé, avez envoyé, ont envoyé
Pluperf.	avais envoyé, avais envoyé, avait envoyé; avions envoyé, aviez envoyé, avaient envoyé
Past Ant.	eus envoyé, eus envoyé, eut envoyé; eûmes envoyé, eûtes envoyé, eurent envoyé
Fut. Perf.	aurai envoyé, auras envoyé, aura envoyé; aurons envoyé, aurez envoyé, auront envoyé
Cond. Perf.	aurais envoyé, aurais envoyé, aurait envoyé; aurions envoyé, auriez envoyé, auraient envoyé
Past Subj.	aie envoyé, aies envoyé, ait envoyé; ayons envoyé, ayez envoyé, aient envoyé
Plup. Subj.	eusse envoyé, eusses envoyé, eût envoyé; eussions envoyé, eussiez envoyé, eussent envoyé
Imperative	envoie, envoyons, envoyez

to save (money)

Pres. Ind.	épargne, épargnes, épargne; épargnons, épargnez, épargnent
Imp. Ind.	épargnais, épargnais, épargnait; épargnions, épargniez, épargnaient
Past Def.	épargnai, épargnas, épargna; épargnâmes, épargnâtes, épargnèrent
Future	épargnerai, épargneras, épargnera; épargnerons, épargnerez, épargneront
Condit.	épargnerais, épargnerais, épargnerait; épargnerions, épargneriez, épargneraient
Pres. Subj.	épargne, épargnes, épargne; épargnions, épargniez, épargnent
Imp. Subj.	épargnasse, épargnasses, épargnât; épargnassions, épargnassiez, épargnassent
Past Indef.	ai épargné, as épargné, a épargné; avons épargné, avez épargné, ont épargné
Plup. Ind.	avais épargné, avais épargné, avait épargné; avions épargné, aviez épargné, avaient épargné
Past Ant.	eus épargné, eus épargné, eut épargné; eûmes épargné, eûtes épargné, eurent épargné
Fut. Perf.	aurai épargné, auras épargné, aura épargné; aurons épargné, aurez épargné, auront épargné
Cond. Perf.	aurais épargné, aurais épargné, aurait épargné; aurions épargné, auriez épargné, auraient épargné
Past Subj.	aie épargné, aies épargné, ait épargné; ayons épargné, ayez épargné, aient épargné
Plup. Subj.	eusse épargné, eusses épargné, eût épargné; eussions épargné, eussiez épargné, eussent épargné
Imperative	épargne, épargnons, épargnez

to marry, wed

Pres. Ind.	épouse, épouses, épouse; épousons, épousez, épousent
Imp. Ind.	épousais, épousais, épousait; épousions, épousiez, épousaient
Past Def.	épousai, épousas, épousa; épousâmes, épousâtes, épousèrent
Future	épouserai, épouseras, épousera; épouserons, épouserez, épouseront
Condit.	épouserais, épouserais, épouserait; épouserions, épouseriez, épouseraient
Pres. Subj.	épouse, épouses, épouse; épousions, épousiez, épousent
Imp. Subj.	épousasse, épousasses, épousât; épousassions, épousassiez, épousassent
Past Indef.	ai épousé, as épousé, a épousé; avons épousé, avez épousé, ont épousé
Plup. Ind.	avais épousé, avais épousé, avait épousé; avions épousé, aviez épousé, avaient épousé
Past Ant.	eus épousé, eus épousé, eut épousé; eûmes épousé, eûtes épousé, eurent épousé
Fut. Perf.	aurai épousé, auras épousé, aura épousé; aurons épousé, aurez épousé, auront épousé
Cond. Perf.	aurais épousé, aurais épousé, aurait épousé; aurions épousé, auriez épousé, auraient épousé
Past Subj.	aie épousé, aies épousé, ait épousé; ayons épousé, ayez épousé, aient épousé
Plup. Subj.	eusse épousé, eusses épousé, eût épousé; eussions épousé, eussiez épousé, eussent épousé
Imperative	épouse, épousons, épousez

to try, test, put to the test, feel, experience

Pres. Ind.	éprouve, éprouves, éprouve; éprouvons, éprouvez, éprouvent
Imp. Ind.	éprouvais, éprouvais, éprouvait; éprouvions, éprouviez, éprouvaient
Past Def.	éprouvai, éprouvas, éprouva; éprouvâmes, éprouvâtes, éprouvèrent
Future	éprouverai, éprouveras, éprouvera; éprouverons, éprouverez, éprouveront
Condit.	éprouverais, éprouverais, éprouverait; éprouverions, éprouveriez, éprouveraient
Pres. Subj.	éprouve, éprouves, éprouve; éprouvions, éprouviez, éprouvent
Imp. Subj.	éprouvasse, éprouvasses, éprouvât; éprouvassions, éprouvassiez, éprouvassent
Past Indef.	ai éprouvé, as éprouvé, a éprouvé; avons éprouvé, avez éprouvé, ont éprouvé
Plup. Ind.	avais éprouvé, avais éprouvé, avait éprouvé; avions éprouvé, aviez éprouvé, avaient éprouvé
Past Ant.	eus éprouvé, eus éprouvé, eut éprouvé; eûmes éprouvé, eûtes éprouvé, eurent éprouvé
Fut. Perf.	aurai éprouvé, auras éprouvé, aura éprouvé; aurons éprouvé, aurez éprouvé, auront éprouvé
Cond. Perf.	aurais éprouvé, aurais éprouvé, aurait éprouvé; aurions éprouvé, auriez éprouvé, auraient éprouvé
Past Subj.	aie éprouvé, aies éprouvé, ait éprouvé; ayons éprouvé, ayez éprouvé, aient éprouvé
Plup. Subj.	eusse éprouvé, eusses éprouvé, eût éprouvé; eussions éprouvé, eussiez éprouvé, eussent éprouvé
Imperative	éprouve, éprouvons, éprouvez

to hope

Pres. Ind.	espère, espères, espère; espérons, espérez, espèrent
Imp. Ind.	espérais, espérais, espérait; espérions, espériez, espéraient
Past Def.	espérai, espéras, espéra; espérâmes, espérâtes, espérèrent
Fut. Ind.	espérerai, espéreras, espérera; espérerons, espérerez, espéreront
Condit.	espérerais, espérerais, espérerait; espérerions, espéreriez, espéreraient
Pres. Subj.	espère, espères, espère; espérions, espériez, espèrent
Imp. Subj.	espérasse, espérasses, espérât; espérassions, espérassiez, espérassent
Past Indef.	ai espéré, as espéré, a espéré; avons espéré, avez espéré, ont espéré
Pluperf.	avais espéré, avais espéré, avait espéré; avions espéré, aviez espéré, avaient espéré
Past Ant.	eus espéré, eus espéré, eut espéré; eûmes espéré, eûtes espéré, eurent espéré
Fut. Perf.	aurai espéré, auras espéré, aura espéré; aurons espéré, aurez espéré, auront espéré
Cond. Perf.	aurais espéré, aurais espéré, aurait espéré; aurions espéré, auriez espéré, auraient espéré
Past Subj.	aie espéré, aies espéré, ait espéré; ayons espéré, ayez espéré, aient espéré
Plup. Subj.	eusse espéré, eusses espéré, eût espéré; eussions espéré, eussiez espéré, eussent espéré
Imperative	espère, espérons, espérez

to try

Pres. Ind.	essaye, essayes, essaye; essayons, essayez, essayent
Imp. Ind.	essayais, essayais, essayait; essayions, essayiez, essayaient
Past Def.	essayai, essayas, essaya; essayâmes, essayâtes, essayèrent
Fut. Ind.	essayerai, essayeras, essayera; essayerons, essayerez, essayeront
Condit.	essayerais, essayerais, essayerait; essayerions, essayeriez, essayeraient
Pres. Subj.	essaye, essayes, essaye; essayions, essayiez, essayent
Imp. Subj.	essayasse, essayasses, essayât; essayassions, essayassiez, essayassent
Past Indef.	ai essayé, as essayé, a essayé; avons essayé, avez essayé, ont essayé
Pluperf.	avais essayé, avais essayé, avait essayé; avions essayé, aviez essayé, avaient essayé
Past Ant.	eus essayé, eus essayé, eut essayé; eûmes essayé, eûtes essayé, eurent essayé
Fut. Perf.	aurai essayé, auras essayé, aura essayé; aurons essayé, aurez essayé, auront essayé
Cond. Perf.	aurais essayé, aurais essayé, aurait essayé; aurions essayé, auriez essayé, auraient essayé
Past Subj.	aie essayé, aies essayé, ait essayé; ayons essayé, ayez essayé, aient essayé
Plup. Subj.	eusse essayé, eusses essayé, eût essayé; eussions essayé, eussiez essayé, eussent essayé
Imperative	essaye, essayons, essayez

to wipe

Pres. Ind.	essuie, essuies, essuie; essuyons, essuyez, essuient
Imp. Ind.	essuyais, essuyais, essuyait; essuyions, essuyiez, essuyaient
Past Def.	essuyai, essuyas, essuya; essuyâmes, essuyâtes, essuyèrent
Fut. Ind.	essuierai, essuieras, essuiera; essuierons, essuierez, essuieront
Condit.	essuierais, essuierais, essuierait; essuierions, essuieriez, essuieraient
Pres. Subj.	essuie, essuies, essuie; essuyions, essuyiez, essuient
Imp. Subj.	essuyasse, essuyasses, essuyât; essuyassions, essuyassiez, essuyassent
Past Indef.	ai essuyé, as essuyé, a essuyé; avons essuyé, avez essuyé, ont essuyé
Pluperf.	avais essuyé, avais essuyé, avait essuyé; avions essuyé, aviez essuyé, avaient essuyé
Past Ant.	eus essuyé, eus essuyé, eut essuyé; eûmes essuyé, eûtes essuyé, eurent essuyé
Fut. Perf.	aurai essuyé, auras essuyé, aura essuyé; aurons essuyé, aurez essuyé, auront essuyé
Cond. Perf.	aurais essuyé, aurais essuyé, aurait essuyé; aurions essuyé, auriez essuyé, auraient essuyé
Past Subj.	aie essuyé, aies essuyé, ait essuyé; ayons essuyé, ayez essuyé, aient essuyé
Plup. Subj.	eusse essuyé, eusses essuyé, eût essuyé; eussions essuyé, eussiez essuyé, eussent essuyé
Imperative	essuie, essuyons, essuyez

to establish

Pres. Ind.	établis, établis, établit; établissons, établissez, établissent
Imp. Ind.	établissais, établissais, établissait; établissions, établissiez, établissaient
Past Def.	établis, établis, établit; établîmes, établîtes, établirent
Future	établirai, établiras, établira; établirons, établirez, établiront
Condit.	établirais, établirais, établirait; établirions, établiriez, établiraient
Pres. Subj.	établisse, établisses, établisse; établissions, établissiez, établissent
Imp. Subj.	établisse, établisses, établît; établissions, établissiez, établissent
Past Indef.	ai établi, as établi, a établi; avons établi, avez établi, ont établi
Pluperf.	avais établi, avais établi, avait établi; avions établi, aviez établi, avaient établi
Past Ant.	eus établi, eus établi, eut établi; eûmes établi, eûtes établi, eurent établi
Fut. Perf.	aurai établi, auras établi, aura établi; aurons établi, aurez établi, auront établi
Cond. Perf.	aurais établi, aurais établi, aurait établi; aurions établi, auriez établi, auraient établi
Past Subj.	aie établi, aies établi, ait établi; ayons établi, ayez établi, aient établi
Plup. Subj.	eusse établi, eusses établi, eût établi; eussions établi, eussiez établi, eussent établi
Imperative	établis, établissons, établissez

to extinguish

Pres. Ind.	éteins, éteins, éteint; éteignons, éteignez, éteignent
Imp. Ind.	éteignais, éteignais, éteignait; éteignions, éteigniez, éteignaient
Past Def.	éteignis, éteignis, éteignit; éteignîmes, éteignîtes, éteignirent
Future	éteindrai, éteindras, éteindra; éteindrons, éteindrez, éteindront
Condit.	éteindrais, éteindrais, éteindrait; éteindrions, éteindriez, éteindraient
Pres. Subj.	éteigne, éteignes, éteigne; éteignions, éteigniez, éteignent
Imp. Subj.	éteignisse, éteignisses, éteignît; éteignissions, éteignissiez, éteignissent
Past Indef.	ai éteint, as éteint, a éteint; avons éteint, avez éteint, ont éteint
Pluperf.	avais éteint, avais éteint, avait éteint; avions éteint, aviez éteint, avaient éteint
Past Ant.	eus éteint, eus éteint, eut éteint; eûmes éteint, eûtes éteint, eurent éteint
Fut. Perf.	aurai éteint, auras éteint, aura éteint; aurons éteint, aurez éteint, auront éteint
Cond. Perf.	aurais éteint, aurais éteint, aurait éteint; aurions éteint, auriez éteint, auraient éteint
Past Subj.	aie éteint, aies éteint, ait éteint; ayons éteint, ayez éteint, aient éteint
Plup. Subj.	eusse éteint, eusses éteint, eût éteint; eussions éteint, eussiez éteint, eussent éteint
Imperative	éteins, éteignons, éteignez

to stretch oneself, stretch out, lie down

Pres. Ind.	m'étends, t'étends, s'étend; nous étendons, vous étendez, s'étendent
Imp. Ind.	m'étendais, t'étendais, s'étendait; nous étendions, vous étendiez, s'étendaient
Past Def.	m'étendis, t'étendis, s'étendit; nous étendîmes, vous étendîtes, s'étendirent
Future	m'étendrai, t'étendras, s'étendra; nous étendrons, vous étendrez, s'étendront
Condit.	m'étendrais, t'étendrais, s'étendrait; nous étendrions, vous étendriez, s'étendraient
Pres. Subj.	m'étende, t'étendes, s'étende; nous étendions, vous étendiez, s'étendent
Imp. Subj.	m'étendisse, t'étendisses, s'étendît; nous étendissions, vous étendissiez, s'étendissent
Past Indef.	me suis étendu(e), t'es étendu(e), s'est étendu(e); nous sommes étendu(e)s, vous êtes étendu(e)(s), se sont étendu(e)s
Plup. Ind.	m'étais étendu(e), t'étais étendu(e), s'était étendu(e); nous étions étendu(e)s, vous étiez étendu(e)(s), s'étaient étendu(e)s
Past Ant.	me fus étendu(e), te fus étendu(e), se fut étendu(e); nous fûmes étendu(e)s, vous fûtes étendu(e)(s), se furent étendu(e)s
Fut. Perf.	me serai étendu(e), te seras étendu(e), se sera étendu(e); nous serons étendu(e)s, vous serez étendu(e)(s), se seront étendu(e)s
Cond. Perf.	me serais étendu(e), te serais étendu(e), se serait étendu(e); nous serions étendu(e)s, vous seriez étendu(e)(s), se seraient étendu(e)s
Past Subj.	me sois étendu(e), te sois étendu(e), se soit étendu(e); nous soyons étendu(e)s, vous soyez étendu(e)(s), se soient étendu(e)s
Plup. Subj.	me fusse étendu(e), te fusses étendu(e), se fût étendu(e); nous fussions étendu(e)s, vous fussiez étendu(e)(s), se fussent étendu(e)s
Imperative	étends-toi, étendons-nous, étendez-vous

to amaze, astonish, stun

Pres. Ind.	étonne, étonnes, étonne; étonnons, étonnez, étonnent
Imp. Ind.	étonnais, étonnais, étonnait; étonnions, étonniez, étonnaient
Past Def.	étonnai, étonnas, étonna; étonnâmes, étonnâtes, étonnèrent
Future	étonnerai, étonneras, étonnera; étonnerons, étonnerez, étonneront
Condit.	étonnerais, étonnerais, étonnerait; étonnerions, étonneriez, étonneraient
Pres. Subj.	étonne, étonnes, étonne; étonnions, étonniez, étonnent
Imp. Subj.	étonnasse, étonnasses, étonnât; étonnassions, étonnassiez, étonnassent
Past Indef.	ai étonné, as étonné, a étonné; avons étonné, avez étonné, ont étonné
Plup. Ind.	avais étonné, avais étonné, avait étonné; avions étonné, aviez étonné, avaient étonné
Past Ant.	eus étonné, eus étonné, eut étonné; eûmes étonné, eûtes étonné, eurent étonné
Fut. Perf.	aurai étonné, auras étonné, aura étonné; aurons étonné, aurez étonné, auront étonné
Cond. Perf.	aurais étonné, aurais étonné, aurait étonné; aurions étonné, auriez étonné, auraient étonné
Past Subj.	aie étonné, aies étonné, ait étonné; ayons étonné, ayez étonné, aient étonné
Plup. Subj.	eusse étonné, eusses étonné, eût étonné; eussions étonné, eussiez étonné, eussent étonné
Imperative	étonne, étonnons, étonnez

to daze, stun, deafen, make dizzy, bewilder

Pres. Ind.	étourdis, étourdis, étourdit; étourdissons, étourdissez, étourdissent
Imp. Ind.	étourdissais, étourdissais, étourdissait; étourdissions, étourdissiez, étourdissaient
Past Def.	étourdis, étourdis, étourdit; étourdîmes, étourdîtes, étourdirent
Future	étourdirai, étourdiras, étourdira; étourdirons, étourdirez, étourdiront
Condit.	étourdirais, étourdirais, étourdirait; étourdirions, étourdiriez, étourdiraient
Pres. Subj.	étourdisse, étourdisses, étourdisse; étourdissions, étourdissiez, étourdissent
Imp. Subj.	étourdisse, étourdisses, étourdît; étourdissions, étourdissiez, étourdissent
Past Indef.	ai étourdi, as étourdi, a étourdi; avons étourdi, avez étourdi, ont étourdi
Pluperf.	avais étourdi, avais étourdi, avait étourdi; avions étourdi, aviez étourdi, avaient étourdi
Past Ant.	eus étourdi, eus étourdi, eut étourdi; eûmes étourdi, eûtes étourdi, eurent étourdi
Fut. Perf.	aurai étourdi, auras étourdi, aura étourdi; aurons étourdi, aurez étourdi, auront étourdi
Cond. Perf.	aurais étourdi, aurais étourdi, aurait étourdi; aurions étourdi, auriez étourdi, auraient étourdi
Past Subj.	aie étourdi, aies étourdi, ait étourdi; ayons étourdi, ayez étourdi, aient étourdi
Plup. Subj.	eusse étourdi, eusses étourdi, eût étourdi; eussions étourdi, eussiez étourdi, eussent étourdi
Imperative	étourdis, étourdissons, étourdissez

to be

Pres. Ind.	suis, es, est; sommes, êtes, sont
Imp. Ind.	étais, étais, était; étions, étiez, étaient
Past Def.	fus, fus, fut; fûmes, fûtes, furent
Fut. Ind.	serai, seras, sera; serons, serez, seront
Condit.	serais, serais, serait; serions, seriez, seraient
Pres. Subj.	sois, sois, soit; soyons, soyez, soient
Imp. Subj.	fusse, fusses, fût; fussions, fussiez, fussent
Past Indef.	ai été, as été, a été; avons été, avez été, ont été
Pluperf.	avais été, avais été, avait été; avions été, aviez été, avaient été
Past Ant.	eus été, eus été, eut été; eûmes été, eûtes été, eurent été
Fut. Perf.	aurai été, auras été, aura été; aurons été, aurez été, auront été
Cond. Perf.	aurais été, aurais été, aurait été; aurions été, auriez été, auraient été
Past Subj.	aie été, aies été, ait été; ayons été, ayez été, aient été
Plup. Subj.	eusse été, eusses été, eût été; eussions été, eussiez été, eussent été
Imperative	sois, soyons, soyez

to embrace, grip

Pres. Ind.	étreins, étreins, étreint; étreignons, étreignez, étreignent
Imp. Ind.	étreignais, étreignais, étreignait; étreignions, étreigniez, étreignaient
Past Def.	étreignis, étreignis, étreignit; étreignîmes, étreignîtes, étreignirent
Future	étreindrai, étreindras, étreindra; étreindrons, étreindrez, étreindront
Condit.	étreindrais, étreindrais, étreindrait; étreindrions, étreindriez, étreindraient
Pres. Subj.	étreigne, étreignes, étreigne; étreignions, étreigniez, étreignent
Imp. Subj.	étreignisse, étreignisses, étreignît; étreignissions, étreignissiez, étreignissent
Past Indef.	ai étreint, as étreint, a étreint; avons étreint, avez étreint, ont étreint
Plup. Ind.	avais étreint, avais étreint, avait étreint; avions étreint, aviez étreint, avaient étreint
Past Ant.	eus étreint, eus étreint, eut étreint; eûmes étreint, eûtes étreint, eurent étreint
Fut. Perf.	aurai étreint, auras étreint, aura étreint; aurons étreint, aurez étreint, auront étreint
Cond. Perf.	aurais étreint, aurais étreint, aurait étreint; aurions étreint, auriez étreint, auraient étreint
Past Subj.	aie étreint, aies étreint, ait étreint; ayons étreint, ayez étreint, aient étreint
Plup. Subj.	eusse étreint, eusses étreint, eût étreint; eussions étreint, eussiez étreint, eussent étreint
Imperative	étreins, étreignons, étreignez

to study

Pres. Ind.	étudie, étudies, étudie; étudions, étudiez, étudient
Imp. Ind.	étudiais, étudiais, étudiait; étudiions, étudiiez, étudiaient
Past Def.	étudiai, étudias, étudia; étudiâmes, étudiâtes, étudièrent
Fut. Ind.	étudierai, étudieras, étudiera; étudierons, étudierez, étudieront
Condit.	étudierais, étudierais, étudierait; étudierions, étudieriez, étudieraient
Pres. Subj.	étudie, étudies, étudie; étudiions, étudiiez, étudient
Imp. Subj.	étudiasse, étudiasses, étudiât; étudiassions, étudiassiez, étudiassent
Past Indef.	ai étudié, as étudié, a étudié; avons étudié, avez étudié, ont étudié
Pluperf.	avais étudié, avais étudié, avait étudié; avions étudié, aviez étudié, avaient étudié
Past Ant.	eus étudié, eus étudié, eut étudié; eûmes étudié, eûtes étudié, eurent étudié
Fut. Perf.	aurai étudié, auras étudié, aura étudié; aurons étudié, aurez étudié, auront étudié
Cond. Perf.	aurais étudié, aurais étudié, aurait étudié; aurions étudié, auriez étudié, auraient étudié
Past Subj.	aie étudié, aies étudié, ait étudié; ayons étudié, ayez étudié, aient étudié
Plup. Subj.	eusse étudié, eusses étudié, eût étudié; eussions étudié, eussiez étudié, eussent étudié
Imperative	étudie, étudions, étudiez

to appraise, assess, estimate, evaluate

Pres. Ind.	évalue, évalues, évalue; évaluons, évaluez, évaluent
Imp. Ind.	évaluais, évaluais, évaluait; évaluions, évaluiez, évaluaient
Past Def.	évaluai, évaluas, évalua; évaluâmes, évaluâtes, évaluèrent
Future	évaluerai, évalueras, évaluera; évaluerons, évaluerez, évalueront
Condit.	évaluerais, évaluerais, évaluerait; évaluerions, évalueriez, évalueraient
Pres. Subj.	évalue, évalues, évalue; évaluions, évaluiez, évaluent
Imp. Subj.	évaluasse, évaluasses, évaluât; évaluassions, évaluassiez, évaluassent
Past Indef.	ai évalué, as évalué, a évalué; avons évalué, avez évalué, ont évalué
Plup. Ind.	avais évalué, avais évalué, avait évalué; avions évalué, aviez évalué, avaient évalué
Past Ant.	eus évalué, eus évalué, eut évalué; eûmes évalué, eûtes évalué, eurent évalué
Fut. Perf.	aurai évalué, auras évalué, aura évalué; aurons évalué, aurez évalué, auront évalué
Cond. Perf.	aurais évalué, aurais évalué, aurait évalué; aurions évalué, auriez évalué, auraient évalué
Past Subj.	aie évalué, aies évalué, ait évalué; ayons évalué, ayez évalué, aient évalué
Plup. Subj.	eusse évalué, eusses évalué, eût évalué; eussions évalué, eussiez évalué, eussent évalué
Imperative	évalue, évaluons, évaluez

to faint, lose consciousness, swoon

Pres. Ind.	m'évanouis, t'évanouis, s'évanouit; nous évanouissons, vous évanouissez, s'évanouissent
Imp. Ind.	m'évanouissais, t'évanouissais, s'évanouissait; nous évanouissions, vous évanouissiez, s'évanouissaient
Past Def.	m'évanouis, t'évanouis, s'évanouit; nous évanouîmes, vous évanouîtes, s'évanouirent
Future	m'évanouirai, t'évanouiras, s'évanouira; nous évanouirons, vous évanouirez, s'évanouiront
Condit.	m'évanouirais, t'évanouirais, s'évanouirait; nous évanouirions, vous évanouiriez, s'évanouiraient
Pres. Subj.	m'évanouisse, t'évanouisses, s'évanouisse; nous évanouissions, vous évanouissiez, s'évanouissent
Imp. Subj.	m'évanouisse, t'évanouisses, s'évanouît; nous évanouissions, vous évanouissiez, s'évanouissent
Past Indef.	me suis évanoui(e), t'es évanoui(e), s'est évanoui(e); nous sommes évanoui(e)s, vous êtes évanoui(e)(s), se sont évanoui(e)s
Plup. Ind.	m'étais évanoui(e), t'étais évanoui(e), s'était évanoui(e); nous étions évanoui(e)s, vous étiez évanoui(e)(s), s'étaient évanoui(e)s
Past Ant.	me fus évanoui(e), te fus évanoui(e), se fut évanoui(e); nous fûmes évanoui(e)s, vous fûtes évanoui(e)(s), se furent évanoui(e)s
Fut. Perf.	me serai évanoui(e), te seras évanoui(e), se sera évanoui(e); nous serons évanoui(e)s, vous serez évanoui(e)(s), se seront évanoui(e)s
Cond. Perf.	me serais évanoui(e), te serais évanoui(e), se serait évanoui(e); nous serions évanoui(e)s, vous seriez évanoui(e)(s), se seraient évanoui(e)s
Past Subj.	me sois évanoui(e), te sois évanoui(e), se soit évanoui(e); nous soyons évanoui(e)s, vous soyez évanoui(e)(s), se soient évanoui(e)s
Plup. Subj.	me fusse évanoui(e), te fusses évanoui(e), se fût évanoui(e); nous fussions évanoui(e)s, vous fussiez évanoui(e)(s), se fussent évanoui(e)s
Imperative	[ordinairement inemployé]

to exclude

Pres. Ind.	exclus, exclus, exclut; excluons, excluez, excluent
Imp. Ind.	excluais, excluais, excluait; excluions, excluiez, excluaient
Past Def.	exclus, exclus, exclut; exclûmes, exclûtes, exclurent
Future	exclurai, excluras, exclura; exclurons, exclurez, excluront
Condit.	exclurais, exclurais, exclurait; exclurions, excluriez, excluraient
Pres. Subj.	exclue, exclues, exclue; excluions, excluiez, excluent
Imp. Subj.	exclusse, exclusses, exclût; exclussions, exclussiez, exclussent
Past Indef.	ai exclu, as exclu, a exclu; avons exclu, avez exclu, ont exclu
Plup. Ind.	avais exclu, avais exclu, avait exclu; avions exclu, aviez exclu, avaient exclu
Past Ant.	eus exclu, eus exclu, eut exclu; eûmes exclu, eûtes exclu, eurent exclu
Fut. Perf.	aurai exclu, auras exclu, aura exclu; aurons exclu, aurez exclu, auront exclu
Cond. Perf.	aurais exclu, aurais exclu, aurait exclu; aurions exclu, auriez exclu, auraient exclu
Past Subj.	aie exclu, aies exclu, ait exclu; ayons exclu, ayez exclu, aient exclu
Plup. Subj.	eusse exclu, eusses exclu, eût exclu; eussions exclu, eussiez exclu, eussent exclu
Imperative	exclus, excluons, excluez

to apologize, excuse oneself

Pres. Ind.	m'excuse, t'excuses, s'excuse; nous excusons, vous excusez, s'excusent
Imp. Ind.	m'excusais, t'excusais, s'excusait; nous excusions, vous excusiez, s'excusaient
Past Def.	m'excusai, t'excusas, s'excusa; nous excusâmes, vous excusâtes, s'excusèrent
Future	m'excuserai, t'excuseras, s'excusera; nous excuserons, vous excuserez, s'excuseront
Condit.	m'excuserais, t'excuserais, s'excuserait; nous excuserions, vous excuseriez, s'excuseraient
Pres. Subj.	m'excuse, t'excuses, s'excuse; nous excusions, vous excusiez, s'excusent
Imp. Subj.	m'excusasse, t'excusasses, s'excusât; nous excusassions, vous excusassiez, s'excusassent
Past Indef.	me suis excusé(e), t'es excusé(e), s'est excusé(e); nous sommes excusé(e)s, vous êtes excusé(e)(s), se sont excusé(e)s
Plup. Ind.	m'étais excusé(e), t'étais excusé(e), s'était excusé(e); nous étions excusé(e)s, vous étiez excusé(e)(s), s'étaient excusé(e)s
Past Ant.	me fus excusé(e), te fus excusé(e), se fut excusé(e); nous fûmes excusé(e)s, vous fûtes excusé(e)(s), se furent excusé(e)s
Fut. Perf.	me serai excusé(e), te seras excusé(e), se sera excusé(e); nous serons excusé(e)s, vous serez excusé(e)(s), se seront excusé(e)s
Cond. Perf.	me serais excusé(e), te serais excusé(e), se serait excusé(e); nous serions excusé(e)s, vous seriez excusé(e)(s), se seraient excusé(e)s
Past Subj.	me sois excusé(e), te sois excusé(e), se soit excusé(e); nous soyons excusé(e)s, vous soyez excusé(e)(s), se soient excusé(e)s
Plup. Subj.	me fusse excusé(e), te fusses excusé(e), se fût excusé(e); nous fussions excusé(e)s, vous fussiez excusé(e)(s), se fussent excusé(e)s
Imperative	excuse-toi, excusons-nous, excusez-vous

to demand, require

Pres. Ind.	exige, exiges, exige; exigeons, exigez, exigent
Imp. Ind.	exigeais, exigeais, exigeait; exigions, exigiez, exigeaient
Past Def.	exigeai, exigeas, exigea; exigeâmes, exigeâtes, exigèrent
Future	exigerai, exigeras, exigera; exigerons, exigerez, exigeront
Condit.	exigerais, exigerais, exigerait; exigerions, exigeriez, exigeraient
Pres. Subj.	exige, exiges, exige; exigions, exigiez, exigent
Imp. Subj.	exigeasse, exigeasses, exigeât; exigeassions, exigeassiez, exigeassent
Past Def.	ai exigé, as exigé, a exigé; avons exigé, avez exigé, ont exigé
Plup. Ind.	avais exigé, avais exigé, avait exigé; avions exigé, aviez exigé, avaient exigé
Past Ant.	eus exigé, eus exigé, eut exigé; eûmes exigé, eûtes exigé, eurent exigé
Fut. Perf.	aurai exigé, auras exigé, aura exigé; aurons exigé, aurez exigé, auront exigé
Cond. Perf.	aurais exigé, aurais exigé, aurait exigé; aurions exigé, auriez exigé, auraient exigé
Past Subj.	aie exigé, aies exigé, ait exigé; ayons exigé, ayez exigé, aient exigé
Plup. Subj.	eusse exigé, eusses exigé, eût exigé; eussions exigé, eussiez exigé, eussent exigé
Imperative	exige, exigeons, exigez

to explain

Pres. Ind.	explique, expliques, explique; expliquons, expliquez, expliquent
Imp. Ind.	expliquais, expliquais, expliquait; expliquions, expliquiez, expliquaient
Past Def.	expliquai, expliquas, expliqua; expliquâmes, expliquâtes, expliquèrent
Future	expliquerai, expliqueras, expliquera; expliquerons, expliquerez, expliqueront
Condit.	expliquerais, expliquerais, expliquerait; expliquerions, expliqueriez, expliqueraient
Pres. Subj.	explique, expliques, explique; expliquions, expliquiez, expliquent
Imp. Subj.	expliquasse, expliquasses, expliquât; expliquassions, expliquassiez, expliquassent
Past Indef.	ai expliqué, as expliqué, a expliqué; avons expliqué, avez expliqué, ont expliqué
Plup. Ind.	avais expliqué, avais expliqué, avait expliqué; avions expliqué, aviez expliqué, avaient expliqué
Past Ant.	eus expliqué, eus expliqué, eut expliqué; eûmes expliqué, eûtes expliqué, eurent expliqué
Fut. Perf.	aurai expliqué, auras expliqué, aura expliqué; aurons expliqué, aurez expliqué, auront expliqué
Cond. Perf.	aurais expliqué, aurais expliqué, aurait expliqué; aurions expliqué, auriez expliqué, auraient expliqué
Past Subj.	aie expliqué, aies expliqué, ait expliqué; ayons expliqué, ayez expliqué, aient expliqué
Plup. Subj.	eusse expliqué, eusses expliqué, eût expliqué; eussions expliqué, eussiez expliqué, eussent expliqué
Imperative	explique, expliquons, expliquez

to express

Pres. Ind.	exprime, exprimes, exprime; exprimons, exprimez, expriment
Imp. Ind.	exprimais, exprimais, exprimait; exprimions, exprimiez, exprimaient
Past Def.	exprimai, exprimas, exprima; exprimâmes, exprimâtes, exprimèrent
Future	exprimerai, exprimeras, exprimera; exprimerons, exprimerez, exprimeront
Condit.	exprimerais, exprimerais, exprimerait; exprimerions, exprimeriez, exprimeraient
Pres. Subj.	exprime, exprimes, exprime; exprimions, exprimiez, expriment
Imp. Subj.	exprimasse, exprimasses, exprimât; exprimassions, exprimassiez, exprimassent
Past Indef.	ai exprimé, as exprimé, a exprimé; avons exprimé, avez exprimé, ont exprimé
Plup. Ind.	avais exprimé, avais exprimé, avait exprimé; avions exprimé, aviez exprimé, avaient exprimé
Past Ant.	eus exprimé, eus exprimé, eut exprimé; eûmes exprimé, eûtes exprimé, eurent exprimé
Fut. Perf.	aurai exprimé, auras exprimé, aura exprimé; aurons exprimé, aurez exprimé, auront exprimé
Cond. Perf.	aurais exprimé, aurais exprimé, aurait exprimé; aurions exprimé, auriez exprimé, auraient exprimé
Past Subj.	aie exprimé, aies exprimé, ait exprimé; ayons exprimé, ayez exprimé, aient exprimé
Plup. Subj.	eusse exprimé, eusses exprimé, eût exprimé; eussions exprimé, eussiez exprimé, eussent exprimé
Imperative	exprime, exprimons, exprimez

to extract

Pres. Ind.	extrais, extrais, extrait; extrayons, extrayez, extraient
Imp. Ind.	extrayais, extrayais, extrayait; extrayions, extrayiez, extrayaient
Past Def.	[inemployé]
Future	extrairai, extrairas, extraira; extrairons, extrairez, extrairont
Condit.	extrairais, extrairais, extrairait; extrairions, extrairiez, extrairaient
Pres. Subj.	extraie, extraies, extraie; extrayions, extrayiez, extraient
Imp. Subj.	[inemployé]
Past Indef.	ai extrait, as extrait, a extrait; avons extrait, avez extrait, ont extrait
Plup. Ind.	avais extrait, avais extrait, avait extrait; avions extrait, aviez extrait, avaient extrait
Past Ant.	eus extrait, eus extrait, eut extrait; eûmes extrait, eûtes extrait, eurent extrait
Fut. Perf.	aurai extrait, auras extrait, aura extrait; aurons extrait, aurez extrait, auront extrait
Cond. Perf.	aurais extrait, aurais extrait, aurait extrait; aurions extrait, auriez extrait, auraient extrait
Past Subj.	aie extrait, aies extrait, ait extrait; ayons extrait, ayez extrait, aient extrait
Plup. Subj.	eusse extrait, eusses extrait, eût extrait; eussions extrait, eussiez extrait, eussent extrait
Imperative	extrais, extrayons, extrayez

to become angry, get angry

Pres. Ind.	me fâche, te fâches, se fâche; nous fâchons, vous fâchez, se fâchent
Imp. Ind.	me fâchais, te fâchais, se fâchait; nous fâchions, vous fâchiez, se fâchaient
Past Def.	me fâchai, te fâchas, se fâcha; nous fâchâmes, vous fâchâtes, se fâchèrent
Fut. Ind.	me fâcherai, te fâcheras, se fâchera; nous fâcherons, vous fâcherez, se fâcheront
Condit.	me fâcherais, te fâcherais, se fâcherait; nous fâcherions, vous fâcheriez, se fâcheraient
Pres. Subj.	me fâche, te fâches, se fâche; nous fâchions, vous fâchiez, se fâchent
Imp. Subj.	me fâchasse, te fâchasses, se fâchât; nous fâchassions, vous fâchassiez, se fâchassent
Past Indef.	me suis fâché(e), t'es fâché(e), s'est fâché(e); nous sommes fâché(e)s, vous êtes fâché(e)(s), se sont fâché(e)s
Pluperf.	m'étais fâché(e), t'étais fâché(e), s'était fâché(e); nous étions fâché(e)s, vous étiez fâché(e)(s), s'étaient fâché(e)s
Past Ant.	me fus fâché(e), te fus fâché(e), se fut fâché(e); nous fûmes fâché(e)s, vous fûtes fâché(e)(s), se furent fâché(e)s
Fut. Perf.	me serai fâché(e), te seras fâché(e), se sera fâché(e); nous serons fâché(e)s, vous serez fâché(e)(s), se seront fâché(e)s
Cond. Perf.	me serais fâché(e), te serais fâché(e), se serait fâché(e); nous serions fâché(e)s, vous seriez fâché(e)(s), se seraient fâché(e)s
Past Subj.	me sois fâché(e), te sois fâché(e), se soit fâché(e); nous soyons fâché(e)s, vous soyez fâché(e)(s), se soient fâché(e)s
Plup. Subj.	me fusse fâché(e), te fusses fâché(e), se fût fâché(e); nous fussions fâché(e)s, vous fussiez fâché(e)(s), se fussent fâché(e)s
Imperative	fâche-toi, fâchons-nous, fâchez-vous [ordinarily not used]

to fail

Pres. Ind.	faux, faux, faut; faillons, faillez, faillent	
Imp. Ind.	faillais, faillais, faillait; faillions, failliez, faillaient	
Past Def.	faillis, faillis, faillit; faillîmes, faillîtes, faillirent	
Fut. Ind.	faillirai, failliras, faillira; faillirons, faillirez, failliront	OR: faudrai, faudras, faudra; faudrons, faudrez, faudront
Condit.	faillirais, faillirais, faillirait; faillirions, failliriez, failliraient	OR: faudrais, faudrais, faudrait; faudrions, faudriez, faudraient
Pres. Subj.	faille, failles, faille; faillions, failliez, faillent	
Imp. Subj.	faillisse, faillisses, faillît; faillissions, faillissiez, faillissent	
Past Indef.	ai failli, as failli, a failli; avons failli, avez failli, ont failli	
Pluperf.	avais failli, avais failli, avait failli; avions failli, aviez failli, avaient failli	
Past Ant.	eus failli, eus failli, eut failli; eûmes failli, eûtes failli, eurent failli	
Fut. Perf.	aurai failli, auras failli, aura failli; aurons failli, aurez failli, auront failli	
Cond. Perf.	aurais failli, aurais failli, aurait failli; aurions failli, auriez failli, auraient failli	
Past Subj.	aie failli, aies failli, ait failli; ayons failli, ayez failli, aient failli	
Plup. Subj.	eusse failli, eusses failli, eût failli; eussions failli, eussiez failli, eussent failli	
Imperative	——	

to do, make

Pres. Ind.	fais, fais, fait; faisons, faites, font
Imp. Ind.	faisais, faisais, faisait; faisions, faisiez, faisaient
Past Def.	fis, fis, fit; fîmes, fîtes, firent
Fut. Ind.	ferai, feras, fera; ferons, ferez, feront
Condit.	ferais, ferais, ferait; ferions, feriez, feraient
Pres. Subj.	fasse, fasses, fasse; fassions, fassiez, fassent
Imp. Subj.	fisse, fisses, fît; fissions, fissiez, fissent
Past Indef.	ai fait, as fait, a fait; avons fait, avez fait, ont fait
Pluperf.	avais fait, avais fait, avait fait; avions fait, aviez fait, avaient fait
Past Ant.	eus fait, eus fait, eut fait; eûmes fait, eûtes fait, eurent fait
Fut. Perf.	aurai fait, auras fait, aura fait; aurons fait, aurez fait, auront fait
Cond. Perf.	aurais fait, aurais fait, aurait fait; aurions fait, auriez fait, auraient fait
Past Subj.	aie fait, aies fait, ait fait; ayons fait, ayez fait, aient fait
Plup. Subj.	eusse fait, eusses fait, eût fait; eussions fait, eussiez fait, eussent fait
Imperative	fais, faisons, faites

to be necessary, must

Pres. Ind.	il faut
Imp. Ind.	il fallait
Past Def.	il fallut
Future	il faudra
Condit.	il faudrait
Pres. Subj.	qu'il faille
Imp. Subj.	qu'il fallût
Past Indef.	il a fallu
Plup. Ind.	il avait fallu
Past Ant.	il eut fallu
Fut. Perf.	il aura fallu
Cond. Perf.	il aurait fallu
Past Subj.	qu'il ait fallu
Plup. Subj.	qu'il eût fallu
Imperative	[inemployé]

to feign, make believe, pretend, simulate

Pres. Ind.	feins, feins, feint; feignons, feignez, feignent
Imp. Ind.	feignais, feignais, feignait; feignions, feigniez, feignaient
Past Def.	feignis, feignis, feignit; feignîmes, feignîtes, feignirent
Future	feindrai, feindras, feindra; feindrons, feindrez, feindront
Condit.	feindrais, feindrais, feindrait; feindrions, feindriez, feindraient
Pres. Subj.	feigne, feignes, feigne; feignions, feigniez, feignent
Imp. Subj.	feignisse, feignisses, feignît; feignissions, feignissiez, feignissent
Past Indef.	ai feint, as feint, a feint; avons feint, avez feint, ont feint
Plup. Ind.	avais feint, avais feint, avait feint; avions feint, aviez feint, avaient feint
Past Ant.	eus feint, eus feint, eut feint; eûmes feint, eûtes feint, eurent feint
Fut. Perf.	aurai feint, auras feint, aura feint; aurons feint, aurez feint, auront feint
Cond. Perf.	aurais feint, aurais feint, aurait feint; aurions feint, auriez feint, auraient feint
Past Subj.	aie feint, aies feint, ait feint; ayons feint, ayez feint, aient feint
Plup. Subj.	eusse feint, eusses feint, eût feint; eussions feint, eussiez feint, eussent feint
Imperative	feins, feignons, feignez

to cleave, crack, split

Pres. Ind.	fends, fends, fend; fendons, fendez, fendent
Imp. Ind.	fendais, fendais, fendait; fendions, fendiez, fendaient
Past Def.	fendis, fendis, fendit; fendîmes, fendîtes, fendirent
Future	fendrai, fendras, fendra; fendrons, fendrez, fendront
Condit.	fendrais, fendrais, fendrait; fendrions, fendriez, fendraient
Pres. Subj.	fende, fendes, fende; fendions, fendiez, fendent
Imp. Subj.	fendisse, fendisses, fendît; fendissions, fendissiez, fendissent
Past Indef.	ai fendu, as fendu, a fendu; avons fendu, avez fendu, ont fendu
Pluperf.	avais fendu, avais fendu, avait fendu; avions fendu, aviez fendu, avaient fendu
Past Ant.	eus fendu, eus fendu, eut fendu; eûmes fendu, eûtes fendu, eurent fendu
Fut. Perf.	aurai fendu, auras fendu, aura fendu; aurons fendu, aurez fendu, auront fendu
Cond. Perf.	aurais fendu, aurais fendu, aurait fendu; aurions fendu, auriez fendu, auraient fendu
Past Subj.	aie fendu, aies fendu, ait fendu; ayons fendu, ayez fendu, aient fendu
Plup. Subj.	eusse fendu, eusses fendu, eût fendu; eussions fendu, eussiez fendu, eussent fendu
Imperative	fends, fendons, fendez

to close

Pres. Ind.	ferme, fermes, ferme; fermons, fermez, ferment
Imp. Ind.	fermais, fermais, fermait; fermions, fermiez, fermaient
Past Def.	fermai, fermas, ferma; fermâmes, fermâtes, fermèrent
Future	fermerai, fermeras, fermera; fermerons, fermerez, fermeront
Condit.	fermerais, fermerais, fermerait; fermerions, fermeriez, fermeraient
Pres. Subj.	ferme, fermes, ferme; fermions, fermiez, ferment
Imp. Subj.	fermasse, fermasses, fermât; fermassions, fermassiez, fermassent
Past Indef.	ai fermé, as fermé, a fermé; avons fermé, avez fermé, ont fermé
Plup. Ind.	avais fermé, avais fermé, avait fermé; avions fermé, aviez fermé, avaient fermé
Past Ant.	eus fermé, eus fermé, eut fermé; eûmes fermé, eûtes fermé, eurent fermé
Fut. Perf.	aurai fermé, auras fermé, aura fermé; aurons fermé, aurez fermé, auront fermé
Cond. Perf.	aurais fermé, aurais fermé, aurait fermé; aurions fermé, auriez fermé, auraient fermé
Past Subj.	aie fermé, aies fermé, ait fermé; ayons fermé, ayez fermé, aient fermé
Plup. Subj.	eusse fermé, eusses fermé, eût fermé; eussions fermé, eussiez fermé, eussent fermé
Imperative	ferme, fermons, fermez

to trust

Pres. Ind.	me fie, te fies, se fie; nous fions, vous fiez, se fient
Imp. Ind.	me fiais, te fiais, se fiait; nous fiions, vous fiiez, se fiaient
Past Def.	me fiai, te fiais, se fia; nous fiâmes, vous fiâtes, se fièrent
Future	me fierai, te fieras, se fiera; nous fierons, vous fierez, se fieront
Condit.	me fierais, te fierais, se fierait; nous fierions, vous fieriez, se fieraient
Pres. Subj.	me fie, te fies, se fie; nous fiions, vous fiiez, se fient
Imp. Subj.	me fiasse, te fiasses, se fiât; nous fiassions, vous fiassiez, se fiassent
Past Indef.	me suis fié(e), t'es fié(e), s'est fié(e); nous sommes fié(e)s, vous êtes fié(e)(s), se sont fié(e)s
Plup. Ind.	m'étais fié(e), t'étais fié(e), s'était fié(e); nous étions fié(e)s, vous étiez fié(e)(s), s'étaient fié(e)s
Past Ant.	me fus fié(e), te fus fié(e), se fut fié(e); nous fûmes fié(e)s, vous fûtes fié(e)(s), se furent fié(e)s
Fut. Perf.	me serai fié(e), te seras fié(e), se sera fié(e); nous serons fié(e)s, vous serez fié(e)(s), se seront fié(e)s
Cond. Perf.	me serais fié(e), te serais fié(e), se serait fié(e); nous serions fié(e)s, vous seriez fié(e)(s), se seraient fié(e)s
Past Subj.	me sois fié(e), te sois fié(e), se soit fié(e); nous soyons fié(e)s, vous soyez fié(e)(s), se soient fié(e)s
Plup. Subj.	me fusse fié(e), te fusses fié(e), se fût fié(e); nous fussions fié(e)s, vous fussiez fié(e)(s), se fussent fié(e)s
Imperative	fie-toi, fions-nous, fiez-vous

to finish, end, terminate, complete

Pres. Ind.	finis, finis, finit; finissons, finissez, finissent
Imp. Ind.	finissais, finissais, finissait; finissions, finissiez, finissaient
Past Def.	finis, finis, finit; finîmes, finîtes, finirent
Fut. Ind.	finirai, finiras, finira; finirons, finirez, finiront
Condit.	finirais, finirais, finirait; finirions, finiriez, finiraient
Pres. Subj.	finisse, finisses, finisse; finissions, finissiez, finissent
Imp. Subj.	finisse, finisses, finît; finissions, finissiez, finissent
Past Indef.	ai fini, as fini, a fini; avons fini, avez fini, ont fini
Pluperf.	avais fini, avais fini, avait fini; avions fini, aviez fini, avaient fini
Past Ant.	eus fini, eus fini, eut fini; eûmes fini, eûtes fini, eurent fini
Fut. Perf.	aurai fini, auras fini, aura fini; aurons fini, aurez fini, auront fini
Cond. Perf.	aurais fini, aurais fini, aurait fini; aurions fini, auriez fini, auraient fini
Past Subj.	aie fini, aies fini, ait fini; ayons fini, ayez fini, aient fini
Plup. Subj.	eusse fini, eusses fini, eût fini; eussions fini, eussiez fini, eussent fini
Imperative	finis, finissons, finissez

to flatter

Pres. Ind.	flatte, flattes, flatte; flattons, flattez, flattent
Imp. Ind.	flattais, flattais, flattait; flattions, flattiez, flattaient
Past Def.	flattai, flattas, flatta; flattâmes, flattâtes, flattèrent
Future	flatterai, flatteras, flattera; flatterons, flatterez, flatteront
Condit.	flatterais, flatterais, flatterait; flatterions, flatteriez, flatteraient
Pres. Subj.	flatte, flattes, flatte; flattions, flattiez, flattent
Imp. Subj.	flattasse, flattasses, flattât; flattassions, flattassiez, flattassent
Past Indef.	ai flatté, as flatté, a flatté; avons flatté, avez flatté, ont flatté
Plup. Ind.	avais flatté, avais flatté, avait flatté; avions flatté, aviez flatté, avaient flatté
Past Ant.	eus flatté, eus flatté, eut flatté; eûmes flatté, eûtes flatté, aurent flatté
Fut. Perf.	aurai flatté, auras flatté, aura flatté; aurons flatté, aurez flatté, euront flatté
Cond. Perf.	aurais flatté, aurais flatté, aurait flatté; aurions flatté, auriez flatté, auraient flatté
Past Subj.	aie flatté, aies flatté, ait flatté; ayons flatté, ayez flatté, aient flatté
Plup. Subj.	eusse flatté, eusses flatté, eût flatté; eussions flatté, eussiez flatté, eussent flatté
Imperative	flatte, flattons, flattez

to float

Pres. Ind.	flotte, flottes, flotte; flottons, flottez, flottent
Imp. Ind.	flottais, flottais, flottait; flottions, flottiez, flottaient
Past Def.	flottai, flottas, flotta; flottâmes, flottâtes, flottèrent
Future	flotterai, flotteras, flottera; flotterons, flotterez, flotteront
Condit.	flotterais, flotterais, flotterait; flotterions, flotteriez, flotteraient
Pres. Subj.	flotte, flottes, flotte; flottions, flottiez, flottent
Imp. Subj.	flottasse, flottasses, flottât; flottassions, flottassiez, flottassent
Past Indef.	ai flotté, as flotté, a flotté; avons flotté, avez flotté, ont flotté
Plup. Ind.	avais flotté, avais flotté, avait flotté; avions flotté, aviez flotté, avaient flotté
Past Ant.	eus flotté, eus flotté, eut flotté; eûmes flotté, eûtes flotté, eurent flotté
Fut. Perf.	aurai flotté, auras flotté, aura flotté; aurons flotté, aurez flotté, auront flotté
Cond. Perf.	aurais flotté, aurais flotté, aurait flotté; aurions flotté, auriez flotté, auraient flotté
Past Subj.	aie flotté, aies flotté, ait flotté; ayons flotté, ayez flotté, aient flotté
Plup. Subj.	eusse flotté, eusses flotté, eût flotté; eussions flotté, eussiez flotté, eussent flotté
Imperative	flotte, flottons, flottez

to found, establish, lay the foundation (of a building)

Pres. Ind.	fonde, fondes, fonde; fondons, fondez, fondent
Imp. Ind.	fondais, fondais, fondait; fondions, fondiez, fondaient
Past Def.	fondai, fondas, fonda; fondâmes, fondâtes, fondèrent
Future	fonderai, fonderas, fondera; fonderons, fonderez, fonderont
Condit.	fonderais, fonderais, fonderait; fonderions, fonderiez, fonderaient
Pres. Subj.	fonde, fondes, fonde; fondions, fondiez, fondent
Imp. Subj.	fondasse, fondasses, fondât; fondassions, fondassiez, fondassent
Past Indef.	ai fondé, as fondé, a fondé; avons fondé, avez fondé, ont fondé
Pluperf.	avais fondé, avais fondé, avait fondé; avions fondé, aviez fondé, avaient fondé
Past Ant.	eus fondé, eus fondé, eut fondé; eûmes fondé, eûtes fondé, eurent fondé
Fut. Perf.	aurai fondé, auras fondé, aura fondé; aurons fondé, aurez fondé, auront fondé
Cond. Perf.	aurais fondé, aurais fondé, aurait fondé; aurions fondé, auriez fondé, auraient fondé
Past Subj.	aie fondé, aies fondé, ait fondé; ayons fondé, ayez fondé, aient fondé
Plup. Subj.	eusse fondé, eusses fondé, eût fondé; eussions fondé, eussiez fondé, eussent fondé
Imperative	fonde, fondons, fondez

to melt, mix (colors)

Pres. Ind.	fonds, fonds, fond; fondons, fondez, fondent
Imp. Ind.	fondais, fondais, fondait; fondions, fondiez, fondaient
Past Def.	fondis, fondis, fondit; fondîmes, fondîtes, fondirent
Future	fondrai, fondras, fondra; fondrons, fondrez, fondront
Condit.	fondrais, fondrais, fondrait; fondrions, fondriez, fondraient
Pres. Subj.	fonde, fondes, fonde; fondions, fondiez, fondent
Imp. Subj.	fondisse, fondisses, fondît; fondissions, fondissiez, fondissent
Past Indef.	ai fondu, as fondu, a fondu; avons fondu, avez fondu, ont fondu
Pluperf.	avais fondu, avais fondu, avait fondu; avions fondu, aviez fondu, avaient fondu
Past Ant.	eus fondu, eus fondu, eut fondu; eûmes fondu, eûtes fondu, eurent fondu
Fut. Perf.	aurai fondu, auras fondu, aura fondu; aurons fondu, aurez fondu, auront fondu
Cond. Perf.	aurais fondu, aurais fondu, aurait fondu; aurions fondu, auriez fondu, auraient fondu
Past Subj.	aie fondu, aies fondu, ait fondu; ayons fondu, ayez fondu, aient fondu
Plup. Subj.	eusse fondu, eusses fondu, eût fondu; eussions fondu, eussiez fondu, eussent fondu
Imperative	fonds, fondons, fondez

to force

Pres. Ind.	force, forces, force; forçons, forcez, forcent
Imp. Ind.	forçais, forçais, forçait; forcions, forciez, forçaient
Past Def.	forçai, forças, força; forçâmes, forçâtes, forcèrent
Future	forcerai, forceras, forcera; forcerons, forcerez, forceront
Condit.	forcerais, forcerais, forcerait; forcerions, forceriez, forceraient
Pres. Subj.	force, forces, force; forcions, forciez, forcent
Imp. Subj.	forçasse, forçasses, forçât; forçassions, forçassiez, forçassent
Past Indef.	ai forcé, as forcé, a forcé; avons forcé, avez forcé, ont forcé
Plup. Ind.	avais forcé, avais forcé, avait forcé; avions forcé, aviez forcé, avaient forcé
Past Ant.	eus forcé, eus forcé, eut forcé; eûmes forcé, eûtes forcé, eurent forcé
Fut. Perf.	aurai forcé, auras forcé, aura forcé; aurons forcé, aurez forcé, auront forcé
Cond. Perf.	aurais forcé, aurais forcé, aurait forcé; aurions forcé, auriez forcé, auraient forcé
Past Subj.	aie forcé, aies forcé, ait forcé; ayons forcé, ayez forcé, aient forcé
Plup. Subj.	eusse forcé, eusses forcé, eût forcé; eussions forcé, eussiez forcé, eussent forcé
Imperative	force, forçons, forcez

to dig, excavate, go deep into

Pres. Ind.	fouille, fouilles, fouille; fouillons, fouillez, fouillent
Imp. Ind.	fouillais, fouillais, fouillait; fouillions, fouilliez, fouillaient
Past Def.	fouillai, fouillas, fouilla; fouillâmes, fouillâtes, fouillèrent
Future	fouillerai, fouilleras, fouillera; fouillerons, fouillerez, fouilleront
Condit.	fouillerais, fouillerais, fouillerait; fouillerions, fouilleriez, fouilleraient
Pres. Subj.	fouille, fouilles, fouille; fouillions, fouilliez, fouillent
Imp. Subj.	fouillasse, fouillasses, fouillât; fouillassions, fouillassiez, fouillassent
Past Indef.	ai fouillé, as fouillé, a fouillé; avons fouillé, avez fouillé, ont fouillé
Plup. Ind.	avais fouillé, avais fouillé, avait fouillé; avions fouillé, aviez fouillé, avaient fouillé
Past Ant.	eus fouillé, eus fouillé, eut fouillé; eûmes fouillé, eûtes fouillé, eurent fouillé
Fut. Perf.	aurai fouillé, auras fouillé, aura fouillé; aurons fouillé, aurez fouillé, auront fouillé
Cond. Perf.	aurais fouillé, aurais fouillé, aurait fouillé; aurions fouillé, auriez fouillé, auraient fouillé
Past Subj.	aie fouillé, aies fouillé, ait fouillé; ayons fouillé, ayez fouillé, aient fouillé
Plup. Subj.	eusse fouillé, eusses fouillé, eût fouillé; eussions fouillé, eussiez fouillé, eussent fouillé
Imperative	fouille, fouillons, fouillez

to furnish

Pres. Ind.	fournis, fournis, fournit; fournissons, fournissez, fournissent
Imp. Ind.	fournissais, fournissais, fournissait; fournissions, fournissiez, fournissaient
Past Def.	fournis, fournis, fournit; fournîmes, fournîtes, fournirent
Future	fournirai, fourniras, fournira; fournirons, fournirez, fourniront
Condit.	fournirais, fournirais, fournirait; fournirions, fourniriez, fourniraient
Pres. Subj.	fournisse, fournisses, fournisse; fournissions, fournissiez, fournissent
Imp. Subj.	fournisse, fournisses, fournît; fournissions, fournissiez, fournissent
Past Indef.	ai fourni, as fourni, a fourni; avons fourni, avez fourni, ont fourni
Plup. Ind.	avais fourni, avais fourni, avait fourni; avions fourni, aviez fourni, avaient fourni
Past Ant.	eus fourni, eus fourni, eut fourni; eûmes fourni, eûtes fourni, eurent fourni
Fut. Perf.	aurai fourni, auras fourni, aura fourni; aurons fourni, aurez fourni, auront fourni
Cond. Perf.	aurais fourni, aurais fourni, aurait fourni; aurions fourni, auriez fourni, auraient fourni
Past Subj.	aie fourni, aies fourni, ait fourni; ayons fourni, ayez fourni, aient fourni
Plup. Subj.	eusse fourni, eusses fourni, eût fourni; eussions fourni, eussiez fourni, eussent fourni
Imperative	fournis, fournissons, fournissez

to shudder

Pres. Ind.	frémis, frémis, frémit; frémissons, frémissez, frémissent
Imp. Ind..	frémissais, frémissais, frémissait; frémissions, frémissiez, frémissaient
Past Def.	frémis, frémis, frémit; frémîmes, frémîtes, frémirent
Future	frémirai, frémiras, frémira; frémirons, frémirez, frémiront
Condit.	frémirais, frémirais, frémirait; frémirions, frémiriez, frémiraient
Pres. Subj.	frémisse, frémisses, frémisse; frémissions, frémissiez, frémissent
Imp. Subj.	frémisse, frémisses, frémît; frémissions, frémissiez, frémissent
Past Indef.	ai frémi, as frémi, a frémi; avons frémi, avez frémi, ont frémi
Plup. Ind.	avais frémi, avais frémi, avait frémi; avions frémi, aviez frémi, avaient frémi
Past Ant.	eus frémi, eus frémi, eut frémi; eûmes frémi, eûtes frémi, eurent frémi
Fut. Perf.	aurai frémi, auras frémi, aura frémi; aurons frémi, aurez frémi, auront frémi
Cond. Perf.	aurais frémi, aurais frémi, aurait frémi; aurions frémi, auriez frémi, auraient frémi
Past Subj.	aie frémi, aies frémi, ait frémi; ayons frémi, ayez frémi, aient frémi
Plup. Subj.	eusse frémi, eusses frémi, eût frémi; eussions frémi, eussiez frémi, eussent frémi
Imperative	frémis, frémissons, frémissez

to fry

Pres. Ind.	fris, fris, frit;
Future	frirai, friras, frira; frirons, frirez, friront
Condit.	frirais, frirais, frirait; féririons, fririez, friraient
Imperative	fris

* This verb is used only in the persons and tenses given above. To supply the forms that are lacking, use the appropriate form of **faire** plus the infinitive **frire**, e.g., the plural of the Present Indicative is: nous faisons frire, vous faites frire, ils font frire.

to flee, fly

Pres. Ind.	fuis, fuis, fuit; fuyons, fuyez, fuient
Imp. Ind.	fuyais, fuyais, fuyait; fuyions, fuyiez, fuyaient
Past Def.	fuis, fuis, fuit; fuîmes, fuîtes, fuirent
Fut. Ind.	fuirai, fuiras, fuira; fuirons, fuirez, fuiront
Condit.	fuirais, fuirais, fuirait; fuirions, fuiriez, fuiraient
Pres. Subj.	fuie, fuies, fuie; fuyions, fuyiez, fuient
Imp. Subj.	fuisse, fuisses, fuît; fuissions, fuissiez, fuissent
Past Indef.	ai fui, as fui, a fui; avons fui, avez fui, ont fui
Pluperf.	avais fui, avais fui, avait fui; avions fui, aviez fui, avaient fui
Past Ant.	eus fui, eus fui, eut fui; eûmes fui, eûtes fui, eurent fui
Fut. Perf.	aurai fui, auras fui, aura fui; aurons fui, aurez fui, auront fui
Cond. Perf.	aurais fui, aurais fui, aurait fui; aurions fui, auriez fui, auraient fui
Past Subj.	aie fui, aies fui, ait fui; ayons fui, ayez fui, aient fui
Plup. Subj.	eusse fui, eusses fui, eût fui; eussions fui, eussiez fui, eussent fui
Imperative	fuis, fuyons, fuyez

to smoke

Pres. Ind.	fume, fumes, fume; fumons, fumez, fument
Imp. Ind.	fumais, fumais, fumait; fumions, fumiez, fumaient
Past Def.	fumai, fumas, fuma; fumâmes, fumâtes, fumèrent
Future	fumerai, fumeras, fumera; fumerons, fumerez, fumeront
Condit.	fumerais, fumerais, fumerait; fumerions, fumeriez, fumeraient
Pres. Subj.	fume, fumes, fume; fumions, fumiez, fument
Imp. Subj.	fumasse, fumasses, fumât; fumassions, fumassiez, fumassent
Past Indef.	ai fumé, as fumé, a fumé; avons fumé, avez fumé, ont fumé
Plup. Ind.	avais fumé, avais fumé, avait fumé; avions fumé, aviez fumé, avaient fumé
Past Ant.	eus fumé, eus fumé, eut fumé; eûmes fumé, eûtes fumé, eurent fumé
Fut. Perf.	aurai fumé, auras fumé, aura fumé; aurons fumé, aurez fumé, auront fumé
Cond. Perf.	aurais fumé, aurais fumé, aurait fumé; aurions fumé, auriez fumé, auraient fumé
Past Subj.	aie fumé, aies fumé, ait fumé; ayons fumé, ayez fumé, aient fumé
Plup. Subj.	eusse fumé, eusses fumé, eût fumé; eussions fumé, eussiez fumé, eussent fumé
Imperative	fume, fumons, fumez

to win, earn, gain

Pres. Ind.	gagne, gagnes, gagne; gagnons, gagnez, gagnent
Imp. Ind.	gagnais, gagnais, gagnait; gagnions, gagniez, gagnaient
Past Def.	gagnai, gagnas, gagna; gagnâmes, gagnâtes, gagnèrent
Fut. Ind.	gagnerai, gagneras, gagnera; gagnerons, gagnerez, gagneront
Condit.	gagnerais, gagnerais, gagnerait; gagnerions, gagneriez, gagneraient
Pres. Subj.	gagne, gagnes, gagne; gagnions, gagniez, gagnent
Imp. Subj.	gagnasse, gagnasses, gagnât; gagnassions, gagnassiez, gagnassent
Past Indef.	ai gagné, as gagné, a gagné; avons gagné, avez gagné, ont gagné
Pluperf.	avais gagné, avais gagné, avait gagné; avions gagné, aviez gagné, avaient gagné
Past Ant.	eus gagné, eus gagné, eut gagné; eûmes gagné, eûtes gagné, eurent gagné
Fut. Perf.	aurai gagné, auras gagné, aura gagné; aurons gagné, aurez gagné, auront gagné
Cond. Perf.	aurais gagné, aurais gagné, aurait gagné; aurions gagné, auriez gagné, auraient gagné
Past Subj.	aie gagné, aies gagné, ait gagné; ayons gagné, ayez gagné, aient gagné
Plup. Subj.	eusse gagné, eusses gagné, eût gagné; eussions gagné, eussiez gagné, eussent gagné
Imperative	gagne, gagnons, gagnez

to guard, keep, retain

Pres. Ind.	garde, gardes, garde; gardons, gardez, gardent
Imp. Ind.	gardais, gardais, gardait; gardions, gardiez, gardaient
Past Def.	gardai, gardas, garda; gardâmes, gardâtes, gardèrent
Future	garderai, garderas, gardera; garderons, garderez, garderont
Condit.	garderais, garderais, garderait; garderions, garderiez, garderaient
Pres. Subj.	garde, gardes, garde; gardions, gardiez, gardent
Imp. Subj.	gardasse, gardasses, gardât; gardassions, gardassiez, gardassent
Past Indef.	ai gardé, as gardé, a gardé; avons gardé, avez gardé, ont gardé
Plup. Ind.	avais gardé, avais gardé, avait gardé; avions gardé, aviez gardé, avaient gardé
Past Ant.	eus gardé, eus gardé, eut gardé; eûmes gardé, eûtes gardé, eurent gardé
Fut. Perf.	aurai gardé, auras gardé, aura gardé; aurons gardé, aurez gardé, auront gardé
Cond. Perf.	aurais gardé, aurais gardé, aurait gardé; aurions gardé, auriez gardé, auraient gardé
Past Subj.	aie gardé, aies gardé, ait gardé; ayons gardé, ayez gardé, aient gardé
Plup. Subj.	eusse gardé, eusses gardé, eût gardé; eussions gardé, eussiez gardé, eussent gardé
Imperative	garde, gardons, gardez

to spoil, damage

Pres. Ind.	gâte, gâtes, gâte; gâtons, gâtez, gâtent
Imp. Ind.	gâtais, gâtais, gâtait; gâtions, gâtiez, gâtaient
Past Def.	gâtai, gâtas, gâta; gâtâmes, gâtâtes, gâtèrent
Future	gâterai, gâteras, gâtera; gâterons, gâterez, gâteront
Condit.	gâterais, gâterais, gâterait; gâterions, gâteriez, gâteraient
Pres. Subj.	gâte, gâtes, gâte; gâtions, gâtiez, gâtent
Imp. Subj.	gâtasse, gâtasses, gâtât; gâtassions, gâtassiez, gâtassent
Past Indef.	ai gâté, as gâté, a gâté; avons gâté, avez gâté, ont gâté
Plup. Ind.	avais gâté, avais gâté, avait gâté; avions gâté, aviez gâté, avaient gâté
Past Ant.	eus gâté, eus gâté, eut gâté; eûmes gâté, eûtes gâté, eurent gâté
Fut. Perf.	aurai gâté, auras gâté, aura gâté; aurons gâté, aurez gâté, auront gâté
Cond. Perf.	aurais gâté, aurais gâté, aurait gâté; aurions gâté, auriez gâté, auraient gâté
Past Subj.	aie gâté, aies gâté, ait gâté; ayons gâté, ayez gâté, aient gâté
Plup. Subj.	eusse gâte, eusses gâté, eût gâté; eussions gâté, eussiez gâté, eussent gâté
Imperative	gâte, gâtons, gâtez

to freeze

Pres. Ind.	il gèle
Imp. Ind.	il gelait
Past Def.	il gela
Future	il gèlera
Condit.	il gèlerait
Pres. Subj.	qu'il gèle
Imp. Subj.	qu'il gelât
Past Indef.	il a gelé
Plup. Ind.	il avait gelé
Past Ant.	il eut gelé
Fut. Perf.	il aura gelé
Cond. Perf.	il aurait gelé
Past Subj.	qu'il ait gelé
Plup. Subj.	qu'il eût gelé
Imperative	[inemployé]

to bother, hamper, hinder, impede, inconvenience

Pres. Ind.	gêne, gênes, gêne; gênons, gênez, gênent
Imp. Ind.	gênais, gênais, gênait; gênions, gêniez, gênaient
Past Def.	gênai, gênas, gêna; gênâmes, gênâtes, gênèrent
Future	gênerai, gêneras, gênera; gênerons, gênerez, gêneront
Condit.	gênerais, gênerais, gênerait; gênerions, gêneriez, gêneraient
Pres. Subj.	gêne, gênes, gêne; gênions, gêniez, gênent
Imp. Subj.	gênasse, gênasses, gênât; gênassions, gênassiez, gênassent
Past Indef.	ai gêné, as gêné, a gêné; avons gêné, avez gêné, ont gêné
Plup. Ind.	avais gêné, avais gêné, avait gêné; avions gêné, aviez gêné, avaient gêné
Past Ant.	eus gêné, eus gêné, eut gêné; eûmes gêné, eûtes gêné, eurent gêné
Fut. Perf.	aurai gêné, auras gêné, aura gêné; aurons gêné, aurez gêné, auront gêné
Cond. Perf.	aurais gêné, aurais gêné, aurait gêné; aurions gêné, auriez gêné, auraient gêné
Past Subj.	aie gêné, aies gêné, ait gêné; ayons gêné, ayez gêné, aient gêné
Plup. Subj.	eusse gêné, eussses gêné, eût gêné; eussions gêné, eussiez gêné, eussent gêné
Imperative	gêne, gênons, gênez

to lie dead, ill

Pres. Ind. gis, gis, gît;
gisons, gisez, gisent

Imp. Ind. gisais, gisais, gisait;
gisions, gisiez, gisaient

* This verb is used only in the above persons and tenses. The following forms are ordinarily used on tombstones: Ci-gît (Here lies) and Ci-gisent (Here lie).

to taste, have a snack

Pres. Ind.	goûte, goûtes, goûte; goûtons, goûtez, goûtent
Imp. Ind.	goûtais, goûtais, goûtait; goûtions, goûtiez, goûtaient
Past Def.	goûtai, goûtas, goûta; goûtâmes, goûtâtes, goûtèrent
Fut. Ind.	goûterai, goûteras, goûtera; goûterons, goûterez, goûteront
Condit.	goûterais, goûterais, goûterait; goûterions, goûteriez, goûteraient
Pres. Subj.	goûte, goûtes, goûte; goûtions, goûtiez, goûtent
Imp. Subj.	goûtasse, goûtasses, goûtât; goûtassions, goûtassiez, goûtassent
Past Indef.	ai goûté, as goûté, a goûté; avons goûté, avez goûté, ont goûté
Pluperf.	avais goûté, avais goûté, avait goûté; avions goûté, aviez goûté, avaient goûté
Past Ant.	eus goûté, eus goûté, eut goûté; eûmes goûté, eûtes goûté, eurent goûté
Fut. Perf.	aurai goûté, auras goûté, aura goûté; aurons goûté, aurez goûté, auront goûté
Cond. Perf.	aurais goûté, aurais goûté, aurait goûté; aurions goûté, auriez goûté, auraient goûté
Past Subj.	aie goûté, aies goûté, ait goûté; ayons goûté, ayez goûté, aient goûté
Plup. Subj.	eusse goûté, eusses goûté, eût goûté; eussions goûté, eussiez goûté, eussent goûté
Imperative	goûte, goûtons, goûtez

to grow (up, taller), increase

Pres. Ind.	grandis, grandis, grandit; grandissons, grandissez, grandissent
Imp. Ind.	grandissais, grandissais, grandissait; grandissions, grandissiez, grandissaient
Past Def.	grandis, grandis, grandit; grandîmes, grandîtes, grandirent
Future	grandirai, grandiras, grandira; grandirons, grandirez, grandiront
Condit.	grandirais, grandirais, grandirait; grandirions, grandiriez, grandiraient
Pres. Subj.	grandisse, grandisses, grandisse; grandissions, grandissiez, grandissent
Imp. Subj.	grandisse, grandisses, grandît; grandissions, grandissiez, grandissent
Past Indef.	ai grandi, as grandi, a grandi; avons grandi, avez grandi, ont grandi
Pluperf.	avais grandi, avais grandi, avait grandi; avions grandi, aviez grandi, avaient grandi
Past Ant.	eus grandi, eus grandi, eut grandi; eûmes grandi, eûtes grandi, eurent grandi
Fut. Perf.	aurai grandi, auras grandi, aura grandi; aurons grandi, aurez grandi, auront grandi
Cond. Perf.	aurais grandi, aurais grandi, aurait grandi; aurions grandi, auriez grandi, auraient grandi
Past Subj.	aie grandi, aies grandi, ait grandi; ayons grandi, ayez grandi, aient grandi
Plup. Subj.	eusse grandi, eusses grandi, eût grandi; eussions grandi, eussiez grandi, eussent grandi
Imperative	grandis, grandissons, grandissez [ordinairement inemployé]

to scrape, scratch

Pres. Ind.	gratte, grattes, gratte; grattons, grattez, grattent
Imp. Ind.	grattais, grattais, grattait; grattions, grattiez, grattaient
Past Def.	grattai, grattas, gratta; grattâmes, grattâtes, grattèrent
Future	gratterai, gratteras, grattera; gratterons, gratterez, gratteront
Condit.	gratterais, gratterais, gratterait; gratterions, gratteriez, gratteraient
Pres. Subj.	gratte, grattes, gratte; grattions, grattiez, grattent
Imp. Subj.	grattasse, grattasses, grattât; grattassions, grattassiez, grattassent
Past Indef.	ai gratté, as gratté, a gratté; avons gratté, avez gratté, ont gratté
Plup. Ind.	avais gratté, avais gratté, avait gratté; avions gratté, aviez gratté, avaient gratté
Past Ant.	eus gratté, eus gratté, eut gratté; eûmes gratté, eûtes gratté, eurent gratté
Fut. Perf.	aurai gratté, auras gratté, aura gratté; aurons gratté, aurez gratté, auront gratté
Cond. Perf.	aurais gratté, aurais gratté, aurait gratté; aurions gratté, auriez gratté, auraient gratté
Past Subj.	aie gratté, aies gratté, ait gratté; ayons gratté, ayez gratté, aient gratté
Plup. Subj.	eusse gratté, eusses gratté, eût gratté; eussions gratté, eussiez gratté, eussent gratté
Imperative	gratte, grattons, grattez

to hail (weather)

Pres. Ind.	il grêle
Imp. Ind.	il grêlait
Past Def.	il grêla
Future	il grêlera
Condit.	il grêlerait
Pres. Subj.	qu'il grêle
Imp. Subj.	qu'il grêlât
Past Indef.	il a grêlé
Plup. Ind.	il avait grêlé
Past Ant.	il eut grêlé
Fut. Perf.	il aura grêlé
Cond. Perf.	il aurait grêlé
Past Subj.	qu'il ait grêlé
Plup. Subj.	qu'il eût grêlé
Imperative	[inemployé]

to climb

Pres. Ind.	grimpe, grimpes, grimpe; grimpons, grimpez, grimpent
Imp. Ind.	grimpais, grimpais, grimpait; grimpions, grimpiez, grimpaient
Past Def.	grimpai, grimpas, grimpa; grimpâmes, grimpâtes, grimpèrent
Future	grimperai, grimperas, grimpera; grimperons, grimperez, grimperont
Condit.	grimperais, grimperais, grimperait; grimperions, grimperiez, grimperaient
Pres. Subj.	grimpe, grimpes, grimpe; grimpions, grimpiez, grimpent
Imp. Subj.	grimpasse, grimpasses, grimpât; grimpassions, grimpassiez, grimpassent
Past Indef.	ai grimpé, as grimpé, a grimpé; avons grimpé, avez grimpé, ont grimpé
Plup. Ind.	avais grimpé, avais grimpé, avait grimpé; avions grimpé, aviez grimpé, avaient grimpé
Past Ant.	eus grimpé, eus grimpé, eut grimpé; eûmes grimpé, eûtes grimpé, eurent grimpé
Fut. Perf.	aurai grimpé, auras grimpé, aura grimpé; aurons grimpé, aurez grimpé, auront grimpé
Cond. Perf.	aurais grimpé, aurais grimpé, aurait grimpé; aurions grimpé, auriez grimpé, auraient grimpé
Past Subj.	aie grimpé, aies grimpé, ait grimpé; ayons grimpé, ayez grimpé, aient grimpé
Plup. Subj.	eusse grimpé, eusses grimpé, eût grimpé; eussions grimpé, eussiez grimpé, eussent grimpé
Imperative	grimpe, grimpons, grimpez

to chide, reprimand, scold

Pres. Ind.	gronde, grondes, gronde; grondons, grondez, grondent
Imp. Ind.	grondais, grondais, grondait; grondions, grondiez, grondaient
Past Def.	grondai, grondas, gronda; grondâmes, grondâtes, grondèrent
Future	gronderai, gronderas, grondera; gronderons, gronderez, gronderont
Condit.	gronderais, gronderais, gronderait; gronderions, gronderiez, gronderaient
Pres. Subj.	gronde, grondes, gronde; grondions, grondiez, grondent
Imp. Subj.	grondasse, grondasses, grondât; grondassions, grondassiez, grondassent
Past Indef.	ai grondé, as grondé, a grondé; avons grondé, avez grondé, ont grondé
Pluperf.	avais grondé, avais grondé, avait grondé; avions grondé, aviez grondé, avaient grondé
Past Ant.	eus grondé, eus grondé, eut grondé; eûmes grondé, eûtes grondé, eurent grondé
Fut. Perf.	aurai grondé, auras grondé, aura grondé; aurons grondé, aurez grondé, auront grondé
Cond. Perf.	aurais grondé, aurais grondé, aurait grondé; aurions grondé, auriez grondé, auraient grondé
Past Subj.	aie grondé, aies grondé, ait grondé; ayons grondé, ayez grondé, aient grondé
Plup. Subj.	eusse grondé, eusses grondé, eût grondé; eussions grondé, eussiez grondé, eussent grondé
Imperative	gronde, grondons, grondez

to cure

Pres. Ind.	guéris, guéris, guérit; guérissons, guérissez, guérissent
Imp. Ind.	guérissais, guérissais, guérissait; guérissions, guérissiez, guérissaient
Past Def.	guéris, guéris, guérit; guérîmes, guérîtes, guérirent
Fut. Ind.	guérirai, guériras, guérira; guérirons, guérirez, guériront
Condit.	guérirais, guérirais, guérirait; guéririons, guéririez, guériraient
Pres. Subj.	guérisse, guérisses, guérisse; guérissions, guérissiez, guérissent
Imp. Subj.	guérisse, guérisses, guérît; guérissions, guérissiez, guérissent
Past Indef.	ai guéri, as guéri, a guéri; avons guéri, avez guéri, ont guéri
Pluperf.	avais guéri, avais guéri, avait guéri; avions guéri, aviez guéri, avaient guéri
Past Ant.	eus guéri, eus guéri, eut guéri; eûmes guéri, eûtes guéri, eurent guéri
Fut. Perf.	aurai guéri, auras guéri, aura guéri; aurons guéri, aurez guéri, auront guéri
Cond. Perf.	aurais guéri, aurais guéri, aurait guéri; aurions guéri, auriez guéri, auraient guéri
Past Subj.	aie guéri, aies guéri, ait guéri; ayons guéri, ayez guéri, aient guéri
Plup. Subj.	eusse guéri, eusses guéri, eût guéri; eussions guéri, eussiez guéri, eussent guéri
Imperative	guéris, guérissons, guérissez

to guide, lead

Pres. Ind.	guide, guides, guide; guidons, guidez, guident
Imp. Ind.	guidais, guidais, guidait; guidions, guidiez, guidaient
Past Def.	guidai, guidas, guida; guidâmes, guidâtes, guidèrent
Future	guiderai, guideras, guidera; guiderons, guiderez, guideront
Condit.	guiderais, guiderais, guiderait; guiderions, guideriez, guideraient
Pres. Subj.	guide, guides, guide; guidions, guidiez, guident
Imp. Subj.	guidasse, guidasses, guidât; guidassions, guidassiez, guidassent
Past Indef.	ai guidé, as guidé, a guidé; avons guidé, avez guidé, ont guidé
Pluperf.	avais guidé, avais guidé, avait guidé; avions guidé, aviez guidé, avaient guidé
Past Ant.	eus guidé, eus guidé, eut guidé; eûmes guidé, eûtes guidé, eurent guidé
Fut. Perf.	aurai guidé, auras guidé, aura guidé; aurons guidé, aurez guidé, auront guidé
Cond. Perf.	aurais guidé, aurais guidé, aurait guidé; aurions guidé, auriez guidé, auraient guidé
Past Subj.	aie guidé, aies guidé, ait guidé; ayons guidé, ayez guidé, aient guidé
Plup. Subj.	eusse guidé, eusses guidé, eût guidé; eussions guidé, eussiez guidé, eussent guidé
Imperative	guide, guidons, guidez

to get dressed, to dress

Pres. Ind.	m'habille, t'habilles, s'habille; nous habillons, vous habillez, s'habillent
Imp. Ind.	m'habillais, t'habillais, s'habillait; nous habillions, vous habilliez, s'habillaient
Past Def.	m'habillai, t'habillas, s'habilla; nous habillâmes, vous habillâtes, s'habillèrent
Fut. Ind.	m'habillerai, t'habilleras, s'habillera; nous habillerons, vous habillerez, s'habilleront
Condit.	m'habillerais, t'habillerais, s'habillerait; nous habillerions, vous habilleriez, s'habilleraient
Pres. Subj.	m'habille, t'habilles, s'habille; nous habillions, vous habilliez, s'habillent
Imp. Subj.	m'habillasse, t'habillasses, s'habillât; nous habillassions, vous habillassiez, s'habillassent
Past Indef.	me suis habillé(e), t'es habillé(e), s'est habillé(e); nous sommes habillé(e)s, vous êtes habillé(e)(s), se sont habillé(e)s
Pluperf.	m'étais habillé(e), t'étais habillé(e), s'était habillé(e); nous étions habillé(e)s, vous étiez habillé(e)(s), s'étaient habillé(e)s
Past Ant.	me fus habillé(e), te fus habillé(e), se fut habillé(e); nous fûmes habillé(e)s, vous fûtes habillé(e)(s), se furent habillé(e)s
Fut. Perf.	me serai habillé(e), te seras habillé(e), se sera habillé(e); nous serons habillé(e)s, vous serez habillé(e)(s), se seront habillé(e)s
Cond. Perf.	me serais habillé(e), te serais habillé(e), se serait habillé(e); nous serions habillé(e)s, vous seriez habillé(e)(s), se seraient habillé(e)s
Past Subj.	me sois habillé(e), te sois habillé(e), se soit habillé(e); nous soyons habillé(e)s, vous soyez habillé(e)(s), se soient habillé(e)s
Plup. Subj.	me fusse habillé(e), te fusses habillé(e), se fût habillé(e); nous fussions habillé(e)s, vous fussiez habillé(e)(s), se fussent habillé(e)s
Imperative	habille-toi, habillons-nous, habillez-vous

to live (in), dwell (in), inhabit

Pres. Ind.	habite, habites, habite; habitons, habitez, habitent
Imp. Ind.	habitais, habitais, habitait; habitions, habitiez, habitaient
Past Def.	habitai, habitas, habita; habitâmes, habitâtes, habitèrent
Fut. Ind.	habiterai, habiteras, habitera; habiterons, habiterez, habiteront
Condit.	habiterais, habiterais, habiterait; habiterions, habiteriez, habiteraient
Pres. Subj.	habite, habites, habite; habitions, habitiez, habitent
Imp. Subj.	habitasse, habitasses, habitât; habitassions, habitassiez, habitassent
Past Indef.	ai habité, as habité, a habité; avons habité, avez habité, ont habité
Pluperf.	avais habité, avais habité, avait habité; avions habité, aviez habité, avaient habité
Past Ant.	eus habité, eus habité, eut habité; eûmes habité, eûtes habité, eurent habité
Fut. Perf.	aurai habité, auras habité, aura habité; aurons habité, aurez habité, auront habité
Cond. Perf.	aurais habité, aurais habité, aurait habité; aurions habité, auriez habité, auraient habité
Past Subj.	aie habité, aies habité, ait habité; ayons habité, ayez habité, aient habité
Plup. Subj.	eusse habité, eusses habité, eût habité; eussions habité, eussiez habité, eussent habité
Imperative	habite, habitons, habitez

to hate

Pres. Ind.	hais, hais, hait; haïssons, haïssez, haïssent
Imp. Ind.	haïssais, haïssais, haïssait; haïssions, haïssiez, haïssaient
Past Def.	haïs, haïs, haït; haïmes, haïtes, haïrent
Fut. Ind.	haïrai, haïras, haïra; haïrons, haïrez, haïront
Condit.	haïrais, haïrais, haïrait; haïrions, haïriez, haïraient
Pres. Subj.	haïsse, haïsses, haïsse; haïssions, haïssiez, haïssent
Imp. Subj.	haïsse, haïsses, haït; haïssions, haïssiez, haïssent
Past Indef.	ai haï, as haï, a haï; avons haï, avez haï, ont haï
Pluperf.	avais haï, avais haï, avait haï; avions haï, aviez haï, avaient haï
Past Ant.	eus haï, eus haï, eut haï; eûmes haï, eûtes haï, eurent haï
Fut. Perf.	aurai haï, auras haï, aura haï; aurons haï, aurez haï, auront haï
Cond. Perf.	aurais haï, aurais haï, aurait haï; aurions haï, auriez haï, auraient haï
Past Subj.	aie haï, aies haï, ait haï; ayons haï, ayez haï, aient haï
Plup. Subj.	eusse haï, eusses haï, eût haï; eussions haï, eussiez haï, eussent haï
Imperative	hais, haïssons, haïssez

to impose

Pres. Ind.	impose, imposes, impose; imposons, imposez, imposent
Imp. Ind.	imposais, imposais, imposait; imposions, imposiez, imposaient
Past Def.	imposai, imposas, imposa; imposâmes, imposâtes, imposèrent
Future	imposerai, imposeras, imposera; imposerons, imposerez, imposeront
Condit.	imposerais, imposerais, imposerait; imposerions, imposeriez, imposeraient
Pres. Subj.	impose, imposes, impose; imposions, imposiez, imposent
Imp. Subj.	imposasse, imposasses, imposât; imposassions, imposassiez, imposassent
Past Indef.	ai imposé, as imposé, a imposé; avons imposé, avez imposé, ont imposé
Plup. Ind.	avais imposé, avais imposé, avait imposé; avions imposé, aviez imposé, avaient imposé
Past Ant.	eus imposé, eus imposé, eut imposé; eûmes imposé, eûtes imposé, eurent imposé
Fut. Perf.	aurai imposé, auras imposé, aura imposé; aurons imposé, aurez imposé, auront imposé
Cond. Perf.	aurais imposé, aurais imposé, aurait imposé; aurions imposé, auriez imposé, auraient imposé
Past Subj.	aie imposé, aies imposé, ait imposé; ayons imposé, ayez imposé, aient imposé
Plup. Subj.	eusse imposé, eusses imposé, eût imposé; eussions imposé, eussiez imposé, eussent imposé
Imperative	impose, imposons, imposez

to include, enclose

Pres. Ind.	inclus, inclus, inclut; incluons, incluez, incluent
Imp. Ind.	incluais, incluais, incluait; incluions, incluiez, incluaient
Past Def.	inclus, inclus, inclut; inclûmes, inclûtes, inclurent
Future	inclurai, incluras, inclura; inclurons, inclurez, incluront
Condit.	inclurais, inclurais, inclurait; inclurions, incluriez, incluraient
Pres. Subj.	inclue, inclues, inclue; incluions, incluiez, incluent
Imp. Subj.	inclusse, inclusses, inclût; inclussions, inclussiez, inclussent
Past Indef.	ai inclus, as inclus, a inclus; avons inclus, avez inclus, ont inclus
Plup. Ind.	avais inclus, avais inclus, avait inclus; avions inclus, aviez inclus, avaient inclus
Past Ant.	eus inclus, eus inclus, eut inclus; eûmes inclus, eûtes inclus, eurent inclus
Fut. Perf.	aurai inclus, auras inclus, aura inclus; aurons inclus, aurez inclus, auront inclus
Cond. Perf.	aurais inclus, aurais inclus, aurait inclus; aurions inclus, auriez inclus, auraient inclus
Past Subj.	aie inclus, aies inclus, ait inclus; ayons inclus, ayez inclus, aient inclus
Plup. Subj.	eusse inclus, eusses inclus, eût inclus; eussions inclus, eussiez inclus, eussent inclus
Imperative	inclus, incluons, incluez

to find out, inquire, make inquiries

Pres. Ind.	m'informe, t'informes, s'informe; nous informons, vous informez, s'informent
Imp. Ind.	m'informais, t'informais, s'informait; nous informions, vous informiez, s'informaient
Past Def.	m'informai, t'informas, s'informa; nous informâmes, vous informâtes, s'informèrent
Future	m'informerai, t'informeras, s'informera; nous informerons, vous informerez, s'informeront
Condit.	m'informerais, t'informerais, s'informerait; nous informerions, vous informeriez, s'informeraient
Pres. Subj.	m'informe, t'informes, s'informe; nous informions, vous informiez, s'informent
Imp. Subj.	m'informasse, t'informasses, s'informât; nous informassions, vous informassiez, s'informassent
Past Indef.	me suis informé(e), t'es informé(e), s'est informé(e); nous sommes informé(e)s, vous êtes informé(e)(s), se sont informé(e)s
Plup. Ind.	m'étais informé(e), t'étais informé(e), s'était informé(e); nous étions informé(e)s, vous étiez informé(e)(s), s'étaient informé(e)s
Past Ant.	me fus informé(e), te fus informé(e), se fut informé(e); nous fûmes informé(e)s, vous fûtes informé(e)(s), se furent informé(e)s
Fut. Perf.	me serai informé(e), te seras informé(e), se sera informé(e); nous serons informé(e)s, vous serez informé(e)(s), se seront informé(e)s
Cond. Perf.	me serais informé(e), te serais informé(e), se serait informé(e); nous serions informé(e)s, vous seriez informé(e)(s), se seraient informé(e)s
Past Subj.	me sois informé(e), te sois informé(e), se soit informé(e); nous soyons informé(e)s, vous soyez informé(e)(s), se soient informé(e)s
Plup. Subj.	me fusse informé(e), te fusses informé(e), se fût informé(e); nous fussions informé(e)s, vous fussiez informé(e)(s), se fussent informé(e)s
Imperative	informe-toi, informons-nous, informez-vous

to insist

Pres. Ind.	insiste, insistes, insiste; insistons, insistez, insistent
Imp. Ind.	insistais, insistais, insistait; insistions, insistiez, insistaient
Past Def.	insistai, insistas, insista; insistâmes, insistâtes, insistèrent
Future	insisterai, insisteras, insistera; insisterons, insisterez, insisteront
Condit.	insisterais, insisterais, insisterait; insisterions, insisteriez, insisteraient
Pres. Subj.	insiste, insistes, insiste; insistions, insistiez, insistent
Imp. Subj.	insistasse, insistasses, insistât; insistassions, insistassiez, insistassent
Past Indef.	ai insisté, as insisté, a insisté; avons insisté, avez insisté, ont insisté
Plup. Ind.	avais insisté, avais insisté, avait insisté; avions insisté, aviez insisté, avaient insisté
Past Ant.	eus insisté, eus insisté, eut insisté; eûmes insisté, eûtes insisté, eurent insisté
Fut. Perf.	aurai insisté, auras insisté, aura insisté; aurons insisté, aurez insisté, auront insisté
Cond. Perf.	aurais insisté, aurais insisté, aurait insisté; aurions insisté, auriez insisté, auraient insisté
Past Subj.	aie insisté, aies insisté, ait insisté; ayons insisté, ayez insisté, aient insisté
Plup. Subj.	eusse insisté, eusses insisté, eût insisté; eussions insisté, eussiez insisté, eussent insisté
Imperative	insiste, insistons, insistez

to instruct

Pres. Ind.	instruis, instruis, instruit; instruisons, instruisez, instruisent
Imp. Ind.	instruisais, instruisais, instruisait; instruisions, instruisiez, instruisaient
Past Def.	instruisis, instruisis, instruisit; instruisîmes, instruisîtes, instruisirent
Future	instruirai, instruiras, instruira; instruirons, instruirez, instruiront
Condit.	instruirais, instruirais, instruirait; instruirions, instruiriez, instruiraient
Pres. Subj.	instruise, instruises, instruise; instruisions, instruisiez, instruisent
Imp. Subj.	instruisisse, instruisisses, instruisît; instruisissions, instruisissiez, instruisissent
Past Indef.	ai instruit, as instruit, a instruit; avons instruit, avez instruit, ont instruit
Plup. Ind.	avais instruit, avais instruit, avait instruit; avions instruit, aviez instruit, avaient instruit
Past Ant.	eus instruit, eus instruit, eut instruit; eûmes instruit, eûtes instruit, eurent instruit
Fut. Perf.	aurai instruit, auras instruit, aura instruit; aurons instruit, aurez instruit, auront instruit
Cond. Perf.	aurais instruit, aurais instruit, aurait instruit; aurions instruit, auriez instruit, auraient instruit
Past Subj.	aie instruit, aies instruit, ait instruit; ayons instruit, ayez instruit, aient instruit
Plup. Subj.	eusse instruit, eusses instruit, eût instruit; eussions instruit, eussiez instruit, eussent instruit
Imperative	instruis, instruisons, instruisez

to forbid, prohibit

Pres. Ind.	interdis, interdis, interdit; interdisons, interdisez, interdisent
Imp. Ind.	interdisais, interdisais, interdisait; interdisions, interdisiez, interdisaient
Past Def.	interdis, interdis, interdit; interdîmes, interdîtes, interdirent
Future	interdirai, interdiras, interdira; interdirons, interdirez, interdiront
Condit.	interdirais, interdirais, interdirait; interdirions, interdiriez, interdiraient
Pres. Subj.	interdise, interdises, interdise; interdisions, interdisiez, interdisent
Imp. Subj.	interdisse, interdisses, interdît; interdissions, interdissiez, interdissent
Past Indef.	ai interdit, as interdit, a interdit; avons interdit, avez interdit, ont interdit
Plup. Ind.	avais interdit, avais interdit, avait interdit; avions interdit, aviez interdit, avaient interdit
Past Ant.	eus interdit, eus interdit, eut interdit; eûmes interdit, eûtes interdit, eurent interdit
Fut. Perf.	aurai interdit, auras interdit, aura interdit; aurons interdit, aurez interdit, auront interdit
Cond. Perf.	aurais interdit, aurais interdit, aurait interdit; aurions interdit, auriez interdit, auraient interdit
Past Subj.	aie interdit, aies interdit, ait interdit; ayons interdit, ayez interdit, aient interdit
Plup. Subj.	eusse interdit, eusses interdit, eût interdit; eussions interdit, eussiez interdit, eussent interdit
Imperative	interdis, interdisons, interdisez

to interrogate, question

Pres. Ind.	interroge, interroges, interroge; interrogeons, interrogez, interrogent
Imp. Ind.	interrogeais, interrogeais, interrogeait; interrogions, interrogiez, interrogeaient
Past Def.	interrogeai, interrogeas, interrogea; interrogeâmes, interrogeâtes, interrogèrent
Fut. Ind.	interrogerai, interrogeras, interrogera; interrogerons, interrogerez, interrogeront
Condit.	interrogerais, interrogerais, interrogerait; interrogerions, interrogeriez, interrogeraient
Pres. Subj.	interroge, interroges, interroge; interrogions, interrogiez, interrogent
Imp. Subj.	interrogeasse, interrogeasses, interrogeât; interrogeassions, interrogeassiez, interrogeassent
Past Indef.	ai interrogé, as interrogé, a interrogé; avons interrogé, avez interrogé, ont interrogé
Pluperf.	avais interrogé, avais interrogé, avait interrogé; avions interrogé, aviez interrogé, avaient interrogé
Past Ant.	eus interrogé, eus interrogé, eut interrogé; eûmes interrogé, eûtes interrogé, eurent interrogé
Fut. Perf.	aurai interrogé, auras interrogé, aura interrogé; aurons interrogé, aurez interrogé, auront interrogé
Cond. Perf.	aurais interrogé, aurais interrogé, aurait interrogé; aurions interrogé, auriez interrogé, auraient interrogé
Past Subj.	aie interrogé, aies interrogé, ait interrogé; ayons interrogé, ayez interrogé, aient interrogé
Plup. Subj.	eusse interrogé, eusses interrogé, eût interrogé; eussions interrogé, eussiez interrogé, eussent interrogé
Imperative	interroge, interrogeons, interrogez

to interrupt

Pres. Ind.	interromps, interromps, interrompt; interrompons, interrompez, interrompent
Imp. Ind.	interrompais, interrompais, interrompait; interrompions, interrompiez, interrompaient
Past Def.	interrompis, interrompis, interrompit; interrompîmes, interrompîtes, interrompirent
Fut. Ind.	interromprai, interrompras, interrompra; interromprons, interromprez, interrompront
Condit.	interromprais, interromprais, interromprait; interromprions, interrompriez, interrompraient
Pres. Subj.	interrompe, interrompes, interrompe; interrompions, interrompiez, interrompent
Imp. Subj.	interrompisse, interrompisses, interrompît; interrompissions, interrompissiez, interrompissent
Past Indef.	ai interrompu, as interrompu, a interrompu; avons interrompu, avez interrompu, ont interrompu
Pluperf.	avais interrompu, avais interrompu, avait interrompu; avions interrompu, aviez interrompu, avaient interrompu
Past Ant.	eus interrompu, eus interrompu, eut interrompu; eûmes interrompu, eûtes interrompu, eurent interrompu
Fut. Perf.	aurai interrompu, auras interrompu, aura interrompu; aurons interrompu, aurez interrompu, auront interrompu
Cond. Perf.	aurais interrompu, aurais interrompu, aurait interrompu; aurions interrompu, auriez interrompu, auraient interrompu
Past Subj.	aie interrompu, aies interrompu, ait interrompu; ayons interrompu, ayez interrompu, aient interrompu
Plup. Subj.	eusse interrompu, eusses interrompu, eût interrompu; eussions interrompu, eussiez interrompu, eussent interrompu
Imperative	interromps, interrompons, interrompez

to introduce, show in

Pres. Ind.	introduis, introduis, introduit; introduisons, introduisez, introduisent
Imp. Ind.	introduisais, introduisais, introduisait; introduisions, introduisiez, introduisaient
Past Def.	introduisis, introduisis, introduisit; introduisîmes, introduisîtes, introduisirent
Future	introduirai, introduiras, introduira; introduirons, introduirez, introduiront
Condit.	introduirais, introduirais, introduirait; introduirions, introduiriez, introduiraient
Pres. Subj.	introduise, introduises, introduise; introduisions, introduisiez, introduisent
Imp. Subj.	introduisisse, introduisisses, introduisît; introduisissions, introduisissiez, introduisissent
Past Indef.	ai introduit, as introduit, a introduit; avons introduit, avez introduit, ont introduit
Plup. Ind.	avais introduit, avais introduit, avait introduit; avions introduit, aviez introduit, avaient introduit
Past Ant.	eus introduit, eus introduit, eut introduit; eûmes introduit, eûtes introduit, eurent introduit
Fut. Perf.	aurai introduit, auras introduit, aura introduit; aurons introduit, aurez introduit, auront introduit
Cond. Perf.	aurais introduit, aurais introduit, aurait introduit; aurions introduit, auriez introduit, auraient introduit
Past Subj.	aie introduit, aies introduit, ait introduit; ayons introduit, ayez introduit, aient introduit
Plup. Subj.	eusse introduit, eusses introduit, eût introduit; eussions introduit, eussiez introduit, eussent introduit
Imperative	introduis, introduisons, introduisez

to invent

Pres. Ind.	invente, inventes, invente; inventons, inventez, inventent
Imp. Ind.	inventais, inventais, inventait; inventions, inventiez, inventaient
Past Def.	inventai, inventas, inventa; inventâmes, inventâtes, inventèrent
Future	inventerai, inventeras, inventera; inventerons, inventerez, inventeront
Condit.	inventerais, inventerais, inventerait; inventerions, inventeriez, inventeraient
Pres. Subj.	invente, inventes, invente; inventions, inventiez, inventent
Imp. Subj.	inventasse, inventasses, inventât; inventassions, inventassiez, inventassent
Past Indef.	ai inventé, as inventé, a inventé; avons inventé, avez inventé, ont inventé
Plup. Ind.	avais inventé, avais inventé, avait inventé; avions inventé, aviez inventé, avaient inventé
Past Ant.	eus inventé, eus inventé, eut inventé; eûmes inventé, eûtes inventé, eurent inventé
Fut. Perf.	aurai inventé, auras inventé, aura inventé; aurons inventé, aurez inventé, auront inventé
Cond. Perf.	aurais inventé, aurais inventé, aurait inventé; aurions inventé, auriez inventé, auraient inventé
Past Subj.	aie inventé, aies inventé, ait inventé; ayons inventé, ayez inventé, aient inventé
Plup. Subj.	eusse inventé, eusses inventé, eût inventé; eussions inventé, eussiez inventé, eussent inventé
Imperative	invente, inventons, inventez

to throw, cast

Pres. Ind.	jette, jettes, jette; jetons, jetez, jettent
Imp. Ind.	jetais, jetais, jetait; jetions, jetiez, jetaient
Past Def.	jetai, jetas, jeta; jetâmes, jetâtes, jetèrent
Fut. Ind.	jetterai, jetteras, jettera; jetterons, jetterez, jetteront
Condit.	jetterais, jetterais, jetterait; jetterions, jetteriez, jetteraient
Pres. Subj.	jette, jettes, jette; jetions, jetiez, jettent
Imp. Subj.	jetasse, jetasses, jetât; jetassions, jetassiez, jetassent
Past Indef.	ai jeté, as jeté, a jeté; avons jeté, avez jeté, ont jeté
Pluperf.	avais jeté, avais jeté, avait jeté; avions jeté, aviez jeté, avaient jeté
Past Ant.	eus jeté, eus jeté, eut jeté; eûmes jeté, eûtes jeté, eurent jeté
Fut. Perf.	aurai jeté, auras jeté, aura jeté; aurons jeté, aurez jeté, auront jeté
Cond. Perf.	aurais jeté, aurais jeté, aurait jeté; aurions jeté, auriez jeté, auraient jeté
Past Subj.	aie jeté, aies jeté, ait jeté; ayons jeté, ayez jeté, aient jeté
Plup. Subj.	eusse jeté, eusses jeté, eût jeté; eussions jeté, eussiez jeté, eussent jeté
Imperative	jette, jetons, jetez

to join

Pres. Ind.	joins, joins, joint; joignons, joignez, joignent
Imp. Ind.	joignais, joignais, joignait; joignions, joigniez, joignaient
Past Def.	joignis, joignis, joignit; joignîmes, joignîtes, joignirent
Fut. Ind.	joindrai, joindras, joindra; joindrons, joindrez, joindront
Condit.	joindrais, joindrais, joindrait; joindrions, joindriez, joindraient
Pres. Subj.	joigne, joignes, joigne; joignions, joigniez, joignent
Imp. Subj.	joignisse, joignisses, joignît; joignissions, joignissiez, joignissent
Past Indef.	ai joint, as joint, a joint; avons joint, avez joint, ont joint
Pluperf.	avais joint, avais joint, avait joint; avions joint, aviez joint, avaient joint
Past Ant.	eus joint, eus joint, eut joint; eûmes joint, eûtes joint, eurent joint
Fut. Perf.	aurai joint, auras joint, aura joint; aurons joint, aurez joint, auront joint
Cond. Perf.	aurais joint, aurais joint, aurait joint; aurions joint, auriez joint, auraient joint
Past Subj.	aie joint, aies joint, ait joint; ayons joint, ayez joint, aient joint
Plup. Subj.	eusse joint, eusses joint, eût joint; eussions joint, eussiez joint, eussent joint
Imperative	joins, joignons, joignez

to play, act (in a play)

Pres. Ind.	joue, joues, joue; jouons, jouez, jouent
Imp. Ind.	jouais, jouais, jouait; jouions, jouiez, jouaient
Past Def.	jouai, jouas, joua; jouâmes, jouâtes, jouèrent
Fut. Ind.	jouerai, joueras, jouera; jouerons, jouerez, joueront
Condit.	jouerais, jouerais, jouerait; jouerions, joueriez, joueraient
Pres. Subj.	joue, joues, joue; jouions, jouiez, jouent
Imp. Subj.	jouasse, jouasses, jouât; jouassions, jouassiez, jouassent
Past Indef.	ai joué, as joué, a joué; avons joué, avez joué, ont joué
Pluperf.	avais joué, avais joué, avait joué; avions joué, aviez joué, avaient joué
Past Ant.	eus joué, eus joué, eut joué; eûmes joué, eûtes joué, eurent joué
Fut. Perf.	aurai joué, auras joué, aura joué; aurons joué, aurez joué, auront joué
Cond. Perf.	aurais joué, aurais joué, aurait joué; aurions joué, auriez joué, auraient joué
Past Subj.	aie joué, aies joué, ait joué; ayons joué, ayez joué, aient joué
Plup. Subj.	eusse joué, eusses joué, eût joué; eussions joué, eussiez joué, eussent joué
Imperative	joue, jouons, jouez

to judge

Pres. Ind.	juge, juges, juge; jugeons, jugez, jugent
Imp. Ind.	jugeais, jugeais, jugeait; jugions, jugiez, jugeaient
Past Def.	jugeai, jugeas, jugea; jugeâmes, jugeâtes, jugèrent
Fut. Ind.	jugerai, jugeras, jugera; jugerons, jugerez, jugeront
Condit.	jugerais, jugerais, jugerait; jugerions, jugeriez, jugeraient
Pres. Subj.	juge, juges, juge; jugions, jugiez, jugent
Imp. Subj.	jugeasse, jugeasses, jugeât; jugeassions, jugeassiez, jugeassent
Past Indef.	ai jugé, as jugé, a jugé; avons jugé, avez jugé, ont jugé
Pluperf.	avais jugé, avais jugé, avait jugé; avions jugé, aviez jugé, avaient jugé
Past Ant.	eus jugé, eus jugé, eut jugé; eûmes jugé, eûtes jugé, eurent jugé
Fut. Perf.	aurai jugé, auras jugé, aura jugé; aurons jugé, aurez jugé, auront jugé
Cond. Perf.	aurais jugé, aurais jugé, aurait jugé; aurions jugé, auriez jugé, auraient jugé
Past Subj.	aie jugé, aies jugé, ait jugé; ayons jugé, ayez jugé, aient jugé
Plup. Subj.	eusse jugé, eusses jugé, eût jugé; eussions jugé, eussiez jugé, eussent jugé
Imperative	juge, jugeons, jugez

to swear, vow

Pres. Ind.	jure, jures, jure; jurons, jurez, jurent
Imp. Ind.	jurais, jurais, jurait; jurions, juriez, juraient
Past Def.	jurai, juras, jura; jurâmes, jurâtes, jurèrent
Future	jurerai, jureras, jurera; jurerons, jurerez, jureront
Condit.	jurerais, jurerais, jurerait; jurerions, jureriez, jureraient
Pres. Subj.	jure, jures, jure; jurions, juriez, jurent
Imp. Subj.	jurasse, jurasses, jurât; jurassions, jurassiez, jurassent
Past Indef.	ai juré, as juré, a juré; avons juré, avez juré, ont juré
Pluperf.	avais juré, avais juré, avait juré; avions juré, aviez juré, avaient juré
Past Ant.	eus juré, eus juré, eut juré; eûmes juré, eûtes juré, eurent juré
Fut. Perf.	aurai juré, auras juré, aura juré; aurons juré, aurez juré, auront juré
Cond. Perf.	aurais juré, aurais juré, aurait juré; aurions juré, auriez juré, auraient juré
Past Subj.	aie juré, aies juré, ait juré; ayons juré, ayez juré, aient juré
Plup. Subj.	eusse juré, eusses juré, eût juré; eussions juré, eussiez juré, eussent juré
Imperative	jure, jurons, jurez

to lace

Pres. Ind.	lace, laces, lace; laçons, lacez, lacent
Imp. Ind.	laçais, laçais, laçait; lacions, laciez, laçaient
Past Def.	laçai, laças, laça; laçâmes, laçâtes, lacèrent
Future	lacerai, laceras, lacera; lacerons, lacerez, laceront
Condit.	lacerais, lacerais, lacerait; lacerions, laceriez, laceraient
Pres. Subj.	lace, laces, lace; lacions, laciez, lacent
Imp. Subj.	laçasse, laçasses, laçât; laçassions, laçassiez, laçassent
Past Indef.	ai lacé, as lacé, a lacé; avons lacé, avez lacé, ont lacé
Plup. Ind.	avais lacé, avais lacé, avait lacé; avions lacé, aviez lacé, avaient lacé
Past Ant.	eus lacé, eus lacé, eut lacé; eûmes lacé, eûtes lacé, eurent lacé
Fut. Perf.	aurai lacé, auras lacé, aura lacé; aurons lacé, aurez lacé, auront lacé
Cond. Perf.	aurais lacé, aurais lacé, aurait lacé; aurions lacé, auriez lacé, auraient lacé
Past Subj.	aie lacé, aies lacé, ait lacé; ayons lacé, ayez lacé, aient lacé
Plup. Subj.	eusse lacé, eusses lacé, eût lacé; eussions lacé, eussiez lacé, eussent lacé
Imperative	lace, laçons, lacez

to let go, leave hold, loosen

Pres. Ind.	lâche, lâches, lâche; lâchons, lâchez, lâchent
Imp. Ind.	lâchais, lâchais, lâchait; lâchions, lâchiez, lâchaient
Past Def.	lâchai, lâchas, lâcha; lâchâmes, lâchâtes, lâchèrent
Future	lâcherai, lâcheras, lâchera; lâcherons, lâcherez, lâcheront
Condit.	lâcherais, lâcherais, lâcherait; lâcherions, lâcheriez, lâcheraient
Pres. Subj.	lâche, lâches, lâche; lâchions, lâchiez, lâchent
Imp. Subj.	lâchasse, lâchasses, lâchât; lâchassions, lâchassiez, lâchassent
Past Indef.	ai lâché, as lâché, a lâché; avons lâché, avez lâché, ont lâché
Plup. Ind.	avais lâché, avais lâché, avait lâché; avions lâché, aviez lâché, avaient lâché
Past Ant.	eus lâché, eus lâché, eut lâché; eûmes lâché, eûtes lâché, eurent lâché
Fut. Perf.	aurai lâché, auras lâché, aura lâché; aurons lâché, aurez lâché, auront lâché
Cond. Perf.	aurais lâché, aurais lâché, aurait lâché; aurions lâché, auriez lâché, auraient lâché
Past Subj.	aie lâché, aies lâché, ait lâché; ayons lâché, ayez lâché, aient lâché
Plup. Subj.	eusse lâché, eusses lâché, eût lâché; eussions lâché, eussiez lâché, eussent lâché
Imperative	lâche, lâchons, lâchez

to leave, let, allow

Pres. Ind.	laisse, laisses, laisse; laissons, laissez, laissent
Imp. Ind.	laissais, laissais, laissait; laissions, laissiez, laissaient
Past Def.	laissai, laissas, laissa; laissâmes, laissâtes, laissèrent
Fut. Ind.	laisserai, laisseras, laissera; laisserons, laisserez, laisseront
Condit.	laisserais, laisserais, laisserait; laisserions, laisseriez, laisseraient
Pres. Subj.	laisse, laisses, laisse; laissions, laissiez, laissent
Imp. Subj.	laissasse, laissasses, laissât; laissassions, laissassiez, laissassent
Past Indef.	ai laissé, as laissé, a laissé; avons laissé, avez laissé, ont laissé
Pluperf.	avais laissé, avais laissé, avait laissé; avions laissé, aviez laissé, avaient laissé
Past Ant.	eus laissé, eus laissé, eut laissé; eûmes laissé, eûtes laissé, eurent laissé
Fut. Perf.	aurai laissé, auras laissé, aura laissé; aurons laissé, aurez laissé, auront laissé
Cond. Perf.	aurais laissé, aurais laissé, aurait laissé; aurions laissé, auriez laissé, auraient laissé
Past Subj.	aie laissé, aies laissé, ait laissé; ayons laissé, ayez laissé, aient laissé
Plup. Subj.	eusse laissé, eusses laissé, eût laissé; eussions laissé, eussiez laissé, eussent laissé
Imperative	laisse, laissons, laissez

to hurl, launch, throw

Pres. Ind.	lance, lances, lance; lançons, lancez, lancent
Imp. Ind.	lançais, lançais, lançait; lancions, lanciez, lançaient
Past Def.	lançai, lanças, lança; lançâmes, lançâtes, lancèrent
Future	lancerai, lanceras, lancera; lancerons, lancerez, lanceront
Condit.	lancerais, lancerais, lancerait; lancerions, lanceriez, lanceraient
Pres. Subj.	lance, lances, lance; lancions, lanciez, lancent
Imp. Subj.	lançasse, lançasses, lançât; lançassions, lançassiez, lançassent
Past Indef.	ai lancé, as lancé, a lancé; avons lancé, avez lancé, ont lancé
Plup. Ind.	avais lancé, avais lancé, avait lancé; avions lancé, aviez lancé, avaient lancé
Past Ant.	eus lancé, eus lancé, eut lancé; eûmes lancé, eûtes lancé, eurent lancé
Fut. Perf.	aurai lancé, auras lancé, aura lancé; aurons lancé, aurez lancé, auront lancé
Cond. Perf.	aurais lancé, aurais lancé, aurait lancé; aurions lancé, auriez lancé, auraient lancé
Past Subj.	aie lancé, aies lancé, ait lancé; ayons lancé, ayez lancé, aient lancé
Plup. Subj.	eusse lancé, eusses lancé, eût lancé; eussions lancé, eussiez lancé, eussent lancé
Imperative	lance, lançons, lancez

to wash oneself

Pres. Ind.	me lave, te laves, se lave; nous lavons, vous lavez, se lavent
Imp. Ind.	me lavais, te lavais, se lavait; nous lavions, vous laviez, se lavaient
Past Def.	me lavai, te lavas, se lava; nous lavâmes, vous lavâtes, se lavèrent
Fut. Ind.	me laverai, te laveras, se lavera; nous laverons, vous laverez, se laveront
Condit.	me laverais, te laverais, se laverait; nous laverions, vous laveriez, se laveraient
Pres. Subj.	me lave, te laves, se lave; nous lavions, vous laviez, se lavent
Imp. Subj.	me lavasse, te lavasses, se lavât; nous lavassions, vous lavassiez, se lavassent
Past Indef.	me suis lavé(e), t'es lavé(e), s'est lavé(e); nous sommes lavé(e)s, vous êtes lavé(e)(s), se sont lavé(e)s
Pluperf.	m'étais lavé(e), t'étais lavé(e), s'était lavé(e); nous étions lavé(e)s, vous étiez lavé(e)(s), s'étaient lavé(e)s
Past Ant.	me fus lavé(e), te fus lavé(e), se fut lavé(e); nous fûmes lavé(e)s, vous fûtes lavé(e)(s), se furent lavé(e)s
Fut. Perf.	me serai lavé(e), te seras lavé(e), se sera lavé(e); nous serons lavé(e)s, vous serez lavé(e)(s), se seront lavé(e)s
Cond. Perf.	me serais lavé(e), te serais lavé(e), se serait lavé(e); nous serions lavé(e)s, vous seriez lavé(e)(s), se seraient lavé(e)s
Past Subj.	me sois lavé(e), te sois lavé(e), se soit lavé(e); nous soyons lavé(e)s, vous soyez lavé(e)(s), se soient lavé(e)s
Plup. Subj.	me fusse lavé(e), te fusses lavé(e), se fût lavé(e); nous fussions lavé(e)s, vous fussiez lavé(e)(s), se fussent lavé(e)s
Imperative	lave-toi, lavons-nous, lavez-vous

to lick

Pres. Ind.	lèche, lèches, lèche; léchons, léchez, lèchent
Imp. Ind.	léchais, léchais, léchait; léchions, léchiez, léchaient
Past Def.	léchai, léchas, lécha; léchâmes, léchâtes, léchèrent
Future	lécherai, lécheras, léchera; lécherons, lécherez, lécheront
Condit.	lécherais, lécherais, lécherait; lécherions, lécheriez, lécheraient
Pres. Subj.	lèche, lèches, lèche; léchions, léchiez, lèchent
Imp. Subj.	léchasse, léchasses, léchât; léchassions, léchassiez, léchassent
Past Indef.	ai léché, as léché, a léché; avons léché, avez léché, ont léché
Pluperf.	avais léché, avais léché, avait léché; avions léché, aviez léché, avaient léché
Past Ant.	eus léché, eus léché, eut léché; eûmes léché, eûtes léché, eurent léché
Fut. Perf.	aurai léché, auras léché, aura léché; aurons léché, aurez léché, auront léché
Cond. Perf.	aurais léché, aurais léché, aurait léché; aurions léché, auriez léché, auraient léché
Past Subj.	aie léché, aies léché, ait léché; ayons léché, ayez léché, aient léché
Plup. Subj.	eusse léché, eusses léché, eût léché; eussions léché, eussiez léché, eussent léché
Imperative	lèche, léchons, léchez

to lift, raise

Pres. Ind.	lève, lèves, lève, levons, levez, lèvent
Imp. Ind.	levais, levais, levait; levions, leviez, levaient
Past Def.	levai, levas, leva; levâmes, levâtes, levèrent
Future	lèverai, lèveras, lèvera; lèverons, lèverez, lèveront
Condit.	lèverais, lèverais, lèverait; lèverions, lèveriez, lèveraient
Pres. Subj.	lève, lèves, lève; levions, leviez, lèvent
Imp. Subj.	levasse, levasses, levât; levassions, levassiez, levassent
Past Indef.	ai levé, as levé, a levé; avons levé, avez levé, ont levé
Plup. Ind.	avais levé, avais levé, avait levé; avions levé, aviez levé, avaient levé
Past Ant.	eus levé, eus levé, eut levé; eûmes levé, eûtes levé, eurent levé
Fut. Perf.	aurai levé, auras levé, aura levé; aurons levé, aurez levé, auront levé
Cond. Perf.	aurais levé, aurais levé, aurait levé; aurions levé, auriez levé, auraient levé
Past Subj.	aie levé, aies levé, ait levé; ayons levé, ayez levé, aient levé
Plup. Subj.	eusse levé, eusses levé, eût levé; eussions levé, eussiez levé, eussent levé
Imperative	lève, levons, levez

to get up

Pres. Ind.	me lève, te lèves, se lève; nous levons, vous levez, se lèvent
Imp. Ind.	me levais, te levais, se levait; nous levions, vous leviez, se levaient
Past Def.	me levai, te levas, se leva; nous levâmes, vous levâtes, se levèrent
Fut. Ind.	me lèverai, te lèveras, se lèvera; nous lèverons, vous lèverez, se lèveront
Condit.	me lèverais, te lèverais, se lèverait; nous lèverions, vous lèveriez, se lèveraient
Pres. Subj.	me lève, te lèves, se lève; nous levions, vous leviez, se lèvent
Imp. Subj.	me levasse, te levasses, se levât; nous levassions, vous levassiez, se levassent
Past Indef.	me suis levé(e), t'es levé(e), s'est levé(e); nous sommes levé(e)s, vous êtes levé(e)(s), se sont levé(e)s
Pluperf.	m'étais levé(e), t'étais levé(e), s'était levé(e); nous étions levé(e)s, vous étiez levé(e)(s), s'étaient levé(e)s
Past Ant.	me fus levé(e), te fus levé(e), se fut levé(e); nous fûmes levé(e)s, vous fûtes levé(e)(s), se furent levé(e)s
Fut. Perf.	me serai levé(e), te seras levé(e), se sera levé(e); nous serons levé(e)s, vous serez levé(e)(s), se seront levé(e)s
Cond. Perf.	me serais levé(e), te serais levé(e), se serait levé(e); nous serions levé(e)s, vous seriez levé(e)(s), se seraient levé(e)s
Past Subj.	me sois levé(e), te sois levé(e), se soit levé(e); nous soyons levé(e)s, vous soyez levé(e)(s), se soient levé(e)s
Plup. Subj.	me fusse levé(e), te fusses levé(e), se fût levé(e); nous fussions levé(e)s, vous fussiez levé(e)(s), se fussent levé(e)s
Imperative	lève-toi, levons-nous, levez-vous

to read

Pres. Ind.	lis, lis, lit; lisons, lisez, lisent
Imp. Ind.	lisais, lisais, lisait; lisions, lisiez, lisaient
Past Def.	lus, lus, lut; lûmes, lûtes, lurent
Fut. Ind.	lirai, liras, lira; lirons, lirez, liront
Condit.	lirais, lirais, lirait; lirions, liriez, liraient
Pres. Subj.	lise, lises, lise; lisions, lisiez, lisent
Imp. Subj.	lusse, lusses, lût; lussions, lussiez, lussent
Past Indef.	ai lu, as lu, a lu; avons lu, avez lu, ont lu
Pluperf.	avais lu, avais lu, avait lu; avions lu, aviez lu, avaient lu
Past Ant.	eus lu, eus lu, eut lu; eûmes lu, eûtes lu, eurent lu
Fut. Perf.	aurai lu, auras lu, aura lu; aurons lu, aurez lu, auront lu
Cond. Perf.	aurais lu, aurais lu, aurait lu; aurions lu, auriez lu, auraient lu
Past Subj.	aie lu, aies lu, ait lu; ayons lu, ayez lu, aient lu
Plup. Subj.	eusse lu, eusses lu, eût lu; eussions lu, eussiez lu, eussent lu
Imperative	lis, lisons, lisez

to praise, rent

Pres. Ind.	loue, loues, loue; louons, louez, louent
Imp. Ind.	louais, louais, louait; louions, louiez, louaient
Past Def.	louai, louas, loua; louâmes, louâtes, louèrent
Future	louerai, loueras, louera; louerons, louerez, loueront
Condit.	louerais, louerais, louerait; louerions, loueriez, loueraient
Pres. Subj.	loue, loues, loue; louions, louiez, louent
Imp. Subj.	louasse, louasses, louât; louassions, louassiez, louassent
Past Indef.	ai loué, as loué, a loué; avons loué, avez loué, ont loué
Plup. Ind.	avais loué, avais loué, avait loué; avions loué, aviez loué, avaient loué
Past Ant.	eus loué, eus loué, eut loué; eûmes loué, eûtes loué, eurent loué
Fut. Perf.	aurai loué, auras loué, aura loué; aurons loué, aurez loué, auront loué
Cond. Perf.	aurais loué, aurais loué, aurait loué; aurions loué, auriez loué, auraient loué
Past Subj.	aie loué, aies loué, ait loué; ayons loué, ayez loué, aient loué
Plup. Subj.	eusse loué, eusses loué, eût loué; eussions loué, eussiez loué, eussent loué
Imperative	loue, louons, louez

to shine

Pres. Ind.	il (elle) luit ils (elles) luisent
Imp. Ind.	il (elle) luisait ils (elles) luisaient
Past Def.	il (elle) luit ils (elles) luirent
Future	il (elle) luira ils (elles) luiront
Condit.	il (elle) luirait ils (elles) luiraient
Pres. Subj.	qu'il (elle) luise qu'ils (elles) luisent
Imp. Subj.	qu'il (elle) luisît qu'ils (elles) luisissent
Past Indef.	il (elle) a lui ils (elles) ont lui
Plup. Ind.	il (elle) avait lui ils (elles) avaient lui
Past Ant.	il (elle) eut lui ils (elles) eurent lui
Fut. Perf.	il (elle) aura lui ils (elles) auront lui
Cond. Perf.	il (elle) aurait lui ils (elles) auraient lui
Past Subj.	qu'il (elle) ait lui qu'ils (elles) aient lui
Plup. Subj.	qu'il (elle) eût lui qu'ils (elles) eussent lui
Imperative	[inemployé]

to reduce (one's weight), grow thin, lose weight

Pres. Ind.	maigris, maigris, maigrit; maigrissons, maigrissez, maigrissent
Imp. Ind.	maigrissais, maigrissais, maigrissait; maigrissions, maigrissiez, maigrissaient
Past Def.	maigris, maigris, maigrit; maigrîmes, maigrîtes, maigrirent
Future	maigrirai, maigriras, maigrira; maigrirons, maigrirez, maigriront
Condit.	maigrirais, maigrirais, maigrirait; maigririons, maigririez, maigriraient
Pres. Subj.	maigrisse, maigrisses, maigrisse; maigrissions, maigrissiez, maigrissent
Imp. Subj.	maigrisse, maigrisses, maigrît; maigrissions, maigrissiez, maigrissent
Past Indef.	ai maigri, as maigri, a maigri; avons maigri, avez maigri, ont maigri
Plup. Ind.	avais maigri, avais maigri, avait maigri; avions maigri, aviez maigri, avaient maigri
Past Ant.	eus maigri, eus maigri, eut maigri; eûmes maigri, eûtes maigri, eurent maigri
Fut. Perf.	aurai maigri, auras maigri, aura maigri; aurons maigri, aurez maigri, auront maigri
Cond. Perf.	aurais maigri, aurais maigri, aurait maigri; aurions maigri, auriez maigri, auraient maigri
Past Subj.	aie maigri, aies maigri, ait maigri; ayons maigri, ayez maigri, aient maigri
Plup. Subj.	eusse maigri, eusses maigri, eût maigri; eussions maigri, eussiez maigri, eussent maigri
Imperative	maigris, maigrissons, maigrissez

to eat

Pres. Ind.	mange, manges, mange; mangeons, mangez, mangent
Imp. Ind.	mangeais, mangeais, mangeait; mangions, mangiez, mangeaient
Past Def.	mangeai, mangeas, mangea; mangeâmes, mangeâtes, mangèrent
Fut. Ind.	mangerai, mangeras, mangera; mangerons, mangerez, mangeront
Condit.	mangerais, mangerais, mangerait; mangerions, mangeriez, mangeraient
Pres. Subj.	mange, manges, mange; mangions, mangiez, mangent
Imp. Subj.	mangeasse, mangeasses, mangeât; mangeassions, mangeassiez, mangeassent
Past Indef.	ai mangé, as mangé, a mangé; avons mangé, avez mangé, ont mangé
Pluperf.	avais mangé, avais mangé, avait mangé; avions mangé, aviez mangé, avaient mangé
Past Ant.	eus mangé, eus mangé, eut mangé; eûmes mangé, eûtes mangé, eurent mangé
Fut. Perf.	aurai mangé, auras mangé, aura mangé; aurons mangé, aurez mangé, auront mangé
Cond. Perf.	aurais mangé, aurais mangé, aurait mangé; aurions mangé, auriez mangé, auraient mangé
Past Subj.	aie mangé, aies mangé, ait mangé; ayons mangé, ayez mangé, aient mangé
Plup. Subj.	eusse mangé, eusses mangé, eût mangé; eussions mangé, eussiez mangé, eussent mangé
Imperative	mange, mangeons, mangez

to miss, lack

Pres. Ind.	manque, manques, manque; manquons, manquez, manquent
Imp. Ind.	manquais, manquais, manquait; manquions, manquiez, manquaient
Past Def.	manquai, manquas, manqua; manquâmes, manquâtes, manquèrent
Future	manquerai, manqueras, manquera; manquerons, manquerez, manqueront
Condit.	manquerais, manquerais, manquerait; manquerions, manqueriez, manqueraient
Pres. Subj.	manque, manques, manque; manquions, manquiez, manquent
Imp. Subj.	manquasse, manquasses, manquât; manquassions, manquassiez, manquassent
Past Indef.	ai manqué, as manqué, a manqué; avons manqué, avez manqué, ont manqué
Pluperf.	avais manqué, avais manqué, avait manqué; avions manqué, aviez manqué, avaient manqué
Past Ant.	eus manqué, eus manqué, eut manqué; eûmes manqué, eûtes manqué, eurent manqué
Fut. Perf.	aurai manqué, auras manqué, aura manqué; aurons manqué, aurez manqué, auront manqué
Cond. Perf.	aurais manqué, aurais manqué, aurait manqué; aurions manqué, auriez manqué, auraient manqué
Past Subj.	aie manqué, aies manqué, ait manqué; ayons manqué, ayez manqué, aient manqué
Plup. Subj.	eusse manqué, eusses manqué, eût manqué; eussions manqué, eussiez manqué, eussent manqué
Imperative	manque, manquons, manquez

to walk, march

Pres. Ind.	marche, marches, marche; marchons, marchez, marchent
Imp. Ind.	marchais, marchais, marchait; marchions, marchiez, marchaient
Past Def.	marchai, marchas, marcha; marchâmes, marchâtes, marchèrent
Future	marcherai, marcheras, marchera; marcherons, marcherez, marcheront
Condit.	marcherais, marcherais, marcherait; marcherions, marcheriez, marcheraient
Pres. Subj.	marche, marches, marche; marchions, marchiez, marchent
Imp. Subj.	marchasse, marchasses, marchât; marchassions, marchassiez, marchassent
Past Indef.	ai marché, as marché, a marché; avons marché, avez marché, ont marché
Plup. Ind.	avais marché, avais marché, avait marché; avions marché, aviez marché, avaient marché
Past Ant.	eus marché, eus marché, eut marché; eûmes marché, eûtes marché, eurent marché
Fut. Perf.	aurai marché, auras marché, aura marché; aurons marché, aurez marché, auront marché
Cond.	aurais marché, aurais marché, aurait marché; aurions marché, auriez marché, auraient marché
Past Subj.	aie marché, aies marché, ait marché; ayons marché, ayez marché, aient marché
Plup. Subj.	eusse marché, eusses marché, eût marché; eussions marché, eussiez marché, eussent marché
Imperative	marche, marchons, marchez

to curse

Pres. Ind.	maudis, maudis, maudit; maudissons, maudissez, maudissent
Imp. Ind.	maudissais, maudissais, maudissait; maudissions, maudissiez, maudissaient
Past Def.	maudis, maudis, maudit; maudîmes, maudîtes, maudirent
Future	maudirai, maudiras, maudira; maudirons, maudirez, maudiront
Condit.	maudirais, maudirais, maudirait; maudirions, maudiriez, maudiraient
Pres. Subj.	maudisse, maudisses, maudisse; maudissions, maudissiez, maudissent
Imp. Subj.	maudisse, maudisses, maudît; maudissions, maudissiez, maudissent
Past Indef.	ai maudit, as maudit, a maudit; avons maudit, avez maudit, ont maudit
Pluperf.	avais maudit, avais maudit, avait maudit; avions maudit, aviez maudit, avaient maudit
Past Ant.	eus maudit, eus maudit, eut maudit; eûmes maudit, eûtes maudit, eurent maudit
Fut. Perf.	aurai maudit, auras maudit, aura maudit; aurons maudit, aurez maudit, auront maudit
Cond. Perf.	aurais maudit, aurais maudit, aurait maudit; aurions maudit, auriez maudit, auraient maudit
Past Subj.	aie maudit, aies maudit, ait maudit; ayons maudit, ayez maudit, aient maudit
Plup. Subj.	eusse maudit, eusses maudit, eût maudit; eussions maudit, eussiez maudit, eussent maudit
Imperative	maudis, maudissons, maudissez

not to know, not to recognize, misjudge, misunderstand

Pres. Ind.	méconnais, méconnais, méconnaît; méconnaissons, méconnaissez, méconnaissent
Imp. Ind.	méconnaissais, méconnaissais, méconnaissait; méconnaissions, méconnaissiez, méconnaissaient
Past Def.	méconnus, méconnus, méconnut; méconnûmes, méconnûtes, méconnurent
Future	méconnaîtrai, méconnaîtras, méconnaîtra; méconnaîtrons, méconnaîtrez, méconnaîtront
Condit.	méconnaîtrais, méconnaîtrais, méconnaîtrait; méconnaîtrions, méconnaîtriez, méconnaîtraient
Pres. Subj.	méconnaisse, méconnaisses, méconnaisse; méconnaissions, méconnaissiez, méconnaissent
Imp. Subj.	méconnusse, méconnusses, méconnût; méconnussions, méconnussiez, méconnussent
Past Indef.	ai méconnu, as méconnu, a méconnu; avons méconnu, avez méconnu, ont méconnu
Plup. Ind.	avais méconnu, avais méconnu, avait méconnu; avions méconnu, aviez méconnu, avaient méconnu
Past Ant.	eus méconnu, eus méconnu, eut méconnu; eûmes méconnu, eûtes méconnu, eurent méconnu
Fut. Perf.	aurai méconnu, auras méconnu, aura méconnu; aurons méconnu, aurez méconnu, auront méconnu
Cond. Perf.	aurais méconnu, aurais méconnu, aurait méconnu; aurions méconnu, auriez méconnu, auraient méconnu
Past Subj.	aie méconnu, aies méconnu, ait méconnu; ayons méconnu, ayez méconnu, aient méconnu
Plup. Subj.	eusse méconnu, eusses méconnu, eût méconnu; eussions méconnu, eussiez méconnu, eussent méconnu
Imperative	méconnais, méconnaissons, méconnaissez

to slander

Pres. Ind.	médis, médis, médit; médisons, médisez, médisent
Imp. Ind.	médisais, médisais, médisait; médisions, médisiez, médisaient
Past Def.	médis, médis, médit; médîmes, médîtes, médirent
Future	médirai, médiras, médira; médirons, médirez, médiront
Condit.	médirais, médirais, médirait; médirions, médiriez, médiraient
Pres. Subj.	médise, médises, médise; médisions, médisiez, médisent
Imp. Subj.	médisse, médisses, médît; médissions, médissiez, médissent
Past Indef.	ai médit, as médit, a médit; avons médit, avez médit, ont médit;
Plup. Ind.	avais médit, avais médit, avait médit; avions médit, aviez médit, avaient médit
Past Ant.	eus médit, eus médit, eut médit; eûmes médit, eûtes médit, eurent médit
Fut. Perf.	aurai médit, auras médit, aura médit; aurons médit, aurez médit, auront médit
Cond. Perf.	aurais médit, aurais médit, aurait médit; aurions médit, auriez médit, auraient médit
Past Subj.	aie médit, aies médit, ait médit; ayons médit, ayez médit, aient médit
Plup. Subj.	eusse médit, eusses médit, eût médit; eussions médit, eussiez médit, eussent médit
Imperative	médis, médisons, médisez

to meditate

Pres. Ind.	médite, médites, médite; méditons, méditez, méditent
Imp. Ind.	méditais, méditais, méditait; méditions, méditiez, méditaient
Past Def.	méditai, méditas, médita; méditâmes, méditâtes, méditèrent
Future	méditerai, méditeras, méditera; méditerons, méditerez, méditeront
Condit.	méditerais, méditerais, méditerait; méditerions, méditeriez, méditeraient
Pres. Subj.	médite, médites, médite; méditions, méditiez, méditent
Imp. Subj.	méditasse, méditasses, méditât; méditassions, méditassiez, méditassent
Past Indef.	ai médité, as médité, a médité; avons médité, avez médité, ont médité
Plup. Ind.	avais médité, avais médité, avait médité; avions médité, aviez médité, avaient médité
Past Ant.	eus médité, eus médité, eut médité; eûmes médité, eûtes médité, eurent médité
Fut. Perf.	aurai médité, auras médité, aura médité; aurons médité, aurez médité, auront médité
Cond. Perf.	aurais médité, aurais médité, aurait médité; aurions médité, auriez médité, auraient médité
Past Subj.	aie médité, aies médité, ait médité; ayons médité, ayez médité, aient médité
Plup. Subj.	eusse médité, eusses médité, eût médité; eussions médité, eussiez médité, eussent médité
Imperative	médite, méditons, méditez

to beware distrust, mistrust

Pres. Ind.	me méfie, te méfies, se méfie; nous méfions, vous méfiez, se méfient
Imp. Ind.	me méfiais, te méfiais, se méfiait; nous méfiions, vous méfiiez, se méfiaient
Past Def.	me méfiai, te méfias, se méfia; nous méfiâmes, vous méfiâtes, se méfièrent
Future	me méfierai, te méfieras, se méfiera; nous méfierons, vous méfierez, se méfieront
Condit.	me méfierais, te méfierais, se méfierait; nous méfierions, vous méfieriez, se méfieraient
Pres. Subj.	me méfie, te méfies, se méfie; nous méfiions, vous méfiiez, se méfient
Imp. Subj.	me méfiasse, te méfiasses, se méfiât; nous méfiassions, vous méfiassiez, se méfiassent
Past Indef.	me suis méfié(e), t'es méfié(e), s'est méfié(e); nous sommes méfié(e)s, vous êtes méfié(e)(s), se sont méfié(e)s
Plup. Ind.	m'étais méfié(e), t'étais méfié(e), s'était méfié(e); nous étions méfié(e)s, vous étiez méfié(e)(s), s'étaient méfié(e)s
Past Ant.	me fus méfié(e), te fus méfié(e), se fut méfié(e); nous fûmes méfié(e)s, vous fûtes méfié(e)(s), se furent méfié(e)s
Fut. Perf.	me serai méfié(e), te seras méfié(e), se sera méfié(e); nous serons méfié(e)s, vous serez méfié(e)(s), se seront méfié(e)s
Cond. Perf.	me serais méfié(e), te serais méfié(e), se serait méfié(e); nous serions méfié(e)s, vous seriez méfié(e)(s), se seraient méfié(e)s
Past Subj.	me sois méfié(e), te sois méfié(e), se soit méfié(e); nous soyons méfié(e)s, vous soyez méfié(e)(s), se soient méfié(e)s
Plup. Subj.	me fusse méfié(e), te fusses méfié(e), se fût méfié(e); nous fussions méfié(e)s, vous fussiez méfié(e)(s), se fussent méfié(e)s
Imperative	méfie-toi, méfions-nous, méfiez-vous

to lead

Pres. Ind.	mène, mènes, mène; menons, menez, mènent
Imp. Ind.	menais, menais, menait; menions, meniez, menaient
Past Def.	menai, menas, mena; menâmes, menâtes, menèrent
Fut. Ind.	mènerai, mèneras, mènera; mènerons, mènerez, mèneront
Condit.	mènerais, mènerais, mènerait; mènerions, mèneriez, mèneraient
Pres. Subj.	mène, mènes, mène; menions, meniez, mènent
Imp. Subj.	menasse, menasses, menât; menassions, menassiez, menassent
Past Indef.	ai mené, as mené, a mené; avons mené, avez mené, ont mené
Pluperf.	avais mené, avais mené, avait mené; avions mené, aviez mené, avaient mené
Past Ant.	eus mené, eus mené, eut mené; eûmes mené, eûtes mené, eurent mené
Fut. Perf.	aurai mené, auras mené, aura mené; aurons mené, aurez mené, auront mené
Cond. Perf.	aurais mené, aurais mené, aurait mené; aurions mené, auriez mené, auraient mené
Past Subj.	aie mené, aies mené, ait mené; ayons mené, ayez mené, aient mené
Plup. Subj.	eusse mené, eusses mené, eût mené; eussions mené, eussiez mené, eussent mené
Imperative	mène, menons, menez

to lie, tell lies

Pres. Ind.	mens, mens, ment; mentons, mentez, mentent
Imp. Ind.	mentais, mentais, mentait; mentions, mentiez, mentaient
Past Def.	mentis, mentis, mentit; mentîmes, mentîtes, mentirent
Fut. Ind.	mentirai, mentiras, mentira; mentirons, mentirez, mentiront
Condit.	mentirais, mentirais, mentirait; mentirions, mentiriez, mentiraient
Pres. Subj.	mente, mentes, mente; mentions, mentiez, mentent
Imp. Subj.	mentisse, mentisses, mentît; mentissions, mentissiez, mentissent
Past Indef.	ai menti, as menti, a menti; avons menti, avez menti, ont menti
Pluperf.	avais menti, avais menti, avait menti; avions menti, aviez menti, avaient menti
Past Ant.	eus menti, eus menti, eut menti; eûmes menti, eûtes menti, eurent menti
Fut. Perf.	aurai menti, auras menti, aura menti; aurons menti, aurez menti, auront menti
Cond. Perf.	aurais menti, aurais menti, aurait menti; aurions menti, auriez menti, auraient menti
Past Subj.	aie menti, aies menti, ait menti; ayons menti, ayez menti, aient menti
Plup. Subj.	eusse menti, eusses menti, eût menti; eussions menti, eussiez menti, eussent menti
Imperative	[Ordinarily not used]

to be mistaken

Pres. Ind.	me méprends, te méprends, se méprend; nous méprenons, vous méprenez, se méprennent
Imp. Ind.	me méprenais, te méprenais, se méprenait; nous méprenions, vous mépreniez, se méprenaient
Past Def.	me mépris, te mépris, se méprit; nous méprîmes, vous méprîtes, se méprirent
Future	me méprendrai, te méprendras, se méprendra; nous méprendrons, vous méprendrez, se méprendront
Condit.	me méprendrais, te méprendrais, se méprendrait; nous méprendrions, vous méprendriez, se méprendraient
Pres. Subj.	me méprenne, te méprennes, se méprenne; nous méprenions, vous mépreniez, se méprennent
Imp. Subj.	me méprisse, te méprisses, se méprît; nous méprissions, vous méprissiez, se méprissent
Past Indef.	me suis mépris(e), t'es mépris(e), s'est mépris(e); nous sommes mépris(es), vous êtes mépris(e)(es), se sont mépris(es)
Plup. Ind.	m'étais mépris(e), t'étais mépris(e), s'était mépris(e); nous étions mépris(es), vous étiez mépris(e)(es), s'étaient mépris(es)
Past Ant.	me fus mépris(e), te fus mépris(e), se fut mépris(e); nous fûmes mépris(es), vous fûtes mépris(e)(es), se furent mépris(es)
Fut. Perf.	me serai mépris(e), te seras mépris(e), se sera mépris(e); nous serons mépris(es), vous serez mépris(e)(es), se seront mépris(es)
Cond. Perf.	me serais mépris(e), te serais mépris(e), se serait mépris(e); nous serions mépris(es), vous seriez mépris(e)(es), se seraient mépris(es)
Past Subj.	me sois mépris(e), te sois mépris(e), se soit mépris(e); nous soyons mépris(e)s, vous soyez mépris(e)(es), se soient mépris(es)
Plup. Subj.	me fusse mépris(e), te fusses mépris(e), se fût mépris(e); nous fussions mépris(es), vous fussiez mépris(e)(es), se fussent mépris(es)
Imperative	[inemployé]

to merit, deserve

Pres. Ind.	mérite, mérites, mérite; méritons, méritez, méritent
Imp. Ind.	méritais, méritais, méritait; méritions, méritiez, méritaient
Past Def.	méritai, méritas, mérita; méritâmes, méritâtes, méritèrent
Future	mériterai, mériteras, méritera; mériterons, mériterez, mériteront
Condit.	mériterais, mériterais, mériterait; mériterions, mériteriez, mériteraient
Pres. Subj.	mérite, mérites, mérite; méritions, méritiez, méritent
Imp. Subj.	méritasse, méritasses, méritât; méritassions, méritassiez, méritassent
Past Indef.	ai mérité, as mérité, a mérité; avons mérité, avez mérité, ont mérité
Plup. Ind.	avais mérité, avais mérité, avait mérité; avions mérité, aviez mérité, avaient mérité
Past Ant.	eus mérité, eus mérité, eut mérité; eûmes mérité, eûtes mérité, eurent mérité
Fut. Perf.	aurai mérité, auras mérité, aura mérité; aurons mérité, aurez mérité, auront mérité
Cond. Perf.	aurais mérité, aurais mérité, aurait mérité; aurions mérité, auriez mérité, auraient mérité
Past Subj.	aie mérité, aies mérité, ait mérité; ayons mérité, ayez mérité, aient mérité
Plup. Subj.	eusse mérité, eusses mérité, eût mérité; eussions mérité, eussiez mérité, eussent mérité
Imperative	mérite, méritons, méritez [ordinairement inemployé]

to put, place

Pres. Ind.	mets, mets, met; mettons, mettez, mettent
Imp. Ind.	mettais, mettais, mettait; mettions, mettiez, mettaient
Past Def.	mis, mis, mit; mîmes, mîtes, mirent
Fut. Ind.	mettrai, mettras, mettra; mettrons, mettrez, mettront
Condit.	mettrais, mettrais, mettrait; mettrions, mettriez, mettraient
Pres. Subj.	mette, mettes, mette; mettions, mettiez, mettent
Imp. Subj.	misse, misses, mît; missions, missiez, missent
Past Indef.	ai mis, as mis, a mis; avons mis, avez mis, ont mis
Pluperf.	avais mis, avais mis, avait mis; avions mis, aviez mis, avaient mis
Past Ant.	eus mis, eus mis, eut mis; eûmes mis, eûtes mis, eurent mis
Fut. Perf.	aurai mis, auras mis, aura mis; aurons mis, aurez mis, auront mis
Cond. Perf.	aurais mis, aurais mis, aurait mis; aurions mis, auriez mis, auraient mis
Past Subj.	aie mis, aies mis, ait mis; ayons mis, ayez mis, aient mis
Plup. Subj.	eusse mis, eusses mis, eût mis; eussions mis, eussiez mis, eussent mis
Imperative	mets, mettons, mettez

to begin, start, place oneself

Pres. Ind.	me mets, te mets, se met; nous mettons, vous mettez, se mettent
Imp. Ind.	me mettais, te mettais, se mettait; nous mettions, vous mettiez, se mettaient
Past Def.	me mis, te mis, se mit; nous mîmes, vous mîtes, se mirent
Future	me mettrai, te mettras, se mettra; nous mettrons, vous mettrez, se mettront
Condit.	me mettrais, te mettrais, se mettrait; nous mettrions, vous mettriez, se mettraient
Pres. Subj.	me mette, te mettes, se mette; nous mettions, vous mettiez, se mettent
Imp. Subj.	me misse, te misses, se mît; nous missions, vous missiez, se missent
Past Indef.	me suis mis(e), t'es mis(e), s'est mis(e); nous sommes mis(es), vous êtes mis(e)(es), se sont mis(es)
Plup. Ind.	m'étais mis(e), t'étais mis(e), s'était mis(e); nous étions mis(es), vous étiez mis(e)(es), s'étaient mis(es)
Past Ant.	me fus mis(e), te fus mis(e), se fut mis(e); nous fûmes mis(es), vous fûtes mis(e)(es), se furent mis(es)
Fut. Perf.	me serai mis(e), te seras mis(e), se sera mis(e); nous serons mis(es), vous serez mis(e)(es), se seront mis(es)
Cond. Perf.	me serais mis(es), te serais mis(e), se serait mis(e); nous serions mis(es), vous seriez mis(es), se seraient mis(es)
Past Subj.	me sois mis(e), te sois mis(e), se soit mis(e); nous soyons mis(es), vous soyez mis(e)(es), se soient mis(es)
Plup. Subj.	me fusse mis(e), te fusses mis(e), se fût mis(e); nous fussions mis(es), vous fussiez mis(e)(es), se fussent mis(es)
Imperative	mets-toi, mettons-nous, mettez-vous

to go up, ascend, take up, bring up

Pres. Ind.	monte, montes, monte; montons, montez, montent
Imp. Ind.	montais, montais, montait; montions, montiez, montaient
Past Def.	montai, montas, monta; montâmes, montâtes, montèrent
Fut. Ind.	monterai, monteras, montera; monterons, monterez, monteront
Condit.	monterais, monterais, monterait; monterions, monteriez, monteraient
Pres. Subj.	monte, montes, monte; montions, montiez, montent
Imp. Subj.	montasse, montasses, montât; montassions, montassiez, montassent
Past Indef.	suis monté(e), es monté(e), est monté(e); sommes monté(e)s, êtes monté(e)(s), sont monté(e)s
Pluperf.	étais monté(e), étais monté(e), était monté(e); étions monté(e)s, étiez monté(e)(s), étaient monté(e)s
Past Ant.	fus monté(e), fus monté(e), fut monté(e); fûmes monté(e)s, fûtes monté(e)(s), furent monté(e)s
Fut. Perf.	serai monté(e), seras monté(e), sera monté(e); serons monté(e)s, serez monté(e)(s), seront monté(e)s
Cond. Perf.	serais monté(e), serais monté(e), serait monté(e); serions monté(e)s, seriez monté(e)(s), seraient monté(e)s
Past Subj.	sois monté(e), sois monté(e), soit monté(e); soyons monté(e)s, soyez monté(e)(s), soient monté(e)s
Plup. Subj.	fusse monté(e), fusses monté(e), fût monté(e); fussions monté(e)s, fussiez monté(e)(s), fussent monté(e)s
Imperative	monte, montons, montez

*** This verb is conjugated with *avoir* when it has a direct object.**
Example: J'ai monté l'escalier.
J'ai monté les valises.

to display, exhibit, show

Pres. Ind.	montre, montres, montre; montrons, montrez, montrent
Imp. Ind.	montrais, montrais, montrait; montrions, montriez, montraient
Past Def.	montrai, montras, montra; montrâmes, montrâtes, montrèrent
Future	montrerai, montreras, montrera; montrerons, montrerez, montreront
Condit.	montrerais, montrerais, montrerait; montrerions, montreriez, montreraient
Pres. Subj.	montre, montres, montre; montrions, montriez, montrent
Imp. Subj.	montrasse, montrasses, montrât; montrassions, montrassiez, montrassent
Past Indef.	ai montré, as montré, a montré; avons montré, avez montré, ont montré
Plup. Ind.	avais montré, avais montré, avait montré; avions montré, aviez montré, avaient montré
Past Ant.	eus montré, eus montré, eut montré; eûmes montré, eûtes montré, eurent montré
Fut. Perf.	aurai montré, auras montré, aura montré; aurons montré, aurez montré, auront montré
Cond. Perf.	aurais montré, aurais montré, aurait montré; aurions montré, auriez montré, auraient montré
Past Subj.	aie montré, aies montré, ait montré; ayons montré, ayez montré, aient montré
Plup. Subj.	eusse montré, eusses montré, eût montré; eussions montré, eussiez montré, eussent montré
Imperative	montre, montrons, montrez

to bite

Pres. Ind.	mords, mords, mord; mordons, mordez, mordent
Imp. Ind.	mordais, mordais, mordait; mordions, mordiez, mordaient
Past Def.	mordis, mordis, mordit; mordîmes, mordîtes, mordirent
Fut. Ind.	mordrai, mordras, mordra; mordrons, mordrez, mordront
Condit.	mordrais, mordrais, mordrait; mordrions, mordriez, mordraient
Pres. Subj.	morde, mordes, morde; mordions, mordiez, mordent
Imp. Subj.	mordisse, mordisses, mordît; mordissions, mordissiez, mordissent
Past Indef.	ai mordu, as mordu, a mordu; avons mordu, avez mordu, ont mordu
Pluperf.	avais mordu, avais mordu, avait mordu; avions mordu, aviez mordu, avaient mordu
Past Ant.	eus mordu, eus mordu, eut mordu; eûmes mordu, eûtes mordu, eurent mordu
Fut. Perf.	aurai mordu, auras mordu, aura mordu; aurons mordu, aurez mordu, auront mordu
Cond. Perf.	aurais mordu, aurais mordu, aurait mordu; aurions mordu, auriez mordu, auraient mordu
Past Subj.	aie mordu, aies mordu, ait mordu; ayons mordu, ayez mordu, aient mordu
Plup. Subj.	eusse mordu, eusses mordu, eût mordu; eussions mordu, eussiez mordu, eussent mordu
Imperative	mords, mordons, mordez

to grind, mill

Pres. Ind.	mouds, mouds, moud; moulons, moulez, moulent
Imp. Ind.	moulais, moulais, moulait; moulions, mouliez, moulaient
Past Def.	moulus, moulus, moulut; moulûmes, moulûtes, moulurent
Future	moudrai, moudras, moudra; moudrons, moudrez, moudront
Condit.	moudrais, moudrais, moudrait; moudrions, moudriez, moudraient
Pres. Subj.	moule, moules, moule; moulions, mouliez, moulent
Imp. Subj.	moulusse, moulusses, moulût; moulussions, moulussiez, moulussent
Past Indef.	ai moulu, as moulu, a moulu; avons moulu, avez moulu, ont moulu
Pluperf.	avais moulu, avais moulu, avait moulu; avions moulu, aviez moulu, avaient moulu
Past Ant.	eus moulu, eus moulu, eut moulu; eûmes moulu, eûtes moulu, eurent moulu
Fut. Perf.	aurai moulu, auras moulu, aura moulu; aurons moulu, aurez moulu, auront moulu
Cond. Perf.	aurais moulu, aurais moulu, aurait moulu; aurions moulu, auriez moulu, auraient moulu
Past Subj.	aie moulu, aies moulu, ait moulu; ayons moulu, ayez moulu, aient moulu
Plup. Subj.	eusse moulu, eusses moulu, eût moulu; eussions moulu, eussiez moulu, eussent moulu
Imperative	mouds, moulons, moulez

to die

Pres. Ind.	meurs, meurs, meurt; mourons, mourez, meurent
Imp. Ind.	mourais, mourais, mourait; mourions, mouriez, mouraient
Past Def.	mourus, mourus, mourut; mourûmes, mourûtes, moururent
Fut. Ind.	mourrai, mourras, mourra; mourrons, mourrez, mourront
Condit.	mourrais, mourrais, mourrait; mourrions, mourriez, mourraient
Pres. Subj.	meure, meures, meure; mourions, mouriez, meurent
Imp. Subj.	mourusse, mourusses, mourût; mourussions, mourussiez, mourussent
Past Indef.	suis mort(e), es mort(e), est mort(e); sommes mort(e)s, êtes mort(e)(s), sont mort(e)s
Pluperf.	étais mort(e), étais mort(e), était mort(e); étions mort(e)s, étiez mort(e)(s), étaient mort(e)s
Past Ant.	fus mort(e), fus mort(e), fut mort(e); fûmes mort(e)s, fûtes mort(e)(s), furent mort(e)s
Fut. Perf.	serai mort(e), seras mort(e), sera mort(e); serons mort(e)s, serez mort(e)(s), seront mort(e)s
Cond. Perf.	serais mort(e), serais mort(e), serait mort(e); serions mort(e)s, seriez mort(e)(s), seraient mort(e)s
Past Subj.	sois mort(e), sois mort(e), soit mort(e); soyons mort(e)s, soyez mort(e)(s), soient mort(e)s
Plup. Subj.	fusse mort(e), fusses mort(e), fût mort(e); fussions mort(e)s, fussiez mort(e)(s), fussent mort(e)s
Imperative	meurs, mourons, mourez

to move

Pres. Ind.	meus, meus, meut; mouvons, mouvez, meuvent
Imp. Ind.	mouvais, mouvais, mouvait; mouvions, mouviez, mouvaient
Past Def.	mus, mus, mut; mûmes, mûtes, murent
Fut. Ind.	mouvrai, mouvras, mouvra; mouvrons, mouvrez, mouvront
Condit.	mouvrais, mouvrais, mouvrait; mouvrions, mouvriez, mouvraient
Pres. Subj.	meuve, meuves, meuve; mouvions, mouviez, meuvent
Imp. Subj.	musse, musses, mût; mussions, mussiez, mussent
Past Indef.	ai mû, as mû, a mû; avons mû, avez mû, ont mû
Pluperf.	avais mû, avais mû, avait mû; avions mû, aviez mû, avaient mû
Past Ant.	eus mû, eus mû, eut mû; eûmes mû, eûtes mû, eurent mû
Fut. Perf.	aurai mû, auras mû, aura mû; aurons mû, aurez mû, auront mû
Cond. Perf.	aurais mû, aurais mû, aurait mû; aurions mû, auriez mû, auraient mû
Past Subj.	aie mû, aies mû, ait mû; ayons mû, ayez mû, aient mû
Plup. Subj.	eusse mû, eusses mû, eût mû; eussions mû, eussiez mû, eussent mû
Imperative	meus, mouvons, mouvez

to murmur, mutter

Pres. Ind.	murmure, murmures, murmure; murmurons, murmurez, murmurent
Imp. Ind.	murmurais, murmurais, murmurait; murmurions, murmuriez, murmuraient
Past Def.	murmurai, murmuras, murmura; murmurâmes, murmurâtes, murmurèrent
Future	murmurerai, murmureras, murmurera; murmurerons, murmurerez, murmureront
Condit.	murmurerais, murmurerais, murmurerait; murmurerions, murmureriez, murmureraient
Pres. Subj.	murmure, murmures, murmure; murmurions, murmuriez, murmurent
Imp. Subj.	murmurasse, murmurasses, murmurât; murmurassions, murmurassiez, murmurassent
Past Indef.	ai murmuré, as murmuré, a murmuré; avons murmuré, avez murmuré, ont murmuré
Plup. Ind.	avais murmuré, avais murmuré, avait murmuré; avions murmuré, aviez murmuré, avaient murmuré
Past Ant.	eus murmuré, eus murmuré, eut murmuré; eûmes murmuré, eûtes murmuré, eurent murmuré
Fut. Perf.	aurai murmuré, auras murmuré, aura murmuré; aurons murmuré, aurez murmuré, auront murmuré
Cond. Perf.	aurais murmuré, aurais murmuré, aurait murmuré; aurions murmuré, auriez murmuré, auraient murmuré
Past Subj.	aie murmuré, aies murmuré, ait murmuré; ayons murmuré, ayez murmuré, aient murmuré
Plup. Subj.	eusse murmuré, eusses murmuré, eût murmuré; eussions murmuré, eussiez murmuré, eussent murmuré
Imperative	murmure, murmurons, murmurez

to swim

Pres. Ind.	nage, nages, nage; nageons, nagez, nagent
Imp. Ind.	nageais, nageais, nageait; nagions, nagiez, nageaient
Past Def.	nageai, nageas, nagea; nageâmes, nageâtes, nagèrent
Fut. Ind.	nagerai, nageras, nagera; nagerons, nagerez, nageront
Condit.	nagerais, nagerais, nagerait; nagerions, nageriez, nageraient
Pres. Subj.	nage, nages, nage; nagions, nagiez, nagent
Imp. Subj.	nageasse, nageasses, nageât; nageassions, nageassiez, nageassent
Past Indef.	ai nagé, as nagé, a nagé; avons nagé, avez nagé, ont nagé
Pluperf.	avais nagé, avais nagé, avait nagé; avions nagé, aviez nagé, avaient nagé
Past Ant.	eus nagé, eus nagé, eut nagé; eûmes nagé, eûtes nagé, eurent nagé
Fut. Perf.	aurai nagé, auras nagé, aura nagé; aurons nagé, aurez nagé, auront nagé
Cond. Perf.	aurais nagé, aurais nagé, aurait nagé; aurions nagé, auriez nagé, auraient nagé
Past Subj.	aie nagé, aies nagé, ait nagé; ayons nagé, ayez nagé, aient nagé
Plup. Subj.	eusse nagé, eusses nagé, eût nagé; eussions nagé, eussiez nagé, eussent nagé
Imperative	nage, nageons, nagez

to be born

Pres. Ind.	nais, nais, naît; naissons, naissez, naissent
Imp. Ind.	naissais, naissais, naissait; naissions, naissiez, naissaient
Past Def.	naquis, naquis, naquit; naquîmes, naquîtes, naquirent
Fut. Ind.	naîtrai, naîtras, naîtra; naîtrons, naîtrez, naîtront
Condit.	naîtrais, naîtrais, naîtrait; naîtrions, naîtriez, naîtraient
Pres. Subj.	naisse, naisses, naisse; naissions, naissiez, naissent
Imp. Subj.	naquisse, naquisses, naquît; naquissions, naquissiez, naquissent
Past Indef.	suis né(e), es né(e), est né(e); sommes né(e)s, êtes né(e)(s), sont né(e)s
Pluperf.	étais né(e), étais né(e), était né(e); étions né(e)s, étiez né(e)(s), étaient né(e)s
Past Ant.	fus né(e), fus né(e), fut né(e); fûmes né(e)s, fûtes né(e)(s), furent né(e)s
Fut. Perf.	serai né(e), seras né(e), sera né(e); serons né(e)s, serez né(e)(s), seront né(e)s
Cond. Perf.	serais né(e), serais né(e), serait né(e); serions né(e)s, seriez né(e)(s), seraient né(e)s
Past Subj.	sois né(e), sois né(e), soit né(e); soyons né(e)s, soyez né(e)(s), soient né(e)s
Plup. Subj.	fusse né(e), fusses né(e), fût né(e); fussions né(e)s, fussiez né(e)(s), fussent né(e)s
Imperative	nais, naissons, naissez

to snow

Pres. Ind.	il neige
Imp. Ind.	il neigeait
Past Def.	il neigea
Future	il neigera
Condit.	il neigerait
Pres. Subj.	qu'il neige
Imp. Subj.	qu'il neigeât
Past Indef.	il a neigé
Plup. Ind.	il avait neigé
Past Ant.	il eut neigé
Fut. Perf.	il aura neigé
Cond. Perf.	il aurait neigé
Past Subj.	qu'il ait neigé
Plup. Subj.	qu'il eût neigé
Imperative	[inemployé]

to clean

Pres. Ind.	nettoie, nettoies, nettoie; nettoyons, nettoyez, nettoient
Imp. Ind.	nettoyais, nettoyais, nettoyait; nettoyions, nettoyiez, nettoyaient
Past Def.	nettoyai, nettoyas, nettoya; nettoyâmes, nettoyâtes, nettoyèrent
Fut. Ind.	nettoierai, nettoieras, nettoiera; nettoierons, nettoierez, nettoieront
Condit.	nettoierais, nettoierais, nettoierait; nettoierions, nettoieriez, nettoieraient
Pres. Subj.	nettoie, nettoies, nettoie; nettoyions, nettoyiez, nettoient
Imp. Subj.	nettoyasse, nettoyasses, nettoyât; nettoyassions, nettoyassiez, nettoyassent
Past Indef.	ai nettoyé, as nettoyé, a nettoyé; avons nettoyé, avez nettoyé, ont nettoyé
Pluperf.	avais nettoyé, avais nettoyé, avait nettoyé; avions nettoyé, aviez nettoyé, avaient nettoyé
Past Ant.	eus nettoyé, eus nettoyé, eut nettoyé; eûmes nettoyé, eûtes nettoyé, eurent nettoyé
Fut. Perf.	aurai nettoyé, auras nettoyé, aura nettoyé; aurons nettoyé, aurez nettoyé, auront nettoyé
Cond. Perf.	aurais nettoyé, aurais nettoyé, aurait nettoyé; aurions nettoyé, auriez nettoyé, auraient nettoyé
Past Subj.	aie nettoyé, aies nettoyé, ait nettoyé; ayons nettoyé, ayez nettoyé, aient nettoyé
Plup. Subj.	eusse nettoyé, eusses nettoyé, eût nettoyé; eussions nettoyé, eussiez nettoyé, eussent nettoyé
Imperative	nettoie, nettoyons, nettoyez

to feed, nourish

Pres. Ind.	nourris, nourris, nourrit; nourrissons, nourrissez, nourrissent
Imp. Ind.	nourrissais, nourrissais, nourrissait; nourrissions, nourrissiez, nourrissaient
Past Def.	nourris, nourris, nourrit; nourrîmes, nourrîtes, nourrirent
Future	nourrirai, nourriras, nourrira; nourrirons, nourrirez, nourriront
Condit.	nourrirais, nourrirais, nourrirait; nourririons, nourririez, nourriraient
Pres. Subj.	nourrisse, nourrisses, nourrisse; nourrissions, nourrissiez, nourrissent
Imp. Subj.	nourrisse, nourrisses, nourrît; nourrissions, nourrissiez, nourrissent
Past Indef.	ai nourri, as nourri, a nourri; avons nourri, avez nourri, ont nourri
Plup. Ind.	avais nourri, avais nourri, avait nourri; avions nourri, aviez nourri, avaient nourri
Past Ant.	eus nourri, eus nourri, eut nourri; eûmes nourri, eûtes nourri, eurent nourri
Fut. Perf.	aurai nourri, auras nourri, aura nourri; aurons nourri, aurez nourri, auront nourri
Cond. Perf.	aurais nourri, aurais nourri, aurait nourri; aurions nourri, auriez nourri, auraient nourri
Past Subj.	aie nourri, aies nourri, ait nourri; ayons nourri, ayez nourri, aient nourri
Plup. Subj.	eusse nourri, eusses nourri, eût nourri; eussions nourri, eussiez nourri, eussent nourri
Imperative	nourris, nourrissons, nourrissez

to harm, hinder

Pres. Ind.	nuis, nuis, nuit; nuisons, nuisez, nuisent
Imp. Ind.	nuisais, nuisais, nuisait; nuisions, nuisiez, nuisaient
Past Def.	nuisis, nuisis, nuisit; nuisîmes, nuisîtes, nuisirent
Fut. Ind.	nuirai, nuiras, nuira; nuirons, nuirez, nuiront
Condit.	nuirais, nuirais, nuirait; nuirions, nuiriez, nuiraient
Pres. Subj.	nuise, nuises, nuise; nuisions, nuisiez, nuisent
Imp. Subj.	nuisisse, nuisisses, nuisît; nuisissions, nuisissiez, nuisissent
Past Indef.	ai nui, as nui, a nui; avons nui, avez nui, ont nui
Pluperf.	avais nui, avais nui, avait nui; avions nui, aviez nui, avaient nui
Past Ant.	eus nui, eus nui, eut nui; eûmes nui, eûtes nui, eurent nui
Fut. Perf.	aurai nui, auras nui, aura nui; aurons nui, aurez nui, auront nui
Cond. Perf.	aurais nui, aurais nui, aurait nui; aurions nui, auriez nui, auraient nui
Past Subj.	aie nui, aies nui, ait nui; ayons nui, ayez nui, aient nui
Plup. Subj.	eusse nui, eusses nui, eût nui; eussions nui, eussiez nui, eussent nui
Imperative	nuis, nuisons, nuisez

to obey

Pres. Ind.	obéis, obéis, obéit; obéissons, obéissez, obéissent
Imp. Ind.	obéissais, obéissais, obéissait; obéissions, obéissiez, obéissaient
Past Def.	obéis, obéis, obéit; obéîmes, obéîtes, obéirent
Fut. Ind.	obéirai, obéiras, obéira; obéirons, obéirez, obéiront
Condit.	obéirais, obéirais, obéirait; obéirions, obéiriez, obéiraient
Pres. Subj.	obéisse, obéisses, obéisse; obéissions, obéissiez, obéissent
Imp. Subj.	obéisse, obéisses, obéît; obéissions, obéissiez, obéissent
Past Indef.	ai obéi, as obéi, a obéi; avons obéi, avez obéi, ont obéi
Pluperf.	avais obéi, avais obéi, avait obéi; avions obéi, aviez obéi, avaient obéi
Past Ant.	eus obéi, eus obéi, eut obéi; eûmes obéi, eûtes obéi, eurent obéi
Fut. Perf.	aurai obéi, auras obéi, aura obéi; aurons obéi, aurez obéi, auront obéi
Cond. Perf.	aurais obéi, aurais obéi, aurait obéi; aurions obéi, auriez obéi, auraient obéi
Past Subj.	aie obéi, aies obéi, ait obéi; ayons obéi, ayez obéi, aient obéi
Plup. Subj.	eusse obéi, eusses obéi, eût obéi; eussions obéi, eussiez obéi, eussent obéi
Imperative	obéis, obéissons, obéissez

to oblige

Pres. Ind.	oblige, obliges, oblige; obligeons, obligez, obligent
Imp. Ind.	obligeais, obligeais, obligeait; obligions, obligiez, obligeaient
Past Def.	obligeai, obligeas, obligea; obligeâmes, obligeâtes, obligèrent
Fut. Ind.	obligerai, obligeras, obligera; obligerons, obligerez, obligeront
Condit.	obligerais, obligerais, obligerait; obligerions, obligeriez, obligeraient
Pres. Subj.	oblige, obliges, oblige; obligions, obligiez, obligent
Imp. Subj.	obligeasse, obligeasses, obligeât; obligeassions, obligeassiez, obligeassent
Past Indef.	ai obligé, as obligé, a obligé; avons obligé, avez obligé, ont obligé
Pluperf.	avais obligé, avais obligé, avait obligé; avions obligé, aviez obligé, avaient obligé
Past Ant.	eus obligé, eus obligé, eut obligé; eûmes obligé, eûtes obligé, eurent obligé
Fut. Perf.	aurai obligé, auras obligé, aura obligé; aurons obligé, aurez obligé, auront obligé
Cond. Perf.	aurais obligé, aurais obligé, aurait obligé; aurions obligé, auriez obligé, auraient obligé
Past Subj.	aie obligé, aies obligé, ait obligé; ayons obligé, ayez obligé, aient obligé
Plup. Subj.	eusse obligé, eusses obligé, eût obligé; eussions obligé, eussiez obligé, eussent obligé
Imperative	oblige, obligeons, obligez

to obtain, get

Pres. Ind.	obtiens, obtiens, obtient; obtenons, obtenez, obtiennent
Imp. Ind.	obtenais, obtenais, obtenait; obtenions, obteniez, obtenaient
Past Def.	obtins, obtins, obtint; obtînmes, obtîntes, obtinrent
Fut. Ind.	obtiendrai, obtiendras, obtiendra; obtiendrons, obtiendrez, obtiendront
Condit.	obtiendrais, obtiendrais, obtiendrait; obtiendrions, obtiendriez, obtiendraient
Pres. Subj.	obtienne, obtiennes, obtienne; obtenions, obteniez, obtiennent
Imp. Subj.	obtinsse, obtinsses, obtînt; obtinssions, obtinssiez, obtinssent
Past Indef.	ai obtenu, as obtenu, a obtenu; avons obtenu, avez obtenu, ont obtenu
Pluperf.	avais obtenu, avais obtenu, avait obtenu; avions obtenu, aviez obtenu, avaient obtenu
Past Ant.	eus obtenu, eus obtenu, eut obtenu; eûmes obtenu, eûtes obtenu, eurent obtenu
Fut. Perf.	aurai obtenu, auras obtenu, aura obtenu; aurons obtenu, aurez obtenu, auront obtenu
Cond. Perf.	aurais obtenu, aurais obtenu, aurait obtenu; aurions obtenu, auriez obtenu, auraient obtenu
Past Subj.	aie obtenu, aies obtenu, ait obtenu; ayons obtenu, ayez obtenu, aient obtenu
Plup. Subj.	eusse obtenu, eusses obtenu, eût obtenu; eussions obtenu, eussiez obtenu, eussent obtenu
Imperative	obtiens, obtenons, obtenez

to occupy

Pres. Ind.	occupe, occupes, occupe; occupons, occupez, occupent
Imp. Ind.	occupais, occupais, occupait; occupions, occupiez, occupaient
Past Def.	occupai, occupas, occupa; occupâmes, occupâtes, occupèrent
Future	occuperai, occuperas, occupera; occuperons, occuperez, occuperont
Condit.	occuperais, occuperais, occuperait; occuperions, occuperiez, occuperaient
Pres. Subj.	occupe, occupes, occupe; occupions, occupiez, occupent
Imp. Subj.	occupasse, occupasses, occupât; occupassions, occupassiez, occupassent
Past Indef.	ai occupé, as occupé, a occupé; avons occupé, avez occupé, ont occupé
Plup. Ind.	avais occupé, avais occupé, avait occupé; avions occupé, aviez occupé, avaient occupé
Past Ant.	eus occupé, eus occupé, eut occupé; eûmes occupé, eûtes occupé, eurent occupé
Fut. Perf.	aurai occupé, auras occupé, aura occupé; aurons occupé, aurez occupé, auront occupé
Cond. Perf.	aurais occupé, aurais occupé, aurait occupé; aurions occupé, auriez occupé, auraient occupé
Past Subj.	aie occupé, aies occupé, ait occupé; ayons occupé, ayez occupé, aient occupé
Plup. Subj.	eusse occupé, eusses occupé, eût occupé; eussions occupé, eussiez occupé, eussent occupé
Imperative	occupe, occupons, occupez

to be busy, keep oneself busy

Pres. Ind.	m'occupe, t'occupes, s'occupe; nous occupons, vous occupez, s'occupent
Imp. Ind.	m'occupais, t'occupais, s'occupait; nous occupions, vous occupiez, s'occupaient
Past Def.	m'occupai, t'occupas, s'occupa; nous occupâmes, vous occupâtes, s'occupèrent
Future	m'occuperai, t'occuperas, s'occupera; nous occuperons, vous occuperez, s'occuperont
Condit.	m'occuperais, t'occuperais, s'occuperait; nous occuperions, vous occuperiez, s'occuperaient
Pres. Subj.	m'occupe, t'occupes, s'occupe; nous occupions, vous occupiez, s'occupent
Imp. Subj.	m'occupasse, t'occupasses, s'occupât; nous occupassions, vous occupassiez, s'occupassent
Past Indef.	me suis occupé(e), t'es occupé(e), s'est occupé(e); nous sommes occupé(e)s, vous êtes occupé(e)(s), se sont occupé(e)s
Plup. Ind.	m'étais occupé(e), t'étais occupé(e), s'était occupé(e); nous étions occupé(e)s, vous étiez occupé(e)(s), s'étaient occupé(e)s
Past Ant.	me fus occupé(e), te fus occupé(e), se fut occupé(e); nous fûmes occupé(e)s, vous fûtes occupé(e)(s), se furent occupé(e)s
Fut. Perf.	me serai occupé(e), te seras occupé(e), se sera occupé(e); nous serons occupé(e)s, vous serez occupé(e)(s), se seront occupé(e)s
Cond. Perf.	me serais occupé(e), te serais occupé(e), se serait occupé(e); nous serions occupé(e)s, vous seriez occupé(e)(s), se seraient occupé(e)s
Past Subj.	me sois occupé(e), te sois occupé(e), se soit occupé(e); nous soyons occupé(e)s, vous soyez occupé(e)(s), se soient occupé(e)s
Plup. Subj.	me fusse occupé(e), te fusses occupé(e), se fût occupé(e); nous fussions occupé(e)s, vous fussiez occupé(e)(s), se fussent occupé(e)s
Imperative	occupe-toi, occupons-nous, occupez-vous

to offer

Pres. Ind.	offre, offres, offre; offrons, offrez, offrent
Imp. Ind.	offrais, offrais, offrait; offrions, offriez, offraient
Past Def.	offris, offris, offrit; offrîmes, offrîtes, offrirent
Fut. Ind.	offrirai, offriras, offrira; offrirons, offrirez, offriront
Condit.	offrirais, offrirais, offrirait; offririons, offririez, offriraient
Pres. Subj.	offre, offres, offre; offrions, offriez, offrent
Imp. Subj.	offrisse, offrisses, offrît; offrissions, offrissiez, offrissent
Past Indef.	ai offert, as offert, a offert; avons offert, avez offert, ont offert
Pluperf.	avais offert, avais offert, avait offert; avions offert, aviez offert, avaient offert
Past Ant.	eus offert, eus offert, eut offert; eûmes offert, eûtes offert, eurent offert
Fut. Perf.	aurai offert, auras offert, aura offert; aurons offert, aurez offert, auront offert
Cond. Perf.	aurais offert, aurais offert, aurait offert; aurions offert, auriez offert, auraient offert
Past Subj.	aie offert, aies offert, ait offert; ayons offert, ayez offert, aient offert
Plup. Subj.	eusse offert, eusses offert, eût offert; eussions offert, eussiez offert, eussent offert
Imperative	offre, offrons, offrez

to omit

Pres. Ind.	omets, omets, omet; omettons, omettez, omettent
Imp. Ind.	omettais, omettais, omettait; omettions, omettiez, omettaient
Past Def.	omis, omis, omit; omîmes, omîtes, omirent
Future	omettrai, omettras, omettra; omettrons, omettrez, omettront
Condit.	omettrais, omettrais, omettrait; omettrions, omettriez, omettraient
Pres. Subj.	omette, omettes, omette; omettions, omettiez, omettent
Imp. Subj.	omisse, omisses, omît; omissions, omissiez, omissent
Past Indef.	ai omis, as omis, a omis; avons omis, avez omis, ont omis
Pluperf.	avais omis, avais omis, avait omis; avions omis, aviez omis, avaient omis
Past Ant.	eus omis, eus omis, eut omis; eûmes omis, eûtes omis, eurent omis
Fut. Perf.	aurai omis, auras omis, aura omis; aurons omis, aurez omis, auront omis
Cond. Perf.	aurais omis, aurais omis, aurait omis; aurions omis, auriez omis, auraient omis
Past Subj.	aie omis, aies omis, ait omis; ayons omis, ayez omis, aient omis
Plup. Subj.	eusse omis, eusses omis, eût omis; eussions omis, eussiez omis, eussent omis
Imperative	omets, omettons, omettez

to dare

Pres. Ind.	ose, oses, ose; osons, osez, osent
Imp. Ind.	osais, osais, osait; osions, osiez, osaient
Past Def.	osai, osas, osa; osâmes, osâtes, osèrent
Fut. Ind.	oserai, oseras, osera; oserons, oserez, oseront
Condit.	oserais, oserais, oserait; oserions, oseriez, oseraient
Pres. Subj.	ose, oses, ose; osions, osiez, osent
Imp. Subj.	osasse, osasses, osât; osassions, osassiez, osassent
Past Indef.	ai osé, as osé, a osé; avons osé, avez osé, ont osé
Pluperf.	avais osé, avais osé, avait osé; avions osé, aviez osé, avaient osé
Past Ant.	eus osé, eus osé, eut osé; eûmes osé, eûtes osé, eurent osé
Fut. Perf.	aurai osé, auras osé, aura osé; aurons osé, aurez osé, auront osé
Cond. Perf.	aurais osé, aurais osé, aurait osé; aurions osé, auriez osé, auraient osé
Past Subj.	aie osé, aies osé, ait osé; ayons osé, ayez osé, aient osé
Plup. Subj.	eusse osé, eusses osé, eût osé; eussions osé, eussiez osé, eussent osé
Imperative	ose, osons, osez

to open

Pres. Ind.	ouvre, ouvres, ouvre; ouvrons, ouvrez, ouvrent
Imp. Ind.	ouvrais, ouvrais, ouvrait; ouvrions, ouvriez, ouvraient
Past Def.	ouvris, ouvris, ouvrit; ouvrîmes, ouvrîtes, ouvrirent
Fut. Ind.	ouvrirai, ouvriras, ouvrira; ouvrirons, ouvrirez, ouvriront
Condit.	ouvrirais, ouvrirais, ouvrirait; ouvririons, ouvririez, ouvriraient
Pres. Subj.	ouvre, ouvres, ouvre; ouvrions, ouvriez, ouvrent
Imp. Subj.	ouvrisse, ouvrisses, ouvrît; ouvrissions, ouvrissiez, ouvrissent
Past Indef.	ai ouvert, as ouvert, a ouvert; avons ouvert, avez ouvert, ont ouvert
Pluperf.	avais ouvert, avais ouvert, avait ouvert; avions ouvert, aviez ouvert, avaient ouvert
Past Ant.	eus ouvert, eus ouvert, eut ouvert; eûmes ouvert, eûtes ouvert, eurent ouvert
Fut. Perf.	aurai ouvert, auras ouvert, aura ouvert; aurons ouvert, aurez ouvert, auront ouvert
Cond. Perf.	aurais ouvert, aurais ouvert, aurait ouvert; aurions ouvert, auriez ouvert, auraient ouvert
Past Subj.	aie ouvert, aies ouvert, ait ouvert; ayons ouvert, ayez ouvert, aient ouvert
Plup. Subj.	eusse ouvert, eusses ouvert, eût ouvert; eussions ouvert, eussiez ouvert, eussent ouvert
Imperative	ouvre, ouvrons, ouvrez

to appear, seem

Pres. Ind.	parais, parais, paraît; paraissons, paraissez, paraissent
Imp. Ind.	paraissais, paraissais, paraissait; paraissions, paraissiez, paraissaient
Past Def.	parus, parus, parut; parûmes, parûtes, parurent
Fut. Ind.	paraîtrai, paraîtras, paraîtra; paraîtrons, paraîtrez, paraîtront
Condit.	paraîtrais, paraîtrais, paraîtrait; paraîtrions, paraîtriez, paraîtraient
Pres. Subj.	paraisse, paraisses, paraisse; paraissions, paraissiez, paraissent
Imp. Subj.	parusse, parusses, parût; parussions, parussiez, parussent
Past Indef.	ai paru, as paru, a paru; avons paru, avez paru, ont paru
Pluperf.	avais paru, avais paru, avait paru; avions paru, aviez paru, avaient paru
Past Ant.	eus paru, eus paru, eut paru; eûmes paru, eûtes paru, eurent paru
Fut. Perf.	aurai paru, auras paru, aura paru; aurons paru, aurez paru, auront paru
Cond. Perf.	aurais paru, aurais paru, aurait paru; aurions paru, auriez paru, auraient paru
Past Subj.	aie paru, aies paru, ait paru; ayons paru, ayez paru, aient paru
Plup. Subj.	eusse paru, eusses paru, eût paru; eussions paru, eussiez paru, eussent paru
Imperative	parais, paraissons, paraissez

to pardon, forgive

Pres. Ind.	pardonne, pardonnes, pardonne; pardonnons, pardonnez, pardonnent
Imp. Ind.	pardonnais, pardonnais, pardonnait; pardonnions, pardonniez, pardonnaient
Past Def.	pardonnai, pardonnas, pardonna; pardonnâmes, pardonnâtes, pardonnèrent
Future	pardonnerai, pardonneras, pardonnera; pardonnerons, pardonnerez, pardonneront
Condit.	pardonnerais, pardonnerais, pardonnerait; pardonnerions, pardonneriez, pardonneraient
Pres. Subj.	pardonne, pardonnes, pardonne; pardonnions, pardonniez, pardonnent
Imp. Subj.	pardonnasse, pardonnasses, pardonnât; pardonnassions, pardonnassiez, pardonnassent
Past Indef.	ai pardonné, as pardonné, a pardonné; avons pardonné, avez pardonné, ont pardonné
Plup. Ind.	avais pardonné, avais pardonné, avait pardonné; avions pardonné, aviez pardonné, avaient pardonné
Past Ant.	eus pardonné, eus pardonné, eut pardonné; eûmes pardonné, eûtes pardonné, eurent pardonné
Fut. Perf.	aurai pardonné, auras pardonné, aura pardonné; aurons pardonné, aurez pardonné, auront pardonné
Cond. Perf.	aurais pardonné, aurais pardonné, aurait pardonné; aurions pardonné, auriez pardonné, auraient pardonné
Past Subj.	aie pardonné, aies pardonné, ait pardonné; ayons pardonné, ayez pardonné, aient pardonné
Plup. Subj.	eusse pardonné, eusses pardonné, eût pardonné; eussions pardonné, eussiez pardonné, eussent pardonné
Imperative	pardonne, pardonnons, pardonnez

to bet, wager

Pres. Ind.	parie, paries, parie; parions, pariez, parient
Imp. Ind.	pariais, pariais, pariait; pariions, pariiez, pariaient
Past Def.	pariai, parias, paria; pariâmes, pariâtes, parièrent
Future	parierai, parieras, pariera; parierons, parierez, parieront
Condit.	parierais, parierais, parierait; parierions, parieriez, parieraient
Pres. Subj.	parie, paries, parie; pariions, pariiez, parient
Imp. Subj.	pariasse, pariasses, pariât; pariassions, pariassiez, pariassent
Past Indef.	ai parié, as parié, a parié; avons parié, avez parié, ont parié
Pluperf.	avais parié, avais parié, avait parié; avions parié, aviez parié, avaient parié
Past Ant.	eus parié, eus parié, eut parié; eûmes parié, eûtes parié, eurent parié
Fut. Perf.	aurai parié, auras parié, aura parié; aurons parié, aurez parié, auront parié
Cond. Perf.	aurais parié, aurais parié, aurait parié; aurions parié, auriez parié, auraient parié
Past Subj.	aie parié, aies parié, ait parié; ayons parié, ayez parié, aient parié
Plup. Subj.	eusse parié, eusses parié, eût parié; eussions parié, eussiez parié, eussent parié
Imperative	parie, parions, pariez

Pres. Ind.	parle, parles, parle; parlons, parlez, parlent	*to speak, talk*
Imp. Ind.	parlais, parlais, parlait; parlions, parliez, parlaient	
Past Def.	parlai, parlas, parla; parlâmes, parlâtes, parlèrent	
Fut. Ind.	parlerai, parleras, parlera; parlerons, parlerez, parleront	
Condit.	parlerais, parlerais, parlerait; parlerions, parleriez, parleraient	
Pres. Subj.	parle, parles, parle; parlions, parliez, parlent	
Imp. Subj.	parlasse, parlasses, parlât; parlassions, parlassiez, parlassent	
Past Indef.	ai parlé, as parlé, a parlé; avons parlé, avez parlé, ont parlé	
Pluperf.	avais parlé, avais parlé, avait parlé; avions parlé, aviez parlé, avaient parlé	
Past Ant.	eus parlé, eus parlé, eut parlé; eûmes parlé, eûtes parlé, eurent parlé	
Fut. Perf.	aurai parlé, auras parlé, aura parlé; aurons parlé, aurez parlé, auront parlé	
Cond. Perf.	aurais parlé, aurais parlé, aurait parlé; aurions parlé, auriez parlé, auraient parlé	
Past Subj.	aie parlé, aies parlé, ait parlé; ayons parlé, ayez parlé, aient parlé	
Plup. Subj.	eusse parlé, eusses parlé, eût parlé; eussions parlé, eussiez parlé, eussent parlé	
Imperative	parle, parlons, parlez	

to leave, depart

Pres. Ind.	pars, pars, part; partons, partez, partent
Imp. Ind.	partais, partais, partait; partions, partiez, partaient
Past Def.	partis, partis, partit; partîmes, partîtes, partirent
Fut. Ind.	partirai, partiras, partira; partirons, partirez, partiront
Condit.	partirais, partirais, partirait; partirions, partiriez, partiraient
Pres. Subj.	parte, partes, parte; partions, partiez, partent
Imp. Subj.	partisse, partisses, partît; partissions, partissiez, partissent
Past Indef.	suis parti(e), es parti(e), est parti(e); sommes parti(e)s, êtes parti(e)(s), sont parti(e)s
Pluperf.	étais parti(e), étais parti(e), était parti(e); étions parti(e)s, étiez parti(e)(s), étaient parti(e)s
Past Ant.	fus parti(e), fus parti(e), fut parti(e); fûmes parti(e)s, fûtes parti(e)(s), furent parti(e)s
Fut. Perf.	serai parti(e), seras parti(e), sera parti(e); serons parti(e)s, serez parti(e)(s), seront parti(e)s
Cond. Perf.	serais parti(e), serais parti(e), serait parti(e); serions parti(e)s, seriez parti(e)(s), seraient parti(e)s
Past Subj.	sois parti(e), sois parti(e), soit parti(e); soyons parti(e)s, soyez parti(e)(s), soient parti(e)s
Plup. Subj.	fusse parti(e), fusses parti(e), fût parti(e); fussions parti(e)s, fussiez parti(e)(s), fussent parti(e)s
Imperative	pars, partons, partez

to pass, spend (time)

Pres. Ind.	passe, passes, passe; passons, passez, passent
Imp. Ind.	passais, passais, passait; passions, passiez, passaient
Past Def.	passai, passas, passa; passâmes, passâtes, passèrent
Future	passerai, passeras, passera; passerons, passerez, passeront
Condit.	passerais, passerais, passerait; passerions, passeriez, passeraient
Pres. Subj.	passe, passes, passe; passions, passiez, passent
Imp. Subj.	passasse, passasses, passât; passassions, passassiez, passassent
Past Indef.	ai passé, as passé, a passé; avons passé, avez passé, ont passé
Plup. Ind.	avais passé, avais passé, avait passé; avions passé, aviez passé, avaient passé
Past Ant.	eus passé, eus passé, eut passé; eûmes passé, eûtes passé, eurent passé
Fut. Perf	aurai passé, auras passé, aura passé; aurons passé, aurez passé, auront passé
Cond. Perf.	aurais passé, aurais passé, aurait passé; aurions passé, auriez passé, auraient passé
Past Subj.	aie passé, aies passé, ait passé; ayons passé, ayez passé, aient passé
Plup. Subj.	eusse passé, eusses passé, eût passé; eussions passé, eussiez passé, eussent passé
Imperative	passe, passons, passez

* This verb is conjugated with **être** to indicate a state. Example: Ses soupçons sont passés en certitudes.

to happen

Pres. Ind.	se passe
Imp. Ind.	se passait
Past Def.	se passa
Future	se passera
Condit.	se passerait
Pres. Subj.	se passe
Imp. Subj.	se passât
Past Indef.	s'est passé
Plup. Ind.	s'était passé
Past Ant.	se fut passé
Fut. Perf.	se sera passé
Cond. Perf.	se serait passé
Past Subj.	se soit passé
Plup. Subj.	se fût passé
Imperative	[inemployé]

to skate (on ice)

Pres. Ind.	patine, patines, patine; patinons, patinez, patinent
Imp. Ind.	patinais, patinais, patinait; patinions, patiniez, patinaient
Past Def.	patinai, patinas, patina; patinâmes, patinâtes, patinèrent
Future	patinerai, patineras, patinera; patinerons, patinerez, patineront
Condit.	patinerais, patinerais, patinerait; patinerions, patineriez, patineraient
Pres. Subj.	patine, patines, patine; patinions, patiniez, patinent
Imp. Subj.	patinasse, patinasses, patinât; patinassions, patinassiez, patinassent
Past Indef.	ai patiné, as patiné, a patiné; avons patiné, avez patiné, ont patiné
Pluperf.	avais patiné, avais patiné, avait patiné; avions patiné, aviez patiné, avaient patiné
Past Ant.	eus patiné, eus patiné, eut patiné; eûmes patiné, eûtes patiné, eurent patiné
Fut. Perf.	aurai patiné, auras patiné, aura patiné; aurons patiné, aurez patiné, auront patiné
Cond. Perf.	aurais patiné, aurais patiné, aurait patiné; aurions patiné, auriez patiné, auraient patiné
Past Subj.	aie patiné, aies patiné, ait patiné; ayons patiné, ayez patiné, aient patiné
Plup. Subj.	eusse patiné, eusses patiné, eût patiné; eussions patiné, eussiez patiné, eussent patiné
Imperative	patine, patinons, patinez

to pay

Pres. Ind.	paye, payes, paye; payons, payez, payent
Imp. Ind.	payais, payais, payait; payions, payiez, payaient
Past Def.	payai, payas, paya; payâmes, payâtes, payèrent
Fut. Ind.	payerai, payeras, payera; payerons, payerez, payeront
Condit.	payerais, payerais, payerait; payerions, payeriez, payeraient
Pres. Subj.	paye, payes, paye; payions, payiez, payent
Imp. Subj.	payasse, payasses, payât; payassions, payassiez, payassent
Past Indef.	ai payé, as payé, a payé; avons payé, avez payé, ont payé
Pluperf.	avais payé, avais payé, avait payé; avions payé, aviez payé, avaient payé
Past Ant.	eus payé, eus payé, eut payé; eûmes payé, eûtes payé, eurent payé
Fut. Perf.	aurai payé, auras payé, aura payé; aurons payé, aurez payé, auront payé
Cond. Perf.	aurais payé, aurais payé, aurait payé; aurions payé, auriez payé, auraient payé
Past Subj.	aie payé, aies payé, ait payé; ayons payé, ayez payé, aient payé
Plup. Subj.	eusse payé, eusses payé, eût payé; eussions payé, eussiez payé, eussent payé
Imperative	paye, payons, payez

to sin, commit sin

Pres. Ind.	pèche, pèches, pèche; péchons, péchez, pèchent
Imp. Ind.	péchais, péchais, péchait; péchions, péchiez, péchaient
Past Def.	péchai, péchas, pécha; péchâmes, péchâtes, péchèrent
Future	pécherai, pécheras, péchera; pécherons, pécherez, pécheront
Condit.	pécherais, pécherais, pécherait; pécherions, pécheriez, pécheraient
Pres. Subj.	pèche, pèches, pèche; péchions, péchiez, pèchent
Imp. Subj.	péchasse, péchasses, péchât; péchassions, péchassiez, péchassent
Past Indef.	ai péché, as péché, a péché; avons péché, avez péché, ont péché
Plup. Ind.	avais péché, avais péché, avait péché; avions péché, aviez péché, avaient péché
Past Ant.	eus péché, eus péché, eut péché; eûmes péché, eûtes péché, eurent péché
Fut. Perf.	aurai péché, auras péché, aura péché; aurons péché, aurez péché, auront péché
Cond. Perf.	aurais péché, aurais péché, aurait péché; aurions péché, auriez péché, auraient péché
Past Subj.	aie péché, aies péché, ait péché; ayons péché, ayez péché, aient péché
Plup. Subj.	eusse péché, eusses péché, eût péché; eussions péché, eussiez péché, eussent péché
Imperative	[ordinairement inemployé]

to fish

Pres. Ind.	pêche, pêches, pêche; pêchons, pêchez, pêchent
Imp. Ind.	pêchais, pêchais, pêchait; pêchions, pêchiez, pêchaient
Past Def.	pêchai, pêchas, pêcha; pêchâmes, pêchâtes, pêchèrent
Future	pêcherai, pêcheras, pêchera; pêcherons, pêcherez, pêcheront
Condit.	pêcherais, pêcherais, pêcherait; pêcherions, pêcheriez, pêcheraient
Pres. Subj.	pêche, pêches, pêche; pêchions, pêchiez, pêchent
Imp. Subj.	pêchasse, pêchasses, pêchât; pêchassions, pêchassiez, pêchassent
Past Indef.	ai pêché, as pêché, a pêché; avons pêché, avez pêché, ont pêché
Plup. Ind.	avais pêché, avais pêché, avait pêché; avions pêché, aviez pêché, avaient pêché
Past Ant.	eus pêché, eus pêché, eut pêché; eûmes pêché, eûtes pêché, eurent pêché
Fut. Perf.	aurai pêché, auras pêché, aura pêché; aurons pêché, aurez pêché, auront pêché
Cond. Perf.	aurais pêché, aurais pêché, aurait pêché; aurions pêché, auriez pêché, auraient pêché
Past Subj.	aie pêché, aies pêché, ait pêché; ayons pêché, ayez pêché, aient pêché
Plup. Subj.	eusse pêché, eusses pêché, eût pêché; eusions pêché, eussiez pêché, eussent pêché
Imperative	pêche, pêchons, pêchez

to comb one's hair

Pres. Ind.	me peigne, te peignes, se peigne; nous peignons, vous peignez, se peignent
Imp. Ind.	me peignais, te peignais, se peignait; nous peignions, vous peigniez, se peignaient
Past Def.	me peignai, te peignas, se peigna; nous peignâmes, vous peignâtes, se peignèrent
Future	me peignerai, te peigneras, se peignera; nous peignerons, vous peignerez, se peigneront
Condit.	me peignerais, te peignerais, se peignerait; nous peignerions, vous peigneriez, se peigneraient
Pres. Subj.	me peigne, te peignes, se peigne; nous peignions, vous peigniez, se peignent
Imp. Subj.	me peignasse, te peignasses, se peignât; nous peignassions, vous peignassiez, se peignassent
Past Indef.	me suis peigné(e), t'es peigné(e), s'est peigné(e); nous sommes peigné(e)s, vous êtes peigné(e)(s), se sont peigné(e)s
Plup. Ind.	m'étais peigné(e), t'étais peigné(e), s'était peigné(e); nous étions peigné(e)s, vous étiez peigné(e)(s), s'étaient peigné(e)s
Past Ant.	me fus peigné(e), te fus peigné(e), se fut peigné(e); nous fûmes peigné(e)s, vous fûtes peigné(e)(s), se furent peigné(e)s
Fut. Perf.	me serai peigné(e), te seras peigné(e), se sera peigné(e); nous serons peigné(e)s, vous serez peigné(e)(s), se seront peigné(e)s
Cond. Perf.	me serais peigné(e), te serais peigné(e), se serait peigné(e); nous serions peigné(e)s, vous seriez peigné(e)(s), se seraient peigné(e)s
Past Subj.	me sois peigné(e), te sois peigné(e), se soit peigné(e); nous soyons peigné(e)s, vous soyez peigné(e)(s), se soient peigné(e)s
Plup. Subj.	me fusse peigné(e), te fusses peigné(e), se fût peigné(e); nous fussions peigné(e)s, vous fussiez peigné(e)(s), se fussent peigné(e)s
Imperative	peigne-toi, peignons-nous, peignez-vous

to paint

Pres. Ind.	peins, peins, peint; peignons, peignez, peignent
Imp. Ind.	peignais, peignais, peignait; peignions, peigniez, peignaient
Past Def.	peignis, peignis, peignit; peignîmes, peignîtes, peignirent
Fut. Ind.	peindrai, peindras, peindra; peindrons, peindrez, peindront
Condit.	peindrais, peindrais, peindrait; peindrions, peindriez, peindraient
Pres. Subj.	peigne, peignes, peigne; peignions, peigniez, peignent
Imp. Subj.	peignisse, peignisses, peignît; peignissions, peignissiez, peignissent
Past Indef.	ai peint, as peint, a peint; avons peint, avez peint, ont peint
Pluperf.	avais peint, avais peint, avait peint; avions peint, aviez peint, avaient peint
Past Ant.	eus peint, eus peint, eut peint; eûmes peint, eûtes peint, eurent peint
Fut. Perf.	aurai peint, auras peint, aura peint; aurons peint, aurez peint, auront peint
Cond. Perf.	aurais peint, aurais peint, aurait peint; aurions peint, auriez peint, auraient peint
Past Subj.	aie peint, aies peint, ait peint; ayons peint, ayez peint, aient peint
Plup. Subj.	eusse peint, eusses peint, eût peint; eussions peint, eussiez peint, eussent peint
Imperative	peins, peignons, peignez

to hang

Pres. Ind.	pends, pends, pend; pendons, pendez, pendent
Imp. Ind.	pendais, pendais, pendait; pendions, pendiez, pendaient
Past Def.	pendis, pendis, pendit; pendîmes, pendîtes, pendirent
Fut. Ind.	pendrai, pendras, pendra; pendrons, pendrez, pendront
Condit.	pendrais, pendrais, pendrait; pendrions, pendriez, pendraient
Pres. Subj.	pende, pendes, pende; pendions, pendiez, pendent
Imp. Subj.	pendisse, pendisses, pendît; pendissions, pendissiez, pendissent
Past Indef.	ai pendu, as pendu, a pendu; avons pendu, avez pendu, ont pendu
Pluperf.	avais pendu, avais pendu, avait pendu; avions pendu, aviez pendu, avaient pendu
Past Ant.	eus pendu, eus pendu, eut pendu; eûmes pendu, eûtes pendu, eurent pendu
Fut. Perf.	aurai pendu, auras pendu, aura pendu; aurons pendu, aurez pendu, auront pendu
Cond. Perf.	aurais pendu, aurais pendu, aurait pendu; aurions pendu, auriez pendu, auraient pendu
Past Subj.	aie pendu, aies pendu, ait pendu; ayons pendu, ayez pendu, aient pendu
Plup. Subj.	eusse pendu, eusses pendu, eût pendu; eussions pendu, eussiez pendu, eussent pendu
Imperative	pends, pendons, pendez

to think

Pres. Ind.	pense, penses, pense; pensons, pensez, pensent
Imp. Ind.	pensais, pensais, pensait; pensions, pensiez, pensaient
Past Def.	pensai, pensas, pensa; pensâmes, pensâtes, pensèrent
Fut. Ind.	penserai, penseras, pensera; penserons, penserez, penseront
Condit.	penserais, penserais, penserait; penserions, penseriez, penseraient
Pres. Subj.	pense, penses, pense; pensions, pensiez, pensent
Imp. Subj.	pensasse, pensasses, pensât; pensassions, pensassiez, pensassent
Past Indef.	ai pensé, as pensé, a pensé; avons pensé, avez pensé, ont pensé
Pluperf.	avais pensé, avais pensé, avait pensé; avions pensé, aviez pensé, avaient pensé
Past Ant.	eus pensé, eus pensé, eut pensé; eûmes pensé, eûtes pensé, eurent pensé
Fut. Perf.	aurai pensé, auras pensé, aura pensé; aurons pensé, aurez pensé, auront pensé
Cond. Perf.	aurais pensé, aurais pensé, aurait pensé; aurions pensé, auriez pensé, auraient pensé
Past Subj.	aie pensé, aies pensé, ait pensé; ayons pensé, ayez pensé, aient pensé
Plup. Subj.	eusse pensé, eusses pensé, eût pensé; eussions pensé, eussiez pensé, eussent pensé
Imperative	pense, pensons, pensez

to lose

Pres. Ind.	perds, perds, perd; perdons, perdez, perdent
Imp. Ind.	perdais, perdais, perdait; perdions, perdiez, perdaient
Past Def.	perdis, perdis, perdit; perdîmes, perdîtes, perdirent
Fut. Ind.	perdrai, perdras, perdra; perdrons, perdrez, perdront
Condit.	perdrais, perdrais, perdrait; perdrions, perdriez, perdraient
Pres. Subj.	perde, perdes, perde; perdions, perdiez, perdent
Imp. Subj.	perdisse, perdisses, perdît; perdissions, perdissiez, perdissent
Past Indef.	ai perdu, as perdu, a perdu; avons perdu, avez perdu, ont perdu
Pluperf.	avais perdu, avais perdu, avait perdu; avions perdu, aviez perdu, avaient perdu
Past Ant.	eus perdu, eus perdu, eut perdu; eûmes perdu, eûtes perdu, eurent perdu
Fut. Perf.	aurai perdu, auras perdu, aura perdu; aurons perdu, aurez perdu, auront perdu
Cond. Perf.	aurais perdu, aurais perdu, aurait perdu; aurions perdu, auriez perdu, auraient perdu
Past Subj.	aie perdu, aies perdu, ait perdu; ayons perdu, ayez perdu, aient perdu
Plup. Subj.	eusse perdu, eusses perdu, eût perdu; eussions perdu, eussiez perdu, eussent perdu
Imperative	perds, perdons, perdez

to perish, die

Pres. Ind.	péris, péris, périt; périssons, périssez, périssent
Imp. Ind.	périssais, périssais, périssait; périssions, périssiez, périssaient
Past Def.	péris, péris, périt; pérîmes, pérîtes, périrent
Fut. Ind.	périrai, périras, périra; périrons, périrez, périront
Condit.	périrais, périrais, périrait; péririons, péririez, périraient
Pres. Subj.	périsse, périsses, périsse; périssions, périssiez, périssent
Imp. Subj.	périsse, périsses, pérît; périssions, périssiez, périssent
Past Indef.	ai péri, as péri, a péri; avons péri, avez péri, ont péri
Pluperf.	avais péri, avais péri, avait péri; avions péri, aviez péri, avaient péri
Past Ant.	eus péri, eus péri, eut péri; eûmes péri, eûtes péri, eurent péri
Fut. Perf.	aurai péri, auras péri, aura péri; aurons péri, aurez péri, auront péri
Cond. Perf.	aurais péri, aurais péri, aurait péri; aurions péri, auriez péri, auraient péri
Past Subj.	aie péri, aies péri, ait péri; ayons péri, ayez péri, aient péri
Plup. Subj.	eusse péri, eusses péri, eût péri; eussions péri, eussiez péri, eussent péri
Imperative	péris, périssons, périssez

to permit, allow, let

Pres. Ind.	permets, permets, permet; permettons, permettez, permettent
Imp. Ind.	permettais, permettais, permettait; permettions, permettiez, permettaient
Past Def.	permis, permis, permit; permîmes, permîtes, permirent
Fut. Ind.	permettrai, permettras, permettra; permettrons, permettrez, permettront
Condit.	permettrais, permettrais, permettrait; permettrions, permettriez, permettraient
Pres. Subj.	permette, permettes, permette; permettions, permettiez, permettent
Imp. Subj.	permisse, permisses, permît; permissions, permissiez, permissent
Past Indef.	ai permis, as permis, a permis; avons permis, avez permis, ont permis
Pluperf.	avais permis, avais permis, avait permis; avions permis, aviez permis, avaient permis
Past Ant.	eus permis, eus permis, eut permis; eûmes permis, eûtes permis, eurent permis
Fut. Perf.	aurai permis, auras permis, aura permis; aurons permis, aurez permis, auront permis
Cond. Perf.	aurais permis, aurais permis, aurait permis; aurions permis, auriez permis, auraient permis
Past Subj.	aie permis, aies permis, ait permis; ayons permis, ayez permis, aient permis
Plup. Subj.	eusse permis, eusses permis, eût permis; eussions permis, eussiez permis, eussent permis
Imperative	permets, permettons, permettez

to weigh

Pres. Ind.	pèse, pèses, pèse; pesons, pesez, pèsent
Imp. Ind.	pesais, pesais, pesait; pesions, pesiez, pesaient
Past Def.	pesai, pesas, pesa; pesâmes, pesâtes, pesèrent
Future	pèserai, pèseras, pèsera; pèserons, pèserez, pèseront
Condit.	pèserais, pèserais, pèserait; pèserions, pèseriez, pèseraient
Pres. Subj.	pèse, pèses, pèse; pesions, pesiez, pèsent
Imp. Subj.	pesasse, pesasses, pesât; pesassions, pesassiez, pesassent
Past Indef.	ai pesé, as pesé, a pesé; avons pesé, avez pesé, ont pesé
Plup. Ind.	avais pesé, avais pesé, avait pesé; avions pesé, aviez pesé, avaient pesé
Past Ant.	eus pesé, eus pesé, eut pesé; eûmes pesé, eûtes pesé, eurent pesé
Fut. Perf.	aurai pesé, auras pesé, aura pesé; aurons pesé, aurez pesé, auront pesé
Cond.	aurais pesé, aurais pesé, aurait pesé; aurions pesé, auriez pesé, auraient pesé
Past Subj.	aie pesé, aies pesé, ait pesé; ayons pesé, ayez pesé, aient pesé
Plup. Subj.	eusse pesé, eusses pesé, eût pesé; eussions pesé, eussiez pesé, eussent pesé
Imperative	pèse, pesons, pesez

to place, put

Pres. Ind.	place, places, place; plaçons, placez, placent
Imp. Ind.	plaçais, plaçais, plaçait; placions, placiez, plaçaient
Past Def.	plaçai, plaças, plaça; plaçâmes, plaçâtes, placèrent
Future	placerai, placeras, placera; placerons, placerez, placeront
Condit.	placerais, placerais, placerait; placerions, placeriez, placeraient
Pres. Subj.	place, places, place; placions, placiez, placent
Imp. Subj.	plaçasse, plaçasses, plaçât; plaçassions, plaçassiez, plaçassent
Past Indef.	ai placé, as placé, a placé; avons placé, avez placé, ont placé
Pluperf.	avais placé, avais placé, avait placé; avions placé, aviez placé, avaient placé
Past Ant.	eus placé, eus placé, eut placé; eûmes placé, eûtes placé, eurent placé
Fut. Perf.	aurai placé, auras placé, aura placé; aurons placé, aurez placé, auront placé
Cond. Perf.	aurais placé, aurais placé, aurait placé; aurions placé, auriez placé, auraient placé
Past Subj.	aie placé, aies placé, ait placé; ayons placé, ayez placé, aient placé
Plup. Subj.	eusse placé, eusses placé, eût placé; eussions placé, eussiez placé, eussent placé
Imperative	place, plaçons, placez

to pity

Pres. Ind.	plains, plains, plaint; plaignons, plaignez, plaignent
Imp. Ind.	plaignais, plaignais, plaignait; plaignions, plaigniez, plaignaient
Past Def.	plaignis, plaignis, plaignit; plaignîmes, plaignîtes, plaignirent
Future	plaindrai, plaindras, plaindra; plaindrons, plaindrez, plaindront
Condit.	plaindrais, plaindrais, plaindrait; plaindrions, plaindriez, plaindraient
Pres. Subj.	plaigne, plaignes, plaigne; plaignions, plaigniez, plaignent
Imp. Subj.	plaignisse, plaignisses, plaignît; plaignissions, plaignissiez, plaignissent
Past Indef.	ai plaint, as plaint, a plaint; avons plaint, avez plaint, ont plaint
Pluperf.	avais plaint, avais plaint, avait plaint; avions plaint, aviez plaint, avaient plaint
Past Ant.	eus plaint, eus plaint, eut plaint; eûmes plaint, eûtes plaint, eurent plaint
Fut. Perf.	aurai plaint, auras plaint, aura plaint; aurons plaint, aurez plaint, auront plaint
Cond. Perf.	aurais plaint, aurais plaint, aurait plaint; aurions plaint, auriez plaint, auraient plaint
Past Subj.	aie plaint, aies plaint, ait plaint; ayons plaint, ayez plaint, aient plaint
Plup. Subj.	eusse plaint, eusses plaint, eût plaint; eussions plaint, eussiez plaint, eussent plaint
Imperative	plains, plaignons, plaignez

to complain, lament, moan

Pres. Ind.	me plains, te plains, se plaint; nous plaignons, vous plaignez, se plaignent
Imp. Ind.	me plaignais, te plaignais, se plaignait; nous plaignions, vous plaigniez, se plaignaient
Past Def.	me plaignis, te plaignis, se plaignit; nous plaignîmes, vous plaignîtes, se plaignirent
Future	me plaindrai, te plaindras, se plaindra; nous plaindrons, vous plaindrez, se plaindront
Condit.	me plaindrais, te plaindrais, se plaindrait; nous plaindrions, vous plaindriez, se plaindraient
Pres. Subj.	me plaigne, te plaignes, se plaigne; nous plaignions, vous plaigniez, se plaignent
Imp. Subj.	me plaignisse, te plaignisses, se plaignît; nous plaignissions, vous plaignissiez, se plaignissent
Past Indef.	me suis plaint(e), t'es plaint(e), s'est plaint(e); nous sommes plaint(e)s, vous êtes plaint(e)(s), se sont plaint(e)s
Pluperf.	m'étais plaint(e), t'étais plaint(e), s'était plaint(e); nous étions plaint(e)s, vous étiez plaint(e)(s), s'étaient plaint(e)s
Past Ant.	me fus plaint(e), te fus plaint(e), se fut plaint(e); nous fûmes plaint(e)s, vous fûtes plaint(e)(s), se furent plaint(e)s
Fut. Perf.	me serai plaint(e), te seras plaint(e), se sera plaint(e); nous serons plaint(e)s, vous serez plaint(e)(s), se seront plaint(e)s
Cond. Perf.	me serais plaint(e), te serais plaint(e), se serait plaint(e); nous serions plaint(e)s, vous seriez plaint(e)(s), se seraient plaint(e)s
Past Subj.	me sois plaint(e), te sois plaint(e), se soit plaint(e); nous soyons plaint(e)s, vous soyez plaint(e)(s), se soient plaint(e)s
Plup. Subj.	me fusse plaint(e), te fusses plaint(e), se fût plaint(e); nous fussions plaint(e)s, vous fussiez plaint(e)(s), se fussent plaint(e)s
Imperative	plains-toi, plaignons-nous, plaignez-vous

to please

Pres. Ind.	plais, plais, plaît; plaisons, plaisez, plaisent
Imp. Ind.	plaisais, plaisais, plaisait; plaisions, plaisiez, plaisaient
Past Def.	plus, plus, plut; plûmes, plûtes, plurent
Fut. Ind.	plairai, plairas, plaira; plairons, plairez, plairont
Condit.	plairais, plairais, plairait; plairions, plairiez, plairaient
Pres. Subj.	plaise, plaises, plaise; plaisions, plaisiez, plaisent
Imp. Subj.	plusse, plusses, plût; plussions, plussiez, plussent
Past Indef.	ai plu, as plu, a plu; avons plu, avez plu, ont plu
Pluperf.	avais plu, avais plu, avait plu; avions plu, aviez plu, avaient plu
Past Ant.	eus plu, eus plu, eut plu; eûmes plu, eûtes plu, eurent plu
Fut. Perf.	aurai plu, auras plu, aura plu; aurons plu, aurez plu, auront plu
Cond. Perf.	aurais plu, aurais plu, aurait plu; aurions plu, auriez plu, auraient plu
Past Subj.	aie plu, aies plu, ait plu; ayons plu, ayez plu, aient plu
Plup. Subj.	eusse plu, eusses plu, eût plu; eussions plu, eussiez plu, eussent plu
Imperative	plais, plaisons, plaisez

to rain

Pres. Ind.	il pleut
Imp. Ind.	il pleuvait
Past Def.	il plut
Future	il pleuvra
Condit.	il pleuvrait
Pres. Subj.	qu'il pleuve
Imp. Subj.	qu'il plût
Past Indef.	il a plu
Plup. Ind.	il avait plu
Past Ant.	il eut plu
Fut. Perf.	il aura plu
Cond. Perf.	il aurait plu
Past Subj.	qu'il ait plu
Plup. Subj.	qu'il eût plu
Imperative	[inemployé]

to wear, carry

Pres. Ind.	porte, portes, porte; portons, portez, portent
Imp. Ind.	portais, portais, portait; portions, portiez, portaient
Past Def.	portai, portas, porta; portâmes, portâtes, portèrent
Fut. Ind.	porterai, porteras, portera; porterons, porterez, porteront
Condit.	porterais, porterais, porterait; porterions, porteriez, porteraient
Pres. Subj.	porte, portes, porte; portions, portiez, portent
Imp. Subj.	portasse, portasses, portât; portassions, portassiez, portassent
Past Indef.	ai porté, as porté, a porté; avons porté, avez porté, ont porté
Pluperf.	avais porté, avais porté, avait porté; avions porté, aviez porté, avaient porté
Past Ant.	eus porté, eus porté, eut porté; eûmes porté, eûtes porté, eurent porté
Fut. Perf.	aurai porté, auras porté, aura porté; aurons porté, aurez porté, auront porté
Cond. Perf.	aurais porté, aurais porté, aurait porté; aurions porté, auriez porté, auraient porté
Past Subj.	aie porté, aies porté, ait porté; ayons porté, ayez porté, aient porté
Plup. Subj.	eusse porté, eusses porté, eût porté; eussions porté, eussiez porté, eussent porté
Imperative	porte, portons, portez

to lay, place, put, set

Pres. Ind.	pose, poses, pose; posons, posez, posent
Imp. Ind.	posais, posais, posait; posions, posiez, posaient
Past Def.	posai, posas, posa; posâmes, posâtes, posèrent
Future	poserai, poseras, posera; poserons, poserez, poseront
Condit.	poserais, poserais, poserait; poserions, poseriez, poseraient
Pres. Subj.	pose, poses, pose; posions, posiez, posent
Imp. Subj.	posasse, posasses, posât; posassions, posassiez, posassent
Past Indef.	ai posé, as posé, a posé; avons posé, avez posé, ont posé
Plup. Ind.	avais posé, avais posé, avait posé; avions posé, aviez posé, avaient posé
Past Ant.	eus posé, eus posé, eut posé; eûmes posé, eûtes posé, eurent posé
Fut. Perf.	aurai posé, auras posé, aura posé; aurons posé, aurez posé, auront posé
Cond. Perf.	aurais posé, aurais posé, aurait posé; aurions posé, auriez posé, auraient posé
Past Subj.	aie posé, aies posé, ait posé; ayons posé, ayez posé, aient posé
Plup. Subj.	eusse posé, eusses posé, eût posé; eussions posé, eussiez posé, eussent posé
Imperative	pose, posons, posez

to pursue, prosecute

Pres. Ind.	poursuis, poursuis, poursuit; poursuivons, poursuivez, poursuivent
Imp. Ind.	poursuivais, poursuivais, poursuivait; poursuivions, poursuiviez, poursuivaient
Past Def.	poursuivis, poursuivis, poursuivit; poursuivîmes, poursuivîtes, poursuivirent
Future	poursuivrai, poursuivras, poursuivra; poursuivrons, poursuivrez, poursuivront
Condit.	poursuivrais, poursuivrais, poursuivrait; poursuivrions, poursuivriez, poursuivraient
Pres. Subj.	poursuive, poursuives, poursuive; poursuivions, poursuiviez, poursuivent
Imp. Subj.	poursuivisse, poursuivisses, poursuivît; poursuivissions, poursuivissiez, poursuivissent
Past Indef.	ai poursuivi, as poursuivi, a poursuivi; avons poursuivi, avez poursuivi, ont poursuivi
Plup. Ind.	avais poursuivi, avais poursuivi, avait poursuivi; avions poursuivi, aviez poursuivi, avaient poursuivi
Past Ant.	eus poursuivi, eus poursuivi, eut poursuivi; eûmes poursuivi, eûtes poursuivi, eurent poursuivi
Fut. Perf.	aurai poursuivi, auras poursuivi, aura poursuivi; aurons poursuivi, aurez poursuivi, auront poursuivi
Cond. Perf.	aurais poursuivi, aurais poursuivi, aurait poursuivi; aurions poursuivi, auriez poursuivi, auraient poursuivi
Past Subj.	aie poursuivi, aies poursuivi, ait poursuivi; ayons poursuivi, ayez poursuivi, aient poursuivi
Plup. Subj.	eusse poursuivi, eusses poursuivi, eût poursuivi; eussions poursuivi, eussiez poursuivi, eussent poursuivi
Imperative	poursuis, poursuivons, poursuivez

to provide

Pres. Ind.	pourvois, pourvois, pourvoit; pourvoyons, pourvoyez, pourvoient
Imp. Ind.	pourvoyais, pourvoyais, pourvoyait; pourvoyions, pourvoyiez, pourvoyaient
Past Def.	pourvus, pourvus, pourvut; pourvûmes, pourvûtes, pourvurent
Fut. Ind.	pourvoirai, pourvoiras, pourvoira; pourvoirons, pourvoirez, pourvoiront
Condit.	pourvoirais, pourvoirais, pourvoirait; pourvoirions, pourvoiriez, pourvoiraient
Pres. Subj.	pourvoie, pourvoies, pourvoie; pourvoyions, pourvoyiez, pourvoient
Imp. Subj.	pourvusse, pourvusses, pourvût; pourvussions, pourvussiez, pourvussent
Past Indef.	ai pourvu, as pourvu, a pourvu; avons pourvu, avez pourvu, ont pourvu
Pluperf.	avais pourvu, avais pourvu, avait pourvu; avions pourvu, aviez pourvu, avaient pourvu
Past Ant.	eus pourvu, eus pourvu, eut pourvu; eûmes pourvu, eûtes pourvu, eurent pourvu
Fut. Perf.	aurai pourvu, auras pourvu, aura pourvu; aurons pourvu, aurez pourvu, auront pourvu
Cond. Perf.	aurais pourvu, aurais pourvu, aurait pourvu; aurions pourvu, auriez pourvu, auraient pourvu
Past Subj.	aie pourvu, aies pourvu, ait pourvu; ayons pourvu, ayez pourvu, aient pourvu
Plup. Subj.	eusse pourvu, eusses pourvu, eût pourvu; eussions pourvu, eussiez pourvu, eussent pourvu
Imperative	pourvois, pourvoyons, pourvoyez

to push

Pres. Ind.	pousse, pousses, pousse; poussons, poussez, poussent
Imp. Ind.	poussais, poussais, poussait; poussions, poussiez, poussaient
Past Def.	poussai, poussas, poussa; poussâmes, poussâtes, poussèrent
Future	pousserai, pousseras, poussera; pousserons, pousserez, pousseront
Condit.	pousserais, pousserais, pousserait; pousserions, pousseriez, poussseraient
Pres. Subj.	pousse, pousses, pousse; poussions, poussiez, poussent
Imp. Subj.	poussasse, poussasses, poussât; poussassions, poussassiez, poussassent
Past Indef.	ai poussé, as poussé, a poussé; avons poussé, avez poussé, ont poussé
Plup. Ind.	avais poussé, avais poussé, avait poussé; avions poussé, aviez poussé, avaient poussé
Past Ant.	eus poussé, eus poussé, eut poussé; eûmes poussé, eûtes poussé, eurent poussé
Fut. Perf.	aurai poussé, auras poussé, aura poussé; aurons poussé, aurez poussé, auront poussé
Cond. Perf.	aurais poussé, aurais poussé, aurait poussé; aurions poussé, auriez poussé, auraient poussé
Past Subj.	aie poussé, aies poussé, ait poussé; ayons poussé, ayez poussé, aient poussé
Plup. Subj.	eusse poussé, eusses poussé, eût poussé; eussions poussé, eussiez poussé, eussent poussé
Imperative	pousse, poussons, poussez

to be able, can

Pres. Ind.	peux *or* puis, peux, peut; pouvons, pouvez, peuvent
Imp. Ind.	pouvais, pouvais, pouvait; pouvions, pouviez, pouvaient
Past Def.	pus, pus, put; pûmes, pûtes, purent
Fut. Ind.	pourrai, pourras, pourra; pourrons, pourrez, pourront
Condit.	pourrais, pourrais, pourrait; pourrions, pourriez, pourraient
Pres. Subj.	puisse, puisses, puisse; puissions, puissiez, puissent
Imp. Subj.	pusse, pusses, pût; pussions, pussiez, pussent
Past Indef.	ai pu, as pu, a pu; avons pu, avez pu, ont pu
Pluperf.	avais pu, avais pu, avait pu; avions pu, aviez pu, avaient pu
Past Ant.	eus pu, eus pu, eut pu; eûmes pu, eûtes pu, eurent pu
Fut. Perf.	aurai pu, auras pu, aura pu; aurons pu, aurez pu, auront pu
Cond. Perf.	aurais pu, aurais pu, aurait pu; aurions pu, auriez pu, auraient pu
Past Subj.	aie pu, aies pu, ait pu; ayons pu, ayez pu, aient pu
Plup. Subj.	eusse pu, eusses pu, eût pu; eussions pu, eussiez pu, eussent pu
Imperative	——

to foretell, predict

Pres. Ind.	prédis, prédis, prédit; prédisons, prédisez, prédisent
Imp. Ind.	prédisais, prédisais, prédisait; prédisions, prédisiez, prédisaient
Past Def.	prédis, prédis, prédit; prédîmes, prédîtes, prédirent
Future	prédirai, prédiras, prédira; prédirons, prédirez, prédiront
Condit.	prédirais, prédirais, prédirait; prédirions, prédiriez, prédiraient
Pres. Subj.	prédise, prédises, prédise; prédisions, prédisiez, prédisent
Imp. Subj.	prédisse, prédisses, prédît; prédissions, prédissiez, prédissent
Past Indef.	ai prédit, as prédit, a prédit; avons prédit, avez prédit, ont prédit
Plup. Ind.	avais prédit, avais prédit, avait prédit; avions prédit, aviez prédit, avaient prédit
Past Ant.	eus prédit, eus prédit, eut prédit; eûmes prédit, eûtes prédit, eurent prédit
Fut. Perf.	aurai prédit, auras prédit, aura prédit; aurons prédit, aurez prédit, auront prédit
Cond. Perf.	aurais prédit, aurais prédit, aurait prédit; aurions prédit, auriez prédit, auraient prédit
Past Subj.	aie prédit, aies prédit, ait prédit; ayons prédit, ayez prédit, aient prédit
Plup. Subj.	eusse prédit, eusses prédit, eût prédit; eussions prédit, eussiez prédit, eussent prédit
Imperative	prédis, prédisons, prédisez

to prefer

Pres. Ind.	préfère, préfères, préfère; préférons, préférez, préfèrent
Imp. Ind.	préférais, préférais, préférait; préférions, préfériez, préféraient
Past Def.	préférai, préféras, préféra; préférâmes, préférâtes, préférèrent
Fut. Ind.	préférerai, préféreras, préférera; préférerons, préférerez, préféreront
Condit.	préférerais, préférerais, préférerait; préférerions, préféreriez, préféreraient
Pres. Subj.	préfère, préfères, préfère; préférions, préfériez, préfèrent
Imp. Subj.	préférasse, préférasses, préférât; préférassions, préférassiez, préférassent
Past Indef.	ai préféré, as préféré, a préféré; avons préféré, avez préféré, ont préféré
Pluperf.	avais préféré, avais préféré, avait préféré; avions préféré, aviez préféré, avaient préféré
Past Ant.	eus préféré, eus préféré, eut préféré; eûmes préféré, eûtes préféré, eurent préféré
Fut. Perf.	aurai préféré, auras préféré, aura préféré; aurons préféré, aurez préféré, auront préféré
Cond. Perf.	aurais préféré, aurais préféré, aurait préféré; aurions préféré, auriez préféré, auraient préféré
Past Subj.	aie préféré, aies préféré, ait préféré; ayons préféré, ayez préféré, aient préféré
Plup. Subj.	eusse préféré, eusses préféré, eût préféré; eussions préféré, eussiez préféré, eussent préféré
Imperative	préfère, préférons, préférez

to take

Pres. Ind.	prends, prends, prend; prenons, prenez, prennent
Imp. Ind.	prenais, prenais, prenait; prenions, preniez, prenaient
Past Def.	pris, pris, prit; prîmes, prîtes, prirent
Fut. Ind.	prendrai, prendras, prendra; prendrons, prendrez, prendront
Condit.	prendrais, prendrais, prendrait; prendrions, prendriez, prendraient
Pres. Subj.	prenne, prennes, prenne; prenions, preniez, prennent
Imp. Subj.	prisse, prisses, prît; prissions, prissiez, prissent
Past Indef.	ai pris, as pris, a pris; avons pris, avez pris, ont pris
Pluperf.	avais pris, avais pris, avait pris; avions pris, aviez pris, avaient pris
Past Ant.	eus pris, eus pris, eut pris; eûmes pris, eûtes pris, eurent pris
Fut. Perf.	aurai pris, auras pris, aura pris; aurons pris, aurez pris, auront pris
Cond. Perf.	aurais pris, aurais pris, aurait pris; aurions pris, auriez pris, auraient pris
Past Subj.	aie pris, aies pris, ait pris; ayons pris, ayez pris, aient pris
Plup. Subj.	eusse pris, eusses pris, eût pris; eussions pris, eussiez pris, eussent pris
Imperative	prends, prenons, prenez

to prepare

Pres. Ind.	prépare, prépares, prépare; préparons, préparez, préparent
Imp. Ind.	préparais, préparais, préparait; préparions, prépariez, préparaient
Past Def.	préparai, préparas, prépara; préparâmes, préparâtes, préparèrent
Future	préparerai, prépareras, préparera; préparerons, préparerez, prépareront
Condit.	préparerais, préparerais, préparerait; préparerions, prépareriez, prépareraient
Pres. Subj.	prépare, prépares, prépare; préparions, prépariez, préparent
Imp. Subj.	préparasse, préparasses, préparât; préparassions, préparassiez, préparassent
Past Indef.	ai préparé, as préparé, a préparé; avons préparé, avez préparé, ont préparé
Plup. Ind.	avais préparé, avais préparé, avait préparé; avions préparé, aviez préparé, avaient préparé
Past Ant.	eus préparé, eus préparé, eut préparé; eûmes préparé, eûtes préparé, eurent préparé
Fut. Perf.	aurai préparé, auras préparé, aura préparé; aurons préparé, aurez préparé, auront préparé
Cond. Perf.	aurais préparé, aurais préparé, aurait préparé; aurions préparé, auriez préparé, auraient préparé
Past Subj.	aie préparé, aies préparé, ait préparé; ayons préparé, ayez préparé, aient préparé
Plup. Subj.	eusse préparé, eusses préparé, eût préparé; eussions préparé, eussiez préparé, eussent préparé
Imperative	prépare, préparons, préparez

to present, introduce (a person)

Pres. Ind.	présente, présentes, présente; présentons, présentez, présentent
Imp. Ind.	présentais, présentais, présentait; présentions, présentiez, présentaient
Past Def.	présentai, présentas, présenta; présentâmes, présentâtes, présentèrent
Future	présenterai, présenteras, présentera; présenterons, présenterez, présenteront
Condit.	présenterais, présenterais, présenterait; présenterions, présenteriez, présenteraient
Pres. Subj.	présente, présentes, présente; présentions, présentiez, présentent
Imp. Subj.	présentasse, présentasses, présentât; présentassions, présentassiez, présentassent
Past Indef.	ai présenté, as présenté, a présenté; avons présenté, avez présenté, ont présenté
Plup. Ind.	avais présenté, avais présenté, avait présenté; avions présenté, aviez présenté, avaient présenté
Past Ant.	eus présenté, eus présenté, eut présenté; eûmes présenté, eûtes présenté, eurent présenté
Fut. Perf.	aurai présenté, auras présenté, aura présenté; aurons présenté, aurez présenté, auront présenté
Cond. Perf.	aurais présenté, aurais présenté, aurait présenté; aurions présenté, auriez présenté, auraient présenté
Past Subj.	aie présenté, aies présenté, ait présenté; ayons présenté, ayez présenté, aient présenté
Plup. Subj.	eusse présenté, eusses présenté, eût présenté; eussions présenté, eussiez présenté, eussent présenté
Imperative	présente, présentons, présentez

to press, squeeze

Pres. Ind.	presse, presses, presse; pressons, pressez, pressent
Imp. Ind.	pressais, pressais, pressait; pressions, pressiez, pressaient
Past Def.	pressai, pressas, pressa; pressâmes, pressâtes, pressèrent
Future	presserai, presseras, pressera; presserons, presserez, presseront
Condit.	presserais, presserais, presserait; presserions, presseriez, presseraient
Pres. Subj.	presse, presses, presse; pressions, pressiez, pressent
Imp. Subj.	pressasse, pressasses, pressât; pressassions, pressassiez, pressassent
Past Indef.	ai pressé, as pressé, a pressé; avons pressé, avez pressé, ont pressé
Plup. Ind.	avais pressé, avais pressé, avait pressé; avions pressé, aviez pressé, avaient pressé
Past Ant.	eus pressé, eus pressé, eut pressé; eûmes pressé, eûtes pressé, eurent pressé
Fut. Perf.	aurai pressé, auras pressé, aura pressé; aurons pressé, aurez pressé, auront pressé
Cond. Perf.	aurais pressé, aurais pressé, aurait pressé; aurions pressé, auriez pressé, auraient pressé
Past Subj.	aie pressé, aies pressé, ait pressé; ayons pressé, ayez pressé, aient pressé
Plup. Subj.	eusse pressé, eusses pressé, eût pressé; eussions pressé, eussiez pressé, eussent pressé
Imperative	presse, pressons, pressez

to be in a hurry, make haste, rush

Pres. Ind.	me presse, te presses, se presse; nous pressons, vous pressez, se pressent
Imp. Ind.	me pressais, te pressais, se pressait; nous pressions, vous pressiez, se pressaient
Past Def.	me pressai, te pressas, se pressa; nous pressâmes, vous pressâtes, se pressèrent
Future	me presserai, te presseras, se pressera; nous presserons, vous presserez, se presseront
Condit.	me presserais, te presserais, se presserait; nous presserions, vous presseriez, se presseraient
Pres. Subj.	me presse, te presses, se presse; nous pressions, vous pressiez, se pressent
Imp. Subj.	me pressasse, te pressasses, se pressât; nous pressassions, vous pressassiez, se pressassent
Past Indef.	me suis pressé(e), t'es pressé(e), s'est pressé(e); nous sommes pressé(e)s, vous êtes pressé(e)(s), se sont pressé(e)s
Plup. Ind.	m'étais pressé(e), t'étais pressé(e), s'était pressé(e); nous étions pressé(e)s, vous étiez pressé(e)(s), s'étaient pressé(e)s
Past Ant.	me fus pressé(e), te fus pressé(e), se fut pressé(e); nous fûmes pressé(e)s, vous fûtes pressé(e)(s), se furent pressé(e)s
Fut. Perf.	me serai pressé(e), te seras pressé(e), se sera pressé(e); nous serons pressé(e)s, vous serez pressé(e)(s), se seront pressé(e)s
Cond. Perf.	me serais pressé(e), te serais pressé(e), se serait pressé(e); nous serions pressé(e)s, vous seriez pressé(e)(s), se seraient pressé(e)s
Past Subj.	me sois pressé(e), te sois pressé(e), se soit pressé(e); nous soyons pressé(e)s, vous soyez pressé(e)(s), se soient pressé(e)s
Plup. Subj.	me fusse pressé(e), te fusses pressé(e), se fût pressé(e); nous fussions pressé(e)s, vous fussiez pressé(e)(s), se fussent pressé(e)s
Imperative	presse-toi, pressons-nous, pressez-vous

to pretend, claim, lay claim

Pres. Ind.	prétends, prétends, prétend; prétendons, prétendez, prétendent
Imp. Ind.	prétendais, prétendais, prétendait; prétendions, prétendiez, prétendaient
Past Def.	prétendis, prétendis, prétendit; prétendîmes, prétendîtes, prétendirent
Future	prétendrai, prétendras, prétendra; prétendrons, prétendrez, prétendront
Condit.	prétendrais, prétendrais, prétendrait; prétendrions, prétendriez, prétendraient
Pres. Subj.	prétende, prétendes, prétende; prétendions, prétendiez, prétendent
Imp. Subj.	prétendisse, prétendisses, prétendît; prétendissions, prétendissiez, prétendissent
Past Indef.	ai prétendu, as prétendu, a prétendu; avons prétendu, avez prétendu, ont prétendu
Plup. Ind.	avais prétendu, avais prétendu, avait prétendu; avions prétendu, aviez prétendu, avaient prétendu
Past Ant.	eus prétendu, eus prétendu, eut prétendu; eûmes prétendu, eûtes prétendu, eurent prétendu
Fut. Perf.	aurai prétendu, auras prétendu, aura prétendu; aurons prétendu, aurez prétendu, auront prétendu
Cond. Perf.	aurais prétendu, aurais prétendu, aurait prétendu; aurions prétendu, auriez prétendu, auraient prétendu
Past Subj.	aie prétendu, aies prétendu, ait prétendu; ayons prétendu, ayez prétendu, aient prétendu
Plup. Subj.	eusse prétendu, eusses prétendu, eût prétendu; eussions prétendu, eussiez prétendu, eussent prétendu
Imperative	prétends, prétendons, prétendez

to lend

Pres. Ind.	prête, prêtes, prête; prêtons, prêtez, prêtent
Imp. Ind.	prêtais, prêtais, prêtait; prêtions, prêtiez, prêtaient
Past Def.	prêtai, prêtas, prêta; prêtâmes, prêtâtes, prêtèrent
Fut. Ind.	prêterai, prêteras, prêtera; prêterons, prêterez, prêteront
Condit.	prêterais, prêterais, prêterait; prêterions, prêteriez, prêteraient
Pres. Subj.	prête, prêtes, prête; prêtions, prêtiez, prêtent
Imp. Subj.	prêtasse, prêtasses, prêtât; prêtassions, prêtassiez, prêtassent
Past Indef.	ai prêté, as prêté, a prêté; avons prêté, avez prêté, ont prêté
Pluperf.	avais prêté, avais prêté, avait prêté; avions prêté, aviez prêté, avaient prêté
Past Ant.	eus prêté, eus prêté, eut prêté; eûmes prêté, eûtes prêté, eurent prêté
Fut. Perf.	aurai prêté, auras prêté, aura prêté; aurons prêté, aurez prêté, auront prêté
Cond. Perf.	aurais prêté, aurais prêté, aurait prêté; aurions prêté, auriez prêté, auraient prêté
Past Subj.	aie prêté, aies prêté, ait prêté; ayons prêté, ayez prêté, aient prêté
Plup. Subj.	eusse prêté, eusses prêté, eût prêté; eussions prêté, eussiez prêté, eussent prêté
Imperative	prête, prêtons, prêtez

to forestall, ward off, warn

Pres. Ind.	préviens, préviens, prévient; prévenons, prévenez, préviennent
Imp. Ind.	prévenais, prévenais, prévenait; prévenions, préveniez, prévenaient
Past Def.	prévins, prévins, prévint; prévînmes, prévîntes, prévinrent
Future	préviendrai, préviendras, préviendra; préviendrons, préviendrez, préviendront
Condit.	préviendrais, préviendrais, préviendrait; préviendrions, préviendriez, préviendraient
Pres. Subj.	prévienne, préviennes, prévienne; prévenions, préveniez, préviennent
Imp. Subj.	prévinsse, prévinsses, prévînt; prévinssions, prévinssiez, prévinssent
Past Indef.	ai prévenu, as prévenu, a prévenu; avons prévenu, avez prévenu, ont prévenu
Pluperf.	avais prévenu, avais prévenu, avait prévenu; avions prévenu, aviez prévenu, avaient prévenu
Past Ant.	eus prévenu, eus prévenu, eut prévenu; eûmes prévenu, eûtes prévenu, eurent prévenu
Fut. Perf.	aurai prévenu, auras prévenu, aura prévenu; aurons prévenu, aurez prévenu, auront prévenu
Cond. Perf.	aurais prévenu, aurais prévenu, aurait prévenu; aurions prévenu, auriez prévenu, auraient prévenu
Past Subj.	aie prévenu, aies prévenu, ait prévenu; ayons prévenu, ayez prévenu, aient prévenu
Plup. Subj.	eusse prévenu, eusses prévenu, eût prévenu; eussions prévenu, eussiez prévenu, eussent prévenu
Imperative	préviens, prévenons, prévenez

to foresee

Pres. Ind.	prévois, prévois, prévoit; prévoyons, prévoyez, prévoient
Imp. Ind.	prévoyais, prévoyais, prévoyait; prévoyions, prévoyiez, prévoyaient
Past Def.	prévis, prévis, prévit; prévîmes, prévîtes, prévirent
Fut. Ind.	prévoirai, prévoiras, prévoira; prévoirons, prévoirez, prévoiront
Condit.	prévoirais, prévoirais, prévoirait; prévoirions, prévoiriez, prévoiraient
Pres. Subj.	prévoie, prévoies, prévoie; prévoyions, prévoyiez, prévoient
Imp. Subj.	prévisse, prévisses, prévît; prévissions, prévissiez, prévissent
Past Indef.	ai prévu, as prévu, a prévu; avons prévu, avez prévu, ont prévu
Pluperf.	avais prévu, avais prévu, avait prévu; avions prévu, aviez prévu, avaient prévu
Past Ant.	eus prévu, eus prévu, eut prévu; eûmes prévu, eûtes prévu, eurent prévu
Fut. Perf.	aurai prévu, auras prévu, aura prévu; aurons prévu, aurez prévu, auront prévu
Cond. Perf.	aurais prévu, aurais prévu, aurait prévu; aurions prévu, auriez prévu, auraient prévu
Past Subj.	aie prévu, aies prévu, ait prévu; ayons prévu, ayez prévu, aient prévu
Plup. Subj.	eusse prévu, eusses prévu, eût prévu; eussions prévu, eussiez prévu, eussent prévu
Imperative	prévois, prévoyons, prévoyez

to pray, beg, supplicate

Pres. Ind.	prie, pries, prie; prions, priez, prient
Imp. Ind.	priais, priais, priait; priions, priiez, priaient
Past Def.	priai, prias, pria; priâmes, priâtes, prièrent
Future	prierai, prieras, priera; prierons, prierez, prieront
Condit.	prierais, prierais, prierait; prierions, prieriez, prieraient
Pres. Subj.	prie, pries, prie; priions, priiez, prient
Imp. Subj.	priasse, priasses, priât; priassions, priassiez, priassent
Past Indef.	ai prié, as prié, a prié; avons prié, avez prié, ont prié
Pluperf.	avais prié, avais prié, avait prié; avions prié, aviez prié, avaient prié
Pust Ant.	eus prié, eus prié, eut prié; eûmes prié, eûtes prié, eurent prié
Fut. Perf.	aurai prié, auras prié, aura prié; aurons prié, aurez prié, auront prié
Cond. Perf.	aurais prié, aurais prié, aurait prié; aurions prié, auriez prié, auraient prié
Past Subj.	aie prié, aies prié, ait prié; ayons prié, ayez prié, aient prié
Plup. Subj.	eusse prié, eusses prié, eût prié; eussions prié, eussiez prié, eussent prié
Imperative	prie, prions, priez

to produce

Pres. Ind.	produis, produis, produit; produisons, produisez, produisent
Imp. Ind.	produisais, produisais, produisait; produisions, produisiez, produisaient
Past Def.	produisis, produisis, produisit; produisîmes, produisîtes, produisirent
Future	produirai, produiras, produira; produirons, produirez, produiront
Condit.	produirais, produirais, produirait; produirions, produiriez, produiraient
Pres. Subj.	produise, produises, produise; produisions, produisiez, produisent
Imp. Subj.	produisisse, produisisses, produisît; produisissions, produisissiez, produisissent
Past Indef.	ai produit, as produit, a produit; avons produit, avez produit, ont produit
Pluperf.	avais produit, avais produit, avait produit; avions produit, aviez produit, avaient produit
Past Ant.	eus produit, eus produit, eut produit; eûmes produit, eûtes produit, eurent produit
Fut. Perf.	aurai produit, auras produit, aura produit; aurons produit, aurez produit, auront produit
Cond. Perf.	aurais produit, aurais produit, aurait produit; aurions produit, auriez produit, auraient produit
Past Subj.	aie produit, aies produit, ait produit; ayons produit, ayez produit, aient produit
Plup. Subj.	eusse produit, eusses produit, eût produit; eussions produit, eussiez produit, eussent produit
Imperative	produis, produisons, produisez

to take a walk

Pres. Ind.	me promène, te promènes, se promène; nous promenons, vous promenez, se promènent
Imp. Ind.	me promenais, te promenais, se promenait; nous promenions, vous promeniez, se promenaient
Past Def.	me promenai, te promenas, se promena; nous promenâmes, vous promenâtes, se promenèrent
Fut. Ind.	me promènerai, te promèneras, se promènera; nous promènerons, vous promènerez, se promèneront
Condit.	me promènerais, te promènerais, se promènerait; nous promènerions, vous promèneriez, se promèneraient
Pres. Subj.	me promène, te promènes, se promène; nous promenions, vous promeniez, se promènent
Imp. Subj.	me promenasse, te promenasses, se promenât; nous promenassions, vous promenassiez, se promenassent
Past Indef.	me suis promené(e), t'es promené(e), s'est promené(e); nous sommes promené(e)s, vous êtes promené(e)(s), se sont promené(e)s
Pluperf.	m'étais promené(e), t'étais promené(e), s'était promené(e); nous étions promené(e)s, vous étiez promené(e)(s), s'étaient promené(e)s
Past Ant.	me fus promené(e), te fus promené(e), se fut promené(e); nous fûmes promené(e)s, vous fûtes promené(e)(s), se furent promené(e)s
Fut. Perf.	me serai promené(e), te seras promené(e), se sera promené(e); nous serons promené(e)s, vous serez promené(e)(s), se seront promené(e)s
Cond. Perf.	me serais promené(e), te serais promené(e), se serait promené(e); nous serions promené(e)s, vous seriez promené(e)(s), se seraient promené(e)s
Past Subj.	me sois promené(e), te sois promené(e), se soit promené(e); nous soyons promené(e)s, vous soyez promené(e)(s), se soient promené(e)s
Plup. Subj.	me fusse promené(e), te fusses promené(e), se fût promené(e); nous fussions promené(e)s, vous fussiez promené(e)(s), se fussent promené(e)s
Imperative	promène-toi, promenons-nous, promenez-vous

to promise

Pres. Ind.	promets, promets, promet; promettons, promettez, promettent
Imp. Ind.	promettais, promettais, promettait; promettions, promettiez, promettaient
Past Def.	promis, promis, promit; promîmes, promîtes, promirent
Fut. Ind.	promettrai, promettras, promettra; promettrons, promettrez, promettront
Condit.	promettrais, promettrais, promettrait; promettrions, promettriez, promettraient
Pres. Subj.	promette, promettes, promette; promettions, promettiez, promettent
Imp. Subj.	promisse, promisses, promît; promissions, promissiez, promissent
Past Indef.	ai promis, as promis, a promis; avons promis, avez promis, ont promis
Pluperf.	avais promis, avais promis, avait promis; avions promis, aviez promis, avaient promis
Past Ant.	eus promis, eus promis, eut promis; eûmes promis, eûtes promis, eurent promis
Fut. Perf.	aurai promis, auras promis, aura promis; aurons promis, aurez promis, auront promis
Cond. Perf.	aurais promis, aurais promis, aurait promis; aurions promis, auriez promis, auraient promis
Past Subj.	aie promis, aies promis, ait promis; ayons promis, ayez promis, aient promis
Plup. Subj.	eusse promis, eusses promis, eût promis; eussions promis, eussiez promis, eussent promis
Imperative	promets, promettons, promettez

to pronounce

Pres. Ind.	prononce, prononces, prononce; prononçons, prononcez, prononcent
Imp. Ind.	prononçais, prononçais, prononçait; prononcions, prononciez, prononçaient
Past Def.	prononçai, prononças, prononça; prononçâmes, prononçâtes, prononcèrent
Fut. Ind.	prononcerai, prononceras, prononcera; prononcerons, prononcerez, prononceront
Condit.	prononcerais, prononcerais, prononcerait; prononcerions, prononceriez, prononceraient
Pres. Subj.	prononce, prononces, prononce; prononcions, prononciez, prononcent
Imp. Subj.	prononçasse, prononçasses, prononçât; prononçassions, prononçassiez, prononçassent
Past Indef.	ai prononcé, as prononcé, a prononcé; avons prononcé, avez prononcé, ont prononcé
Pluperf.	avais prononcé, avais prononcé, avait prononcé; avions prononcé, aviez prononcé, avaient prononcé
Past Ant.	eus prononcé, eus prononcé, eut prononcé; eûmes prononcé, eûtes prononcé, eurent prononcé
Fut. Perf.	aurai prononcé, auras prononcé, aura prononcé; aurons prononcé, aurez prononcé, auront prononcé
Cond. Perf.	aurais prononcé, aurais prononcé, aurait prononcé; aurions prononcé, auriez prononcé, auraient prononcé
Past Subj.	aie prononcé, aies prononcé, ait prononcé; ayons prononcé, ayez prononcé, aient prononcé
Plup. Subj.	eusse prononcé, eusses prononcé, eût prononcé; eussions prononcé, eussiez prononcé, eussent prononcé
Imperative	prononce, prononçons, prononcez

to prove

Pres. Ind.	prouve, prouves, prouve; prouvons, prouvez, prouvent
Imp. Ind.	prouvais, prouvais, prouvait; prouvions, prouviez, prouvaient
Past Def.	prouvai, prouvas, prouva; prouvâmes, prouvâtes, prouvèrent
Future	prouverai, prouveras, prouvera; prouverons, prouverez, prouveront
Condit.	prouverais, prouverais, prouverait; prouverions, prouveriez, prouveraient
Pres. Subj.	prouve, prouves, prouve; prouvions, prouviez, prouvent
Imp. Subj.	prouvasse, prouvasses, prouvât; prouvassions, prouvassiez, prouvassent
Past Indef.	ai prouvé, as prouvé, a prouvé; avons prouvé, avez prouvé, ont prouvé
Plup. Ind.	avais prouvé, avais prouvé, avait prouvé; avions prouvé, aviez prouvé, avaient prouvé
Past Ant.	eus prouvé, eus prouvé, eut prouvé; eûmes prouvé, eûtes prouvé, eurent prouvé
Fut. Perf.	aurai prouvé, auras prouvé, aura prouvé; aurons prouvé, aurez prouvé, auront prouvé
Cond. Perf.	aurais prouvé, aurais prouvé, aurait prouvé; aurions prouvé, auriez prouvé, auraient prouvé
Past Subj.	aie prouvé, aies prouvé, ait prouvé; ayons prouvé, ayez prouvé, aient prouvé
Plup. Subj.	eusse prouvé, eusses prouvé, eût prouvé; eussions prouvé, eussiez prouvé, eussent prouvé
Imperative	prouve, prouvons, prouvez

to stink

Pres. Ind.	pue, pues, pue; puons, puez, puent
Imp. Ind.	puais, puais, puait; puions, puiez, puaient
Future	puerai, pueras, puera; puerons, puerez, pueront
Condit.	puerais, puerais, puerait; puerions, pueriez, pueraient

* This verb is used mainly in the above tenses.

to punish

Pres. Ind.	punis, punis, punit; punissons, punissez, punissent
Imp. Ind.	punissais, punissais, punissait; punissions, punissiez, punissaient
Past Def.	punis, punis, punit; punîmes, punîtes, punirent
Fut. Ind.	punirai, puniras, punira; punirons, punirez, puniront
Condit.	punirais, punirais, punirait; punirions, puniriez, puniraient
Pres. Subj.	punisse, punisses, punisse; punissions, punissiez, punissent
Imp. Subj.	punisse, punisses, punît; punissions, punissiez, punissent
Past Indef.	ai puni, as puni, a puni; avons puni, avez puni, ont puni
Pluperf.	avais puni, avais puni, avait puni; avions puni, aviez puni, avaient puni
Past Ant.	eus puni, eus puni, eut puni; eûmes puni, eûtes puni, eurent puni
Fut. Perf.	aurai puni, auras puni, aura puni; aurons puni, aurez puni, auront puni
Cond. Perf.	aurais puni, aurais puni, aurait puni; aurions puni, auriez puni, auraient puni
Past Subj.	aie puni, aies puni, ait puni; ayons puni, ayez puni, aient puni
Plup. Subj.	eusse puni, eusses puni, eût puni; eussions puni, eussiez puni, eussent puni
Imperative	punis, punissons, punissez

to leave

Pres. Ind.	quitte, quittes, quitte; quittons, quittez, quittent
Imp. Ind.	quittais, quittais, quittait; quittions, quittiez, quittaient
Past Def.	quittai, quittas, quitta; quittâmes, quittâtes, quittèrent
Fut. Ind.	quitterai, quitteras, quittera; quitterons, quitterez, quitteront
Condit.	quitterais, quitterais, quitterait; quitterions, quitteriez, quitteraient
Pres. Subj.	quitte, quittes, quitte; quittions, quittiez, quittent
Imp. Subj.	quittasse, quittasses, quittât; quittassions, quittassiez, quittassent
Past Indef.	ai quitté, as quitté, a quitté; avons quitté, avez quitté, ont quitté
Pluperf.	avais quitté, avais quitté, avait quitté; avions quitté, aviez quitté, avaient quitté
Past Ant.	eus quitté, eus quitté, eut quitté; eûmes quitté, eûtes quitté, eurent quitté
Fut. Perf.	aurai quitté, auras quitté, aura quitté; aurons quitté, aurez quitté, auront quitté
Cond. Perf.	aurais quitté, aurais quitté, aurait quitté; aurions quitté, auriez quitté, auraient quitté
Past Subj.	aie quitté, aies quitté, ait quitté; ayons quitté, ayez quitté, aient quitté
Plup. Subj.	eusse quitté, eusses quitté, eût quitté; eussions quitté, eussiez quitté, eussent quitté
Imperative	quitte, quittons, quittez

to relate, tell about

Pres. Ind.	raconte, racontes, raconte; racontons, racontez, racontent
Imp. Ind.	racontais, racontais, racontait; racontions, racontiez, racontaient
Past Def.	racontai, racontas, raconta; racontâmes, racontâtes, racontèrent
Fut. Ind.	raconterai, raconteras, racontera; raconterons, raconterez, raconteront
Condit.	raconterais, raconterais, raconterait; raconterions, raconteriez, raconteraient
Pres. Subj.	raconte, racontes, raconte; racontions, racontiez, racontent
Imp. Subj.	racontasse, racontasses, racontât; racontassions, racontassiez, racontassent
Past Indef.	ai raconté, as raconté, a raconté; avons raconté, avez raconté, ont raconté
Pluperf.	avais raconté, avais raconté, avait raconté; avions raconté, aviez raconté, avaient raconté
Past Ant.	eus raconté, eus raconté, eut raconté; eûmes raconté, eûtes raconté, eurent raconté
Fut. Perf.	aurai raconté, auras raconté, aura raconté; aurons raconté, aurez raconté, auront raconté
Cond. Perf.	aurais raconté, aurais raconté, aurait raconté; aurions raconté, auriez raconté, auraient raconté
Past Subj.	aie raconté, aies raconté, ait raconté; ayons raconté, ayez raconté, aient raconté
Plup. Subj.	eusse raconté, eusses raconté, eût raconté; eussions raconté, eussiez raconté, eussent raconté
Imperative	raconte, racontons, racontez

to call again, call back, recall, remind

Pres. Ind.	rappelle, rappelles, rappelle; rappelons, rappelez, rappellent
Imp. Ind.	rappelais, rappelais, rappelait; rappelions, rappeliez, rappelaient
Past Def.	rappelai, rappelas, rappela; rappelâmes, rappelâtes, rappelèrent
Future	rappellerai, rappelleras, rappellera; rappellerons, rappellerez, rappelleront
Condit.	rappellerais, rappellerais, rappellerait; rappellerions, rappelleriez, rappelleraient
Pres. Subj.	rappelle, rappelles, rappelle; rappelions, rappeliez, rappellent
Imp. Subj.	rappelasse, rappelasses, rappelât; rappelassions, rappelassiez, rappelassent
Past Indef.	ai rappelé, as rappelé, a rappelé; avons rappelé, avez rappelé, ont rappelé
Pluperf.	avais rappelé, avais rappelé, avait rappelé; avions rappelé, aviez rappelé, avaient rappelé
Past Ant.	eus rappelé, eus rappelé, eut rappelé; eûmes rappelé, eûtes rappelé, eurent rappelé
Fut. Perf.	aurai rappelé, auras rappelé, aura rappelé; aurons rappelé, aurez rappelé, auront rappelé
Cond. Perf.	aurais rappelé, aurais rappelé, aurait rappelé; aurions rappelé, auriez rappelé, auraient rappelé
Past Subj.	aie rappelé, aies rappelé, ait rappelé; ayons rappelé, ayez rappelé, aient rappelé
Plup. Subj.	eusse rappelé, eusses rappelé, eût rappelé; eussions rappelé, eussiez rappelé, eussent rappelé
Imperative	rappelle, rappelons, rappelez

to remember, recall, recollect

Pres. Ind.	me rappelle, te rappelles, se rappelle; nous rappelons, vous rappelez, se rappellent
Imp. Ind.	me rappelais, te rappelais, se rappelait; nous rappelions, vous rappeliez, se rappelaient
Past Def.	me rappelai, te rappelas, se rappela; nous rappelâmes, vous rappelâtes, se rappelèrent
Future	me rappellerai, te rappelleras, se rappellera; nous rappellerons, vous rappellerez, se rappelleront
Condit.	me rappellerais, te rappellerais, se rappellerait; nous rappellerions, vous rappelleriez, se rappelleraient
Pres. Subj.	me rappelle, te rappelles, se rappelle; nous rappelions, vous rappeliez, se rappellent
Imp. Subj.	me rappelasse, te rappelasses, se rappelât; nous rappelassions, vous rappelassiez, se rappelassent
Past Indef.	me suis rappelé(e), t'es rappelé(e), s'est rappelé(e); nous sommes rappelé(e)s, vous êtes rappelé(e)(s), se sont rappelé(e)s
Pluperf.	m'étais rappelé(e), t'étais rappelé(e), s'était rappelé(e); nous étions rappelé(e)s, vous étiez rappelé(e)(s), s'étaient rappelé(e)s
Past Ant.	me fus rappelé(e), te fus rappelé(e), se fut rappelé(e); nous fûmes rappelé(e)s, vous fûtes rappelé(e)(s), se furent rappelé(e)s
Fut. Perf.	me serai rappelé(e), te seras rappelé(e), se sera rappelé(e); nous serons rappelé(e)s, vous serez rappelé(e)(s), se seront rappelé(e)s
Cond. Perf.	me serais rappelé(e), te serais rappelé(e), se serait rappelé(e); nous serions rappelé(e)s, vous seriez rappelé(e)(s), se seraient rappelé(e)s
Past Subj.	me sois rappelé(e), te sois rappelé(e), se soit rappelé(e); nous soyons rappelé(e)s, vous soyez rappelé(e)(s), se soient rappelé(e)s
Plup. Subj.	me fusse rappelé(e), te fusses rappelé(e), se fût rappelé(e); nous fussions rappelé(e)s, vous fussiez rappelé(e)(s), se fussent rappelé(e)s
Imperative	rappelle-toi, rappelons-nous, rappelez-vous

to receive, get

Pres. Ind.	reçois, reçois, reçoit; recevons, recevez, reçoivent
Imp. Ind.	recevais, recevais, recevait; recevions, receviez, recevaient
Past Def.	reçus, reçus, reçut; reçûmes, reçûtes, reçurent
Fut. Ind.	recevrai, recevras, recevra; recevrons, recevrez, recevront
Condit.	recevrais, recevrais, recevrait; recevrions, recevriez, recevraient
Pres. Subj.	reçoive, reçoives, reçoive; recevions, receviez, reçoivent
Imp. Subj.	reçusse, reçusses, reçût; reçussions, reçussiez, reçussent
Past Indef.	ai reçu, as reçu, a reçu; avons reçu, avez reçu, ont reçu
Pluperf.	avais reçu, avais reçu, avait reçu; avions reçu, aviez reçu, avaient reçu
Past Ant.	eus reçu, eus reçu, eut reçu; eûmes reçu, eûtes reçu, eurent reçu
Fut. Perf.	aurai reçu, auras reçu, aura reçu; aurons reçu, aurez reçu, auront reçu
Cond. Perf.	aurais reçu, aurais reçu, aurait reçu; aurions reçu, auriez reçu, auraient reçu
Past Subj.	aie reçu, aies reçu, ait reçu; ayons reçu, ayez reçu, aient reçu
Plup. Subj.	eusse reçu, eusses reçu, eût reçu; eussions reçu, eussiez reçu, eussent reçu
Imperative	reçois, recevons, recevez

to recognize, acknowledge

Pres. Ind.	reconnais, reconnais, reconnaît; reconnaissons, reconnaissez, reconnaissent
Imp. Ind.	reconnaissais, reconnaissais, reconnaissait; reconnaissions, reconnaissiez, reconnaissaient
Past Def.	reconnus, reconnus, reconnut; reconnûmes, reconnûtes, reconnurent
Future	reconnaîtrai, reconnaîtras, reconnaîtra; reconnaîtrons, reconnaîtrez, reconnaîtront
Condit.	reconnaîtrais, reconnaîtrais, reconnaîtrait; reconnaîtrions, reconnaîtriez, reconnaîtraient
Pres. Subj.	reconnaisse, reconnaisses, reconnaisse; reconnaissions, reconnaissiez, reconnaissent
Imp. Subj.	reconnusse, reconnusses, reconnût; reconnussions, reconnussiez, reconnussent
Past Indef.	ai reconnu, as reconnu, a reconnu; avons reconnu, avez reconnu, ont reconnu
Pluperf.	avais reconnu, avais reconnu, avait reconnu; avions reconnu, aviez reconnu, avaient reconnu
Past Ant.	eus reconnu, eus reconnu, eut reconnu; eûmes reconnu, eûtes reconnu, eurent reconnu
Fut. Perf.	aurai reconnu, auras reconnu, aura reconnu; aurons reconnu, aurez reconnu, auront reconnu
Cond. Perf.	aurais reconnu, aurais reconnu, aurait reconnu; aurions reconnu, auriez reconnu, auraient reconnu
Past Subj.	aie reconnu, aies reconnu, ait reconnu; ayons reconnu, ayez reconnu, aient reconnu
Plup. Subj.	eusse reconnu, eusses reconnu, eût reconnu; eussions reconnu, eussiez reconnu, eussent reconnu
Imperative	reconnais, reconnaissons, reconnaissez

to collect, gather, harvest

Pres. Ind.	recueille, recueilles, recueille; recueillons, recueillez, recueillent
Imp. Ind.	recueillais, recueillais, recueillait; recueillions, recueilliez, recueillaient
Past Def.	recueillis, recueillis, recueillit; recueillîmes, recueillîtes, recueillirent
Future	recueillerai, recueilleras, recueillera; recueillerons, recueillerez, recueilleront
Condit.	recueillerais, recueillerais, recueillerait; recueillerions, recueilleriez, recueilleraient
Pres. Subj.	recueille, recueilles, recueille; recueillions, recueilliez, recueillent
Imp. Subj.	recueillisse, recueillisses, recueillît; recueillissions, recueillissiez, recueillissent
Past Indef.	ai recueilli, as recueilli, a recueilli; avons recueilli, avez recueilli, ont recueilli
Pluperf.	avais recueilli, avais recueilli, avait recueilli; avions recueilli, aviez recueilli, avaient recueilli
Past Ant.	eus recueilli, eus recueilli, eut recueilli; eûmes recueilli, eûtes recueilli, eurent recueilli
Fut. Perf.	aurai recueilli, auras recueilli, aura recueilli; aurons recueilli, aurez recueilli, auront recueilli
Cond. Perf.	aurais recueilli, aurais recueilli, aurait recueilli; aurions recueilli, auriez recueilli, auraient recueilli
Past Subj.	aie recueilli, aies recueilli, ait recueilli; ayons recueilli, ayez recueilli, aient recueilli
Plup. Subj.	eusse recueilli, eusses recueilli, eût recueilli; eussions recueilli, eussiez recueilli, eussent recueilli
Imperative	recueille, recueillons, recueillez

to reduce, decrease, diminish

Pres. Ind.	réduis, réduis, réduit; réduisons, réduisez, réduisent
Imp. Ind.	réduisais, réduisais, réduisait; réduisions, réduisiez, réduisaient
Past Def.	réduisis, réduisis, réduisit; réduisîmes, réduisîtes, réduisirent
Future	réduirai, réduiras, réduira; réduirons, réduirez, réduiront
Condit.	réduirais, réduirais, réduirait; réduirions, réduiriez, réduiraient
Pres. Subj.	réduise, réduises, réduise; réduisions, réduisiez, réduisent
Imp. Subj.	réduisisse, réduisisses, réduisît; réduisissions, réduisissiez, réduisissent
Past Indef.	ai réduit, as réduit, a réduit; avons réduit, avez réduit, ont réduit
Plup. Ind.	avais réduit, avais réduit, avait réduit; avions réduit, aviez réduit, avaient réduit
Past Ant.	eus réduit, eus réduit, eut réduit; eûmes réduit, eûtes réduit, eurent réduit
Fut. Perf.	aurai réduit, auras réduit, aura réduit; aurons réduit, aurez réduit, auront réduit
Cond. Perf.	aurais réduit, aurais réduit, aurait réduit; aurions réduit, auriez réduit, auraient réduit
Past Subj.	aie réduit, aies réduit, ait réduit; ayons réduit, ayez réduit, aient réduit
Plup. Subj.	eusse réduit, eusses réduit, eût réduit; eussions réduit, eussiez réduit, eussent réduit
Imperative	réduis, réduisons, réduisez

to think, meditate, reflect

Pres. Ind.	réfléchis, réfléchis, réfléchit; réfléchissons, réfléchissez, réfléchissent
Imp. Ind.	réfléchissais, réfléchissais, réfléchissait; réfléchissions, réfléchissiez, réfléchissaient
Past Def.	réfléchis, réfléchis, réfléchit; réfléchîmes, réfléchîtes, réfléchirent
Future	réfléchirai, réfléchiras, réfléchira; réfléchirons, réfléchirez, réfléchiront
Condit.	réfléchirais, réfléchirais, réfléchirait; réfléchirions, réfléchiriez, réfléchiraient
Pres. Subj.	réfléchisse, réfléchisses, réfléchisse; réfléchissions, réfléchissiez, réfléchissent
Imp. Subj.	réfléchisse, réfléchisses, réfléchît; réfléchissions, réfléchissiez, réfléchissent
Past Indef.	ai réfléchi, as réfléchi, a réfléchi; avons réfléchi, avez réfléchi, ont réfléchi
Plup. Ind.	avais réfléchi, avais réfléchi, avait réfléchi; avions réfléchi, aviez réfléchi, avaient réfléchi
Past Ant.	eus réfléchi, eus réfléchi, eut réfléchi; eûmes réfléchi, eûtes réfléchi, eurent réfléchi
Fut. Perf.	aurai réfléchi, auras réfléchi, aura réfléchi; aurons réfléchi, aurez réfléchi, auront réfléchi
Cond. Perf.	aurais réfléchi, aurais réfléchi, aurait réfléchi; aurions réfléchi, auriez réfléchi, auraient réfléchi
Past Subj.	aie réfléchi, aies réfléchi, ait réfléchi; ayons réfléchi, ayez réfléchi, aient réfléchi
Plup. Subj.	eusse réfléchi, eusses réfléchi, eût réfléchi; eussions réfléchi, eussiez réfléchi, eussent réfléchi
Imperative	réfléchis, réfléchissons, réfléchissez

to refuse

Pres. Ind.	refuse, refuses, refuse; refusons, refusez, refusent
Imp. Ind.	refusais, refusais, refusait; refusions, refusiez, refusaient
Past Def.	refusai, refusas, refusa; refusâmes, refusâtes, refusèrent
Future	refuserai, refuseras, refusera; refuserons, refuserez, refuseront
Condit.	refuserais, refuserais, refuserait; refuserions, refuseriez, refuseraient
Pres. Subj.	refuse, refuses, refuse; refusions, refusiez, refusent
Imp. Subj.	refusasse, refusasses, refusât; refusassions, refusassiez, refusassent
Past Indef.	ai refusé, as refusé, a refusé; avons refusé, avez refusé, ont refusé
Plup. Ind.	avais refusé, avais refusé, avait refusé; avions refusé, aviez refusé, avaient refusé
Past Ant.	eus refusé, eus refusé, eut refusé; eûmes refusé, eûtes refusé, eurent refusé
Fut. Perf.	aurai refusé, auras refusé, aura refusé; aurons refusé, aurez refusé, auront refusé
Cond. Perf.	aurais refusé, aurais refusé, aurait refusé; aurions refusé, auriez refusé, auraient refusé
Past Subj.	aie refusé, aies refusé, ait refusé; ayons refusé, ayez refusé, aient refusé
Plup. Subj.	eusse refusé, eusses refusé, eût refusé; eussions refusé, eussiez refusé, eussent refusé
Imperative	refuse, refusons, refusez

to look (at), watch

Pres. Ind.	regarde, regardes, regarde; regardons, regardez, regardent
Imp. Ind.	regardais, regardais, regardait; regardions, regardiez, regardaient
Past Def.	regardai, regardas, regarda; regardâmes, regardâtes, regardèrent
Fut. Ind.	regarderai, regarderas, regardera; regarderons, regarderez, regarderont
Condit.	regarderais, regarderais, regarderait; regarderions, regarderiez, regarderaient
Pres. Subj.	regarde, regardes, regarde; regardions, regardiez, regardent
Imp. Subj.	regardasse, regardasses, regardât; regardassions, regardassiez, regardassent
Past Indef.	ai regardé, as regardé, a regardé; avons regardé, avez regardé, ont regardé
Pluperf.	avais regardé, avais regardé, avait regardé; avions regardé, aviez regardé, avaient regardé
Past Ant.	eus regardé, eus regardé, eut regardé; eûmes regardé, eûtes regardé, eurent regardé
Fut. Perf.	aurai regardé, auras regardé, aura regardé; aurons regardé, aurez regardé, auront regardé
Cond. Perf.	aurais regardé, aurais regardé, aurait regardé; aurions regardé, auriez regardé, auraient regardé
Past Subj.	aie regardé, aies regardé, ait regardé; ayons regardé, ayez regardé, aient regardé
Plup. Subj.	eusse regardé, eusses regardé, eût regardé; eussions regardé, eussiez regardé, eussent regardé
Imperative	regarde, regardons, regardez

to freeze again

Pres. Ind.	il regèle
Imp. Ind.	il regelait
Past Def.	il regela
Future	il regèlera
Condit.	il regèlerait
Pres. Subj.	qu'il regèle
Imp. Subj.	qu'il regelât
Past Indef.	il a regelé
Plup. Ind.	il avait regelé
Past Ant.	il eut regelé
Fut. Perf.	il aura regelé
Cond. Perf.	il aurait regelé
Past Subj.	qu'il ait regelé
Plup. Subj.	qu'il eût regelé
Imperative	[inemployé]

to read again

Pres. Ind.	relis, relis, relit; relisons, relisez, relisent
Imp. Ind.	relisais, relisais, relisait; relisions, relisiez, relisaient
Past Def.	relus, relus, relut; relûmes, relûtes, relurent
Future	relirai, reliras, relira; relirons, relirez, reliront
Condit.	relirais, relirais, relirait; relirions, reliriez, reliraient
Pres. Subj.	relise, relises, relise; relisions, relisiez, relisent
Imp. Subj.	relusse, relusses, relût; relussions, relussiez, relussent
Past Indef.	ai relu, as relu, a relu; avons relu, avez relu, ont relu
Plup. Ind.	avais relu, avais relu, avait relu; avions relu, aviez relu, avaient relu
Past Ant.	eus relu, eus relu, eut relu; eûmes relu, eûtes relu, eurent relu
Fut. Perf.	aurai relu, auras relu, aura relu; aurons relu, aurez relu, auront relu
Cond. Perf.	aurais relu, aurais relu, aurait relu; aurions relu, auriez relu, auraient relu
Past Subj.	aie relu, aies relu, ait relu; ayons relu, ayez relu, aient relu
Plup. Subj.	eusse relu, eusses relu, eût relu; eussions relu, eussiez relu, eussent relu
Imperative	relis, relisons, relisez

to notice, observe

Pres. Ind.	remarque, remarques, remarque; remarquons, remarquez, remarquent
Imp. Ind.	remarquais, remarquais, remarquait; remarquions, remarquiez, remarquaient
Past Def.	remarquai, remarquas, remarqua; remarquâmes, remarquâtes, remarquèrent
Fut. Ind.	remarquerai, remarqueras, remarquera; remarquerons, remarquerez, remarqueront
Condit.	remarquerais, remarquerais, remarquerait; remarquerions, remarqueriez, remarqueraient
Pres. Subj.	remarque, remarques, remarque; remarquions, remarquiez, remarquent
Imp. Subj.	remarquasse, remarquasses, remarquât; remarquassions, remarquassiez, remarquassent
Past Indef.	ai remarqué, as remarqué, a remarqué; avons remarqué, avez remarqué, ont remarqué
Pluperf.	avais remarqué, avais remarqué, avait remarqué; avions remarqué, aviez remarqué, avaient remarqué
Past Ant.	eus remarqué, eus remarqué, eut remarqué; eûmes remarqué, eûtes remarqué, eurent remarqué
Fut. Perf.	aurai remarqué, auras remarqué, aura remarqué; aurons remarqué, aurez remarqué, auront remarqué
Cond. Perf.	aurais remarqué, aurais remarqué, aurait remarqué; aurions remarqué, auriez remarqué, auraient remarqué
Past Subj.	aie remarqué, aies remarqué, ait remarqué; ayons remarqué, ayez remarqué, aient remarqué
Plup. Subj.	eusse remarqué, eusses remarqué, eût remarqué; eussions remarqué, eussiez remarqué, eussent remarqué
Imperative	remarque, remarquons, remarquez

to put (on) again, replace, put back, give back

Pres. Ind.	remets, remets, remet; remettons, remettez, remettent
Imp. Ind.	remettais, remettais, remettait; remettions, remettiez, remettaient
Past Def.	remis, remis, remit; remîmes, remîtes, remirent
Future	remettrai, remettras, remettra; remettrons, remettrez, remettront
Condit.	remettrais, remettrais, remettrait; remettrions, remettriez, remettraient
Pres. Subj.	remette, remettes, remette; remettions, remettiez, remettent
Imp. Subj.	remisse, remisses, remît; remissions, remissiez, remissent
Past Indef.	ai remis, as remis, a remis; avons remis, avez remis, ont remis
Pluperf.	avais remis, avais remis, avait remis; avions remis, aviez remis, avaient remis
Past Ant.	eus remis, eus remis, eut remis; eûmes remis, eûtes remis, eurent remis
Fut. Perf.	aurai remis, auras remis, aura remis; aurons remis, aurez remis, auront remis
Cond. Perf.	aurais remis, aurais remis, aurait remis; aurions remis, auriez remis, auraient remis
Past Subj.	aie remis, aies remis, ait remis; ayons remis, ayez remis, aient remis
Plup. Subj.	eusse remis, eusses remis, eût remis; eussions remis, eussiez remis, eussent remis
Imperative	remets, remettons, remettez

to replace

Pres. Ind.	remplace, remplaces, remplace; remplaçons, remplacez, remplacent
Imp. Ind.	remplaçais, remplaçais, remplaçait; remplacions, remplaciez, remplaçaient
Past Def.	remplaçai, remplaças, remplaça; remplaçâmes, remplaçâtes, remplacèrent
Fut. Ind.	remplacerai, remplaceras, remplacera; remplacerons, remplacerez, remplaceront
Condit.	remplacerais, remplacerais, remplacerait; remplacerions, remplaceriez, remplaceraient
Pres. Subj.	remplace, remplaces, remplace; remplacions, remplaciez, remplacent
Imp. Subj.	remplaçasse, remplaçasses, remplaçât; remplaçassions, remplaçassiez, remplaçassent
Past Indef.	ai remplacé, as remplacé, a remplacé; avons remplacé, avez remplacé, ont remplacé
Pluperf.	avais remplacé, avais remplacé, avait remplacé; avions remplacé, aviez remplacé, avaient remplacé
Past Ant.	eus remplacé, eus remplacé, eut remplacé; eûmes remplacé, eûtes remplacé, eurent remplacé
Fut. Perf.	aurai remplacé, auras remplacé, aura remplacé; aurons remplacé, aurez remplacé, auront remplacé
Cond. Perf.	aurais remplacé, aurais remplacé, aurait remplacé; aurions remplacé, auriez remplacé, auraient remplacé
Past Subj.	aie remplacé, aies remplacé, ait remplacé; ayons remplacé, ayez remplacé, aient remplacé
Plup. Subj.	eusse remplacé, eusses remplacé, eût remplacé; eussions remplacé, eussiez remplacé, eussent remplacé
Imperative	remplace, remplaçons, remplacez

to fill

Pres. Ind.	remplis, remplis, remplit; remplissons, remplissez, remplissent
Imp. Ind.	remplissais, remplissais, remplissait; remplissions, remplissiez, remplissaient
Past Def.	remplis, remplis, remplit; remplîmes, remplîtes, remplirent
Fut. Ind.	remplirai, rempliras, remplira; remplirons, remplirez, rempliront
Condit.	remplirais, remplirais, remplirait; remplirions, rempliriez, rempliraient
Pres. Subj.	remplisse, remplisses, remplisse; remplissions, remplissiez, remplissent
Imp. Subj.	remplisse, remplisses, remplît; remplissions, remplissiez, remplissent
Past Indef.	ai rempli, as rempli, a rempli; avons rempli, avez rempli, ont rempli
Pluperf.	avais rempli, avais rempli, avait rempli; avions rempli, aviez rempli, avaient rempli
Past Ant.	eus rempli, eus rempli, eut rempli; eûmes rempli, eûtes rempli, eurent rempli
Fut. Perf.	aurai rempli, auras rempli, aura rempli; aurons rempli, aurez rempli, auront rempli
Cond. Perf.	aurais rempli, aurais rempli, aurait rempli; aurions rempli, auriez rempli, auraient rempli
Past Subj.	aie rempli, aies rempli, ait rempli; ayons rempli, ayez rempli, aient rempli
Plup. Subj.	eusse rempli, eusses rempli, eût rempli; eussions rempli, eussiez rempli, eussent rempli
Imperative	remplis, remplissons, remplissez

to meet

Pres. Ind.	rencontre, rencontres, rencontre; rencontrons, rencontrez, rencontrent
Imp. Ind.	rencontrais, rencontrais, rencontrait; rencontrions, rencontriez, rencontraient
Past Def.	rencontrai, rencontras, rencontra; rencontrâmes, rencontrâtes, rencontrèrent
Future	rencontrerai, rencontreras, rencontrera; rencontrerons, rencontrerez, rencontreront
Condit.	rencontrerais, rencontrerais, rencontrerait; rencontrerions, rencontreriez, rencontreraient
Pres. Subj.	rencontre, rencontres, rencontre; rencontrions, rencontriez, rencontrent
Imp. Subj.	rencontrasse, rencontrasses, rencontrât; rencontrassions, rencontrassiez, rencontrassent
Past Indef.	ai rencontré, as rencontré, a rencontré; avons rencontré, avez rencontré, ont rencontré
Plup. Ind.	avais rencontré, avais rencontré, avait rencontré; avions rencontré, aviez rencontré, avaient rencontré
Past Ant.	eus rencontré, eus rencontré, eut rencontré; eûmes rencontré, eûtes rencontré, eurent rencontré
Fut. Perf.	aurai rencontré, auras rencontré, aura rencontré; aurons rencontré, aurez rencontré, auront rencontré
Cond. Perf.	aurais rencontré, aurais rencontré, aurait rencontré; aurions rencontré, auriez rencontré, auraient rencontré
Past Subj.	aie rencontré, aies rencontré, ait rencontré; ayons rencontré, ayez rencontré, aient rencontré
Plup. Subj.	eusse rencontré, eusses rencontré, eût rencontré; eussions rencontré, eussiez rencontré, eussent rencontré
Imperative	rencontre, rencontrons, rencontrez

to give back, return (something), render

Pres. Ind.	rends, rends, rend; rendons, rendez, rendent
Imp. Ind.	rendais, rendais, rendait; rendions, rendiez, rendaient
Past Def.	rendis, rendis, rendit; rendîmes, rendîtes, rendirent
Fut. Ind.	rendrai, rendras, rendra; rendrons, rendrez, rendront
Condit.	rendrais, rendrais, rendrait; rendrions, rendriez, rendraient
Pres. Subj.	rende, rendes, rende; rendions, rendiez, rendent
Imp. Subj.	rendisse, rendisses, rendît; rendissions, rendissiez, rendissent
Past Indef.	ai rendu, as rendu, a rendu; avons rendu, avez rendu, ont rendu
Pluperf.	avais rendu, avais rendu, avait rendu; avions rendu, aviez rendu, avaient rendu
Past Ant.	eus rendu, eus rendu, eut rendu; eûmes rendu, eûtes rendu, eurent rendu
Fut. Perf.	aurai rendu, auras rendu, aura rendu; aurons rendu, aurez rendu, auront rendu
Cond. Perf.	aurais rendu, aurais rendu, aurait rendu; aurions rendu, auriez rendu, auraient rendu
Past Subj.	aie rendu, aies rendu, ait rendu; ayons rendu, ayez rendu, aient rendu
Plup. Subj.	eusse rendu, eusses rendu, eût rendu; eussions rendu, eussiez rendu, eussent rendu
Imperative	rends, rendons, rendez

to return

Pres. Ind.	rentre, rentres, rentre; rentrons, rentrez, rentrent
Imp. Ind.	rentrais, rentrais, rentrait; rentrions, rentriez, rentraient
Past Def.	rentrai, rentras, rentra; rentrâmes, rentrâtes, rentrèrent
Fut. Ind.	rentrerai, rentreras, rentrera; rentrerons, rentrerez, rentreront
Condit.	rentrerais, rentrerais, rentrerait; rentrerions, rentreriez, rentreraient
Pres. Subj.	rentre, rentres, rentre; rentrions, rentriez, rentrent
Imp. Subj.	rentrasse, rentrasses, rentrât; rentrassions, rentrassiez, rentrassent
Past Indef.	suis rentré(e), es rentré(e), est rentré(e); sommes rentré(e)s, êtes rentré(e)(s), sont rentré(e)s
Pluperf.	étais rentré(e), étais rentré(e), était rentré(e); étions rentré(e)s, étiez rentré(e)(s), étaient rentré(e)s
Past Ant.	fus rentré(e), fus rentré(e), fut rentré(e); fûmes rentré(e)s, fûtes rentré(e)(s), furent rentré(e)s
Fut. Perf.	serai rentré(e), seras rentré(e), sera rentré(e); serons rentré(e)s, serez rentré(e)(s), seront rentré(e)s
Cond. Perf.	serais rentré(e), serais rentré(e), serait rentré(e); serions rentré(e)s, seriez rentré(e)(s), seraient rentré(e)s
Past Subj.	sois rentré(e), sois rentré(e), soit rentré(e); soyons rentré(e)s, soyez rentré(e)(s), soient rentré(e)s
Plup. Subj.	fusse rentré(e), fusses rentré(e), fût rentré(e); fussions rentré(e)s, fussiez rentré(e)(s), fussent rentré(e)s
Imperative	rentre, rentrons, rentrez

to spread

Pres. Ind.	répands, répands, répand; répandons, répandez, répandent
Imp. Ind.	répandais, répandais, répandait; répandions, répandiez, répandaient
Past Def.	répandis, répandis, répandit; répandîmes, répandîtes, répandirent
Future	répandrai, répandras, répandra; répandrons, répandrez, répandront
Condit.	répandrais, répandrais, répandrait; répandrions, répandriez, répandraient
Pres. Subj.	répande, répandes, répande; répandions, répandiez, répandent
Imp. Subj.	répandisse, répandisses, répandît; répandissions, répandissiez, répandissent
Past Indef.	ai répandu, as répandu, a répandu; avons répandu, avez répandu, ont répandu
Plup. Ind.	avais répandu, avais répandu, avait répandu; avions répandu, aviez répandu, avaient répandu
Past Ant.	eus répandu, eus répandu, eut répandu; eûmes répandu, eûtes répandu, eurent répandu
Fut. Perf.	aurai répandu, auras répandu, aura répandu; aurons répandu, aurez répandu, auront répandu
Cond. Perf.	aurais répandu, aurais répandu, aurait répandu; aurions répandu, auriez répandu, auraient répandu
Past Subj.	aie répandu, aies répandu, ait répandu; ayons répandu, ayez répandu, aient répandu
Plup. Subj.	eusse répandu, eusses répandu, eût répandu; eussions répandu, eussiez répandu, eussent répandu
Imperative	répands, répandons, répandez

to reappear, appear again

Pres. Ind.	reparais, reparais, reparaît; reparaissons, reparaissez, reparaissent
Imp. Ind.	reparaissais, reparaissais, reparaissait; reparaissions, reparaissiez, reparaissaient
Past Def.	reparus, reparus, reparut; reparûmes, reparûtes, reparurent
Future	reparaîtrai, reparaîtras, reparaîtra; reparaîtrons, reparaîtrez, reparaîtront
Condit.	reparaîtrais, reparaîtrais, reparaîtrait; reparaîtrions, reparaîtriez, reparaîtraient
Pres. Subj.	reparaisse, reparaisses, reparaisse; reparaissions, reparaissiez, reparaissent
Imp. Subj.	reparusse, reparusses, reparût; reparussions, reparussiez, reparussent
Past Indef.	ai reparu, as reparu, a reparu; avons reparu, avez reparu, ont reparu
Plup. Ind.	avais reparu, avais reparu, avait reparu; avions reparu, aviez reparu, avaient reparu
Past Ant.	eus reparu, eus reparu, eut reparu; eûmes reparu, eûtes reparu, eurent reparu
Fut. Perf.	aurai reparu, auras reparu, aura reparu; aurons reparu, aurez reparu, auront reparu
Cond. Perf.	aurais reparu, aurais reparu, aurait reparu; aurions reparu, auriez reparu, auraient reparu
Past Subj.	aie reparu, aies reparu, ait reparu; ayons reparu, ayez reparu, aient reparu
Plup. Subj.	eusse reparu, eusses reparu, eût reparu; eussions reparu, eussiez reparu, eussent reparu
Imperative	reparais, reparaissons, reparaissez

to repair

Pres. Ind.	répare, répares, répare; réparons, réparez, réparent
Imp. Ind.	réparais, réparais, réparait; réparions, répariez, réparaient
Past Def.	réparai, réparas, répara; réparâmes, réparâtes, réparèrent
Future	réparerai, répareras, réparera; réparerons, réparerez, répareront
Condit.	réparerais, réparerais, réparerait; réparerions, répareriez, répareraient
Pres. Subj.	répare, répares, répare; réparions, répariez, réparent
Imp. Subj.	réparasse, réparasses, réparât; réparassions, réparassiez, réparassent
Past Indef.	ai réparé, as réparé, a réparé; avons réparé, avez réparé, ont réparé
Plup. Ind.	avais réparé, avais réparé, avait réparé; avions réparé, aviez réparé, avaient réparé
Past Ant.	eus réparé, eus réparé, eut réparé; eûmes réparé, eûtes réparé, eurent réparé
Fut. Perf.	aurai réparé, auras réparé, aura réparé; aurons réparé, aurez réparé, auront réparé
Cond. Perf.	aurais réparé, aurais réparé, aurait réparé; aurions réparé, auriez réparé, auraient réparé
Past Subj.	aie réparé, aies réparé, ait réparé; ayons réparé, ayez réparé, aient réparé
Plup. Subj.	eusse réparé, eusses réparé, eût réparé; eussions réparé, eussiez réparé, eussent réparé
Imperative	répare, réparons, réparez

to iron

Pres. Ind.	repasse, repasses, repasse; repassons, repassez, repassent
Imp. Ind.	repassais, repassais, repassait; repassions, repassiez, repassaient
Past Def.	repassai, repassas, repassa; repassâmes, repassâtes, repassèrent
Future	repasserai, repasseras, repassera; repasserons, repasserez, repasseront
Condit.	repasserais, repasserais, repasserait; repasserions, repasseriez, repasseraient
Pres. Subj.	repasse, repasses, repasse; repassions, repassiez, repassent
Imp. Subj.	repassasse, repassasses, repassât; repassassions, repassassiez, repassassent
Past Indef.	ai repassé, as repassé, a repassé; avons repassé, avez repassé, ont repassé
Plup. Ind.	avais repassé, avais repassé, avait repassé; avions repassé, aviez repassé, avaient repassé
Past Ant.	eus repassé, eus repassé, eut repassé; eûmes repassé, eûtes repassé, eurent repassé
Fut. Perf.	aurai repassé, auras repassé, aura repassé; aurons repassé, aurez repassé, auront repassé
Cond. Perf.	aurais repassé, aurais repassé, aurait repassé; aurions repassé, auriez repassé, auraient repassé
Past Subj.	aie repassé, aies repassé, ait repassé; ayons repassé, ayez repassé, aient repassé
Plup. Subj.	eusse repassé, eusses repassé, eût repassé; eussions repassé, eussiez repasssé, eussent repassé
Imperative	repasse, repassons, repassez

to repeat

Pres. Ind.	répète, répètes, répète; répétons, répétez, répètent
Imp. Ind.	répétais, répétais, répétait; répétions, répétiez, répétaient
Past Def.	répétai, répétas, répéta; répétâmes, répétâtes, répétèrent
Fut. Ind.	répéterai, répéteras, répétera; répéterons, répéterez, répéteront
Condit.	répéterais, répéterais, répéterait; répéterions, répéteriez, répéteraient
Pres. Subj.	répète, répètes, répète; répétions, répétiez, répètent
Imp. Subj.	répétasse, répétasses, répétât; répétassions, répétassiez, répétassent
Past Indef.	ai répété, as répété, a répété; avons répété, avez répété, ont répété
Pluperf.	avais répété, avais répété, avait répété; avions répété, aviez répété, avaient répété
Past Ant.	eus répété, eus répété, eut répété; eûmes répété, eûtes répété, eurent répété
Fut. Perf.	aurai répété, auras répété, aura répété; aurons répété, aurez répété, auront répété
Cond. Perf.	aurais répété, aurais répété, aurait répété; aurions répété, auriez répété, auraient répété
Past Subj.	aie répété, aies répété, ait répété; ayons répété, ayez répété, aient répété
Plup. Subj.	eusse répété, eusses répété, eût répété; eussions répété, eussiez répété, eussent répété
Imperative	répète, répétons, répétez

to reply, answer

Pres. Ind.	réponds, réponds, répond; répondons, répondez, répondent
Imp. Ind.	répondais, répondais, répondait; répondions, répondiez, répondaient
Past Def.	répondis, répondis, répondit; répondîmes, répondîtes, répondirent
Fut. Ind.	répondrai, répondras, répondra; répondrons, répondrez, répondront
Condit.	répondrais, répondrais, répondrait; répondrions, répondriez, répondraient
Pres. Subj.	réponde, répondes, réponde; répondions, répondiez, répondent
Imp. Subj.	répondisse, répondisses, répondît; répondissions, répondissiez, répondissent
Past Indef.	ai répondu, as répondu, a répondu; avons répondu, avez répondu, ont répondu
Pluperf.	avais répondu, avais répondu, avait répondu; avions répondu, aviez répondu, avaient répondu
Past Ant.	eus répondu, eus répondu, eut répondu; eûmes répondu, eûtes répondu, eurent répondu
Fut. Perf.	aurai répondu, auras répondu, aura répondu; aurons répondu, aurez répondu, auront répondu
Cond. Perf.	aurais répondu, aurais répondu, aurait répondu; aurions répondu, auriez répondu, auraient répondu
Past Subj.	aie répondu, aies répondu, ait répondu; ayons répondu, ayez répondu, aient répondu
Plup. Subj.	eusse répondu, eusses répondu, eût répondu; eussions répondu, eussiez répondu, eussent répondu
Imperative	réponds, répondons, répondez

to rest

Pres. Ind.	me repose, te reposes, se repose; nous reposons, vous reposez, se reposent
Imp. Ind.	me reposais, te reposais, se reposait; nous reposions, vous reposiez, se reposaient
Past Def.	me reposai, te reposas, se reposa; nous reposâmes, vous reposâtes, se reposèrent
Future	me reposerai, te reposeras, se reposera; nous reposerons, vous reposerez, se reposeront
Condit.	me reposerais, te reposerais, se reposerait; nous reposerions, vous reposeriez, se reposeraient
Pres. Subj.	me repose, te reposes, se repose; nous reposions, vous reposiez, se reposent
Imp. Subj.	me reposasse, te reposasses, se reposât; nous reposassions, vous reposassiez, se reposassent
Past Indef.	me suis reposé(e), t'es reposé(e), s'est reposé(e); nous sommes reposé(e)s, vous êtes reposé(e)(s), se sont reposé(e)s
Pluperf.	m'étais reposé(e), t'étais reposé(e), s'était reposé(e); nous étions reposé(e)s, vous étiez reposé(e)(s), s'étaient reposé(e)s
Past Ant.	me fus reposé(e), te fus reposé(e), se fut reposé(e); nous fûmes reposé(e)s, vous fûtes reposé(e)(s), se furent reposé(e)s
Fut. Perf.	me serai reposé(e), te seras reposé(e), se sera reposé(e); nous serons reposé(e)s, vous serez reposé(e)(s), se seront reposé(e)s
Cond. Perf.	me serais reposé(e), te serais reposé(e), se serait reposé(e); nous serions reposé(e)s, vous seriez reposé(e)(s), se seraient reposé(e)s
Past Subj.	me sois reposé(e), te sois reposé(e), se soit reposé(e); nous soyons reposé(e)s, vous soyez reposé(e)(s), se soient reposé(e)s
Plup. Subj.	me fusse reposé(e), te fusses reposé(e), se fût reposé(e); nous fussions reposé(e)s, vous fussiez reposé(e)(s), se fussent reposé(e)s
Imperative	repose-toi, reposons-nous, reposez-vous

to take again, take back, recover, resume

Pres. Ind.	reprends, reprends, reprend; reprenons, reprenez, reprennent
Imp. Ind.	reprenais, reprenais, reprenait; reprenions, repreniez, reprenaient
Past Def.	repris, repris, reprit; reprîmes, reprîtes, reprirent
Future	reprendrai, reprendras, reprendra; reprendrons, reprendrez, reprendront
Condit.	reprendrais, reprendrais, reprendrait; reprendrions, reprendriez, reprendraient
Pres. Subj.	reprenne, reprennes, reprenne; reprenions, repreniez, reprennent
Imp. Subj.	reprisse, reprisses, reprît; reprissions, reprissiez, reprissent
Past Indef.	ai repris, as repris, a repris; avons repris, avez repris, ont repris
Plup. Ind.	avais repris, avais repris, avait repris; avions repris, aviez repris, avaient repris
Past Ant.	eus repris, eus repris, eut repris; eûmes repris, eûtes repris, eurent repris
Fut. Perf.	aurai repris, auras repris, aura repris; aurons repris, aurez repris, auront repris
Cond. Perf.	aurais repris, aurais repris, aurait repris; aurions repris, auriez repris, auraient repris
Past Subj.	aie repris, aies repris, ait repris; ayons repris, ayez repris, aient repris
Plup. Subj.	eusse repris, eusses repris, eût repris; eussions repris, eussiez repris, eussent repris
Imperative	reprends, reprenons, reprenez

to reprimand, rebuke

Pres. Ind.	réprimande, réprimandes, réprimande; réprimandons, réprimandez, réprimandent
Imp. Ind.	réprimandais, réprimandais, réprimandait; réprimandions, réprimandiez, réprimandaient
Past Def.	réprimandai, réprimandas, réprimanda; réprimandâmes, réprimandâtes, réprimandèrent
Future	réprimanderai, réprimanderas, réprimandera; réprimanderons, réprimanderez, réprimanderont
Condit.	réprimanderais, réprimanderais, réprimanderait; réprimanderions, réprimanderiez, réprimanderaient
Pres. Subj.	réprimande, réprimandes, réprimande; réprimandions, réprimandiez, réprimandent
Imp. Subj.	réprimandasse, réprimandasses, réprimandât; réprimandassions, réprimandassiez, réprimandassent
Past Indef.	ai réprimandé, as réprimandé, a réprimandé; avons réprimandé, avez réprimandé, ont réprimandé
Plup. Ind.	avais réprimandé, avais réprimandé, avait réprimandé; avions réprimandé, aviez réprimandé, avaient réprimandé
Past Ant.	eus réprimandé, eus réprimandé, eut réprimandé; eûmes réprimandé, eûtes réprimandé, eurent réprimandé
Fut. Perf.	aurai réprimandé, auras réprimandé, aura réprimandé; aurons réprimandé, aurez réprimandé, auront réprimandé
Cond. Perf.	aurais réprimandé, aurais réprimandé, aurait réprimandé; aurions réprimandé, auriez réprimandé, auraient réprimandé
Past Subj.	aie réprimandé, aies réprimandé, ait réprimandé; ayons réprimandé, ayez réprimandé, aient réprimandé
Plup. Subj.	eusse réprimandé, eusses réprimandé, eût réprimandé; eussions réprimandé, eussiez réprimandé, eussent réprimandé
Imperative	réprimande, réprimandons, réprimandez

to reproduce

Pres. Ind.	reproduis, reproduis, reproduit; reproduisons, reproduisez, reproduisent
Imp. Ind.	reproduisais, reproduisais, reproduisait; reproduisions, reproduisiez, reproduisaient
Past Def.	reproduisis, reproduisis, reproduisit; reproduisîmes, reproduisîtes, reproduisirent
Future	reproduirai, reproduiras, reproduira; reproduirons, reproduirez, reproduiront
Condit.	reproduirais, reproduirais, reproduirait; reproduirions, reproduiriez, reproduiraient
Pres. Subj.	reproduise, reproduises, reproduise; reproduisions, reproduisiez, reproduisent
Imp. Subj.	reproduisisse, reproduisisses, reproduisît; reproduisissions, reproduisissiez, reproduisissent
Past Indef.	ai reproduit, as reproduit, a reproduit; avons reproduit, avez reproduit, ont reproduit
Plup. Ind.	avais reproduit, avais reproduit, avait reproduit; avions reproduit, aviez reproduit, avaient reproduit
Past Ant.	eus reproduit, eus reproduit, eut reproduit; eûmes reproduit, eûtes reproduit, eurent reproduit
Fut. Perf.	aurai reproduit, auras reproduit, aura reproduit; aurons reproduit, aurez reproduit, auront reproduit
Cond. Perf.	aurais reproduit, aurais reproduit, aurait reproduit; aurions reproduit, auriez reproduit, auraient reproduit
Past Subj.	aie reproduit, aies reproduit, ait reproduit; ayons reproduit, ayez reproduit, aient reproduit
Plup. Subj.	eusse reproduit, eusses reproduit, eût reproduit; eussions reproduit, eussiez reproduit, eussent reproduit
Imperative	reproduis, reproduisons, reproduisez

to resolve, solve

Pres. Ind.	résous, résous, résout; résolvons, résolvez, résolvent
Imp. Ind.	résolvais, résolvais, résolvait; résolvions, résolviez, résolvaient
Past Def.	résolus, résolus, résolut; résolûmes, résolûtes, résolurent
Fut. Ind.	résoudrai, résoudras, résoudra; résoudrons, résoudrez, résoudront
Condit.	résoudrais, résoudrais, résoudrait; résoudrions, résoudriez, résoudraient
Pres. Subj.	résolve, résolves, résolve; résolvions, résolviez, résolvent
Imp. Subj.	résolusse, résolusses, résolût; résolussions, résolussiez, résolussent
Past Indef.	ai résolu, as résolu, a résolu; avons résolu, avez résolu, ont résolu
Pluperf.	avais résolu, avais résolu, avait résolu; avions résolu, aviez résolu, avaient résolu
Past Ant.	eus résolu, eus résolu, eut résolu; eûmes résolu, eûtes résolu, eurent résolu
Fut. Perf.	aurai résolu, auras résolu, aura résolu; aurons résolu, aurez résolu, auront résolu
Cond. Perf.	aurais résolu, aurais résolu, aurait résolu; aurions résolu, auriez résolu, auraient résolu
Past Subj.	aie résolu, aies résolu, ait résolu; ayons résolu, ayez résolu, aient résolu
Plup. Subj.	eusse résolu, eusses résolu, eût résolu; eussions résolu, eussiez résolu, eussent résolu
Imperative	résous, résolvons, résolvez

to resemble, be like, look like

Pres. Ind.	ressemble, ressembles, ressemble; ressemblons, ressemblez, ressemblent
Imp. Ind.	ressemblais, ressemblais, ressemblait; ressemblions, ressembliez, ressemblaient
Past Def.	ressemblai, ressemblas, ressembla; ressemblâmes, ressemblâtes, ressemblèrent
Future	ressemblerai, ressembleras, ressemblera; ressemblerons, ressemblerez, ressembleront
Condit.	ressemblerais, ressemblerais, ressemblerait; ressemblerions, ressembleriez, ressembleraient
Pres. Subj.	ressemble, ressembles, ressemble; ressemblions, ressembliez, ressemblent
Imp. Subj.	ressemblasse, ressemblasses, ressemblât; ressemblassions, ressemblassiez, ressemblassent
Past Indef.	ai ressemblé, as ressemblé, a ressemblé; avons ressemblé, avez ressemblé, ont ressemblé
Plup. Ind.	avais ressemblé, avais ressemblé, avait ressemblé; avions ressemblé, aviez ressemblé, avaient ressemblé
Past Ant.	eus ressemblé, eus ressemblé, eut ressemblé; eûmes ressemblé, eûtes ressemblé, eurent ressemblé
Fut. Perf.	aurai ressemblé, auras ressemblé, aura ressemblé; aurons ressemblé, aurez ressemblé, auront ressemblé
Cond. Perf.	aurais ressemblé, aurais ressemblé, aurait ressemblé; aurions ressemblé, auriez ressemblé, auraient ressemblé
Past Subj.	aie ressemblé, aies ressemblé, ait ressemblé; ayons ressemblé, ayez ressemblé, aient ressemblé
Plup. Subj.	eusse ressemblé, eusses ressemblé, eût ressemblé; eussions ressemblé, eussiez ressemblé, eussent ressemblé
Imperative	[ordinairement inemployé]

to remain, stay

Pres. Ind.	reste, restes, reste; restons, restez, restent
Imp. Ind.	restais, restais, restait; restions, restiez, restaient
Past Def.	restai, restas, resta; restâmes, restâtes, restèrent
Fut. Ind.	resterai, resteras, restera; resterons, resterez, resteront
Condit.	resterais, resterais, resterait; resterions, resteriez, resteraient
Pres. Subj.	reste, restes, reste; restions, restiez, restent
Imp. Subj.	restasse, restasses, restât; restassions, restassiez, restassent
Past Indef.	suis resté(e), es resté(e), est resté(e); sommes resté(e)s, êtes resté(e)(s), sont resté(e)s
Pluperf.	étais resté(e), étais resté(e), était resté(e); étions resté(e)s, étiez resté(e)(s), étaient resté(e)s
Past Ant.	fus resté(e), fus resté(e), fut resté(e); fûmes resté(e)s, fûtes resté(e)(s), furent resté(e)s
Fut. Perf.	serai resté(e), seras resté(e), sera resté(e); serons resté(e)s, serez resté(e)(s), seront resté(e)s
Cond. Perf.	serais resté(e), serais resté(e), serait resté(e); serions resté(e)s, seriez resté(e)(s), seraient resté(e)s
Past Subj.	sois resté(e), sois resté(e), soit resté(e); soyons resté(e)s, soyez resté(e)(s), soient resté(e)s
Plup. Subj.	fusse resté(e), fusses resté(e), fût resté(e); fussions resté(e)s, fussiez resté(e)(s), fussent resté(e)s
Imperative	reste, restons, restez

to retain, keep, detain

Pres. Ind.	retiens, retiens, retient; retenons, retenez, retiennent
Imp. Ind.	retenais, retenais, retenait; retenions, reteniez, retenaient
Past Def.	retins, retins, retint; retînmes, retîntes, retinrent
Future	retiendrai, retiendras, retiendra; retiendrons, retiendrez, retiendront
Condit.	retiendrais, retiendrais, retiendrait; retiendrions, retiendriez, retiendraient
Pres. Subj.	retienne, retiennes, retienne; retenions, reteniez, retiennent
Imp. Subj.	retinsse, retinsses, retînt; retinssions, retinssiez, retinssent
Past Indef.	ai retenu, as retenu, a retenu; avons retenu, avez retenu, ont retenu
Pluperf.	avais retenu, avais retenu, avait retenu; avions retenu, aviez retenu, avaient retenu
Past Ant.	eus retenu, eus retenu, eut retenu; eûmes retenu, eûtes retenu, eurent retenu
Fut. Perf.	aurai retenu, auras retenu, aura retenu; aurons retenu, aurez retenu, auront retenu
Cond. Perf.	aurais retenu, aurais retenu, aurait retenu; aurions retenu, auriez retenu, auraient retenu
Past Subj.	aie retenu, aies retenu, ait retenu; ayons retenu, ayez retenu, aient retenu
Plup. Subj.	eusse retenu, eusses retenu, eût retenu; eussions retenu, eussiez retenu, eussent retenu
Imperative	retiens, retenons, retenez

to draw (out) again, pull again

Pres. Ind.	retire, retires, retire; retirons, retirez, retirent
Imp. Ind.	retirais, retirais, retirait; retirions, retiriez, retiraient
Past Def.	retirai, retiras, retira; retirâmes, retirâtes, retirèrent
Future	retirerai, retireras, retirera; retirerons, retirerez, retireront
Condit.	retirerais, retirerais, retirerait; retirerions, retireriez, retireraient
Pres. Subj.	retire, retires, retire; retirions, retiriez, retirent
Imp. Subj.	retirasse, retirasses, retirât; retirassions, retirassiez, retirassent
Past Indef.	ai retiré, as retiré, a retiré; avons retiré, avez retiré, ont retiré
Plup. Ind.	avais retiré, avais retiré, avait retiré; avions retiré, aviez retiré, avaient retiré
Past Ant.	eus retiré, eus retiré, eut retiré; eûmes retiré, eûtes retiré, eurent retiré
Fut. Perf.	aurai retiré, auras retiré, aura retiré; aurons retiré, aurez retiré, auront retiré
Cond. Perf.	aurais retiré, aurais retiré, aurait retiré; aurions retiré, auriez retiré, auraient retiré
Past Subj.	aie retiré. aies retiré, ait retiré; ayons retiré, ayez retiré, aient retiré
Plup. Subj.	eusse retiré, eusses retiré, eût retiré; eussions retiré, eussiez retiré, eussent retiré
Imperative	retire, retirons, retirez

to retire, withdraw

Pres. Ind.	me retire, te retires, se retire; nous retirons, vous retirez, se retirent
Imp. Ind.	me retirais, te retirais, se retirait; nous retirions, vous retiriez, se retiraient
Past Def.	me retirai, te retiras, se retira; nous retirâmes, vous retirâtes, se retirèrent
Future	me retirerai, te retireras, se retirera; nous retirerons, vous retirerez, se retireront
Condit.	me retirerais, te retirerais, se retirerait; nous retirerions, vous retireriez, se retireraient
Pres. Subj.	me retire, te retires, se retire; nous retirions, vous retiriez, se retirent
Imp. Subj.	me retirasse, te retirasses, se retirât; nous retirassions, vous retirassiez, se retirassent
Past Indef.	me suis retiré(e), t'es retiré(e), s'est retiré(e); nous sommes retiré(e)s, vous êtes retiré(e)(s), se sont retiré(e)s
Plup. Ind.	m'étais retiré(e), t'étais retiré(e), s'était retiré(e); nous étions retiré(e)s, vous étiez retiré(e)(s), s'étaient retiré(e)s
Past Ant.	me fus retiré(e), te fus retiré(e), se fut retiré(e); nous fûmes retiré(e)s, vous fûtes retiré(e)(s), se furent retiré(e)s
Fut. Perf.	me serai retiré(e), te seras retiré(e), se sera retiré(e); nous serons retiré(e)s, vous serez retiré(e)(s), se seront retiré(e)s
Cond. Perf.	me serais retiré(e), te serais retiré(e), se serait retiré(e); nous serions retiré(e)s, vous seriez retiré(e)(s), se seraient retiré(e)s
Past Subj.	me sois retiré(e), te sois retiré(e), se soit retiré(e); nous soyons retiré(e)s, vous soyez retiré(e)(s), se soient retiré(e)s
Plup. Subj.	me fusse retiré(e), te fusses retiré(e), se fût retiré(e); nous fussions retiré(e)s, vous fussiez retiré(e)(s), se fussent retiré(e)s
Imperative	retire-toi, retirons-nous, retirez-vous

to return, go back

Pres. Ind.	retourne, retournes, retourne; retournons, retournez, retournent
Imp. Ind.	retournais, retournais, retournait; retournions, retourniez, retournaient
Past Def.	retournai, retournas, retourna; retournâmes, retournâtes, retournèrent
Fut. Ind.	retournerai, retourneras, retournera; retournerons, retournerez, retourneront
Condit.	retournerais, retournerais, retournerait; retournerions, retourneriez, retourneraient
Pres. Subj.	retourne, retournes, retourne; retournions, retourniez, retournent
Imp. Subj.	retournasse, retournasses, retournât; retournassions, retournassiez, retournassent
Past Indef.	suis retourné(e), es retourné(e), est retourné(e); sommes retourné(e)s, êtes retourné(e)(s), sont retourné(e)s
Pluperf.	étais retourné(e), étais retourné(e), était retourné(e); étions retourné(e)s, étiez retourné(e)(s), étaient retourné(e)s
Past Ant.	fus retourné(e), fus retourné(e), fut retourné(e); fûmes retourné(e)s, fûtes retourné(e)(s), furent retourné(e)s
Fut. Perf.	serai retourné(e), seras retourné(e), sera retourné(e); serons retourné(e)s, serez retourné(e)(s), seront retourné(e)s
Cond. Perf.	serais retourné(e), serais retourné(e), serait retourné(e); serions retourné(e)s, seriez retourné(e)(s), seraient retourné(e)s
Past Subj.	sois retourné(e), sois retourné(e), soit retourné(e); soyons retourné(e)s, soyez retourné(e)(s), soient retourné(e)s
Plup. Subj.	fusse retourné(e), fusses retourné(e), fût retourné(e); fussions retourné(e)s, fussiez retourné(e)(s), fussent retourné(e)s
Imperative	retourne, retournons, retournez

to succeed

Pres. Ind.	réussis, réussis, réussit; réussissons, réussissez, réussissent
Imp. Ind.	réussissais, réussissais, réussissait; réussissions, réussissiez, réussissaient
Past Def.	réussis, réussis, réussit; réussîmes, réussîtes, réussirent
Fut. Ind.	réussirai, réussiras, réussira; réussirons, réussirez, réussiront
Condit.	réussirais, réussirais, réussirait; réussirions, réussiriez, réussiraient
Pres. Subj.	réussisse, réussisses, réussisse; réussissions, réussissiez, réussissent
Imp. Subj.	réussisse, réussisses, réussît; réussissions, réussissiez, réussissent
Past Indef.	ai réussi, as réussi, a réussi; avons réussi, avez réussi, ont réussi
Pluperf.	avais réussi, avais réussi, avait réussi; avions réussi, aviez réussi, avaient réussi
Past Ant.	eus réussi, eus réussi, eut réussi; eûmes réussi, eûtes réussi, eurent réussi
Fut. Perf.	aurai réussi, auras réussi, aura réussi; aurons réussi, aurez réussi, auront réussi
Cond. Perf.	aurais réussi, aurais réussi, aurait réussi; aurions réussi, auriez réussi, auraient réussi
Past Subj.	aie réussi, aies réussi, ait réussi; ayons réussi, ayez réussi, aient réussi
Plup. Subj.	eusse réussi, eusses réussi, eût réussi; eussions réussi, eussiez réussi, eussent réussi
Imperative	réussis, réussissons, réussissez

to wake up

Pres. Ind.	me réveille, te réveilles, se réveille; nous réveillons, vous réveillez, se réveillent
Imp. Ind.	me réveillais, te réveillais, se réveillait; nous réveillions, vous réveilliez, se réveillaient
Past Def.	me réveillai, te réveillas, se réveilla; nous réveillâmes, vous réveillâtes, se réveillèrent
Fut. Ind.	me réveillerai, te réveilleras, se réveillera; nous réveillerons, vous réveillerez, se réveilleront
Condit.	me réveillerais, te réveillerais, se réveillerait; nous réveillerions, vous réveilleriez, se réveilleraient
Pres. Subj.	me réveille, te réveilles, se réveille; nous réveillions, vous réveilliez, se réveillent
Imp. Subj.	me réveillasse, te réveillasses, se réveillât; nous réveillassions, vous réveillassiez, se réveillassent
Past Indef.	me suis réveillé(e), t'es réveillé(e), s'est réveillé(e); nous sommes réveillé(e)s, vous êtes réveillé(e)(s), se sont réveillé(e)s
Pluperf.	m'étais réveillé(e), t'étais réveillé(e), s'était réveillé(e); nous étions réveillé(e)s, vous étiez réveillé(e)(s), s'étaient réveillé(e)s
Past Ant.	me fus réveillé(e), te fus réveillé(e), se fut réveillé(e); nous fûmes réveillé(e)s, vous fûtes réveillé(e)(s), se furent réveillé(e)s
Fut. Perf.	me serai réveillé(e), te seras réveillé(e), se sera réveillé(e); nous serons réveillé(e)s, vous serez réveillé(e)(s), se seront réveillé(e)s
Cond. Perf.	me serais réveillé(e), te serais réveillé(e), se serait réveillé(e); nous serions réveillé(e)s, vous seriez réveillé(e)(s), se seraient réveillé(e)s
Past Subj.	me sois réveillé(e), te sois réveillé(e), se soit réveillé(e); nous soyons réveillé(e)s, vous soyez réveillé(e)(s), se soient réveillé(e)s
Plup. Subj.	me fusse réveillé(e), te fusses réveillé(e), se fût réveillé(e); nous fussions réveillé(e)s, vous fussiez réveillé(e)(s), se fussent réveillé(e)s
Imperative	réveille-toi, réveillons-nous, réveillez-vous

to come back

Pres. Ind.	reviens, reviens, revient; revenons, revenez, reviennent
Imp. Ind.	revenais, revenais, revenait; revenions, reveniez, revenaient
Past Def.	revins, revins, revint; revînmes, revîntes, revinrent
Fut. Ind.	reviendrai, reviendras, reviendra; reviendrons, reviendrez, reviendront
Condit.	reviendrais, reviendrais, reviendrait; reviendrions, reviendriez, reviendraient
Pres. Subj.	revienne, reviennes, revienne; revenions, reveniez, reviennent
Imp. Subj.	revinsse, revinsses, revînt; revinssions, revinssiez, revinssent
Past Indef.	suis revenu(e), es revenu(e), est revenu(e); sommes revenu(e)s, êtes revenu(e)(s), sont revenu(e)s
Pluperf.	étais revenu(e), étais revenu(e), était revenu(e); étions revenu(e)s, étiez revenu(e)(s), étaient revenu(e)s
Past Ant.	fus revenu(e), fus revenu(e), fut revenu(e); fûmes revenu(e)s, fûtes revenu(e)(s), furent revenu(e)s
Fut. Perf.	serai revenu(e), seras revenu(e), sera revenu(e); serons revenu(e)s, serez revenu(e)(s), seront revenu(e)s
Cond. Perf.	serais revenu(e), serais revenu(e), serait revenu(e); serions revenu(e)s, seriez revenu(e)(s), seraient revenu(e)s
Past Subj.	sois revenu(e), sois revenu(e), soit revenu(e); soyons revenu(e)s, soyez revenu(e)(s), soient revenu(e)s
Plup. Subj.	fusse revenu(e), fusses revenu(e), fût revenu(e); fussions revenu(e)s, fussiez revenu(e)(s), fussent revenu(e)s
Imperative	reviens, revenons, revenez

to see again, see once more

Pres. Ind.	revois, revois, revoit; revoyons, revoyez, revoient
Imp. Ind.	revoyais, revoyais, revoyait; revoyions, revoyiez, revoyaient
Past Def.	revis, revis, revit; revîmes, revîtes, revirent
Future	reverrai, reverras, reverra; reverrons, reverrez, reverront
Condit.	reverrais, reverrais, reverrait; reverrions, reverriez, reverraient
Pres. Subj.	revoie, revoies, revoie; revoyions, revoyiez, revoient
Imp. Subj.	revisse, revisses, revît; revissions, revissiez, revissent
Past Indef.	ai revu, as revu, a revu; avons revu, avez revu, ont revu
Plup. Ind.	avais revu, avais revu, avait revu; avions revu, aviez revu, avaient revu
Past Ant.	eus revu, eus revu, eut revu; eûmes revu, eûtes revu, eurent revu
Fut. Perf.	aurai revu, auras revu, aura revu; aurons revu, aurez revu, auront revu
Cond. Perf.	aurais revu, aurais revu, aurait revu; aurions revu, auriez revu, auraient revu
Past Subj.	aie revu, aies revu, ait revu; ayons revu, ayez revu, aient revu
Plup. Subj.	eusse revu, eusses revu, eût revu; eussions revu, eussiez revu, eussent revu
Imperative	revois, revoyons, revoyez

to ridicule

Pres. Ind.	ridiculise, ridiculises, ridiculise; ridiculisons, ridiculisez, ridiculisent
Imp. Ind.	ridiculisais, ridiculisais, ridiculisait; ridiculisions, ridiculisiez, ridiculisaient
Past Ant.	ridiculisai, ridiculisas, ridiculisa; ridiculisâmes, ridiculisâtes, ridiculisèrent
Future	ridiculiserai, ridiculiseras, ridiculisera; ridiculiserons, ridiculiserez, ridiculiseront
Condit.	ridiculiserais, ridiculiserais, ridiculiserait; ridiculiserions, ridiculiseriez, ridiculiseraient
Pres. Subj.	ridiculise, ridiculises, ridiculise; ridiculisions, ridiculisiez, ridiculisent
Imp. Subj.	ridiculisasse, ridiculisasses, ridiculisât; ridiculisassions, ridiculisassiez, ridiculisassent
Past Indef.	ai ridiculisé, as ridiculisé, a ridiculisé; avons ridiculisé, avez ridiculisé, ont ridiculisé
Plup. Ind.	avais ridiculisé, avais ridiculisé, avait ridiculisé; avions ridiculisé, aviez ridiculisé, avaient ridiculisé
Past Ant.	eus ridiculisé, eus ridiculisé, eut ridiculisé; eûmes ridiculisé, eûtes ridiculisé, eurent ridiculisé
Fut. Perf.	aurai ridiculisé, auras ridiculisé, aura ridiculisé; aurons ridiculisé, aurez ridiculisé, auront ridiculisé
Cond. Perf.	aurais ridiculisé, aurais ridiculisé, aurait ridiculisé; aurions ridiculisé, auriez ridiculisé, auraient ridiculisé
Past Subj.	aie ridiculisé, aies ridiculisé, ait ridiculisé; ayons ridiculisé, ayez ridiculisé, aient ridiculisé
Plup. Subj.	eusse ridiculisé, eusses ridiculisé, eût ridiculisé; eussions ridiculisé, eussiez ridiculisé, eussent ridiculisé
Imperative	ridiculise, ridiculisons, ridiculisez

to laugh

Pres. Ind.	ris, ris, rit; rions, riez, rient
Imp. Ind.	riais, riais, riait; riions, riiez, riaient
Past Def.	ris, ris, rit; rîmes, rîtes, rirent
Fut. Ind.	rirai, riras, rira; rirons, rirez, riront
Condit.	rirais, rirais, rirait; ririons, ririez, riraient
Pres. Subj.	rie, ries, rie; riions, riiez, rient
Imp. Subj.	risse, risses, rît; rissions, rissiez, rissent
Past Indef.	ai ri, as ri, a ri; avons ri, avez ri, ont ri
Pluperf.	avais ri, avais ri, avait ri; avions ri, aviez ri, avaient ri
Past Ant.	eus ri, eus ri, eut ri; eûmes ri, eûtes ri, eurent ri
Fut. Perf.	aurai ri, auras ri, aura ri; aurons ri, aurez ri, auront ri
Cond. Perf.	aurais ri, aurais ri, aurait ri; aurions ri, auriez ri, auraient ri
Past Subj.	aie ri, aies ri, ait ri; ayons ri, ayez ri, aient ri
Plup. Subj.	eusse ri, eusses ri, eût ri; eussions ri, eussiez ri, eussent ri
Imperative	ris, rions, riez

to break, burst, shatter

Pres. Ind.	romps, romps, rompt; rompons, rompez, rompent
Imp. Ind.	rompais, rompais, rompait; rompions, rompiez, rompaient
Past Def.	rompis, rompis, rompit; rompîmes, rompîtes, rompirent
Fut. Ind.	romprai, rompras, rompra; romprons, romprez, rompront
Condit.	romprais, romprais, romprait; romprions, rompriez, rompraient
Pres. Subj.	rompe, rompes, rompe; rompions, rompiez, rompent
Imp. Subj.	rompisse, rompisses, rompît; rompissions, rompissiez, rompissent
Past Indef.	ai rompu, as rompu, a rompu; avons rompu, avez rompu, ont rompu
Pluperf.	avais rompu, avais rompu, avait rompu; avions rompu, aviez rompu, avaient rompu
Past Ant.	eus rompu, eus rompu, eut rompu; eûmes rompu, eûtes rompu, eurent rompu
Fut. Perf.	aurai rompu, auras rompu, aura rompu; aurons rompu, aurez rompu, auront rompu
Cond. Perf.	aurais rompu, aurais rompu, aurait rompu; aurions rompu, auriez rompu, auraient rompu
Past Subj.	aie rompu, aies rompu, ait rompu; ayons rompu, ayez rompu, aient rompu
Plup. Subj.	eusse rompu, eusses rompu, eût rompu; eussions rompu, eussiez rompu, eussent rompu
Imperative	romps, rompons, rompez

to blush

Pres. Ind.	rougis, rougis, rougit; rougissons, rougissez, rougissent
Imp. Ind.	rougissais, rougissais, rougissait; rougissions, rougissiez, rougissaient
Past Def.	rougis, rougis, rougit; rougîmes, rougîtes, rougirent
Fut. Ind.	rougirai, rougiras, rougira; rougirons, rougirez, rougiront
Condit.	rougirais, rougirais, rougirait; rougirions, rougiriez, rougiraient
Pres. Subj.	rougisse, rougisses, rougisse; rougissions, rougissiez, rougissent
Imp. Subj.	rougisse, rougisses, rougît; rougissions, rougissiez, rougissent
Past Indef.	ai rougi, as rougi, a rougi; avons rougi, avez rougi, ont rougi
Pluperf.	avais rougi, avais rougi, avait rougi; avions rougi, aviez rougi, avaient rougi
Past Ant.	eus rougi, eus rougi, eut rougi; eûmes rougi, eûtes rougi, eurent rougi
Fut. Perf.	aurai rougi, auras rougi, aura rougi; aurons rougi, aurez rougi, auront rougi
Cond. Perf.	aurais rougi, aurais rougi, aurait rougi; aurions rougi, auriez rougi, auraient rougi
Past Subj.	aie rougi, aies rougi, ait rougi; ayons rougi, ayez rougi, aient rougi
Plup. Subj.	eusse rougi, eusses rougi, eût rougi; eussions rougi, eussiez rougi, eussent rougi
Imperative	rougis, rougissons, rougissez

to roll, roll along, drive (a car)

Pres. Ind.	roule, roules, roule; roulons, roulez, roulent
Imp. Ind.	roulais, roulais, roulait; roulions, rouliez, roulaient
Past Def.	roulai, roulas, roula; roulâmes, roulâtes, roulèrent
Future	roulerai, rouleras, roulera; roulerons, roulerez, rouleront
Condit.	roulerais, roulerais, roulerait; roulerions, rouleriez, rouleraient
Pres. Subj.	roule, roules, roule; roulions, rouliez, roulent
Imp. Subj.	roulasse, roulasses, roulât; roulassions, roulassiez, roulassent
Past Indef.	ai roulé, as roulé, a roulé; avons roulé, avez roulé, ont roulé
Plup. Ind.	avais roulé, avais roulé, avait roulé; avions roulé, aviez roulé, avaient roulé
Past Ant.	eus roulé, eus roulé, eut roulé; eûmes roulé, eûtes roulé, eurent roulé
Fut. Perf.	aurai roulé, auras roulé, aura roulé; aurons roulé, aurez roulé, auront roulé
Cond. Perf.	aurais roulé, aurais roulé, aurait roulé; aurions roulé, auriez roulé, auraient roulé
Past Subj.	aie roulé, aies roulé, ait roulé; ayons roulé, ayez roulé, aient roulé
Plup. Subj.	eusse roulé, eusses roulé, eût roulé; eussions roulé, eussiez roulé, eussent roulé
Imperative	roule, roulons, roulez

to seize, grasp

Pres. Ind.	saisis, saisis, saisit; saisissons, saisissez, saisissent
Imp. Ind.	saisissais, saisissais, saisissait; saisissions, saisissiez, saisissaient
Past Def.	saisis, saisis, saisit; saisîmes, saisîtes, saisirent
Future	saisirai, saisiras, saisira; saisirons, saisirez, saisiront
Condit.	saisirais, saisirais, saisirait; saisirions, saisiriez, saisiraient
Pres. Subj.	saisisse, saisisses, saisisse; saisissions, saisissiez, saisissent
Imp. Subj.	saisisse, saisisses, saisît; saisissions, saisissiez, saisissent
Past Indef.	ai saisi, as saisi, a saisi; avons saisi, avez saisi, ont saisi
Plup. Ind.	avais saisi, avais saisi, avait saisi; avions saisi, aviez saisi, avaient saisi
Past Ant.	eus saisi, eus saisi, eut saisi; eûmes saisi, eûtes saisi, eurent saisi
Fut. Perf.	aurai saisi, auras saisi, aura saisi; aurons saisi, aurez saisi, auront saisi
Cond. Perf.	aurais saisi, aurais saisi, aurait saisi; aurions saisi, auriez saisi, auraient saisi
Past Subj.	aie saisi, aies saisi, ait saisi; ayons saisi, ayez saisi, aient saisi
Plup. Subj.	eusse saisi, eusses saisi, eût saisi; eussions saisi, eussiez saisi, eussent saisi
Imperative	saisis, saisissons, saisissez

to soil, dirty

Pres. Ind.	salis, salis, salit; salissons, salissez, salissent
Imp. Ind.	salissais, salissais, salissait; salissions, salissiez, salissaient
Past Def.	salis, salis, salit; salîmes, salîtes, salirent
Fut. Ind.	salirai, saliras, salira; salirons, salirez, saliront
Condit.	salirais, salirais, salirait; salirions, saliriez, saliraient
Pres. Subj.	salisse, salisses, salisse; salissions, salissiez, salissent
Imp. Subj.	salisse, salisses, salît; salissions, salissiez, salissent
Past Indef.	ai sali, as sali, a sali; avons sali, avez sali, ont sali
Pluperf.	avais sali, avais sali, avait sali; avions sali, aviez sali, avaient sali
Past Ant.	eus sali, eus sali, eut sali; eûmes sali, eûtes sali, eurent sali
Fut. Perf.	aurai sali, auras sali, aura sali; aurons sali, aurez sali, auront sali
Cond. Perf.	aurais sali, aurais sali, aurait sali; aurions sali, auriez sali, auraient sali
Past Subj.	aie sali, aies sali, ait sali; ayons sali, ayez sali, aient sali
Plup. Subj.	eusse sali, eusses sali, eût sali; eussions sali, eussiez sali, eussent sali
Imperative	salis, salissons, salissez

to satisfy

Pres. Ind.	satisfais, satisfais, satisfait; satisfaisons, satisfaites, satisfont
Imp. Ind.	satisfaisais, satisfaisais, satisfaisait; satisfaisions, satisfaisiez, satisfaisaient
Past Def.	satisfis, satisfis, satisfit; satisfîmes, satisfîtes, satisfirent
Future	satisferai, satisferas, satisfera; satisferons, satisferez, satisferont
Condit.	satisferais, satisferais, satisferait; satisferions, satisferiez, satisferaient
Pres. Subj.	satisfasse, satisfasses, satisfasse; satisfassions, satisfassiez, satisfassent
Imp. Subj.	satisfisse, satisfisses, satisfît; satisfissions, satisfissiez, satisfissent
Past Indef.	ai satisfait, as satisfait, a satisfait; avons satisfait, avez satisfait, ont satisfait
Pluperf.	avais satisfait, avais satisfait, avait satisfait; avions satisfait, aviez satisfait, avaient satisfait
Past Ant.	eus satisfait, eus satisfait, eut satisfait; eûmes satisfait, eûtes satisfait, eurent satisfait
Fut. Perf.	aurai satisfait, auras satisfait, aura satisfait; aurons satisfait, aurez satisfait, auront satisfait
Cond. Perf.	aurais satisfait, aurais satisfait, aurait satisfait; aurions satisfait, auriez satisfait, auraient satisfait
Past Subj.	aie satisfait, aies satisfait, ait satisfait; ayons satisfait, ayez satisfait, aient satisfait
Plup. Subj.	eusse satisfait, eusses satisfait, eût satisfait; eussions satisfait, eussiez satisfait, eussent satisfait
Imperative	satisfais, satisfaisons, satisfaites

to jump, leap

Pres. Ind.	saute, sautes, saute; sautons, sautez, sautent
Imp. Ind.	sautais, sautais, sautait; sautions, sautiez, sautaient
Past Def.	sautai, sautas, sauta; sautâmes, sautâtes, sautèrent
Fut. Ind.	sauterai, sauteras, sautera; sauterons, sauterez, sauteront
Condit.	sauterais, sauterais, sauterait; sauterions, sauteriez, sauteraient
Pres. Subj.	saute, sautes, saute; sautions, sautiez, sautent
Imp. Subj.	sautasse, sautasses, sautât; sautassions, sautassiez, sautassent
Past Indef.	ai sauté, as sauté, a sauté; avons sauté, avez sauté, ont sauté
Pluperf.	avais sauté, avais sauté, avait sauté; avions sauté, aviez sauté, avaient sauté
Past Ant.	eus sauté, eus sauté, eut sauté; eûmes sauté, eûtes sauté, eurent sauté
Fut. Perf.	aurai sauté, auras sauté, aura sauté; aurons sauté, aurez sauté, auront sauté
Cond. Perf.	aurais sauté, aurais sauté, aurait sauté; aurions sauté, auriez sauté, auraient sauté
Past Subj.	aie sauté, aies sauté, ait sauté; ayons sauté, ayez sauté, aient sauté
Plup. Subj.	eusse sauté, eusses sauté, eût sauté; eussions sauté, eussiez sauté, eussent sauté
Imperative	saute, sautons, sautez

to rescue, save

Pres. Ind.	sauve, sauves, sauve; sauvons, sauvez, sauvent
Imp. Ind.	sauvais, sauvais, sauvait; sauvions, sauviez, sauvaient
Past Def.	sauvai, sauvas, sauva; sauvâmes, sauvâtes, sauvèrent
Future	sauverai, sauveras, sauvera; sauverons, sauverez, sauveront
Condit.	sauverais, sauverais, sauverait; sauverions, sauveriez, sauveraient
Pres. Subj.	sauve, sauves, sauve; sauvions, sauviez, sauvent
Imp. Subj.	sauvasse, sauvasses, sauvât; sauvassions, sauvassiez, sauvassent
Past Indef.	ai sauvé, as sauvé, a sauvé; avons sauvé, avez sauvé, ont sauvé
Plup. Ind.	avais sauvé, avais sauvé, avait sauvé; avions sauvé, aviez sauvé, avaient sauvé
Past Ant.	eus sauvé, eus sauvé, eut sauvé; eûmes sauvé, eûtes sauvé, eurent sauvé
Fut. Perf.	aurai sauvé, auras sauvé, aura sauvé; aurons sauvé, aurez sauvé, auront sauvé
Cond. Perf.	aurais sauvé, aurais sauvé, aurait sauvé; aurions sauvé, auriez sauvé, auraient sauvé
Past Subj.	aie sauvé, aies sauvé, ait sauvé; ayons sauvé, ayez sauvé, aient sauvé
Plup. Subj.	eusse sauvé, eusses sauvé, eût sauvé; eussions sauvé, eussiez sauvé, eussent sauvé
Imperative	sauve, sauvons, sauvez

to run away

Pres. Ind.	me sauve, te sauves, se sauve; nous sauvons, vous sauvez, se sauvent
Imp. Ind.	me sauvais, te sauvais, se sauvait; nous sauvions, vous sauviez, se sauvaient
Past Def.	me sauvai, te sauvas, se sauva; nous sauvâmes, vous sauvâtes, se sauvèrent
Future	me sauverai, te sauveras, se sauvera; nous sauverons, vous sauverez, se sauveront
Condit.	me sauverais, te sauverais, se sauverait; nous sauverions, vous sauveriez, se sauveraient
Pres. Subj.	me sauve, te sauves, se sauve; nous sauvions, vous sauviez, se sauvent
Imp. Subj.	me sauvasse, te sauvasses, se sauvât; nous sauvassions, vous sauvassiez, se sauvassent
Past Indef.	me suis sauvé(e), t'es sauvé(e), s'est sauvé(e); nous sommes sauvé(e)s, vous êtes sauvé(e)(s), se sont sauvé(e)s
Plup. Ind.	m'étais sauvé(e), t'étais sauvé(e), s'était sauvé(e); nous étions sauvé(e)s, vous étiez sauvé(e)(s), s'étaient sauvé(e)s
Past Ant.	me fus sauvé(e), te fus sauvé(e), se fut sauvé(e); nous fûmes sauvé(e)s, vous fûtes sauvé(e)(s), se furent sauvé(e)s
Fut. Perf.	me serai sauvé(e), te seras sauvé(e), se sera sauvé(e); nous serons sauvé(e)s, vous serez sauvé(e)(s), se seront sauvé(e)s
Cond. Perf.	me serais sauvé(e), te serais sauvé(e), se serait sauvé(e); nous serions sauvé(e)s, vous seriez sauvé(e)(s), se seraient sauvé(e)s
Past Subj.	me sois sauvé(e), te sois sauvé(e), se soit sauvé(e); nous soyons sauvé(e)s, vous soyez sauvé(e)(s), se soient sauvé(e)s
Plup. Subj.	me fusse sauvé(e), te fusses sauvé(e), se fût sauvé(e); nous fussions sauvé(e)s, vous fussiez sauvé(e)(s), se fussent sauvé(e)s
Imperative	sauve-toi, sauvons-nous, sauvez-vous

to know (how)

Pres. Ind.	sais, sais, sait; savons, savez, savent
Imp. Ind.	savais, savais, savait; savions, saviez, savaient
Past Def.	sus, sus, sut; sûmes, sûtes, surent
Fut. Ind.	saurai, sauras, saura; saurons, saurez, sauront
Condit.	saurais, saurais, saurait; saurions, sauriez, sauraient
Pres. Subj.	sache, saches, sache; sachions, sachiez, sachent
Imp. Subj.	susse, susses, sût; sussions, sussiez, sussent
Past Indef.	ai su, as su, a su; avons su, avez su, ont su
Pluperf.	avais su, avais su, avait su; avions su, aviez su, avaient su
Past Ant.	eus su, eus su, eut su; eûmes su, eûtes su, eurent su
Fut. Perf.	aurai su, auras su, aura su; aurons su, aurez su, auront su
Cond. Perf.	aurais su, aurais su, aurait su; aurions su, auriez su, auraient su
Past Subj.	aie su, aies su, ait su; ayons su, ayez su, aient su
Plup. Subj.	eusse su, eusses su, eût su; eussions su, eussiez su, eussent su
Imperative	sache, sachons, sachez

to shake, shake down (off)

Pres. Ind.	secoue, secoues, secoue; secouons, secouez, secouent
Imp. Ind.	secouais, secouais, secouait; secouions, secouiez, secouaient
Past Def.	secouai, secouas, secoua; secouâmes, secouâtes, secouèrent
Future	secouerai, secoueras, secouera; secouerons, secouerez, secoueront
Condit.	secouerais, secouerais, secouerait; secouerions, secoueriez, secoueraient
Pres. Subj.	secoue, secoues, secoue; secouions, secouiez, secouent
Imp. Subj.	secouasse, secouasses, secouât; secouassions, secouassiez, secouassent
Past Indef.	ai secoué, as secoué, a secoué; avons secoué, avez secoué, ont secoué
Plup. Ind.	avais secoué, avais secoué, avait secoué; avions secoué, aviez secoué, avaient secoué
Past Ant.	eus secoué, eus secoué, eut secoué; eûmes secoué, eûtes secoué, eurent secoué
Fut. Perf.	aurai secoué, auras secoué, aura secoué; aurons secoué, aurez secoué, auront secoué
Cond. Perf.	aurais secoué, aurais secoué, aurait secoué; aurions secoué, auriez secoué, auraient secoué
Past Subj.	aie secoué, aies secoué, ait secoué; ayons secoué, ayez secoué, aient secoué
Plup. Subj.	eusse secoué, eusses secoué, eût secoué; eussions secoué, eussiez secoué, eussent secoué
Imperative	secoue, secouons, secouez

to help, relieve, succor

Pres. Ind.	secours, secours, secourt; secourons, secourez, secourent
Imp. Ind.	secourais, secourais, secourait; secourions, secouriez, secouraient
Past Def.	secourus, secourus, secourut; secourûmes, secourûtes, secoururent
Future	secourrai, secourras, secourra; secourrons, secourrez, secourront
Condit.	secourrais, secourrais, secourrait; secourrions, secourriez, secourraient
Pres. Subj.	secoure, secoures, secoure; secourions, secouriez, secourent
Imp. Subj.	secourusse, secourusses, secourût; secourussions, secourussiez, secourussent
Past Indef.	ai secouru, as secouru, a secouru; avons secouru, avez secouru, ont secouru
Pluperf.	avais secouru, avais secouru, avait secouru; avions secouru, aviez secouru, avaient secouru
Past Ant.	eus secouru, eus secouru, eut secouru; eûmes secouru, eûtes secouru, eurent secouru
Fut. Perf.	aurai secouru, auras secouru, aura secouru; aurons secouru, aurez secouru, auront secouru
Cond.	aurais secouru, aurais secouru, aurait secouru; aurions secouru, auriez secouru, auraient secouru
Past Subj.	aie secouru, aies secouru, ait secouru; ayons secouru, ayez secouru, aient secouru
Plup. Subj.	eusse secouru, eusses secouru, eût secouru; eussions secouru, eussiez secouru, eussent secouru
Imperative	secours, secourons, secourez

to seduce

Pres. Ind.	séduis, séduis, séduit; séduisons, séduisez, séduisent
Imp. Ind.	séduisais, séduisais, séduisait; séduisions, séduisiez, séduisaient
Past Def.	séduisis, séduisis, séduisit; séduisîmes, séduisîtes, séduisirent
Future	séduirai, séduiras, séduira; séduirons, séduirez, séduiront
Condit.	séduirais, séduirais, séduirait; séduirions, séduiriez, séduiraient
Pres. Subj.	séduise, séduises, séduise; séduisions, séduisiez, séduisent
Imp. Subj.	séduisisse, séduisisses, séduisît; séduisissions, séduisissiez, séduisissent
Past Indef.	ai séduit, as séduit, a séduit; avons séduit, avez séduit, ont séduit
Plup. Ind.	avais séduit, avais séduit, avait séduit; avions séduit, aviez séduit, avaient séduit
Past Ant.	eus séduit, eus séduit, eut séduit; eûmes séduit, eûtes séduit, eurent séduit
Fut. Perf.	aurai séduit, auras séduit, aura séduit; aurons séduit, aurez séduit, auront séduit
Cond. Perf.	aurais séduit, aurais séduit, aurait séduit; aurions séduit, auriez séduit, auraient séduit
Past Subj.	aie séduit, aies séduit, ait séduit; ayons séduit, ayez séduit, aient séduit
Plup. Subj.	eusse séduit, eusses séduit, eût séduit; eussions séduit, eussiez séduit, eussent séduit
Imperative	séduis, séduisons, séduisez

to sojourn, live somewhere temporarily

Pres. Ind.	séjourne, séjournes, séjourne; séjournons, séjournez, séjournent
Imp. Ind.	séjournais, séjournais, séjournait; séjournions, séjourniez, séjournaient
Past Def.	séjournai, séjournas, séjourna; séjournâmes, séjournâtes, séjournèrent
Future	séjournerai, séjourneras, séjournera; séjournerons, séjournerez, séjourneront
Condit.	séjournerais, séjournerais, séjournerait; séjournerions, séjourneriez, séjourneraient
Pres. Subj.	séjourne, séjournes, séjourne; séjournions, séjourniez, séjournent
Imp. Subj.	séjournasse, séjournasses, séjournât; séjournassions, séjournassiez, séjournassent
Past Indef.	ai séjourné, as séjourné, a séjourné; avons séjourné, avez séjourné, ont séjourné
Plup. Ind.	avais séjourné, avais séjourné, avait séjourné; avions séjourné, aviez séjourné, avaient séjourné
Past Ant.	eus séjourné, eus séjourné, eut séjourné; eûmes séjourné, eûtes séjourné, eurent séjourné
Fut. Perf.	aurai séjourné, auras séjourné, aura séjourné; aurons séjourné, aurez séjourné, auront séjourné
Cond. Perf.	aurais séjourné, aurais séjourné, aurait séjourné; aurions séjourné, auriez séjourné, auraient séjourné
Past Subj.	aie séjourné, aies séjourné, ait séjourné; ayons séjourné, ayez séjourné, aient séjourné
Plup. Subj.	eusse séjourné, eusses séjourné, eût séjourné; eussions séjourné, eussiez séjourné, eussent séjourné
Imperative	séjourne, séjournons, séjournez

to seem

Pres. Ind.	il semble
Imp. Ind.	il semblait
Past Def.	il sembla
Future	il semblera
Condit.	il semblerait
Pres. Subj.	qu'il semble
Imp. Subj.	qu'il semblât
Past Indef.	il a semblé
Plup. Ind.	il avait semblé
Past Ant.	il eut semblé
Fut. Perf.	il aura semblé
Cond. Perf.	il aurait semblé
Past Subj.	qu'il ait semblé
Plup. Subj.	qu'il eût semblé
Imperative	[inemployé]

to feel, smell

Pres. Ind.	sens, sens, sent; sentons, sentez, sentent
Imp. Ind.	sentais, sentais, sentait; sentions, sentiez, sentaient
Past Def.	sentis, sentis, sentit; sentîmes, sentîtes, sentirent
Fut. Ind.	sentirai, sentiras, sentira; sentirons, sentirez, sentiront
Condit.	sentirais, sentirais, sentirait; sentirions, sentiriez, sentiraient
Pres. Subj.	sente, sentes, sente; sentions, sentiez, sentent
Imp. Subj.	sentisse, sentisses, sentît; sentissions, sentissiez, sentissent
Past Indef.	ai senti, as senti, a senti; avons senti, avez senti, ont senti
Pluperf.	avais senti, avais senti, avait senti; avions senti, aviez senti, avaient senti
Past Ant.	eus senti, eus senti, eut senti; eûmes senti, eûtes senti, eurent senti
Fut. Perf.	aurai senti, auras senti, aura senti; aurons senti, aurez senti, auront senti
Cond. Perf.	aurais senti, aurais senti, aurait senti; aurions senti, auriez senti, auraient senti
Past Subj.	aie senti, aies senti, ait senti; ayons senti, ayez senti, aient senti
Plup. Subj.	eusse senti, eusses senti, eût senti; eussions senti, eussiez senti, eussent senti
Imperative	sens, sentons, sentez

to be becoming, suit

Pres. Ind.	il sied; ils siéent
Imp. Ind.	il seyait; ils seyaient
Future	il siéra; ils siéront
Condit.	il siérait; ils siéraient
Pres. Subj.	qu'il siée; qu'ils siéent

* This verb is used only in the above persons and tenses.

to grasp, press, shake (hands), squeeze

Pres. Ind.	serre, serres, serre; serrons, serrez, serrent
Imp. Ind.	serrais, serrais, serrait; serrions, serriez, serraient
Past Def.	serrai, serras, serra; serrâmes, serrâtes, serrèrent
Future	serrerai, serreras, serrera; serrerons, serrerez, serreront
Condit.	serrerais, serrerais, serrerait; serrerions, serreriez, serreraient
Pres. Subj.	serre, serres, serre; serrions, serriez, serrent
Imp. Subj.	serrasse, serrasses, serrât; serrassions, serrassiez, serrassent
Past Indef.	ai serré, as serré, a serré; avons serré, avez serré, ont serré
Plup. Ind.	avais serré, avais serré, avait serré; avions serré, aviez serré, avaient serré
Past Ant.	eus serré, eus serré, eut serré; eûmes serré, eûtes serré, eurent serré
Fut. Perf.	aurai serré, auras serré, aura serré; aurons serré, aurez serré, auront serré
Cond. Perf.	aurais serré, aurais serré, aurait serré; aurions serré, auriez serré, auraient serré
Past Subj.	aie serré, aies serré, ait serré; ayons serré, ayez serré, aient serré
Plup. Subj.	eusse serré, eusses serré, eût serré; eussions serré, eussiez serré, eussent serré
Imperative	serre, serrons, serrez

to serve

Pres. Ind.	sers, sers, sert; servons, servez, servent
Imp. Ind.	servais, servais, servait; servions, serviez, servaient
Past Def.	servis, servis, servit; servîmes, servîtes, servirent
Fut. Ind.	servirai, serviras, servira; servirons, servirez, serviront
Condit.	servirais, servirais, servirait; servirions, serviriez, serviraient
Pres. Subj.	serve, serves, serve; servions, serviez, servent
Imp. Subj.	servisse, servisses, servît; servissions, servissiez, servissent
Past Indef.	ai servi, as servi, a servi; avons servi, avez servi, ont servi
Pluperf.	avais servi, avais servi, avait servi; avions servi, aviez servi, avaient servi
Past Ant.	eus servi, eus servi, eut servi; eûmes servi, eûtes servi, eurent servi
Fut. Perf.	aurai servi, auras servi, aura servi; aurons servi, aurez servi, auront servi
Cond. Perf.	aurais servi, aurais servi, aurait servi; aurions servi, auriez servi, auraient servi
Past Subj.	aie servi, aies servi, ait servi; ayons servi, ayez servi, aient servi
Plup. Subj.	eusse servi, eusses servi, eût servi; eussions servi, eussiez servi, eussent servi
Imperative	sers, servons, servez

to serve oneself, help oneself (to food and drink)

Pres. Ind.	me sers, te sers, se sert; nous servons, vous servez, se servent
Imp. Ind.	me servais, te servais, se servait; nous servions, vous serviez, se servaient
Past Def.	me servis, te servis, se servit; nous servîmes, vous servîtes, se servirent
Future	me servirai, te serviras, se servira; nous servirons, vous servirez, se serviront
Condit.	me servirais, te servirais, se servirait; nous servirions, vous serviriez, se serviraient
Pres. Subj.	me serve, te serves, se serve; nous servions, vous serviez, se servent
Imp. Subj.	me servisse, te servisses, se servît; nous servissions, vous servissiez, se servissent
Past Indef.	me suis servi(e), t'es servi(e), s'est servi(e); nous sommes servi(e)s, vous êtes servi(e)(s), se sont servi(e)s
Plup. Ind.	m'étais servi(e), t'étais servi(e), s'était servi(e); nous étions servi(e)s, vous étiez servi(e)(s), s'étaient servi(e)s
Past Ant.	me fus servi(e), te fus servi(e), se fut servi(e); nous fûmes servi(e)s, vous fûtes servi(e)(s), se furent servi(e)s
Fut. Perf.	me serai servi(e), te seras servi(e), se sera servi(e); nous serons servi(e)s, vous serez servi(e)(s), se seront servi(e)s
Cond. Perf.	me serais servi(e), te serais servi(e), se serait servi(e); nous serions servi(e)s, vous seriez servi(e)(s), se seraient servi(e)s
Past Subj.	me sois servi(e), te sois servi(e), se soit servi(e); nous soyons servi(e)s, vous soyez servi(e)(s), se soient servi(e)s
Plup. Subj.	me fusse servi(e), te fusses servi(e), se fût servi(e); nous fussions servi(e)s, vous fussiez servi(e)(s), se fussent servi(e)s
Imperative	sers-toi, servons-nous, servez-vous

to whistle, hiss

Pres. Ind.	siffle, siffles, siffle; sifflons, sifflez, sifflent
Imp. Ind.	sifflais, sifflais, sifflait; sifflions, siffliez, sifflaient
Past Def.	sifflai, sifflas, siffla; sifflâmes, sifflâtes, sifflèrent
Future	sifflerai, siffleras, sifflera; sifflerons, sifflerez, siffleront
Condit.	sifflerais, sifflerais, sifflerait; sifflerions, siffleriez, siffleraient
Pres. Subj.	siffle, siffles, siffle; sifflions, siffliez, sifflent
Imp. Subj.	sifflasse, sifflasses, sifflât; sifflassions, sifflassiez, sifflassent
Past Indef.	ai sifflé, as sifflé, a sifflé; avons sifflé, avez sifflé, ont sifflé
Pluperf.	avais sifflé, avais sifflé, avait sifflé; avions sifflé, aviez sifflé, avaient sifflé
Past Ant.	eus sifflé, eus sifflé, eut sifflé; eûmes sifflé, eûtes sifflé, eurent sifflé
Fut. Perf.	aurai sifflé, auras sifflé, aura sifflé; aurons sifflé, aurez sifflé, auront sifflé
Cond. Perf.	aurais sifflé, aurais sifflé, aurait sifflé; aurions sifflé, auriez sifflé, auraient sifflé
Past Subj.	aie sifflé, aies sifflé, ait sifflé; ayons sifflé, ayez sifflé, aient sifflé
Plup. Subj.	eusse sifflé, eusses sifflé, eût sifflé; eussions sifflé, eussiez sifflé, eussent sifflé
Imperative	siffle, sifflons, sifflez

to dream, think

Pres. Ind.	songe, songes, songe; songeons, songez, songent
Imp. Ind.	songeais, songeais, songeait; songions, songiez, songeaient
Past Def.	songeai, songeas, songea; songeâmes, songeâtes, songèrent
Fut. Ind.	songerai, songeras, songera; songerons, songerez, songeront
Condit.	songerais, songerais, songerait; songerions, songeriez, songeraient
Pres. Subj.	songe, songes, songe; songions, songiez, songent
Imp. Subj.	songeasse, songeasses, songeât; songeassions, songeassiez, songeassent
Past Indef.	ai songé, as songé, a songé; avons songé, avez songé, ont songé
Pluperf.	avais songé, avais songé, avait songé; avions songé, aviez songé, avaient songé
Past Ant.	eus songé, eus songé, eut songé; eûmes songé, eûtes songé, eurent songé
Fut. Perf.	aurai songé, auras songé, aura songé; aurons songé, aurez songé, auront songé
Cond. Perf.	aurais songé, aurais songé, aurait songé; aurions songé, auriez songé, auraient songé
Past Subj.	aie songé, aies songé, ait songé; ayons songé, ayez songé, aient songé
Plup. Subj.	eusse songé, eusses songé, eût songé; eussions songé, eussiez songé, eussent songé
Imperative	songe, songeons, songez

to go out, leave

Pres. Ind.	sors, sors, sort; sortons, sortez, sortent
Imp. Ind.	sortais, sortais, sortait; sortions, sortiez, sortaient
Past Def.	sortis, sortis, sortit; sortîmes, sortîtes, sortirent
Fut. Ind.	sortirai, sortiras, sortira; sortirons, sortirez, sortiront
Condit.	sortirais, sortirais, sortirait; sortirions, sortiriez, sortiraient
Pres. Subj.	sorte, sortes, sorte; sortions, sortiez, sortent
Imp. Subj.	sortisse, sortisses, sortît; sortissions, sortissiez, sortissent
Past Indef.	suis sorti(e), es sorti(e), est sorti(e); sommes sorti(e)s, êtes sorti(e)(s), sont sorti(e)s
Pluperf.	étais sorti(e), étais sorti(e), était sorti(e); étions sorti(e)s, étiez sorti(e)(s), étaient sorti(e)s
Past Ant.	fus sorti(e), fus sorti(e), fut sorti(e); fûmes sorti(e)s, fûtes sorti(e)(s), furent sorti(e)s
Fut. Perf.	serai sorti(e), seras sorti(e), sera sorti(e); serons sorti(e)s, serez sorti(e)(s), seront sorti(e)s
Cond. Perf.	serais sorti(e), serais sorti(e), serait sorti(e); serions sorti(e)s, seriez sorti(e)(s), seraient sorti(e)s
Past Subj.	sois sorti(e), sois sorti(e), soit sorti(e); soyons sorti(e)s, soyez sorti(e)(s), soient sorti(e)s
Plup. Subj.	fusse sorti(e), fusses sorti(e), fût sorti(e); fussions sorti(e)s, fussiez sorti(e)(s), fussent sorti(e)s
Imperative	sors, sortons, sortez

to blow, pant, prompt (an actor with a cue)

Pres. Ind.	souffle, souffles, souffle; soufflons, soufflez, soufflent
Imp. Ind.	soufflais, soufflais, soufflait; soufflions, souffliez, soufflaient
Past Def.	soufflai, soufflas, souffla; soufflâmes, soufflâtes, soufflèrent
Future	soufflerai, souffleras, soufflera; soufflerons, soufflerez, souffleront
Condit.	soufflerais, soufflerais, soufflerait; soufflerions, souffleriez, souffleraient
Pres. Subj.	souffle, souffles, souffle; soufflions, souffliez, soufflent
Imp. Subj.	soufflasse, soufflasses, soufflât; soufflassions, soufflassiez, soufflassent
Past Indef.	ai soufflé, as soufflé, a soufflé; avons soufflé, avez soufflé, ont soufflé
Pluperf.	avais soufflé, avais soufflé, avait soufflé; avions soufflé, aviez soufflé, avaient soufflé
Past Ant.	eus soufflé, eus soufflé, eut soufflé; eûmes soufflé, eûtes soufflé, eurent soufflé
Fut. Perf.	aurai soufflé, auras soufflé, aura soufflé; aurons soufflé, aurez soufflé, auront soufflé
Cond. Perf.	aurais soufflé, aurais soufflé, aurait soufflé; aurions soufflé, auriez soufflé, auraient soufflé
Past Subj.	aie soufflé, aies soufflé, ait soufflé; ayons soufflé, ayez soufflé, aient soufflé
Plup. Subj.	eusse soufflé, eusses soufflé, eût soufflé; eussions soufflé, eussiez soufflé, eussent soufflé
Imperative	souffle, soufflons, soufflez

to wish

Pres. Ind.	souhaite, souhaites, souhaite; souhaitons, souhaitez, souhaitent
Imp. Ind.	souhaitais, souhaitais, souhaitait; souhaitions, souhaitiez, souhaitaient
Past Def.	souhaitai, souhaitas, souhaita; souhaitâmes, souhaitâtes, souhaitèrent
Future	souhaiterai, souhaiteras, souhaitera; souhaiterons, souhaiterez, souhaiteront
Condit.	souhaiterais, souhaiterais, souhaiterait; souhaiterions, souhaiteriez, souhaiteraient
Pres. Subj.	souhaite, souhaites, souhaite; souhaitions, souhaitiez, souhaitent
Imp. Subj.	souhaitasse, souhaitasses, souhaitât; souhaitassions, souhaitassiez, souhaitassent
Past Indef.	ai souhaité, as souhaité, a souhaité; avons souhaité, avez souhaité, ont souhaité
Plup. Ind.	avais souhaité, avais souhaité, avait souhaité; avions souhaité, aviez souhaité, avaient souhaité
Past Ant.	eus souhaité, eus souhaité, eut souhaité; eûmes souhaité, eûtes souhaité, eurent souhaité
Fut. Perf.	aurai souhaité, auras souhaité, aura souhaité; aurons souhaité, aurez souhaité, auront souhaité
Cond. Perf.	aurais souhaité, aurais souhaité, aurait souhaité; aurions souhaité, auriez souhaité, auraient souhaité
Past Subj.	aie souhaité, aies souhaité, ait souhaité; ayons souhaité, ayez souhaité, aient souhaité
Plup. Subj.	eusse souhaité, eusses souhaité, eût souhaité; eussions souhaité, eussiez souhaité, eussent souhaité
Imperative	souhaite, souhaitons, souhaitez

to dirty, muddy, soil

Pres. Ind.	souille, souilles, souille; souillons, souillez, souillent
Imp. Ind.	souillais, souillais, souillait; souillions, souilliez, souillaient
Past Def.	souillai, souillas, souilla; souillâmes, souillâtes, souillèrent
Future	souillerai, souilleras, souillera; souillerons, souillerez, souilleront
Condit.	souillerais, souillerais, souillerait; souillerions, souilleriez, souilleraient
Pres. Subj.	souille, souilles, souille; souillions, souilliez, souillent
Imp. Subj.	souillasse, souillasses, souillât; souillassions, souillassiez, souillassent
Past Indef.	ai souillé, as souillé, a souillé; avons souillé, avez souillé, ont souillé
Plup. Ind.	avais souillé, avais souillé, avait souillé; avions souillé, aviez souillé, avaient souillé
Past Ant.	eus souillé, eus souillé, eut souillé; eûmes souillé, eûtes souillé, eurent souillé
Fut. Perf.	aurai souillé, auras souillé, aura souillé; aurons souillé, aurez souillé, auront souillé
Cond. Perf.	aurais souillé, aurais souillé, aurait souillé; aurions souillé, auriez souillé, auraient souillé
Past Subj.	aie souillé, aies souillé, ait souillé; ayons souillé, ayez souillé, aient souillé
Plup. Subj.	eusse souillé, eusses souillé, eût souillé; eussions souillé, eussiez souillé, eussent souillé
Imperative	souille, souillons, souillez

to submit

Pres. Ind.	soumets, soumets, soumet; soumettons, soumettez, soumettent
Imp. Ind.	soumettais, soumettais, soumettait; soumettions, soumettiez, soumettaient
Past Def.	soumis, soumis, soumit; soumîmes, soumîtes, soumirent
Future	soumettrai, soumettras, soumettra; soumettrons, soumettrez, soumettront
Condit.	soumettrais, soumettrais, soumettrait; soumettrions, soumettriez, soumettraient
Pres. Subj.	soumette, soumettes, soumette; soumettions, soumettiez, soumettent
Imp. Subj.	soumisse, soumisses, soumît; soumissions, soumissiez, soumissent
Past Indef.	ai soumis, as soumis, a soumis; avons soumis, avez soumis, ont soumis
Pluperf.	avais soumis, avais soumis, avait soumis; avions soumis, aviez soumis, avaient soumis
Past Ant.	eus soumis, eus soumis, eut soumis; eûmes soumis, eûtes soumis, eurent soumis
Fut. Perf.	aurai soumis, auras soumis, aura soumis; aurons soumis, aurez soumis, auront soumis
Cond. Perf.	aurais soumis, aurais soumis, aurait soumis; aurions soumis, auriez soumis, auraient soumis
Past Subj.	aie soumis, aies soumis, ait soumis; ayons soumis, ayez soumis, aient soumis
Plup. Subj.	eusse soumis, eusses soumis, eût soumis; eussions soumis, eussiez soumis, eussent soumis
Imperative	soumets, soumettons, soumettez

to sup, have supper

Pres. Ind.	soupe, soupes, soupe; soupons, soupez, soupent
Imp. Ind.	soupais, soupais, soupait; soupions, soupiez, soupaient
Past Def.	soupai, soupas, soupa; soupâmes, soupâtes, soupèrent
Future	souperai, souperas, soupera; souperons, souperez, souperont
Condit.	souperais, souperais, souperait; souperions, souperiez, souperaient
Pres. Subj.	soupe, soupes, soupe; soupions, soupiez, soupent
Imp. Subj.	soupasse, soupasses, soupât; soupassions, soupassiez, soupassent
Past Indef.	ai soupé, as soupé, a soupé; avons soupé, avez soupé, ont soupé
Plup. Ind.	avais soupé, avais soupé, avait soupé; avions soupé, aviez soupé, avaient soupé
Past Ant.	eus soupé, eus soupé, eut soupé; eûmes soupé, eûtes soupé, eurent soupé
Fut. Perf.	aurai soupé, auras soupé, aura soupé; aurons soupé, aurez soupé, auront soupé
Cond. Perf.	aurais soupé, aurais soupé, aurait soupé; aurions soupé, auriez soupé, auraient soupé
Past Subj.	aie soupé, aies soupé, ait soupé; ayons soupé, ayez soupé, aient soupé
Plup. Subj.	eusse soupé, eusses soupé, eût soupé; eussions soupé, eussiez soupé, eussent soupé
Imperative	soupe, soupons, soupez

to sigh

Pres. Ind.	soupire, soupires, soupire; soupirons, soupirez, soupirent
Imp. Ind.	soupirais, soupirais, soupirait; soupirions, soupiriez, soupiraient
Past Def.	soupirai, soupiras, soupira; soupirâmes, soupirâtes, soupirèrent
Future	soupirerai, soupireras, soupirera; soupirerons, soupirerez, soupireront
Condit.	soupirerais, soupirerais, soupirerait; soupirerions, soupireriez, soupireraient
Pres. Subj.	soupire, soupires, soupire; soupirions, soupiriez, soupirent
Imp. Subj.	soupirasse, soupirasses, soupirât; soupirassions, soupirassiez, soupirassent
Past Indef.	ai soupiré, as soupiré, a soupiré; avons soupiré, avez soupiré, ont soupiré
Plup. Ind.	avais soupiré, avais soupiré, avait soupiré; avions soupiré, aviez soupiré, avaient soupiré
Past Ant.	eus soupiré, eus soupiré, eut soupiré; eûmes soupiré, eûtes soupiré, eurent soupiré
Fut. Perf.	aurai soupiré, auras soupiré, aura soupiré; aurons soupiré, aurez soupiré, auront soupiré
Cond. Perf.	aurais soupiré, aurais soupiré, aurait soupiré; aurions soupiré, auriez soupiré, auraient soupiré
Past Subj.	aie soupiré, aies soupiré, ait soupiré; ayons soupiré, ayez soupiré, aient soupiré
Plup. Subj.	eusse soupiré, eusses soupiré, eût soupiré; eussions soupiré, eussiez soupiré, eussent soupiré
Imperative	soupire, soupirons, soupirez

to smile

Pres. Ind.	souris, souris, sourit; sourions, souriez, sourient
Imp. Ind.	souriais, souriais, souriait; souriions, souriiez, souriaient
Past Def.	souris, souris, sourit; sourîmes, sourîtes, souriren
Future	sourirai, souriras, sourira; sourirons, sourirez, souriront
Condit.	sourirais, sourirais, sourirait; souririons, souririez, souriraient
Pres. Subj.	sourie, souries, sourie; souriions, souriiez, sourient
Imp. Subj.	sourisse, sourisses, sourît; sourissions, sourissiez, sourissent
Past Indef.	ai souri, as souri, a souri; avons souri, avez souri, ont souri
Pluperf.	avais souri, avais souri, avait souri; avions souri, aviez souri, avaient souri
Past Ant.	eus souri, eus souri, eut souri; eûmes souri, eûtes souri, eurent souri
Fut. Perf.	aurai souri, auras souri, aura souri; aurons souri, aurez souri, auront souri
Cond. Perf.	aurais souri, aurais souri, aurait souri; aurions souri, auriez souri, auraient souri
Past Subj.	aie souri, aies souri, ait souri; ayons souri, ayez souri, aient souri
Plup. Subj.	eusse souri, eusses souri, eût souri; eussions souri, eussiez souri, eussent souri
Imperative	souris, sourions, souriez

to remember, recall

Pres. Ind.	me souviens, te souviens, se souvient; nous souvenons, vous souvenez, se souviennent
Imp. Ind.	me souvenais, te souvenais, se souvenait; nous souvenions, vous souveniez, se souvenaient
Past Def.	me souvins, te souvins, se souvint; nous souvînmes, vous souvîntes, se souvinrent
Future	me souviendrai, te souviendras, se souviendra; nous souviendrons, vous souviendrez, se souviendront
Condit.	me souviendrais, te souviendrais, se souviendrait; nous souviendrions, vous souviendriez, se souviendraient
Pres. Subj.	me souvienne, te souviennes, se souvienne; nous souvenions, vous souveniez, se souviennent
Imp. Subj.	me souvinsse, te souvinsses, se souvînt; nous souvinssions, vous souvinssiez, se souvinssent
Past Indef.	me suis souvenu(e), t'es souvenu(e), s'est souvenu(e); nous sommes souvenu(e)s, vous êtes souvenu(e)(s), se sont souvenu(e)s
Pluperf.	m'étais souvenu(e), t'étais souvenu(e), s'était souvenu(e); nous étions souvenu(e)s, vous étiez souvenu(e)(s), s'étaient souvenu(e)s
Past Ant.	me fus souvenu(e), te fus souvenu(e), se fut souvenu(e); nous fûmes souvenu(e)s, vous fûtes souvenu(e)(s), se furent souvenu(e)s
Fut. Perf.	me serai souvenu(e), te seras souvenu(e), se sera souvenu(e); nous serons souvenu(e)s, vous serez souvenu(e)(s), se seront souvenu(e)s
Cond. Perf.	me serais souvenu(e), te serais souvenu(e), se serait souvenu(e); nous serions souvenu(e)s, vous seriez souvenu(e)(s), se seraient souvenu(e)s
Past Subj.	me sois souvenu(e), te sois souvenu(e), se soit souvenu(e); nous soyons souvenu(e)s, vous soyez souvenu(e)(s), se soient souvenu(e)s
Plup. Subj.	me fusse souvenu(e), te fusses souvenu(e), se fût souvenu(e); nous fussions souvenu(e)s, vous fussiez souvenu(e)(s), se fussent souvenu(e)s
Imperative	souviens-toi, souvenons-nous, souvenez-vous

to station, park (a car)

Pres. Ind.	stationne, stationnes, stationne; stationnons, stationnez, stationnent
Imp. Ind.	stationnais, stationnais, stationnait; stationnions, stationniez, stationnaient
Past Def.	stationnai, stationnas, stationna; stationnâmes, stationnâtes, stationnèrent
Future	stationnerai, stationneras, stationnera; stationnerons, stationnerez, stationneront
Condit.	stationnerais, stationnerais, stationnerait; stationnerions, stationneriez, stationneraient
Pres. Subj.	stationne, stationnes, stationne; stationnions, stationniez, stationnent
Imp. Subj.	stationnasse, stationnasses, stationnât; stationnassions, stationnassiez, stationnassent
Past Indef.	ai stationné, as stationné, a stationné; avons stationné, avez stationné, ont stationné
Plup. Ind.	avais stationné, avais stationné, avait stationné; avions stationné, aviez stationné, avaient stationné
Past Ant.	eus stationné, eus stationné, eut stationné; eûmes stationné, eûtes stationné, eurent stationné
Fut. Perf.	aurai stationné, auras stationné, aura stationné; aurons stationné, aurez stationné, auront stationné
Cond. Perf.	aurais stationné, aurais stationné, aurait stationné; aurions stationné, auriez stationné, auraient stationné
Past Subj.	aie stationné, aies stationné, ait stationné; ayons stationné, ayez stationné, aient stationné
Plup. Subj.	eusse stationné, eusses stationné, eût stationné; eussions stationné, eussiez stationné, eussent stationné
Imperative	stationne, stationnons, stationnez

to suck

Pres. Ind.	suce, suces, suce; suçons, sucez, sucent
Imp. Ind.	suçais, suçais, suçait; sucions, suciez, suçaient
Past Def.	suçai, suças, suça; suçâmes, suçâtes, sucèrent
Future	sucerai, suceras, sucera; sucerons, sucerez, suceront
Condit.	sucerais, sucerais, sucerait; sucerions, suceriez, suceraient
Pres. Subj.	suce, suces, suce; sucions, suciez, sucent
Imp. Subj.	suçasse, suçasses, suçât; suçassions, suçassiez, suçassent
Past Indef.	ai sucé, as sucé, a sucé; avons sucé, avez sucé, ont sucé
Pluperf.	avais sucé, avais sucé, avait sucé; avions sucé, aviez sucé, avaient sucé
Past Ant.	eus sucé, eus sucé, eut sucé; eûmes sucé, eûtes sucé, eurent sucé
Fut. Perf.	aurai sucé, auras sucé, aura sucé; aurons sucé, aurez sucé, auront sucé
Cond. Perf.	aurais sucé, aurais sucé, aurait sucé; aurions sucé, auriez sucé, auraient sucé
Past Subj.	aie sucé, aies sucé, ait sucé; ayons sucé, ayez sucé, aient sucé
Plup. Subj.	eusse sucé, eusses sucé, eût sucé; eussions sucé, eussiez sucé, eussent sucé
Imperative	suce, suçons, sucez

to suffice,
be sufficient,
be enough

Pres. Ind.	il suffit
Imp. Ind.	il suffisait
Past Def.	il suffit
Future	il suffira
Condit.	il suffirait
Pres. Subj.	qu'il suffise
Imp. Subj.	qu'll suffît
Past Indef.	il a suffi
Plup. Ind.	il avait suffi
Past Ant.	il eut suffi
Fut. Perf.	il aura suffi
Cond. Perf.	il aurait suffi
Past Subj.	qu'il ait suffi
Plup. Subj.	qu'il eût suffi
Imperative	[inemployé]

to follow

Pres. Ind.	suis, suis, suit; suivons, suivez, suivent
Imp. Ind.	suivais, suivais, suivait; suivions, suiviez, suivaient
Past Def.	suivis, suivis, suivit; suivîmes, suivîtes, suivirent
Fut. Ind.	suivrai, suivras, suivra; suivrons, suivrez, suivront
Condit.	suivrais, suivrais, suivrait; suivrions, suivriez, suivraient
Pres. Subj.	suive, suives, suive; suivions, suiviez, suivent
Imp. Subj.	suivisse, suivisses, suivît; suivissions, suivissiez, suivissent
Past Indef.	ai suivi, as suivi, a suivi; avons suivi, avez suivi, ont suivi
Pluperf.	avais suivi, avais suivi, avait suivi; avions suivi, aviez suivi, avaient suivi
Past Ant.	eus suivi, eus suivi, eut suivi; eûmes suivi, eûtes suivi, eurent suivi
Fut. Perf.	aurai suivi, auras suivi, aura suivi; aurons suivi, aurez suivi, auront suivi
Cond. Perf.	aurais suivi, aurais suivi, aurait suivi; aurions suivi, auriez suivi, auraient suivi
Past Subj.	aie suivi, aies suivi, ait suivi; ayons suivi, ayez suivi, aient suivi
Plup. Subj.	eusse suivi, eusses suivi, eût suivi; eussions suivi, eussiez suivi, eussent suivi
Imperative	suis, suivons, suivez

to beg, beseech, implore, supplicate

Pres. Ind.	supplie, supplies, supplie; supplions, suppliez, supplient
Imp. Ind.	suppliais, suppliais, suppliait; suppliions, suppliiez, suppliaient
Past Def.	suppliai, supplias, supplia; suppliâmes, suppliâtes, supplièrent
Future	supplierai, supplieras, suppliera; supplierons, supplierez, supplieront
Condit.	supplierais, supplierais, supplierait; supplierions, supplieriez, supplieraient
Pres. Subj.	supplie, supplies, supplie; suppliions, suppliiez, supplient
Imp. Subj.	suppliasse, suppliasses, suppliât; suppliassions, suppliassiez, suppliassent
Past Indef.	ai supplié, as supplié, a supplié; avons supplié, avez supplié, ont supplié
Plup. Ind.	avais supplié, avais supplié, avait supplié; avions supplié, aviez supplié, avaient supplié
Past Ant.	eus supplié, eus supplié, eut supplié; eûmes supplié, eûtes supplié, eurent supplié
Fut. Perf.	aurai supplié, auras supplié, aura supplié; aurons supplié, aurez supplié, auront supplié
Cond. Perf.	aurais supplié, aurais supplié, aurait supplié; aurions supplié, auriez supplié, auraient supplié
Past Subj.	aie supplié, aies supplié, ait supplié; ayons supplié, ayez supplié, aient supplié
Plup. Subj.	eusse supplié, eusses supplié, eût supplié; eussions supplié, eussiez supplié, eussent supplié
Imperative	supplie, supplions, suppliez

to hold up, prop up, support

Pres. Ind.	supporte, supportes, supporte; supportons, supportez, supportent
Imp. Ind.	supportais, supportais, supportait; supportions, supportiez, supportaient
Past Def.	supportai, supportas, supporta; supportâmes, supportâtes, supportèrent
Future	supporterai, supporteras, supportera; supporterons, supporterez, supporteront
Condit.	supporterais, supporterais, supporterait; supporterions, supporteriez, supporteraient
Pres. Subj.	supporte, supportes, supporte; supportions, supportiez, supportent
Imp. Subj.	supportasse, supportasses, supportât; supportassions, supportassiez, supportassent
Past Indef.	ai supporté, as supporté, a supporté; avons supporté, avez supporté, ont supporté
Plup. Ind.	avais supporté, avais supporté, avait supporté; avions supporté, aviez supporté, avaient supporté
Past Ant.	eus supporté, eus supporté, eut supporté; eûmes supporté, eûtes supporté, eurent supporté
Fut. Perf.	aurai supporté, auras supporté, aura supporté; aurons supporté, aurez supporté, auront supporté
Cond. Perf.	aurais supporté, aurais supporté. aurait supporté; aurions supporté, auriez supporté, auraient supporté
Past Subj.	aie supporté, aies supporté, ait supporté; ayons supporté, ayez supporté, aient supporté
Plup. Subj.	eusse supporté, eusses supporté, eût supporté; eussions supporté, eussiez supporté, eussent supporté
Imperative	supporte, supportons, supportez

to suppose

Pres. Ind.	suppose, supposes, suppose; supposons, supposez, supposent
Imp. Ind.	supposais, supposais, supposait; supposions, supposiez, supposaient
Past Def.	supposai, supposas, supposa; supposâmes, supposâtes, supposèrent
Future	supposerai, supposeras, supposera; supposerons, supposerez, supposeront
Condit.	supposerais, supposerais, supposerait; supposerions, supposeriez, supposeraient
Pres. Subj.	suppose, supposes, suppose; supposions, supposiez, supposent
Imp. Subj.	supposasse, supposasses, supposât; supposassions, supposassiez, supposassent
Past Indef.	ai supposé, as supposé, a supposé; avons supposé, avez supposé, ont supposé
Plup. Ind.	avais supposé, avais supposé, avait supposé; avions supposé, aviez supposé, avaient supposé
Past Ant.	eus supposé, eus supposé, eut supposé; eûmes supposé, eûtes supposé, eurent supposé
Fut. Perf.	aurai supposé, auras supposé, aura supposé; aurons supposé, aurez supposé, auront supposé
Cond. Perf.	aurais supposé, aurais supposé, aurait supposé; aurions supposé, auriez supposé, auraient supposé
Past Subj.	aie supposé, aies supposé, ait supposé; ayons supposé, ayez supposé, aient supposé
Plup. Subj.	eusse supposé, eusses supposé, eût supposé; eussions supposé, eussiez supposé, eussent supposé
Imperative	suppose, supposons, supposez

to surprise

Pres. Ind.	surprends, surprends, surprend; surprenons, surprenez, surprennent
Imp. Ind.	surprenais, surprenais, surprenait; surprenions, surpreniez, surprenaient
Past Def.	surpris, surpris, surprit; surprîmes, surprîtes, surprirent
Future	surprendrai, surprendras, surprendra; surprendrons, surprendrez, surprendront
Condit.	surprendrais, surprendrais, surprendrait; surprendrions, surprendriez, surprendraient
Pres. Subj.	surprenne, surprennes, surprenne; surprenions, surpreniez, surprennent
Imp. Subj.	surprisse, surprisses, surprît; surprissions, surprissiez, surprissent
Past Indef.	ai surpris, as surpris, a surpris; avons surpris, avez surpris, ont surpris
Plup. Ind.	avais surpris, avais surpris, avait surpris; avions surpris, aviez surpris, avaient surpris
Past Ant.	eus surpris, eus surpris, eut surpris; eûmes surpris, eûtes surpris, eurent surpris
Fut. Perf.	aurai surpris, auras surpris, aura surpris; aurons surpris, aurez surpris, auront surpris
Cond. Perf.	aurais surpris, aurais surpris, aurait surpris; aurions surpris, auriez surpris, auraient surpris
Past Subj.	aie surpris, aies surpris, ait surpris; ayons surpris, ayez surpris, aient surpris
Plup. Subj.	eusse surpris, eusses surpris, eût surpris; eussions surpris, eussiez surpris, eussent surpris
Imperative	surprends, surprenons, surprenez

to survive

Pres. Ind.	survis, survis, survit; survivons, survivez, survivent
Imp. Ind.	survivais, survivais, survivait; survivions, surviviez, survivaient
Past Def.	survécus, survécus, survécut; survécûmes, survécûtes, survécurent
Future	survivrai, survivras, survivra; survivrons, survivrez, survivront
Condit.	survivrais, survivrais, survivrait; survivrions, survivriez, survivraient
Pres. Subj.	survive, survives, survive; survivions, surviviez, survivent
Imp. Subj.	survécusse, survécusses, survécût; survécussions, survécussiez, survécussent
Past Indef.	ai survécu, as survécu, a survécu; avons survécu, avez survécu, ont survécu
Plup. Ind.	avais survécu, avais survécu, avait survécu; avions survécu, aviez survécu, avaient survécu
Past Ant.	eus survécu, eus survécu, eut survécu; eûmes survécu, eûtes survécu, eurent survécu
Fut. Perf.	aurai survécu, auras survécu, aura survécu; aurons survécu, aurez survécu, auront survécu
Cond. Perf.	aurais survécu, aurais survécu, aurait survécu; aurions survécu, auriez survécu, auraient survécu
Past Subj.	aie survécu, aies survécu, ait survécu; ayons survécu, ayez survécu, aient survécu
Plup. Subj.	eusse survécu, eusses survécu, eût survécu; eussions survécu, eussiez survécu, eussent survécu
Imperative	survis, survivons, survivez

to fly over

Pres. Ind.	survole, survoles, survole; survolons, survolez, survolent
Imp. Ind.	survolais, survolais, survolait; survolions, survoliez, survolaient
Past Def.	survolai, survolas, survola; survolâmes, survolâtes, survolèrent
Future	survolerai, survoleras, survolera; survolerons, survolerez, survoleront
Condit.	survolerais, survolerais, survolerait; survolerions, survoleriez, survoleraient
Pres. Subj.	survole, survoles, survole; survolions, survoliez, survolent
Imp. Subj.	survolasse, survolasses, survolât; survolassions, survolassiez, survolassent
Past Indef.	ai survolé, as survolé, a survolé; avons survolé, avez survolé, ont survolé
Plup. Ind.	avais survolé, avais survolé, avait survolé; avions survolé, aviez survolé, avaient survolé
Past Ant.	eus survolé, eus survolé, eut survolé; eûmes survolé, eûtes survolé, eurent survolé
Fut. Perf.	aurai survolé, auras survolé, aura survolé; aurons survolé, aurez survolé, auront survolé
Cond. Perf.	aurais survolé, aurais survolé, aurait survolé; aurions survolé, auriez survolé, auraient survolé
Past Subj.	aie survolé, aies survolé, ait survolé; ayons survolé, ayez survolé, aient survolé
Plup. Subj.	eusse survolé, eusses survolé, eût survolé; eussions survolé, eussiez survolé, eussent survolé
Imperative	survole, survolons, survolez

to clip, cut (out), trim

Pres. Ind.	taille, tailles, taille; taillons, taillez, taillent
Imp. Ind.	taillais, taillais, taillait; taillions, tailliez, taillaient
Past Def.	taillai, taillas, tailla; taillâmes, taillâtes, taillèrent
Future	taillerai, tailleras, taillera; taillerons, taillerez, tailleront
Condit.	taillerais, taillerais, taillerait; taillerions, tailleriez, tailleraient
Pres. Subj.	taille, tailles, taille; taillions, tailliez, taillent
Imp. Subj.	taillasse, taillasses, taillât; taillassions, taillassiez, taillassent
Past Indef.	ai talllé, as taillé, a taillé; avons taillé, avez taillé, ont taillé
Plup. Ind.	avais taillé, avais taillé, avait taillé; avions taillé, aviez taillé, avaient taillé
Past Ant.	eus taillé, eus taillé, eut taillé; eûmes taillé, eûtes taillé, eurent taillé
Fut. Perf.	aurai taillé, auras taillé, aura taillé; aurons taillé, aurez taillé, auront taillé
Cond. Perf.	aurais taillé, aurais taillé, aurait taillé; aurions taillé, auriez taillé, auraient taillé
Past Subj.	aie taillé, aies taillé, ait taillé; ayons taillé, ayez taillé, aient taillé
Plup. Subj.	eusse taillé, eusses taillé, eût taillé; eussions taillé, eussiez taillé, eussent taillé
Imperative	taille, taillons, taillez

to be silent, be quiet, not to speak

Pres. Ind.	me tais, te tais, se tait; nous taisons, vous taisez, se taisent
Imp. Ind.	me taisais, te taisais, se taisait; nous taisions, vous taisiez, se taisaient
Past Def.	me tus, te tus, se tut; nous tûmes, vous tûtes, se turent
Fut. Ind.	me tairai, te tairas, se taira; nous tairons, vous tairez, se tairont
Condit.	me tairais, te tairais, se tairait; nous tairions, vous tairiez, se tairaient
Pres. Subj.	me taise, te taises, se taise; nous taisions, vous taisiez, se taisent
Imp. Subj.	me tusse, te tusses, se tût; nous tussions, vous tussiez, se tussent
Past Indef.	me suis tu(e), t'es tu(e), s'est tu(e); nous sommes tu(e)s, vous êtes tu(e)(s), se sont tu(e)s
Pluperf.	m'étais tu(e), t'étais tu(e), s'était tu(e); nous étions tu(e)s, vous étiez tu(e)(s), s'étaient tu(e)s
Past Ant.	me fus tu(e), te fus tu(e), se fut tu(e); nous fûmes tu(e)s, vous fûtes tu(e)(s), se furent tu(e)s
Fut. Perf.	me serai tu(e), te seras tu(e), se sera tu(e); nous serons tu(e)s, vous serez tu(e)(s), se seront tu(e)s
Cond. Perf.	me serais tu(e), te serais tu(e), se serait tu(e); nous serions tu(e)s, vous seriez tu(e)(s), se seraient tu(e)s
Past Subj.	me sois tu(e), te sois tu(e), se soit tu(e); nous soyons tu(e)s, vous soyez tu(e)(s), se soient tu(e)s
Plup. Subj.	me fusse tu(e) te fusses tu(e), se fût tu(e); nous fussions tu(e)s, vous fussiez tu(e)(s), se fussent tu(e)s
Imperative	tais-toi, taisons-nous, taisez-vous

to tap, rap, smack, strike, hit

Pres. Ind.	tape, tapes, tape; tapons, tapez, tapent
Imp. Ind.	tapais, tapais, tapait; tapions, tapiez, tapaient
Past Def.	tapai, tapas, tapa; tapâmes, tapâtes, tapèrent
Future	taperai, taperas, tapera; taperons, taperez, taperont
Condit.	taperais, taperais, taperait; taperions, taperiez, taperaient
Pres. Subj.	tape, tapes, tape; tapions, tapiez, tapent
Imp. Subj.	tapasse, tapasses, tapât; tapassions, tapassiez, tapassent
Past Indef.	ai tapé, as tapé, a tapé; avons tapé, avez tapé, ont tapé
Plup. Ind.	avais tapé, avais tapé, avait tapé; avions tapé, aviez tapé, avaient tapé
Past Ant.	eus tapé, eus tapé, eut tapé; eûmes tapé, eûtes tapé, eurent tapé
Fut. Perf.	aurai tapé, auras tapé, aura tapé; aurons tapé, aurez tapé, auront tapé
Cond. Perf.	aurais tapé, aurais tapé, aurait tapé; aurions tapé, auriez tapé, auraient tapé
Past Subj.	aie tapé, aies tapé, ait tapé; ayons tapé, ayez tapé, aient tapé
Plup. Subj.	eusse tapé, eusses tapé, eût tapé; eussions tapé, eussiez tapé, eussent tapé
Imperative	tape, tapons, tapez

to crouch, lie flat, squat, stoop low

Pres. Ind.	me tapis, te tapis, se tapit; nous tapissons, vous tapissez, se tapissent
Imp. Ind.	me tapissais, te tapissais, se tapissait; nous tapissions, vous tapissiez, se tapissaient
Past Def.	me tapis, te tapis, se tapit; nous tapîmes, vous tapîtes, se tapirent
Future	me tapirai, te tapiras, se tapira; nous tapirons, vous tapirez, se tapiront
Condit.	me tapirais, te tapirais, se tapirait; nous tapirions, vous tapiriez, se tapiraient
Pres. Subj.	me tapisse, te tapisses, se tapisse; nous tapissions, vous tapissiez, se tapissent
Imp. Subj.	me tapisse, te tapisses, se tapît; nous tapissions, vous tapissiez, se tapissent
Past Indef.	me suis tapi(e), t'es tapi(e), s'est tapi(e); nous sommes tapi(e)s, vous êtes tapi(e)(s), se sont tapi(e)s
Plup. Ind.	m'étais tapi(e), t'étais tapi(e), s'était tapi(e); nous étions tapi(e)s, vous étiez tapi(e)(s), s'étaient tapi(e)s
Past Ant.	me fus tapi(e), te fus tapi(e), se fut tapi(e); nous fûmes tapi(e)s, vous fûtes tapi(e)(s), se furent tapi(e)s
Fut. Perf.	me serai tapi(e), te seras tapi(e), se sera tapi(e); nous serons tapi(e)s, vous serez tapi(e)(s), se seront tapi(e)s
Cond. Perf.	me serais tapi(e), te serais tapi(e), se serait tapi(e); nous serions tapi(e)s, vous seriez tapi(e)(s), se seraient tapi(e)s
Past Subj.	me sois tapi(e), te sois tapi(e), se soit tapi(e); nous soyons tapi(e)s, vous soyez tapi(e)(s), se soient tapi(e)s
Plup. Subj.	me fusse tapi(e), te fusses tapi(e), se fût tapi(e); nous fussions tapi(e)s, vous fussiez tapi(e)(s), se fussent tapi(e)s
Imperative	tapis-toi, tapissons-nous, tapissez-vous

to dye

Pres. Ind.	teins, teins, teint; teignons, teignez, teignent
Imp. Ind.	teignais, teignais, teignait; teignions, teigniez, teignaient
Past Def.	teignis, teignis, teignit; teignîmes, teignîtes, teignirent
Future	teindrai, teindras, teindra; teindrons, teindrez, teindront
Condit.	teindrais, teindrais, teindrait; teindrions, teindriez, teindraient
Pres. Subj.	teigne, teignes, teigne; teignions, teigniez, teignent
Imp. Subj.	teignisse, teignisses, teignît; teignissions, teignissiez, teignissent
Past Indef.	ai teint, as teint, a teint; avons teint, avez teint, ont teint
Plup. Ind.	avais teint, avais teint, avait teint; avions teint, aviez teint, avaient teint
Past Ant.	eus teint, eus teint, eut teint; eûmes teint, eûtes teint, eurent teint
Fut. Perf.	aurai teint, auras teint, aura teint; aurons teint, aurez teint, auront teint
Cond. Perf.	aurais teint, aurais teint, aurait teint; aurions teint, auriez teint, auraient teint
Past Subj.	aie teint, aies teint, ait teint; ayons teint, ayez teint, aient teint
Plup. Subj.	eusse teint, eusses teint, eût teint; eussions teint, eussiez teint, eussent teint
Imperative	teins, teignons, teignez

to telephone

Pres. Ind.	téléphone, téléphones, téléphone; téléphonons, téléphonez, téléphonent
Imp. Ind.	téléphonais, téléphonais, téléphonait; téléphonions, téléphoniez, téléphonaient
Past Def.	téléphonai, téléphonas, téléphona; téléphonâmes, téléphonâtes, téléphonèrent
Future	téléphonerai, téléphoneras, téléphonera; téléphonerons, téléphonerez, téléphoneront
Condit.	téléphonerais, téléphonerais, téléphonerait; téléphonerions, téléphoneriez, téléphoneraient
Pres. Subj.	téléphone, téléphones, téléphone; téléphonions, téléphoniez, téléphonent
Imp. Subj.	téléphonasse, téléphonasses, téléphonât; téléphonassions, téléphonassiez, téléphonassent
Past Indef.	ai téléphoné, as téléphoné, a téléphoné; avons téléphoné, avez téléphoné, ont téléphoné
Plup. Ind.	avais téléphoné, avais téléphoné, avait téléphoné; avions téléphoné, aviez téléphoné, avaient téléphoné
Past Ant.	eus téléphoné, eus téléphoné, eut téléphoné; eûmes téléphoné, eûtes téléphoné, eurent téléphoné
Fut. Perf.	aurai téléphoné, auras téléphoné, aura téléphoné; aurons téléphoné, aurez téléphoné, auront téléphoné
Cond. Perf.	aurais téléphoné, aurais téléphoné, aurait téléphoné; aurions téléphoné, auriez téléphoné, auraient téléphoné
Past Subj.	aie téléphoné, aies téléphoné, ait téléphoné; ayons téléphoné, ayez téléphoné, aient téléphoné
Plup. Subj.	eusse téléphoné, eusses téléphoné, eût téléphoné; eussions téléphoné, eussiez téléphoné, eussent téléphoné
Imperative	téléphone, téléphonons, téléphonez

to strain, stretch, tighten

Pres. Ind.	tends, tends, tend; tendons, tendez, tendent
Imp. Ind.	tendais, tendais, tendait; tendions, tendiez, tendaient
Past Def.	tendis, tendis, tendit; tendîmes, tendîtes, tendirent
Future	tendrai, tendras, tendra; tendrons, tendrez, tendront
Condit.	tendrais, tendrais, tendrait; tendrions, tendriez, tendraient
Pres. Subj.	tende, tendes, tende; tendions, tendiez, tendent
Imp. Subj.	tendisse, tendisses, tendît; tendissions, tendissiez, tendissent
Past Indef.	ai tendu, as tendu, a tendu; avons tendu, avez tendu, ont tendu
Plup. Ind.	avais tendu, avais tendu, avait tendu; avions tendu, aviez tendu, avaient tendu
Past Ant.	eus tendu, eus tendu, eut tendu; eûmes tendu, eûtes tendu, eurent tendu
Fut. Perf.	aurai tendu, auras tendu, aura tendu; aurons tendu, aurez tendu, auront tendu
Cond. Perf.	aurais tendu, aurais tendu, aurait tendu; aurions tendu, auriez tendu, auraient tendu
Past Subj.	aie tendu, aies tendu, ait tendu; ayons tendu, ayez tendu, aient tendu
Plup. Subj.	eusse tendu, eusses tendu, eût tendu; eussions tendu, eussiez tendu, eussent tendu
Imperative	tends, tendons, tendez

to hold, have

Pres. Ind.	tiens, tiens, tient; tenons, tenez, tiennent
Imp. Ind.	tenais, tenais, tenait; tenions, teniez, tenaient
Past Def.	tins, tins, tint; tînmes, tîntes, tinrent
Fut. Ind.	tiendrai, tiendras, tiendra; tiendrons, tiendrez, tiendront
Condit.	tiendrais, tiendrais, tiendrait; tiendrions, tiendriez, tiendraient
Pres. Subj.	tienne, tiennes, tienne; tenions, teniez, tiennent
Imp. Subj.	tinsse, tinsses, tînt; tinssions, tinssiez, tinssent
Past Indef.	ai tenu, as tenu, a tenu; avons tenu, avez tenu, ont tenu
Pluperf.	avais tenu, avais tenu, avait tenu; avions tenu, aviez tenu, avaient tenu
Past Ant.	eus tenu, eus tenu, eut tenu; eûmes tenu, eûtes tenu, eurent tenu
Fut. Perf.	aurai tenu, auras tenu, aura tenu; aurons tenu, aurez tenu, auront tenu
Cond. Perf.	aurais tenu, aurais tenu, aurait tenu; aurions tenu, auriez tenu, auraient tenu
Past Subj.	aie tenu, aies tenu, ait tenu; ayons tenu, ayez tenu, aient tenu
Plup. Subj.	eusse tenu, eusses tenu, eût tenu; eussions tenu, eussiez tenu, eussent tenu
Imperative	tiens, tenons, tenez

to attempt, tempt

Pres. Ind.	tente, tentes, tente; tentons, tentez, tentent
Imp. Ind.	tentais, tentais, tentait; tentions, tentiez, tentaient
Past Def.	tentai, tentas, tenta; tentâmes, tentâtes, tentèrent
Future	tenterai, tenteras, tentera; tenterons, tenterez, tenteront
Condit.	tenterais, tenterais, tenterait; tenterions, tenteriez, tenteraient
Pres. Subj.	tente, tentes, tente; tentions, tentiez, tentent
Imp. Subj.	tentasse, tentasses, tentât; tentassions, tentassiez, tentassent
Past Indef.	ai tenté, as tenté, a tenté; avons tenté, avez tenté, ont tenté
Plup. Ind.	avais tenté, avais tenté, avait tenté; avions tenté, aviez tenté, avaient tenté
Past Ant.	eus tenté, eus tenté, eut tenté; eûmes tenté, eûtes tenté, eurent tenté
Fut. Perf.	aurai tenté, auras tenté, aura tenté; aurons tenté, aurez tenté, auront tenté
Cond. Perf.	aurais tenté, aurais tenté, aurait tenté; aurions tenté, auriez tenté, auraient tenté
Past Subj.	aie tenté, aies tenté, ait tenté; ayons tenté, ayez tenté, aient tenté
Plup. Subj.	eusse tenté, eusses tenté, eût tenté; eussions tenté, eussiez tenté, eussent tenté
Imperative	tente, tentons, tentez

to terminate, finish, end

Pres. Ind.	termine, termines, termine; terminons, terminez, terminent
Imp. Ind.	terminais, terminais, terminait; terminions, terminiez, terminaient
Past Def.	terminai, terminas, termina; terminâmes, terminâtes, terminèrent
Future	terminerai, termineras, terminera; terminerons, terminerez, termineront
Condit.	terminerais, terminerais, terminerait; terminerions, termineriez, termineraient
Pres. Subj.	termine, termines, termine; terminions, terminiez, terminent
Imp. Subj.	terminasse, terminasses, terminât; terminassions, terminassiez, terminassent
Past Indef.	ai terminé, as terminé, a terminé; avons terminé, avez terminé, ont terminé
Plup. Ind.	avais terminé, avais terminé, avait terminé; avions terminé, aviez terminé, avaient terminé
Past Ant.	eus terminé, eus terminé, eut terminé; eûmes terminé, eûtes terminé, eurent terminé
Fut. Perf.	aurai terminé, auras terminé, aura terminé; aurons terminé, aurez terminé, auront terminé
Cond. Perf.	aurais terminé, aurais terminé, aurait terminé; aurions terminé, auriez terminé, auraient terminé
Past Subj.	aie terminé, aies terminé, ait terminé; ayons terminé, ayez terminé, aient terminé
Plup. Subj.	eusse terminé, eusses terminé, eût terminé; eussions terminé, eussiez terminé, eussent terminé
Imperative	termine, terminons, terminez

to draw (out), pull

Pres. Ind.	tire, tires, tire; tirons, tirez, tirent
Imp. Ind.	tirais, tirais, tirait; tirions, tiriez, tiraient
Past Def.	tirai, tiras, tira; tirâmes, tirâtes, tirèrent
Future	tirerai, tireras, tirera; tirerons, tirerez, tireront
Condit.	tirerais, tirerais, tirerait; tirerions, tireriez, tireraient
Pres. Subj.	tire, tires, tire; tirions, tiriez, tirent
Imp. Subj.	tirasse, tirasses, tirât; tirassions, tirassiez, tirassent
Past Indef.	ai tiré, as tiré, a tiré; avons tiré, avez tiré, ont tiré
Plup. Ind.	avais tiré, avais tiré, avait tiré; avions tiré, aviez tiré, avaient tiré
Past Ant.	eus tiré, eus tiré, eut tiré; eûmes tiré, eûtes tiré, eurent tiré
Fut. Perf.	aurai tiré, auras tiré, aura tiré; aurons tiré, aurez tiré, auront tiré
Cond. Perf.	aurais tiré, aurais tiré, aurait tiré; aurions tiré, auriez tiré, auraient tiré
Past Subj.	aie tiré, aies tiré, ait tiré; ayons tiré, ayez tiré, aient tiré
Plup. Subj.	eusse tiré, eusses tiré, eût tiré; eussions tiré, eussiez tiré, eussent tiré
Imperative	tire, tirons, tirez

to fall

Pres. Ind.	tombe, tombes, tombe; tombons, tombez, tombent
Imp. Ind.	tombais, tombais, tombait; tombions, tombiez, tombaient
Past Def.	tombai, tombas, tomba; tombâmes, tombâtes, tombèrent
Fut. Ind.	tomberai, tomberas, tombera; tomberons, tomberez, tomberont
Condit.	tomberais, tomberais, tomberait; tomberions, tomberiez, tomberaient
Pres. Subj.	tombe, tombes, tombe; tombions, tombiez, tombent
Imp. Subj.	tombasse, tombasses, tombât; tombassions, tombassiez, tombassent
Past Indef.	suis tombé(e), es tombé(e), est tombé(e); sommes tombé(e)s, êtes tombé(e)(s), sont tombé(e)s
Pluperf.	étais tombé(e), étais tombé(e), était tombé(e); étions tombé(e)s, étiez tombé(e)(s), étaient tombé(e)s
Past Ant.	fus tombé(e), fus tombé(e), fut tombé(e); fûmes tombé(e)s, fûtes tombé(e)(s), furent tombé(e)s
Fut. Perf.	serai tombé(e), seras tombé(e), sera tombé(e); serons tombé(e)s, serez tombé(e)(s), seront tombé(e)s
Cond. Perf.	serais tombé(e), serais tombé(e), serait tombé(e); serions tombé(e)s, seriez tombé(e)(s), seraient tombé(e)s
Past Subj.	sois tombé(e), sois tombé(e), soit tombé(e); soyons tombé(e)s, soyez tombé(e)(s), soient tombé(e)s
Plup. Subj.	fusse tombé(e), fusses tombé(e), fût tombé(e); fussions tombé(e)s, fussiez tombé(e)(s), fussent tombé(e)s
Imperative	tombe, tombons, tombez

to thunder

Pres. Ind.	il tonne
Imp. Ind.	il tonnait
Past Def.	il tonna
Future	il tonnera
Condit.	il tonnerait
Pres. Subj.	qu'il tonne
Imp. Subj.	qu'il tonnât
Past Indef.	il a tonné
Plup. Ind.	il avait tonné
Past Ant.	il eut tonné
Fut. Perf.	il aura tonné
Cond. Perf.	il aurait tonné
Past Subj.	qu'il ait tonné
Plup. Subj.	qu'il eût tonné
Imperative	[inemployé]

to twist

Pres. Ind.	tords, tords, tord; tordons, tordez, tordent
Imp. Ind.	tordais, tordais, tordait; tordions, tordiez, tordaient
Past Def.	tordis, tordis, tordit; tordîmes, tordîtes, tordirent
Future	tordrai, tordras, tordra; tordrons, tordrez, tordront
Condit.	tordrais, tordrais, tordrait; tordrions, tordriez, tordraient
Pres. Subj.	torde, tordes, torde; tordions, tordiez, tordent
Imp. Subj.	tordisse, tordisses, tordît; tordissions, tordissiez, tordissent
Past Indef.	ai tordu, as tordu, a tordu; avons tordu, avez tordu, ont tordu
Plup. Ind.	avais tordu, avais tordu, avait tordu; avions tordu, aviez tordu, avaient tordu
Past Ant.	eus tordu, eus tordu, eut tordu; eûmes tordu, eûtes tordu, eurent tordu
Fut. Perf.	aurai tordu, auras tordu, aura tordu; aurons tordu, aurez tordu, auront tordu
Cond. Perf.	aurais tordu, aurais tordu, aurait tordu; aurions tordu, auriez tordu, auraient tordu
Past Subj.	aie tordu, aies tordu, ait tordu; ayons tordu, ayez tordu, aient tordu
Plup. Subj.	eusse tordu, eusses tordu, eût tordu; eussions tordu, eussiez tordu, eussent tordu
Imperative	tords, tordons, tordez

to touch

Pres. Ind.	touche, touches, touche; touchons, touchez, touchent
Imp. Ind.	touchais, touchais, touchait; touchions, touchiez, touchaient
Past Def.	touchai, touchas, toucha; touchâmes, touchâtes, touchèrent
Future	toucherai, toucheras, touchera; toucherons, toucherez, toucheront
Condit.	toucherais, toucherais, toucherait; toucherions, toucheriez, toucheraient
Pres. Subj.	touche, touches, touche; touchions, touchiez, touchent
Imp. Subj.	touchasse, touchasses, touchât; touchassions, touchassiez, touchassent
Past Indef.	ai touché, as touché, a touché; avons touché, avez touché, ont touché
Plup. Ind.	avais touché, avais touché, avait touché; avions touché, aviez touché, avaient touché
Past Ant.	eus touché, eus touché, eut touché; eûmes touché, eûtes touché, eurent touché
Fut. Perf.	aurai touché, auras touché, aura touché; aurons touché, aurez touché, auront touché
Cond. Perf.	aurais touché, aurais touché, aurait touché; aurions touché, auriez touché, auraient touché
Past Subj.	aie touché, aies touché, ait touché; ayons touché, ayez touché, aient touché
Plup. Subj.	eusse touché, eusses touché, eût touché; eussions touché, eussiez touché, eussent touché
Imperative	touche, touchons, touchez

to cough

Pres. Ind.	tousse, tousses, tousse; toussons, toussez, toussent
Imp. Ind.	toussais, toussais, toussait; toussions, toussiez, toussaient
Past Def.	toussai, toussas, toussa; toussâmes, toussâtes, toussèrent
Future	tousserai, tousseras, toussera; tousserons, tousserez, tousseront
Condit.	tousserais, tousserais, tousserait; tousserions, tousseriez, tousseraient
Pres. Subj.	tousse, tousses, tousse; toussions, toussiez, toussent
Imp. Subj.	toussasse, toussasses, toussât; toussassions, toussassiez, toussassent
Past Indef.	ai toussé, as toussé, a toussé; avons toussé, avez toussé, ont toussé
Plup. Ind.	avais toussé, avais toussé, avait toussé; avions toussé, aviez toussé, avaient toussé
Past Ant.	eus toussé, eus toussé, eut toussé; eûmes toussé, eûtes toussé, eurent toussé
Fut. Perf.	aurai toussé, auras toussé, aura toussé; aurons toussé, aurez toussé, auront toussé
Cond. Perf.	aurais toussé, aurais toussé, aurait toussé; aurions toussé, auriez toussé, auraient toussé
Past Subj.	aie toussé, aies toussé, ait toussé; ayons toussé, ayez toussé, aient toussé
Plup. Subj.	eusse toussé, eusses toussé, eût toussé; eussions toussé, eussiez toussé, eussent toussé
Imperative	tousse, toussons, toussez

to translate

Pres. Ind.	traduis, traduis, traduit; traduisons, traduisez, traduisent
Imp. Ind.	traduisais, traduisais, traduisait; traduisions, traduisiez, traduisaient
Past Def.	traduisis, traduisis, traduisit; traduisîmes, traduisîtes, traduisirent
Fut. Ind.	traduirai, traduiras, traduira; traduirons, traduirez, traduiront
Condit.	traduirais, traduirais, traduirait; traduirions, traduiriez, traduiraient
Pres. Subj.	traduise, traduises, traduise; traduisions, traduisiez, traduisent
Imp. Subj.	traduisisse, traduisisses, traduisît; traduisissions, traduisissiez, traduisissent
Past Indef.	ai traduit, as traduit, a traduit; avons traduit, avez traduit, ont traduit
Pluperf.	avais traduit, avais traduit, avait traduit; avions traduit, aviez traduit, avaient traduit
Past Ant.	eus traduit, eus traduit, eut traduit; eûmes traduit, eûtes traduit, eurent traduit
Fut. Perf.	aurai traduit, auras traduit, aura traduit; aurons traduit, aurez traduit, auront traduit
Cond. Perf.	aurais traduit, aurais traduit, aurait traduit; aurions traduit, auriez traduit, auraient traduit
Past Subj.	aie traduit, aies traduit, ait traduit; ayons traduit, ayez traduit, aient traduit
Plup. Subj.	eusse traduit, eusses traduit, eût traduit; eussions traduit, eussiez traduit, eussent traduit
Imperative	traduis, traduisons, traduisez

to betray

Pres. Ind.	trahis, trahis, trahit; trahissons, trahissez, trahissent
Imp. Ind.	trahissais, trahissais, trahissait; trahissions, trahissiez, trahissaient
Past Def.	trahis, trahis, trahit; trahîmes, trahîtes, trahirent
Future	trahirai, trahiras, trahira; trahirons, trahirez, trahiront
Condit.	trahirais, trahirais, trahirait; trahirions, trahiriez, trahiraient
Pres. Subj.	trahisse, trahisses, trahisse; trahissions, trahissiez, trahissent
Imp. Subj.	trahisse, trahisses, trahît; trahissions, trahissiez, trahissent
Past Indef.	ai trahi, as trahi, a trahi; avons trahi, avez trahi, ont trahi
Plup. Ind.	avais trahi, avais trahi, avait trahi; avions trahi, aviez trahi, avaient trahi
Past Ant.	eus trahi, eus trahi, eut trahi; eûmes trahi, eûtes trahi, eurent trahi
Fut. Perf.	aurai trahi, auras trahi, aura trahi; aurons trahi, aurez trahi, auront trahi
Cond. Perf.	aurais trahi, aurais trahi, aurait trahi; aurions trahi, auriez trahi, auraient trahi
Past Subj.	aie trahi, aies trahi, ait trahi; ayons trahi, ayez trahi, aient trahi
Plup. Subj.	eusse trahi, eusses trahi, eût trahi; eussions trahi, eussiez trahi, eussent trahi
Imperative	trahis, trahissons, trahissez

to milk

Pres. Ind.	trais, trais, trait; trayons, trayez, traient
Imp. Ind.	trayais, trayais, trayait; trayions, trayiez, trayaient
Past Def.	[inemployé]
Future	trairai, trairas, traira; trairons, trairez, trairont
Condit.	trairais, trairais, trairait; trairions, trairiez, trairaient
Pres. Subj.	traie, traies, traie; trayions, trayiez, traient
Imp. Subj.	[inemployé]
Past Indef.	ai trait, as trait, a trait; avons trait, avez trait, ont trait
Pluperf.	avais trait, avais trait, avait trait; avions trait, aviez trait, avaient trait
Past Ant.	eus trait, eus trait, eut trait; eûmes trait, eûtes trait, eurent trait
Fut. Perf.	aurai trait, auras trait, aura trait; aurons trait, aurez trait, auront trait
Cond. Perf.	aurais trait, aurais trait, aurait trait; aurions trait, auriez trait, auraient trait
Past Subj.	aie trait, aies trait, ait trait; ayons trait, ayez trait, aient trait
Plup. Subj.	eusse trait, eusses trait, eût trait; eussions trait, eussiez trait, eussent trait
Imperative	trais, trayons, trayez

to transmit

Pres. Ind.	transmets, transmets, transmet; transmettons, transmettez, transmettent
Imp. Ind.	transmettais, transmettais, transmettait; transmettions, transmettiez, transmettaient
Past Def.	transmis, transmis, transmit; transmîmes, transmîtes, transmirent
Future	transmettrai, transmettras, transmettra; transmettrons, transmettrez, transmettront
Condit.	transmettrais, transmettrais, transmettrait; transmettrions, transmettriez, transmettraient
Pres. Subj.	transmette, transmettes, transmette; transmettions, transmettiez, transmettent
Imp. Subj.	transmisse, transmisses, transmît; transmissions, transmissiez, transmissent
Past Indef.	ai transmis, as transmis, a transmis; avons transmis, avez transmis, ont transmis
Plup. Ind.	avais transmis, avais transmis, avait transmis; avions transmis, aviez transmis, avaient transmis
Past Ant.	eus transmis, eus transmis, eut transmis; eûmes transmis, eûtes transmis, eurent transmis
Fut. Perf.	aurai transmis, auras transmis, aura transmis; aurons transmis, aurez transmis, auront transmis
Cond. Perf.	aurais transmis, aurais transmis, aurait transmis; aurions transmis, auriez transmis, auraient transmis
Past Subj.	aie transmis, aies transmis, ait transmis; ayons transmis, ayez transmis, aient transmis
Plup. Subj.	eusse transmis, eusses transmis, eût transmis; eussions transmis, eussiez transmis, eussent transmis
Imperative	transmets, transmettons, transmettez

to work

Pres. Ind.	travaille, travailles, travaille; travaillons, travaillez, travaillent
Imp. Ind.	travaillais, travaillais, travaillait; travaillions, travailliez, travaillaient
Past Def.	travaillai, travaillas, travailla; travaillâmes, travaillâtes, travaillèrent
Fut. Ind.	travaillerai, travailleras, travaillera; travaillerons, travaillerez, travailleront
Condit.	travaillerais, travaillerais, travaillerait; travaillerions, travailleriez, travailleraient
Pres. Subj.	travaille, travailles, travaille; travaillions, travailliez, travaillent
Imp. Subj.	travaillasse, travaillasses, travaillât; travaillassions, travaillassiez, travaillassent
Past Indef.	ai travaillé, as travaillé, a travaillé; avons travaillé, avez travaillé, ont travaillé
Pluperf.	avais travaillé, avais travaillé, avait travaillé; avions travaillé, aviez travaillé, avaient travaillé
Past Ant.	eus travaillé, eus travaillé, eut travaillé; eûmes travaillé, eûtes travaillé, eurent travaillé
Fut. Perf.	aurai travaillé, auras travaillé, aura travaillé; aurons travaillé, aurez travaillé, auront travaillé
Cond. Perf.	aurais travaillé, aurais travaillé, aurait travaillé; aurions travaillé, auriez travaillé, auraient travaillé
Past Subj.	aie travaillé, aies travaillé, ait travaillé; ayons travaillé, ayez travaillé, aient travaillé
Plup. Subj.	eusse travaillé, eusses travaillé, eût travaillé; eussions travaillé, eussiez travaillé, eussent travaillé
Imperative	travaille, travaillons, travaillez

to cheat, trick

Pres. Ind.	triche, triches, triche; trichons, trichez, trichent
Imp. Ind.	trichais, trichais, trichait; trichions, trichiez, trichaient
Past Def.	trichai, trichas, tricha; trichâmes, trichâtes, trichèrent
Future	tricherai, tricheras, trichera; tricherons, tricherez, tricheront
Condit.	tricherais, tricherais, tricherait; tricherions, tricheriez, tricheraient
Pres. Subj.	triche, triches, triche; trichions, trichiez, trichent
Imp. Subj.	trichasse, trichasses, trichât; trichassions, trichassiez, trichassent
Past Indef.	ai triché, as triché, a triché; avons triché, avez triché, ont triché
Plup. Ind.	avais triché, avais triché, avait triché; avions triché, aviez triché, avaient triché
Past Ant.	eus triché, eus triché, eut triché; eûmes triché, eûtes triché, eurent triché
Fut. Perf.	aurai triché, auras triché, aura triché; aurons triché, aurez triché, auront triché
Cond. Perf.	aurais triché, aurais triché, aurait triché; aurions triché, auriez triché, auraient triché
Past Subj.	aie triché, aies triché, ait triché; ayons triché, ayez triché, aient triché
Plup. Subj.	eusse triché, eusses triché, eût triché; eussions triché, eussiez triché, eussent triché
Imperative	triche, trichons, trichez

to be mistaken

Pres. Ind.	me trompe, te trompes, se trompe; nous trompons, vous trompez, se trompent
Imp. Ind.	me trompais, te trompais, se trompait; nous trompions, vous trompiez, se trompaient
Past Def.	me trompai, te trompas, se trompa; nous trompâmes, vous trompâtes, se trompèrent
Future	me tromperai, te tromperas, se trompera; nous tromperons, vous tromperez, se tromperont
Condit.	me tromperais, te tromperais, se tromperait; nous tromperions, vous tromperiez, se tromperaient
Pres. Subj.	me trompe, te trompes, se trompe; nous trompions, vous trompiez, se trompent
Imp. Subj.	me trompasse, te trompasses, se trompât; nous trompassions, vous trompassiez, se trompassent
Past Indef.	me suis trompé(e), t'es trompé(e), s'est trompé(e); nous sommes trompé(e)s, vous êtes trompé(e)(s), se sont trompé(e)s
Plup. Ind.	m'étais trompé(e), t'étais trompé(e), s'était trompé(e); nous étions trompé(e)s, vous étiez trompé(e)(s), s'étaient trompé(e)s
Past Ant.	me fus trompé(e), te fus trompé(e), se fut trompé(e); nous fûmes trompé(e)s, vous fûtes trompé(e)(s), se furent trompé(e)s
Fut. Perf.	me serai trompé(e), te seras trompé(e), se sera trompé(e); nous serons trompé(e)s, vous serez trompé(e)(s), se seront trompé(e)s
Cond. Perf.	me serais trompé(e), te serais trompé(e), se serait trompé(e); nous serions trompé(e)s, vous seriez trompé(e)(s), se seraient trompé(e)s
Past Subj.	me sois trompé(e), te sois trompé(e), se soit trompé(e); nous soyons trompé(e)s, vous soyez trompé(e)(s), se soient trompé(e)s
Plup. Subj.	me fusse trompé(e), te fusses trompé(e), se fût trompé(e); nous fussions trompé(e)s, vous fussiez trompé(e)(s), se fussent trompé(e)s
Imperative	trompe-toi, trompons-nous, trompez-vous [ordinairement inemployé]

to find

Pres. Ind.	trouve, trouves, trouve; trouvons, trouvez, trouvent
Imp. Ind.	trouvais, trouvais, trouvait; trouvions, trouviez, trouvaient
Past Def.	trouvai, trouvas, trouva; trouvâmes, trouvâtes, trouvèrent
Fut. Ind.	trouverai, trouveras, trouvera; trouverons, trouverez, trouveront
Condit.	trouverais, trouverais, trouverait; trouverions, trouveriez, trouveraient
Pres. Subj.	trouve, trouves, trouve; trouvions, trouviez, trouvent
Imp. Subj.	trouvasse, trouvasses, trouvât; trouvassions trouvassiez, trouvassent
Past Indef.	ai trouvé, as trouvé, a trouvé; avons trouvé, avez trouvé, ont trouvé
Pluperf.	avais trouvé, avais trouvé, avait trouvé; avions trouvé, aviez trouvé, avaient trouvé
Past Ant.	eus trouvé, eus trouvé, eut trouvé; eûmes trouvé, eûtes trouvé, eurent trouvé
Fut. Perf.	aurai trouvé, auras trouvé, aura trouvé; aurons trouvé, aurez trouvé, auront trouvé
Cond. Perf.	aurais trouvé, aurais trouvé, aurait trouvé; aurions trouvé, auriez trouvé, auraient trouvé
Past Subj.	aie trouvé, aies trouvé, ait trouvé; ayons trouvé, ayez trouvé, aient trouvé
Plup. Subj.	eusse trouvé, eusses trouvé, eût trouvé; eussions trouvé, eussiez trouvé, eussent trouvé
Imperative	trouve, trouvons, trouvez

to fake

Pres. Ind.	truque, truques, truque; truquons, truquez, truquent
Imp. Ind.	truquais, truquais, truquait; truquions, truquiez, truquaient
Past Def.	truquai, truquas, truqua; truquâmes, truquâtes, truquèrent
Future	truquerai, truqueras, truquera; truquerons, truquerez, truqueront
Condit.	truquerais, truquerais, truquerait; truquerions, truqueriez, truqueraient
Pres. Subj.	truque, truques, truque; truquions, truquiez, truquent
Imp. Subj.	truquasse, truquasses, truquât; truquassions, truquassiez, truquassent
Past Indef.	ai truqué, as truqué, a truqué; avons truqué, avez truqué, ont truqué
Plup. Ind.	avais truqué, avais truqué, avait truqué; avions truqué, aviez truqué, avaient truqué
Past Ant.	eus truqué, eus truqué, eut truqué; eûmes truqué, eûtes truqué, eurent truqué
Fut. Perf.	aurai truqué, auras truqué, aura truqué; aurons truqué, aurez truqué, auront truqué
Cond. Perf.	aurais truqué, aurais truqué, aurait truqué; aurions truqué, auriez truqué, auraient truqué
Past Subj.	aie truqué, aies truqué, ait truqué; ayons truqué, ayez truqué, aient truqué
Plup. Subj.	eusse truqué, eusses truqué, eût truqué; eussions truqué, eussiez truqué, eussent truqué
Imperative	truque, truquons, truquez

to kill

Pres. Ind.	tue, tues, tue; tuons, tuez, tuent
Imp. Ind.	tuais, tuais, tuait; tuions, tuiez, tuaient
Past Def.	tuai, tuas, tua; tuâmes, tuâtes, tuèrent
Future	tuerai, tueras, tuera; tuerons, tuerez, tueront
Condit.	tuerais, tuerais, tuerait; tuerions, tueriez, tueraient
Pres. Subj.	tue, tues, tue; tuions, tuiez, tuent
Imp. Subj.	tuasse, tuasses, tuât; tuassions, tuassiez, tuassent
Past Indef.	ai tué, as tué, a tué; avons tué, avez tué, ont tué
Plup. Ind.	avais tué, avais tué, avait tué; avions tué, aviez tué, avaient tué
Past Ant.	eus tué, eus tué, eut tué; eûmes tué, eûtes tué, eurent tué
Fut. Perf.	aurai tué, auras tué, aura tué; aurons tué, aurez tué, auront tué
Cond. Perf.	aurais tué, aurais tué, aurait tué; aurions tué, auriez tué, auraient tué
Past Subj.	aie tué, aies tué, ait tué; ayons tué, ayez tué, aient tué
Plup. Subj.	eusse tué, eusses tué, eût tué; eussions tué, eussiez tué, eussent tué
Imperative	tue, tuons, tuez

to unite

Pres. Ind.	unis, unis, unit; unissons, unissez, unissent
Imp. Ind.	unissais, unissais, unissait; unissions, unissiez, unissaient
Past Def.	unis, unis, unit; unîmes, unîtes, unirent
Future	unirai, uniras, unira; unirons, unirez, uniront
Condit.	unirais, unirais, unirait; unirions, uniriez, uniraient
Pres. Subj.	unisse, unisses, unisse; unissions, unissiez, unissent
Imp. Subj.	unisse, unisses, unît; unissions, unissiez, unissent
Past Indef.	ai uni, as uni, a uni; avons uni, avez uni, ont uni
Plup. Ind.	avais uni, avais uni, avait uni; avions uni, aviez uni, avaient uni
Past Ant.	eus uni, eus uni, eut uni; eûmes uni, eûtes uni, eurent uni
Fut. Perf.	aurai uni, auras uni, aura uni; aurons uni, aurez uni, auront uni
Cond. Perf.	aurais uni, aurais uni, aurait uni; aurions uni, auriez uni, auraient uni
Past Subj.	aie uni, aies uni, ait uni; ayons uni, ayez uni, aient uni
Plup. Subj.	eusse uni, eusses uni, eût uni; eussions uni, eussiez uni, eussent uni
Imperative	unis, unissons, unissez

to use, utilize, make use of, put to use

Pres. Ind.	utilise, utilises, utilise; utilisons, utilisez, utilisent
Imp. Ind.	utilisais, utilisais, utilisait; utilisions, utilisiez, utilisaient
Past Def.	utilisai, utilisas, utilisa; utilisâmes, utilisâtes, utilisèrent
Future	utiliserai, utiliseras, utilisera; utiliserons, utiliserez, utiliseront
Condit.	utiliserais, utiliserais, utiliserait; utiliserions, utiliseriez, utiliseraient
Pres. Subj.	utilise, utilises, utilise; utilisions, utilisiez, utilisent
Imp. Subj.	utilisasse, utilisasses, utilisât; utilisassions, utilisassiez, utilisassent
Past Indef.	ai utilisé, as utilisé, a utilisé; avons utilisé, avez utilisé, ont utilisé
Plup. Ind.	avais utilisé, avais utilisé, avait utilisé; avions utilisé, aviez utilisé, avaient utilisé
Past Ant.	eus utilisé, eus utilisé, eut utilisé; eûmes utilisé, eûtes utilisé, eurent utilisé
Fut. Perf.	aurai utilisé, auras utilisé, aura utilisé; aurons utilisé, aurez utilisé, auront utilisé
Cond. Perf.	aurais utilisé, aurais utilisé, aurait utilisé; aurions utilisé, auriez utilisé, auraient utilisé
Past Subj.	aie utilisé, aies utilisé, ait utilisé; ayons utilisé, ayez utilisé, aient utilisé
Plup. Subj.	eusse utilisé, eusses utilisé, eût utilisé; eussions utilisé, eussiez utilisé, eussent utilisé
Imperative	utilise, utilisons, utilisez

to conquer, vanquish

Pres. Ind.	vaincs, vaincs, vainc; vainquons, vainquez, vainquent
Imp. Ind.	vainquais, vainquais, vainquait; vainquions, vainquiez, vainquaient
Past Def.	vainquis, vainquis, vainquit; vainquîmes, vainquîtes, vainquirent
Fut. Ind.	vaincrai, vaincras, vaincra; vaincrons, vaincrez, vaincront
Condit.	vaincrais, vaincrais, vaincrait; vaincrions, vaincriez, vaincraient
Pres. Subj.	vainque, vainques, vainque; vainquions, vainquiez, vainquent
Imp. Subj.	vainquisse, vainquisses, vainquît; vainquissions, vainquissiez, vainquissent
Past Indef.	ai vaincu, as vaincu, a vaincu; avons vaincu, avez vaincu, ont vaincu
Pluperf.	avais vaincu, avais vaincu, avait vaincu; avions vaincu, aviez vaincu, avaient vaincu
Past Ant.	eus vaincu, eus vaincu, eut vaincu; eûmes vaincu, eûtes vaincu, eurent vaincu
Fut. Perf.	aurai vaincu, auras vaincu, aura vaincu; aurons vaincu, aurez vaincu, auront vaincu
Cond. Perf.	aurais vaincu, aurais vaincu, aurait vaincu; aurions vaincu, auriez vaincu, auraient vaincu
Past Subj.	aie vaincu, aies vaincu, ait vaincu; ayons vaincu, ayez vaincu, aient vaincu
Plup. Subj.	eusse vaincu, eusses vaincu, eût vaincu; eussions vaincu, eussiez vaincu, eussent vaincu
Imperative	vaincs, vainquons, vainquez

to be worth, be as good as, deserve, merit

Pres. Ind.	vaux, vaux, vaut; valons, valez, valent
Imp. Ind.	valais, valais, valait; valions, valiez, valaient
Past Def.	valus, valus, valut; valûmes, valûtes, valurent
Fut. Ind.	vaudrai, vaudras, vaudra; vaudrons, vaudrez, vaudront
Condit.	vaudrais, vaudrais, vaudrait; vaudrions, vaudriez, vaudraient
Pres. Subj.	vaille, vailles, vaille; valions, valiez, vaillent
Imp. Subj.	valusse, valusses, valût; valussions, valussiez, valussent
Past Indef.	ai valu, as valu, a valu; avons valu, avez valu, ont valu
Pluperf.	avais valu, avais valu, avait valu; avions valu, aviez valu, avaient valu
Past Ant.	eus valu, eus valu, eut valu; eûmes valu, eûtes valu, eurent valu
Fut. Perf.	aurai valu, auras valu, aura valu; aurons valu, aurez valu, auront valu
Perf. Cond.	aurais valu, aurais valu, aurait valu; aurions valu, auriez valu, auraient valu
Past Subj.	aie valu, aies valu, ait valu; ayons valu, ayez valu, aient valu
Plup. Subj.	eusse valu, eusses valu, eût valu; eussions valu, eussiez valu, eussent valu
Imperative	vaux, valons, valez

to sell

Pres. Ind.	vends, vends, vend; vendons, vendez, vendent
Imp. Ind.	vendais, vendais, vendait; vendions, vendiez, vendaient
Past Def.	vendis, vendis, vendit; vendîmes, vendîtes, vendirent
Fut. Ind.	vendrai, vendras, vendra; vendrons, vendrez, vendront
Condit.	vendrais, vendrais, vendrait; vendrions, vendriez, vendraient
Pres. Subj.	vende, vendes, vende; vendions, vendiez, vendent
Imp. Subj.	vendisse, vendisses, vendît; vendissions, vendissiez, vendissent
Past Indef.	ai vendu, as vendu, a vendu; avons vendu, avez vendu, ont vendu
Pluperf.	avais vendu, avais vendu, avait vendu; avions vendu, aviez vendu, avaient vendu
Past Ant.	eus vendu, eus vendu, eut vendu; eûmes vendu, eûtes vendu, eurent vendu
Fut. Perf.	aurai vendu, auras vendu, aura vendu; aurons vendu, aurez vendu, auront vendu
Perf. Cond.	aurais vendu, aurais vendu, aurait vendu; aurions vendu, auriez vendu, auraient vendu
Past Subj.	aie vendu, aies vendu, ait vendu; ayons vendu, ayez vendu, aient vendu
Plup. Subj.	eusse vendu, eusses vendu, eût vendu; eussions vendu, eussiez vendu, eussent vendu
Imperative	vends, vendons, vendez

to avenge

Pres. Ind.	venge, venges, venge; vengeons, vengez, vengent
Imp. Ind.	vengeais, vengeais, vengeait; vengions, vengiez, vengeaient
Past Def.	vengeai, vengeas, vengea; vengeâmes, vengeâtes, vengèrent
Future	vengerai, vengeras, vengera; vengerons, vengerez, vengeront
Condit.	vengerais, vengerais, vengerait; vengerions, vengeriez, vengeraient
Pres. Subj.	venge, venges, venge; vengions, vengiez, vengent
Imp. Subj.	vengeasse, vengeasses, vengeât; vengeassions, vengeassiez, vengeassent
Past Indef.	ai vengé, as vengé, a vengé; avons vengé, avez vengé, ont vengé
Plup. Ind.	avais vengé, avais vengé, avait vengé; avions vengé, aviez vengé, avaient vengé
Past Ant.	eus vengé, eus vengé, eut vengé; eûmes vengé, eûtes vengé, eurent vengé
Fut. Perf.	aurai vengé, auras vengé, aura vengé; aurons vengé, aurez vengé, auront vengé
Cond. Perf.	aurais vengé, aurais vengé, aurait vengé; aurions vengé, auriez vengé, auraient vengé
Past Subj.	aie vengé, aies vengé, ait vengé; ayons vengé, ayez vengé, aient vengé
Plup. Subj.	eusse vengé, eusses vengé, eût vengé; eussions vengé, eussiez vengé, eussent vengé
Imperative	venge, vengeons, vengez

to come

Pres. Ind.	viens, viens, vient; venons, venez, viennent
Imp. Ind.	venais, venais, venait; venions, veniez, venaient
Past Def.	vins, vins, vint; vînmes, vîntes, vinrent
Fut. Ind.	viendrai, viendras, viendra; viendrons, viendrez, viendront
Condit.	viendrais, viendrais, viendrait; viendrions, viendriez, viendraient
Pres. Subj.	vienne, viennes, vienne; venions, veniez, viennent
Imp. Subj.	vinsse, vinsses, vînt; vinssions, vinssiez, vinssent
Past Indef.	suis venu(e), es venu(e), est venu(e); sommes venu(e)s, êtes venu(e)(s), sont venu(e)s
Pluperf.	étais venu(e), étais venu(e), était venu(e); étions venu(e)s, étiez venu(e)(s), étaient venu(e)s
Past Ant.	fus venu(e), fus venu(e), fut venu(e); fûmes venu(e)s, fûtes venu(e)(s), furent venu(e)s
Fut. Perf.	serai venu(e), seras venu(e), sera venu(e); serons venu(e)s, serez venu(e)(s), seront venu(e)s
Cond. Perf.	serais venu(e), serais venu(e), serait venu(e); serions venu(e)s, seriez venu(e)(s), seraient venu(e)s
Past Subj.	sois venu(e), sois venu(e), soit venu(e); soyons venu(e)s, soyez venu(e)(s), soient venu(e)s
Plup. Subj.	fusse venu(e), fusses venu(e), fût venu(e); fussions venu(e)s, fussiez venu(e)(s), fussent venu(e)s
Imperative	viens, venons, venez

to pour

Pres. Ind.	verse, verses, verse; versons, versez, versent
Imp. Ind.	versais, versais, versait; versions, versiez, versaient
Past Def.	versai, versas, versa; versâmes, versâtes, versèrent
Future	verserai, verseras, versera; verserons, verserez, verseront
Condit.	verserais, verserais, verserait; verserions, verseriez, verseraient
Pres. Subj.	verse, verses, verse; versions, versiez, versent
Imp. Subj.	versasse, versasses, versât; versassions, versassiez, versassent
Past Indef.	ai versé, as versé, a versé; avons versé, avez versé, ont versé
Plup. Ind.	avais versé, avais versé, avait versé; avions versé, aviez versé, avaient versé
Past Ant.	eus versé, eus versé, eut versé; eûmes versé, eûtes versé, eurent versé
Fut. Perf.	aurai versé, auras versé, aura versé; aurons versé, aurez versé, auront versé
Cond. Perf.	aurais versé, aurais versé, aurait versé; aurions versé, auriez versé, auraient versé
Past Subj.	aie versé, aies versé, ait versé; ayons versé, ayez versé, aient versé
Plup. Subj.	eusse versé, eusses versé, eût versé; eussions versé, eussiez versé, eussent versé
Imperative	verse, versons, versez

to clothe, dress

Pres. Ind.	vêts, vêts, vêt; vêtons, vêtez, vêtent
Imp. Ind.	vêtais, vêtais, vêtait; vêtions, vêtiez, vêtaient
Past Def.	vêtis, vêtis, vêtit; vêtîmes, vêtîtes, vêtirent
Fut. Ind.	vêtirai, vêtiras, vêtira; vêtirons, vêtirez, vêtiront
Condit.	vêtirais, vêtirais, vêtirait; vêtirions, vêtiriez, vêtiraient
Pres. Subj.	vête, vêtes, vête; vêtions, vêtiez, vêtent
Imp. Subj.	vêtisse, vêtisses, vêtît; vêtissions, vêtissiez, vêtissent
Past Indef.	ai vêtu, as vêtu, a vêtu; avons vêtu, avez vêtu, ont vêtu
Pluperf.	avais vêtu, avais vêtu, avait vêtu; avions vêtu, aviez vêtu, avaient vêtu
Past Ant.	eus vêtu, eus vêtu, eut vêtu; eûmes vêtu, eûtes vêtu, eurent vêtu
Fut. Perf.	aurai vêtu, auras vêtu, aura vêtu; aurons vêtu, aurez vêtu, auront vêtu
Cond. Perf.	aurais vêtu, aurais vêtu, aurait vêtu; aurions vêtu, auriez vêtu, auraient vêtu
Past Subj.	aie vêtu, aies vêtu, ait vêtu; ayons vêtu, ayez vêtu, aient vêtu
Plup. Subj.	eusse vêtu, eusses vêtu, eût vêtu; eussions vêtu, eussiez vêtu, eussent vêtu
Imperative	vêts, vêtons, vêtez

to grow old, become old, age

Pres. Ind.	vieillis, vieillis, vieillit; vieillissons, vieillissez, vieillissent
Imp. Ind.	vieillissais, vieillissais, vieillissait; vieillissions, vieillissiez, vieillissaient
Past Def.	vieillis, vieillis, vieillit; vieillîmes, vieillîtes, vieillirent
Future	vieillirai, vieilliras, vieillira; vieillirons, vieillirez, vieilliront
Condit.	vieillirais, vieillirais, vieillirait; vieillirions, vieilliriez, vieilliraient
Pres. Subj.	vieillisse, vieillisses, vieillisse; vieillissions, vieillissiez, vieillissent
Imp. Subj.	vieillisse, vieillisses, vieillît; vieillissions, vieillissiez, vieillissent
Past Indef.	ai vieilli, as vieilli, a vieilli; avons vieilli, avez vieilli, ont vieilli
Plup. Ind.	avais vieilli, avais vieilli, avait vieilli; avions vieilli, aviez vieilli, avaient vieilli
Past Ant.	eus vieilli, eus vieilli, eut vieilli; eûmes vieilli, eûtes vieilli, eurent vieilli
Fut. Perf.	aurai vieilli, auras vieilli, aura vieilli; aurons vieilli, aurez vieilli, auront vieilli
Cond. Perf.	aurais vieilli, aurais vieilli, aurait vieilli; aurions vieilli, auriez vieilli, auraient vieilli
Past Subj.	aie vieilli, aies vieilli, ait vieilli; ayons vieilli, ayez vieilli, aient vieilli
Plup. Subj.	eusse vieilli, eusses vieilli, eût vieilli; eussions vieilli, eussiez vieilli, eussent vieilli
Imperative	vieillis, vieillissons, vieillissez [ordinairement inemployé]

to visit

Pres. Ind.	visite, visites, visite; visitons, visitez, visitent
Imp. Ind.	visitais, visitais, visitait; visitions, visitiez, visitaient
Past Def.	visitai, visitas, visita; visitâmes, visitâtes, visitèrent
Future	visiterai, visiteras, visitera; visiterons, visiterez, visiteront
Condit.	visiterais, visiterais, visiterait; visiterions, visiteriez, visiteraient
Pres. Subj.	visite, visites, visite; visitions, visitiez, visitent
Imp. Subj.	visitasse, visitasses, visitât; visitassions, visitassiez, visitassent
Past Indef.	ai visité, as visité, a visité; avons visité, avez visité, ont visité
Plup. Ind.	avais visité, avais visité, avait visité; avions visité, aviez visité, avaient visité
Past Ant.	eus visité, eus visité, eut visité; eûmes visité, eûtes visité, eurent visité
Fut. Perf.	aurai visité, auras visité, aura visité; aurons visité, aurez visité, auront visité
Cond. Perf.	aurais visité, aurais visité, aurait visité; aurions visité, auriez visité, auraient visité
Past Subj.	aie visité, aies visité, ait visité; ayons visité, ayez visité, aient visité
Plup. Subj.	eusse visité, eusses visité, eût visité; eussions visité, eussiez visité, eussent visité
Imperative	visite, visitons, visitez

to live

Pres. Ind.	vis, vis, vit; vivons, vivez, vivent
Imp. Ind.	vivais, vivais, vivait; vivions, viviez, vivaient
Past Def.	vécus, vécus, vécut; vécûmes, vécûtes, vécurent
Fut. Ind.	vivrai, vivras, vivra; vivrons, vivrez, vivront
Condit.	vivrais, vivrais, vivrait; vivrions, vivriez, vivraient
Pres. Subj.	vive, vives, vive; vivions, viviez, vivent
Imp. Subj.	vécusse, vécusses, vécût; vécussions, vécussiez, vécussent
Past Indef.	ai vécu, as vécu, a vécu; avons vécu, avez vécu, ont vécu
Pluperf.	avais vécu, avais vécu, avait vécu; avions vécu, aviez vécu, avaient vécu
Past Ant.	eus vécu, eus vécu, eut vécu; eûmes vécu, eûtes vécu, eurent vécu
Fut. Perf.	aurai vécu, auras vécu, aura vécu; aurons vécu, aurez vécu, auront vécu
Cond. Perf.	aurais vécu, aurais vécu, aurait vécu; aurions vécu, auriez vécu, auraient vécu
Past Subj.	aie vécu, aies vécu, ait vécu; ayons vécu, ayez vécu, aient vécu
Plup. Subj.	eusse vécu, eusses vécu, eût vécu; eussions vécu, eussiez vécu, eussent vécu
Imperative	vis, vivons, vivez

to drift, row, sail, wander

Pres. Ind.	vogue, vogues, vogue; voguons, voguez, voguent
Imp. Ind.	voguais, voguais, voguait; voguions, voguiez, voguaient
Past Def.	voguai, voguas, vogua; voguâmes, voguâtes, voguèrent
Future	voguerai, vogueras, voguera; voguerons, voguerez, vogueront
Condit.	voguerais, voguerais, voguerait; voguerions, vogueriez, vogueraient
Pres. Subj.	vogue, vogues, vogue; voguions, voguiez, voguent
Imp. Subj.	voguasse, voguasses, voguât; voguassions, voguassiez, voguassent
Past Indef.	ai vogué, as vogué, a vogué; avons vogué, avez vogué, ont vogué
Plup. Ind.	avais vogué, avais vogué, avait vogué; avions vogué, aviez vogué, avaient vogué
Past Ant.	eus vogué, eus vogué, eut vogué; eûmes vogué, eûtes vogué, eurent vogué
Fut. Perf.	aurai vogué, auras vogué, aura vogué; aurons vogué, aurez vogué, auront vogué
Cond. Perf.	aurais vogué, aurais vogué, aurait vogué; aurions vogué, auriez vogué, auraient vogué
Past Subj.	aie vogué, aies vogué, ait vogué; ayons vogué, ayez vogué, aient vogué
Plup. Subj.	eusse vogué, eusses vogué, eût vogué; eussions vogué, eussiez vogué, eussent vogué
Imperative	vogue, voguons, voguez

to see

Pres. Ind.	vois, vois, voit; voyons, voyez, voient
Imp. Ind.	voyais, voyais, voyait; voyions, voyiez, voyaient
Past Def.	vis, vis, vit; vîmes, vîtes, virent
Fut. Ind.	verrai, verras, verra; verrons, verrez, verront
Condit.	verrais, verrais, verrait; verrions, verriez, verraient
Pres. Subj.	voie, voies, voie; voyions, voyiez, voient
Imp. Subj.	visse, visses, vît; vissions, vissiez, vissent
Past Indef.	ai vu, as vu, a vu; avons vu, avez vu, ont vu
Pluperf.	avais vu, avais vu, avait vu; avions vu, aviez vu, avaient vu
Past Ant.	eus vu, eus vu, eut vu; eûmes vu, eûtes vu, eurent vu
Fut. Perf.	aurai vu, auras vu, aura vu; aurons vu, aurez vu, auront vu
Cond. Perf.	aurais vu, aurais vu, aurait vu; aurions vu, auriez vu, auraient vu
Past Subj.	aie vu, aies vu, ait vu; ayons vu, ayez vu, aient vu
Plup. Subj.	eusse vu, eusses vu, eût vu; eussions vu, eussiez vu, eussent vu
Imperative	vois, voyons, voyez

to fly, steal

Pres. Ind.	vole, voles, vole; volons, volez, volent
Imp. Ind.	volais, volais, volait; volions, voliez, volaient
Past Def.	volai, volas, vola; volâmes, volâtes, volèrent
Fut. Ind.	volerai, voleras, volera; volerons, volerez, voleront
Condit.	volerais, volerais, volerait; volerions, voleriez, voleraient
Pres. Subj.	vole, voles, vole; volions, voliez, volent
Imp. Subj.	volasse, volasses, volât; volassions, volassiez, volassent
Past Indef.	ai volé, as volé, a volé; avons volé, avez volé, ont volé
Pluperf.	avais volé, avais volé, avait volé; avions volé, aviez volé, avaient volé
Past Ant.	eus volé, eus volé, eut volé; eûmes volé, eûtes volé, eurent volé
Fut. Perf.	aurai volé, auras volé, aura volé; aurons volé, aurez volé, auront volé
Cond. Perf.	aurais volé, aurais volé, aurait volé; aurions volé, auriez volé, auraient volé
Past Subj.	aie volé, aies volé, ait volé; ayons volé, ayez volé, aient volé
Plup. Subj.	eusse volé, eusses volé, eût volé; eussions volé, eussiez volé, eussent volé
Imperative	vole, volons, volez

to want, wish

Pres. Ind.	veux, veux, veut; voulons, voulez, veulent
Imp. Ind.	voulais, voulais, voulait; voulions, vouliez, voulaient
Past Def.	voulus, voulus, voulut; voulûmes, voulûtes, voulurent
Fut. Ind.	voudrai, voudras, voudra; voudrons, voudrez, voudront
Condit.	voudrais, voudrais, voudrait; voudrions, voudriez, voudraient
Pres. Subj.	veuille, veuilles, veuille; voulions, vouliez, veuillent
Imp. Subj.	voulusse, voulusses, voulût; voulussions, voulussiez, voulussent
Past Indef.	ai voulu, as voulu, a voulu; avons voulu, avez voulu, ont voulu
Pluperf.	avais voulu, avais voulu, avait voulu; avions voulu, aviez voulu, avaient voulu
Past Ant.	eus voulu, eus voulu, eut voulu; eûmes voulu, eûtes voulu, eurent voulu
Fut. Perf.	aurai voulu, auras voulu, aura voulu; aurons voulu, aurez voulu, auront voulu
Cond. Perf.	aurais voulu, aurais voulu, aurait voulu; aurions voulu, auriez voulu, auraient voulu
Past Subj.	aie voulu, aies voulu, ait voulu; ayons voulu, ayez voulu, aient voulu
Plup. Subj.	eusse voulu, eusses voulu, eût voulu; eussions voulu, eussiez voulu, eussent voulu
Imperative	veuille, veuillez

to travel

Pres. Ind.	voyage, voyages, voyage; voyageons, voyagez, voyagent
Imp. Ind.	voyageais, voyageais, voyageait; voyagions, voyagiez, voyageaient
Past Def.	voyageai, voyageas, voyagea; voyageâmes, voyageâtes, voyagèrent
Fut. Ind.	voyagerai, voyageras, voyagera; voyagerons, voyagerez, voyageront
Condit.	voyagerais, voyagerais, voyagerait; voyagerions, voyageriez, voyageraient
Pres. Subj.	voyage, voyages, voyage; voyagions, voyagiez, voyagent
Imp. Subj.	voyageasse, voyageasses, voyageât; voyageassions, voyageassiez, voyageassent
Past Indef.	ai voyagé, as voyagé, a voyagé; avons voyagé, avez voyagé, ont voyagé
Pluperf.	avais voyagé, avais voyagé, avait voyagé; avions voyagé, aviez voyagé, avaient voyagé
Past Ant.	eus voyagé, eus voyagé, eut voyagé; eûmes voyagé, eûtes voyagé, eurent voyagé
Fut. Perf.	aurai voyagé, auras voyagé, aura voyagé; aurons voyagé, aurez voyagé, auront voyagé
Cond. Perf.	aurais voyagé, aurais voyagé, aurait voyagé; aurions voyagé, auriez voyagé, auraient voyagé
Past Subj.	aie voyagé, aies voyagé, ait voyagé; ayons voyagé, ayez voyagé, aient voyagé
Plup. Subj.	eusse voyagé, eusses voyagé, eût voyagé; eussions voyagé, eussiez voyagé, eussent voyagé
Imperative	voyage, voyageons, voyagez

English — French Verb Index

If the French verb you want is reflexive (*e.g.*, **s'appeler**), you will find it listed alphabetically in the preceding pages under the first letter of the verb and not under the reflexive pronoun *s'* or *se*.

A

abandon **abandonner**
able, be **pouvoir**
abolish **abolir**
absolve **absoudre**
abstain **s'abstenir**
abstract **abstraire**
accept **accepter**
acclaim **acclamer**
accompany **accompagner**
accuse **accuser**
achieve **achever**
acknowledge **convenir, reconnaître**
acquainted with, be **connaître**
acquire **acquérir**
act **agir**
act (in a play) **jouer**
adjoin **adjoindre**
admire **admirer**
admit **admettre**
adore **adorer**
advance **avancer**
afraid, be **craindre**
age **vieillir**
agree **convenir**
aid **aider**
allow **laisser, permettre**
allure **attirer, attraire**
amaze **étonner**
amuse **amuser, égayer**
amuse oneself **s'amuser**
angry, become **se fâcher**
annoy **agacer, ennuyer**
answer **répondre**
apologize **s'excuser**
appear **apparaître, paraître**
appear again **reparaître**
appease **adoucir**
applaud **acclamer**
appraise **évaluer**
appropriate, be **convenir**
approve (of) **approuver**
arrange **arranger**
arrest **arrêter**
arrive **arriver**
ascend **monter**
ascertain **constater**
ask (for) **demander**
assail **assaillir**
assault **assaillir**
assess **évaluer**
assist **aider**
assist (at) **assister**
assure **assurer**
assure oneself **s'assurer**
astonish **étonner**
attain **atteindre**
attempt **tenter**

attend **assister**
attest **certifier**
attract **attirer, attraire**
augment **augmenter**
avenge **venger**

B

babble **bavarder**
balance **balancer**
be **être**
be a question of **s'agir**
be able **pouvoir**
be acquainted with **connaître**
be afraid **craindre**
be appropriate **convenir**
be as good as **valoir**
be becoming (in appearance) **seoir**
be born **naître**
be busy **s'occuper**
be dependent **dépendre**
be enough **suffire**
be in a hurry **se presser**
be like **ressembler**
be mistaken **se méprendre, se tromper**
be named **s'appeler**
be necessary **falloir**
be present (at) **assister**
be quiet **se taire**
be silent **se taire**
be sufficient **suffire**
be suitable **convenir**
be the matter **s'agir**
be worth **valoir**
beat **battre**
become **devenir**
become angry **se fâcher**
become old **vieillir**
becoming, be (in appearance) **seoir**
beg **prier, supplier**
begin **commencer, se mettre**
behave **agir**
believe **croire**
belong **appartenir**
beseech **supplier**
bet **parier**
betray **trahir**
beware **se méfier**
bewilder **abasourdir, étourdir**
bite **mordre**
blame **blâmer**
bless **bénir**
blow **souffler**
blush **rougir**
boil **bouillir**
bore **ennuyer**
born, be **naître**
borrow **emprunter**
bother **gêner**
break **casser, rompre**
bring **amener, apporter**
bring down **descendre**
bring up (raise) **élever**
bring up (take up) **monter**
brush **brosser**
brush oneself **se brosser**
budge **bouger**
build **bâtir, construire**
burden **charger**
burn **brûler**
burst **rompre**
bury **enterrer**
busy, be **s'occuper**
buy **acheter**

C

call **appeler**
call again **rappeler**
call back **rappeler**
call oneself **s'appeler**

can **pouvoir**
carry **porter**
carry away **enlever**
cast **jeter**
catch **attraper**
cause **causer**
cease **cesser**
certify **certifier, constater**
change **changer**
charge **charger**
chase **chasser**
chat **bavarder, causer**
chatter **bavarder**
cheat **tricher**
cheer **acclamer**
cheer up **égayer**
cherish **chérir**
chide **gronder**
choose **choisir**
claim **prétendre**
class **classer**
classify **classer**
clean **nettoyer**
cleave **fendre**
climb **grimper**
clip **tailler**
close **fermer**
clothe **vêtir**
collect **recueillir**
comb one's hair **se peigner**
combat **combattre**
come **venir**
come back **revenir**
come in **entrer**
come to pass **advenir**
command **commander**
commence **commencer**
commit **commettre**
commit sin **pécher**
compare **comparer**
compel **contraindre**
complain **se plaindre**
complete **finir**
compromise **compromettre**
conceive **concevoir**
conclude **conclure**
concur **concourir**
condescend **s'abaisser**
conduct **conduire**
conquer **conquérir, vaincre**
consent **consentir**
constrain **contraindre**
construct **construire, bâtir**
contain **contenir**
continue **continuer**
contradict **contredire**
convince **convaincre**
cook **cuire**
correct **corriger**
corrupt **corrompre**
cost **coûter**
cough **tousser**
count **compter**
cover **couvrir**
crack **fendre**
create **créer**
crouch **se tapir**
cure **guérir**
curse **maudire**
cut **couper**
cut (out) **tailler**

D

damage **gâter**
dance **danser**
dare **oser**
daze **abasourdir, étourdir**
deafen **abasourdir, étourdir**
decay (decline) **déchoir**
deceive **décevoir**
decline **déchoir**
decrease **décroître, diminuer, réduire**

deduce **déduire**
deduct **déduire**
defend **défendre**
demand **exiger**
demolish **démolir**
depart **partir**
depend **dépendre**
dependent, be **dépendre**
depict **dépeindre**
descend **descendre**
describe **décrire, dépeindre**
desert **abandonner**
deserve **mériter, valoir**
desire **désirer**
destroy **détruire**
detain **retenir**
detest **détester**
develop **développer**
die **mourir, périr**
dig **fouiller**
diminish **décroître, diminuer, réduire**
dine **dîner**
dirty **salir, souiller**
disappear **disparaître**
discourse **discourir**
discover **découvrir**
dishearten **abattre**
dislike **détester**
display **montrer**
displease **déplaire**
dissuade **dissuader**
distract **distraire**
distrust **se méfier**
divest **dévêtir**
do **faire**
do away with **abolir**
doubt **douter**
draw (sketch) **dessiner**
draw (out) **tirer**
draw (out) again **retirer**
dream **songer**
dress **vêtir**
dress oneself **s'habiller**
drift **voguer**
drink **boire**
drive **conduire**
drive (a car) **conduire, rouler**
drive out **chasser**
drizzle **bruiner**
dwell (in) **habiter**
dye **teindre**

E

earn **gagner**
eat **manger**
elect **élire**
embrace **étreindre**
employ **employer**
enclose **inclure**
encourage **encourager**
end **finir, terminer**
engage upon **entreprendre**
enjoy oneself **s'amuser**
enliven **égayer**
enough, be **suffire**
ensure **assurer**
enter **entrer**
entertain **amuser, égayer**
entice **attraire**
escape **s'enfuir**
establish **établir, fonder**
estimate **évaluer**
evaluate **évaluer**
excavate **fouiller**
excite **émouvoir**
exclude **exclure**
excuse oneself **s'excuser**
exhibit **montrer**
experience **éprouver**
explain **expliquer**
express **exprimer**

extinguish **éteindre**
extract **extraire**

F

fail **échouer, faillir**
faint **s'évanouir**
fake **truquer**
fall **tomber**
fall off (decay, decline) **déchoir**
fear **craindre**
feed **nourrir**
feel **sentir**
feel (experience) **éprouver**
feign **feindre**
fight **se battre, combattre**
fill **remplir**
find **trouver**
find out **s'informer**
finish **achever, finir, terminer**
fish **pêcher**
flatter **flatter**
flee **s'enfuir, fuir**
float **flotter**
fly **s'enfuir, fuir, voler**
fly off **s'envoler**
fly over **survoler**
follow **suivre**
forbid **défendre, interdire**
force **forcer**
foresee **prévoir**
forestall **prévenir**
foretell **prédire**
forgive **pardonner**
found (establish) **fonder**
freeze **geler**
freeze again **regeler**
frighten **effrayer**
fry **frire**
furnish **fournir**

G

gain **gagner**
gather **cueillir, recueillir**
get **obtenir, recevoir**
get angry **se fâcher**
get dressed **s'habiller**
get up **se lever**
give **donner**
give back **remettre, rendre**
go **aller**
go away **s'en aller**
go back **retourner**
go deep into **fouiller**
go down **descendre**
go forward **avancer**
go in **entrer**
go out **sortir**
go to bed **se coucher**
go up **monter**
gossip **bavarder**
grasp **saisir, serrer**
greet **accueillir**
grind **moudre**
grip **étreindre**
grow **croître**
grow (up, grow taller) **grandir**
grow old **vieillir**
grow thin **maigrir**
guarantee **assurer, certifier**
guard **garder**
guide **guider**

H

hail (weather) **grêler**
hamper **gêner**
hang **accrocher, pendre**
happen **advenir, se passer**
harm **blesser, nuire**
harvest **recueillir**

hasten **se dépêcher**
hate **haïr**
have **avoir**
have (hold) **tenir**
have a good time **s'amuser**
have a snack **goûter**
have dinner **dîner**
have lunch **déjeuner**
have supper **souper**
have to **devoir**
hear **entendre**
help **aider, secourir**
help oneself (to food and drink) **se servir**
hide **cacher**
hide oneself **se cacher**
hinder **empêcher, gêner, nuire**
hiss **siffler**
hit **battre, taper**
hold **tenir**
hold up **supporter**
hope **espérer**
humble **abaisser**
humble oneself **s'abaisser**
humiliate **abaisser**
hunt **chasser**
hurl **lancer**
hurry **se dépêcher**
hurry (be in a hurry) **se presser**
hurt **blesser**
hurt oneself **se blesser**

I

impede **gêner**
implore **supplier**
impose **imposer**
include **inclure**
inconvenience **gêner**
increase **accroître, augmenter, grandir**
infer **déduire**
inhabit **habiter**
injure **blesser**
injure oneself **se blesser**
inquire **s'informer**
insist **insister**
instruct **instruire**
insure **assurer**
insure oneself **s'assurer**
intend **compter**
interrogate **interroger**
interrupt **interrompre**
introduce **introduire**
introduce (a person) **présenter**
invent **inventer**
iron **repasser**
irritate **agacer**

J

join **joindre**
judge **juger**
jump **sauter**

K

keep **garder, retenir**
keep oneself busy **s'occuper**
kill **tuer**
knock down **abattre**
know **connaître**
know (how) **savoir**
know, not to **méconnaître**

L

lace **lacer**
lack **manquer**
lament **se plaindre**

laugh **rire**
launch **lancer**
lay **coucher, poser**
lay claim **prétendre**
lay the foundation (of a building) **fonder**
lead **amener, conduire, guider, mener**
leap **sauter**
learn **apprendre**
leave **laisser, partir, quitter, sortir**
leave hold **lâcher**
lend **prêter**
let **laisser, permettre**
let go **lâcher**
lick **lécher**
lie dead **gésir**
lie down **s'étendre**
lie flat **se tapir**
lie ill **gésir**
lie, tell a **mentir**
lift **lever**
like **aimer**
listen (to) **écouter**
live **vivre**
live (reside) **demeurer**
live (in) **habiter**
live somewhere temporarily **séjourner**
load **charger**
look (at) **regarder**
look for **chercher**
look like **ressembler**
loosen **lâcher**
lose **perdre**
lose consciousness **s'évanouir**
lose weight **maigrir**
love **aimer**
lower **abaisser**
lower oneself **s'abaisser**
lunch **déjeuner**

M

make **faire**
make believe **feindre**
make dizzy **étourdir**
make greater **accroître**
make haste **se presser**
make inquiries **s'informer**
make sure **s'assurer**
make use of **utiliser**
march **marcher**
marry **épouser**
matter, be the **s'agir**
meditate **méditer, réfléchir**
meet **rencontrer**
melt **fondre**
merit **mériter, valoir**
milk **traire**
mill **moudre**
misjudge **méconnaître**
miss **manquer**
mistaken, be **se méprendre, se tromper**
mistrust **se méfier**
misunderstand **méconnaître**
mix (colors) **fondre**
moan **se plaindre**
move **mouvoir**
move (budge) **bouger**
move out (change residence) **déménager**
muddy **souiller**
murmur **murmurer**
must **devoir, falloir**
mutter **murmurer**

N

name **appeler**
named, be **s'appeler**
necessary, be **falloir**

not to know **méconnaître**
not to recognize **méconnaître**
not to speak **se taire**
notice **remarquer**
nourish **nourrir**

O

obey **obéir**
oblige **obliger**
observe **constater, remarquer**
obtain **obtenir**
occupy **occuper**
occur **advenir**
offer **offrir**
omit **omettre**
open **ouvrir**
order **commander**
ought **devoir**
owe **devoir**

P

paint **peindre**
pant **souffler**
pardon **pardonner**
park (a car) **stationner**
pass **passer**
pay **payer**
perceive **apercevoir**
perish **périr**
permit **permettre**
pester **agacer**
pick (choose) **choisir**
pick (gather) **cueillir**
pickle **confire**
pity **plaindre**
place **mettre, placer, poser**
place oneself **se mettre**
play **jouer**
please **plaire**
pour **verser**
praise **louer**
pray **prier**
predict **prédire**
prefer **préférer**
prepare **préparer**
present **présenter**
present (at), be **assister**
preserve **confire**
press **presser, serrer**
pretend **feindre, prétendre**
prevent **empêcher**
produce **produire**
prohibit **défendre, interdire**
promise **promettre**
prompt (an actor with a cue) **souffler**
pronounce **prononcer**
prop up **supporter**
prosecute **poursuivre**
prove **prouver**
provide **pourvoir**
pull **tirer**
pull again **retirer**
pull up **arracher**
punish **punir**
purchase **acheter**
pursue **chasser, poursuivre**
push **pousser**
put **mettre, placer, poser**
put back **remettre**
put (on) again **remettre**
put to bed **coucher**
put to the test **éprouver**
put to use **utiliser**

Q

question **interroger**
question (be a question of) **s'agir**
quiet, be **se taire**

R

rain **pleuvoir**
raise (bring up) **élever**
raise (lift) **lever**
rap **taper**
read **lire**
read again **relire**
reappear **reparaître**
rear **élever**
rebuke **réprimander**
recall **rappeler, se rappeler, se souvenir**
receive **recevoir**
recognize **reconnaître**
recognize, not to **méconnaître**
recollect **se rappeler**
recover **reprendre**
reduce **abaisser, réduire**
reduce (one's weight) **maigrir**
reflect **réfléchir**
refuse **refuser**
relate **conter, raconter**
relieve **secourir**
remain **rester**
remember **se rappeler, se souvenir**
remind **rappeler**
rend **déchirer**
render **rendre**
rent **louer**
repair **réparer**
repeat **répéter**
replace **remettre, remplacer**
reply **répondre**
reprimand **gronder, réprimander**
reproduce **reproduire**
request **demander**
require **exiger**
rescue **sauver**
resemble **ressembler**
reside **demeurer**
resolve **résoudre**
rest **se reposer**
resume **reprendre**
retain **garder, retenir**
retire **se retirer**
return **rentrer, retourner**
return (something) **rendre**
ridicule **ridiculiser**
rip **déchirer**
roll **rouler**
roll along **rouler**
rouse **émouvoir**
row **voguer**
run **courir**
run away **s'enfuir, se sauver**
run to **accourir**
run up to **accourir**
rush **se presser**

S

sail **voguer**
satisfy **satisfaire**
save (money) **épargner**
save (rescue) **sauver**
say **dire**
scold **gronder**
scrape **gratter**
scratch **gratter**
search **chercher**
seduce **séduire**
see **apercevoir, voir**
see again **revoir**
see once more **revoir**
seem **paraître, sembler**
seize **saisir**
select **choisir**
sell **vendre**
send **envoyer**
serve **servir**
serve oneself **se servir**

set **poser**
sew **coudre**
shake **secouer**
shake down (off) **secouer**
shake (hands) **serrer**
shatter **rompre**
shine **luire**
should **devoir**
show **montrer**
show in **introduire**
shudder **frémir**
sigh **soupirer**
silent, be **se taire**
simulate **feindre**
sin **pécher**
sing **chanter**
sit down **s'asseoir**
skate (on ice) **patiner**
sketch **dessiner**
slander **médire**
sleep **dormir**
slip away **s'enfuir**
smack **taper**
smell **sentir**
smile **sourire**
smoke **fumer**
smooth **adoucir**
snow **neiger**
soften **adoucir**
soil **salir, souiller**
sojourn **séjourner**
solve **résoudre**
sort **classer**
speak **parler**
speak, not to **se taire**
spend (money) **dépenser**
spend (time) **passer**
split **fendre**
spoil **gâter**
spread **répandre**
squat **se tapir**
squeeze **presser, serrer**
start **commencer, se mettre**
station **stationner**
stay **rester**
steal **voler**
stink **puer**
stir **émouvoir**
stoop low **se tapir**
stop (oneself) **s'arrêter**
stop (someone or something) **arrêter**
strain **tendre**
stretch **tendre**
stretch (oneself) **s'étendre**
stretch out (oneself) **s'étendre**
strike (beat) **battre**
strike down **abattre**
strike (hit) **battre, taper**
strip **dévêtir**
study **étudier**
stun **abasourdir, étonner, étourdir**
stupefy **abasourdir**
submit **soumettre**
succeed **réussir**
succor **secourir**
suck **sucer**
suffice **suffire**
sufficient, be **suffire**
suit **convenir, seoir**
suitable, be **convenir**
sup **souper**
supplicate **prier, supplier**
support **supporter**
suppose **supposer**
surprise **surprendre**
survive **survivre**
swallow **avaler**
sway **balancer**
swear **jurer**
sweep **balayer**
swim **nager**
swing **balancer**
swoon **s'évanouir**

T

take prendre
take a walk se promener
take again reprendre
take away enlever
take back reprendre
take down descendre
take flight s'envoler
take off (airplaine) s'envoler
take up (carry up) monter
take wing s'envoler
talk parler
tap taper
taste goûter
teach enseigner
tear déchirer
telephone téléphoner
tell dire
tell about raconter
tell lies mentir
tempt tenter
terminate finir, terminer
test éprouver
thaw dégeler
think penser, réfléchir, songer
throw jeter, lancer
thunder tonner
tighten tendre
touch toucher
translate traduire
transmit transmettre
travel voyager
trick tricher
trim tailler
trust se fier
try éprouver, essayer
turn aside détourner
turn (oneself) aside, away se détourner
turn away détourner
twist tordre

U

uncover découvrir
understand comprendre, entendre
undertake entreprendre
undo défaire
unite unir
unlace délacer
unsew découdre
unstitch découdre
untie défaire
uproot arracher
use employer, utiliser
utilize utiliser

V

vanquish vaincre
visit visiter
vow jurer

W

wager parier
wait (for) attendre
wake up se réveiller
walk marcher
walk, take a se promener
wander voguer
want vouloir
ward off prévenir
warn prévenir
wash oneself se laver
watch regarder
wear porter
weary ennuyer
wed épouser
weigh peser
welcome accueillir
whisper chuchoter

whistle **siffler**
whiten **blanchir**
win **gagner**
wipe **essuyer**
wish **vouloir, souhaiter**
withdraw **se retirer**
work **travailler**
worth, be **valoir**
wound **blesser**
wound oneself **se blesser**
write **écrire**

Y

yield **céder**

Index of Verb Forms Identified by Infinitive

The purpose of this index is to help you identify those verb forms which cannot be readily identified. Verb forms whose first three or four letters are the same as the infinitive have not been included because they can easily be identified by referring to the alphabetical listing of the 501 verbs in this book.

dois **devoir**
doive, *etc.* **devoir**
dors **dormir**
dû, due **devoir**
dûmes **devoir**
dus, dussent **devoir**
dut, dût **devoir**

E

es **être**
est **être**
étais, *etc.* **être**
été **être**
êtes **être**
étiez **être**
eu **avoir**
eûmes **avoir**
eurent **avoir**
eus **avoir**
eusse, *etc.* **avoir**
eut, eût **avoir**
eûtes **avoir**

F

faille **faillir, falloir**
fais, *etc.* **faire**
fasse, *etc.* **faire**
faudra **faillir, falloir**
faudrait **faillir, falloir**
faut **faillir, falloir**
faux **faillir**
ferai, *etc.* **faire**
fîmes **faire**
firent **faire**
fis, *etc.* **faire**
font **faire**
fûmes **être**
furent **être**
fus, *etc.* **être**
fut, fût **être**
fuyais, *etc.* **fuir**

G

gisons, *etc.* **gésir**
gît **gésir**

I

ira, irai, iras, *etc.* **aller**

L

lis, *etc.* **lire**
lu **lire**
lus, *etc.* **lire**

M

meure, *etc.* **mourir**
meus, *etc.* **mouvoir**
mîmes **mettre**
mirent **mettre**
mis **mettre**
misses, *etc.* **mettre**
mit **mettre**
mort **mourir**
moulons, *etc.* **moudre**
moulu **moudre**
mû, mue **mouvoir**
mussent **mouvoir**
mut **mouvoir**

N

naquîmes, *etc.* **naître**
né **naître**

O

omis **omettre**
ont **avoir**

P

pars **partir**
paru **paraître**
peignis, *etc.* **peindre**
peuvent **pouvoir**
peux, *etc.* **pouvoir**
plu **plaire, pleuvoir**
plurent **plaire**
plut, plût **plaire, pleuvoir**
plûtes **plaire**
pourrai, *etc.* **pouvoir**
prîmes **prendre**
prirent **prendre**
pris **prendre**
prisse, *etc.* **prendre**
pu **pouvoir**
puis **pouvoir**
puisse, *etc.* **pouvoir**
pûmes, *etc.* **pouvoir**
purent **pouvoir**
pus **pouvoir**
pusse **pouvoir**
put, pût **pouvoir**

R

reçois, *etc.* **recevoir**
reçûmes, *etc.* **recevoir**
relu **relire**
reviens, *etc.* **revenir**
revins, *etc.* **revenir**
riiez **rire**
ris, *etc.* **rire**

S

sache, *etc.* **savoir**
sais, *etc.* **savoir**
saurai, *etc.* **savoir**
séant **seoir**
serai, *etc.* **être**
sers, *etc.* **servir**
seyant **seoir**
sied **seoir**
siéent **seoir**
siéra, *etc.* **seoir**
sois, *etc.* **être**
sommes **être**
sont **être**
sors, *etc.* **sortir**
soyez **être**
soyons **être**
su **savoir**
suis **être, suivre**
suit **suivre**
sûmes **savoir**
surent **savoir**
survécu **survivre**
susse, *etc.* **savoir**
sut, sût **savoir**

T

tiendrai, *etc.* **tenir**
tienne, *etc.* **tenir**
tînmes **tenir**
tins, *etc.* **tenir**
trayant **traire**
tu **taire**
tûmes **taire**
turent **taire**
tus **taire**
tusse, *etc.* **taire**
tut, tût **taire**

V

va **aller**
vaille **valoir**
vais **allez**
vas **aller**
vaudrai, *etc.* **valoir**
vaux, *etc.* **valoir**
vécu **vivre**
vécûmes, *etc.* **vivre**
verrai, *etc.* **voir**
veuille, *etc.* **vouloir**
veulent **vouloir**
veux, *etc.* **vouloir**
viendrai, *etc.* **venir**
vienne, *etc.* **venir**
viens, *etc.* **venir**
vîmes **voir**
vînmes **venir**
vinrent **venir**
vins, *etc.* **venir**
virent **voir**
vis **vivre, voir**
visse, *etc.* **voir**
vit **vivre, voir**
vît **voir**
vîtes **voir**
vont **aller**
voudrai, *etc.* **vouloir**
voyais, *etc.* **voir**
vu **voir**

List of French Verbs Conjugated Like Model Verbs Among the 501

The number after each verb is the page number where a model verb is shown fully conjugated.

A

B

C

D

E

F

G

H

I

J

K

L

M

Q

R

S

T

U

V